Preface:

This is a book of trucking knowledge.

Complied is 10 year's worth of direct experience plus 100's years of combined experience that was collected.

I dedicate this book to Clint Douglas, family friend, my late mom Charlotte Ray, to the younger version of me that went through with trucking, to who wanted to help support in the creation of this project, and to you the reader. You are holding something that is real. It is a message. I the writer am the messenger.

Do what you can to take nothing like the wording personal in this book, positive intentions only here and thank you for your time. I know time can be the hardest thing to get back but remember this is a reference book too, and that the contents are thorough and can be skipped around in.

BLESS BLESS BLESS I wish you much success, strength and peace. I pray you and your business insulated from famine and your life to be charging with increasing potential at all times.

Setbacks are almost guaranteed but do what you can to not focus on them and just prepare and execute. "An ounce of preparation is worth a pound of cure"

Edition: 1 2022 Distributed with

love, truth, peace, freedom and justice

from Georgia and or Louisiana.

Overcome using S.T.R.E.N.G.T.H

Save Money.

Take Profitable Loads.

Remember to be Easy on Your Truck.

Enter a Positive State of Mind.

Never Give Up.

Give Yourself Time.

Teach Yourself Constantly.

Have Tools in your Truck.

Table of Protents: (because con- usually alludes to negative or against progress (right...right!))

This is a self teaching and stand alone text book.

Welcome to How to be Successful in Trucking the FIRST edition physically printed text book! (or KDP Kindle!)

How to be Successful in Trucking starts with an entire chapter dedicated to what's it's like in the day to day of being owner operator already with own authority. For one week, see move by move what decisions and deals I made and why. See what happened that week, how I handled it and how much money I was able to make in simple profit.

(2020 Q4 time frame is when this publication was written, released in pdf format February 2, 2021 self published)

HOW TO BE SUCCESFUL IN TRUCKING

Written by Andrew W. Higgins

CHAPTER 1: A WEEK IN MY SHOES

Wednesday: 4:30AM- My clock is set for 5am, but I wake early as I usually do when I'm leaving from home time. 😁

Something about getting back on the road excites me to the point where if I wake up early, I find it difficult to go back to sleep and I usually decide to get a head start so I don't have to rush as much. **Rushing is not good**! Some of the biggest mistakes I've made happened when I allowed myself to get into too much of a rush. Anything past a modest rush tends to increase the chances of making a mistake… and in this business, mistakes can mean points on your license, damaging your equipment, hurting yourself or others, missing your exit or something simple that will cost you money, and etc. I'm pretty sure you've experienced the mistakes and frustrations when it comes to rushing! 🚚

I've been home for about 5 weeks, enjoying my home time, visited Grand Canyon, got a series of minor work and upgrades done on my truck, fixed some hurricane damage around my property, received about 10 checks from loads I did on my last go around, and etc. →I book this load from Fort Polk, LA to Fort Bragg, NC. **We make a deal for $3,500 on about 1000 miles**, so about $3.50 a mile ($3500 divided by 1000 miles), <u>not bad</u>! I did have a 150-mile deadhead, so $3500 divided by 1150 miles is still $3.04 a mile for all miles, still, pretty well considering I'm delivering to Fayetteville, NC area; which is not a bad reload area factoring in Durham, Raleigh, Greenville, Wilmington, Florence and Myrtle Beach all being as close as they are. $

My math says I'll make about **$3,125** on this load in two days. It's **really simple** how I got this number. First, I find out how much I'm spending on fuel. I take my empty miles of 150 + loaded miles of 1000 = 1150 total miles. Next, I divide 1150 total miles by 6 miles per gallon = about 192 gallons of fuel will be needed. Next, I take 192 gallons and X (multiply) it by $1.95 (the cost of fuel) = $375. Then I simply take the total revenue of the load $3500 and - $375 = $3125! Since there's no tolls on this route, and good estimation of simple profit (without other expenses) is $3,125. Then you can take this number and divide it by the amount of days it took to run it and see what you made or will make per day, or just use it to gauge your income, negotiations, and decision making. + − ÷ ×

Everything's already packed from day before, my tools are loaded up, I shower, grab my refrigerator and freezer food; my wife, she wakes up to help me do this. I power on my truck motor to warm, load up my truck fridge, and log the pre-trip. It's 150 miles to Fort Polk, all state roads with no interstate, so I plan accordingly with a little extra time to get there; Can't budget time on the state roads that have towns, stops and terrain like how time is estimated for interstate travel right! 🚚

5:25- I leave out by now and enjoy catching the sunrise as it starts and enjoying getting back on the road. ☀️

8:30-9:00- I make it to Fort Polk. I get checked in by the young soldiers, go to the big motor pool, load my 2 hum-vees and one trailer. 10 chains, 11 binders, and I'm out of there by 12. I don't have a load for Friday yet, so I'm glancing on Truckstop.com – Load Board and Freight Management on auto refresh as I go. **Got to stay vigilant on self dispatch!** ✔️

2:30 PM- About 175 miles later I stop at TA in Tallulah, fuel is $1.90 with my NASTC discount, pump price was $2.23, that's .33 cents off, <u>not bad</u>! I fill all the way up; 72 gallons X .33 discount means I saved $23 this fill up. I love saving money right! **I get 96% of my fuel from only TA or Petro**. I trust their fuel, I get my biggest discounts there, and I prefer the environment. TA Petro tends to attract more experienced, professional and owner drivers, unlike the swift truck at pilot whose been parked at the pump for 30 minutes getting food or taking a shower or something ok! 😂

I do my own IFTA reporting, which is **very easy** by the way, so I need to keep track of my gallons purchased in each state, and the fuel receipt does this just fine or digital fuel card reporting is even better. It's all interstate from here, I-20 basically all the way across then I-95. Flatter routes like this was always perfered by me to keep easy on the truck. It's much better on fuel and driveline in my opinion. I have about 4 hours left I can drive, so I plan to stop at TA in Tuscaloosa or at the big L&B Travel Plaza in Livingston, AL exit 17 if I don't have enough time to make TA. I drive pretty slow! I'm still looking for loads at this time and taking calls for my posted truck. No North East for me right now due to the current and traditional lack of outbound freight, and Monday is Labor Day- dang! I'll figure it out. Oh, I snack some homemade plant base potato salad 😁

6:00 PM- I stop. I had one hour of drive time left, but 60 miles to reach TA in Tuscaloosa. It would have been **better** to deliver tomorrow and be empty first thing Friday morning. Why would it be better to go ahead and be empty? Well first, this is a big unit military move, **there's a lot of trucks involved**.   It takes time to get into the base, then you just never really know how many trucks will be in front of you on larger moves like this. So, by me delivering on Thursday, <u>I would have more time to drive further empty to my next load if need be</u>. It's going to be Friday and I don't want to get stuck over the WEEKEND without a load, especially on a long Labor Day weekend. 💲 💲

        I'll deliver Friday early morning, like originally planned, and aim to be empty by 9-10 am if I get there right a 6:30-7. **This takes initiative**! This will limit my load booking a bit though. I will not book a load further than 150-175 miles away, because if the unloading goes all the way until 12, I'll still have a 3-4 hour drive to pick up my next load before the end of the business day (usually around 4-5 PM). The closer the load picks up the better of course, not only will it be less fuel & time used, but will lower the stress level on Friday for sure. <u>When I make a deal, I hold my end of the bargain!</u> A big part of this is to not over-commit to schedules and circumstances that are too close in time. I would always give myself "wiggle room", and budget my committed travel times to about 50-55mph. I wouldn't commit to much more than 500 miles a day. All this pick at 9 am on Monday and deliver 1200 miles away Wednesday at 6am wasn't the loads I was trying to subject myself to!

That is when the **cost effecting** habit of driving 70+ miles per hour starts. If the load really really pays, yes there's room for exception and Justification. But there's no way I'm trying to drive 65 mph + for $2.50 a mile or less freight. That number should be closer to $4 a mile if I'm going to rush myself like that and put more wear, tear and vibration on my truck.

      L&B Travel Plaza in Livingston, AL has a pretty good Indian food restaurant. I'll order Channa Masala, and research trading stock options for about 2 hours and get about 8 or so hours of sleep. 5:25 AM to 6 PM, 12 hours today. Average. After eating inside, I power on my generator and set up my home made "apu", I read some more and sleep!

Thursday: 4:00 AM CST- I decide to wake up **early** again. There is still a slim chance I can get to fort Bragg by 4pm EST, so I'll take it! If I don't get there in time, I'll have plenty of time to do whatever I want later today when I stop. I put up my apu, log a pre-trip, look over the truck, use the bathroom, pour me some cold coffee from my fridge and get going!

7:00- I stop at exit 165, the I-20 truck stop in Lincoln, AL. It's not time to fuel yet or I would of stopped at TA in Lincoln. I need to use the bathroom only, so I choose the I-20 Truckstop because it is on the south side of the interstate and an easy on and off. 90% of the time I don't cross over the interstate or take truck stop's further off the interstate for simple things like using bathroom, it's too much unnecessary fuel and time used when you consider the big picture of doing it every day for a year. For restrooms I prefer rest areas. **Rest areas** are the easiest, quickest and most economical on and offs. There was an added benefit to this stop at I-20 Truckstop though, I hadn't been eating this early in the morning but they had Vidalia boiled peanuts! This brand can be hard to find outside of Georgia and I enjoy them much more than the Peanut Patch brand! 😁

10:00- I'm in Atlanta on the 285 loop and I get a call in saying troops will be active until 8 pm tonight and to come on in and get unloaded. **Great**! My early morning haste has paid off. This will open more opportunities for tomorrow. They originally would only receive until 4 pm, and my eta is 5:00. 360 miles to go, 6 hours and 17 minutes of drive time, and a 30 minute break I must take. This is one of those exceptions to my normal speed, I will go 63-67 mph now.

11:15- I stop in TA Madison for fuel. I only run one fuel tank; I get fuel every day. It's a personal preference of mine, but it's not something one has to do. 512 miles \ 75 gallons = 6.8 mpg. Not bad! As you see, I always estimate at 6 mpg, but aim to do better based off my driving habits. Now I must take my mandatory 30 min break even though I don't want to! I use this time to make this certain salad I enjoy making over the road. Romaine lettuce, broccoli slaw, one avocado, a can of chic-peas, avocado oil, Ms. Dash and some fresh cracked Himalayan sea salt! **I use this time also to search the load board for opportunities**. I think I got one that'll work fine lined up with Trident. I'll hear back in a few. 😊

3:55 PM- I'm blazing up the road, faster than I usually go, but this weekend has a lot riding on it because Labor Day makes it a 4 day weekend. I **cannot** be empty all weekend, or doing some lousy $1200 load. That is not good use of a weekend! Especially on a 4 day weekend being gone from home. So, I'm taking advantage of delivering early so I can be ready first thing tomorrow for freight.

I'm 10 miles from delivery, and I stop at a red light. <u>My clutch pedal won't go down!</u> **Jeez**!!!! Now mind you, I put a new clutch in about 4 months ago and have put few miles on it since, so I know it's not the clutch. **This is where knowing your truck comes in.** I know my truck has a 'hydraulic assist' clutch, no linkage. It's a master and slave cylinder, a small reservoir, and a hydraulic line for the fluid. It's a good system and is bullet proof for the most part. I push the clutch pedal down harder to see if maybe it's a fluke, or had some air trapped in it somehow. The pedal hits the floor, no there's no clutch at all, no resistance that is. I'm on a busy 6 lane highway right at the traffic light. <u>Don't panic</u>! Keep cool, put your flashers on, and go ahead and create some space by putting your safety triangles out and get to **THINKING FAST!** 😵

I **don't** like to call police or **any one** right away in these situations because usually <u>the first thing they're going to suggest and eventually stick to is "you need to call a tow truck"</u>. Well tow trucks are **expensive** and **I'm going to fix the truck or get it going myself if at all possible**. The more tools and spare items you keep, the higher the chance you can fix it yourself and keep more of your hard earned cash at home. Plus, they might even try to write you a ticket or get aggressive with you, even though you're the one in the unpleasant situation! If you're leased to a company, you want these people (police) out of your business, because negative reports like this from police to your company make you look delinquent, or like you don't know what you're doing, making you in trouble more with them. **Call firefighters** if anyone, if your polite and don't rush them, they'll be way more kind and forgiving. Then let them introduce the cops, & state police if need be.

I **hurry up** and get to problem solving asap, when you're the boss, the show is all on you! Will you **fumble** the ball under pressure, or will you **hold it** tight and take the hit? Or even better break the tackle and keep running. The line runs from my driver's side firewall (master cylinder), down the frame rail to the slave cylinder that is bolted to transmission on my driver's side as well. This will be my problem area I'm pretty sure, so I start here. It didn't long, I see a puddle of fluid below my transmission area. One reason I choose this truck is because of its simple design and easy access to almost everything on the truck. I don't have full farrings in the way, or under carriage exhaust pipes and emissions cans in the way. I can literally crouch under the truck, and **easily** put my hand right over the transmission if need be.

I have a **tiny** hole in my line. But sometimes that's all it takes when it comes to fluids. No brake fluid, no working clutch! At this point I'm under the truck, and over the transmission looking at the line and feeling around, moving the line to see exactly where the leak is, and to see if I can come up with a solution. I **burn** my arm pretty good on the exhaust pipe behind me, everything is super hot. Be **more careful**! I know I got some stuff in my truck that might help, but really there's not much I can do for a steel braided line that's under pressure once it has a hole. Not thinking that once the hydraulic assist loses fluid, the air has to be bled out before it will take the new fluid, I continue to think JB Weld, repair tape, JB Weld putty steel, **SOMETHING** right! 👻

It's been about **20** minutes now, I've burnt myself a few times, but I do get good people in Fayetteville to stop and ask if I need help. A man on a motorcycle spends about ten minutes with me. That **boosts** my morale! I'm calm, staying optimistic, but am rapidly searching for solutions. I try repair tape, no good. I try the putty steel, no good. I decide on mixing some quick setting JB Weld, and hoping it will fill the hole, and be good enough to take fluid. I'm not very confident in it but I must do something, I'm **not** paying a wrecker to $800 to haul me 20 miles if I can help it. 9 years and I've never been hooked to a wrecker! BUT. I do know a trick to get the truck moving without a clutch if need be. 🍶

I'm **making** a lot of calls now. I pull up the app "find trucker service", they have one of the Best collections of places to call when in a pinch. I'm 15 miles from a Volvo dealer, but they **don't** have the line and **can't** get it until Tuesday. Remember, I still have a load and a customer waiting on me. I do make a good connection with **Charles**; he runs an independent shop called Justice Towing in Saint Pauls, NC. He was **very** helpful, I called him like 7 times and he picked up every time, what a guy I say! We make backup plans and he tells me he'll leave his gate unlocked for me. While I'm waiting on the JB self to dry, I'm making a **ton** of phone calls to find who has my part. I eventually find the line I need, except it's in Greensboro, 100 miles away. Better that than waiting until Tuesday or Wednesday. 🚚

The JB weld dries pretty good, I fill the reservoir back up with brake fluid, then the **duh** moment comes where I realize, so what? It's going to take two people to bleed the air out to even be able to use the fluid. I **decide** to use my trick to get truck moving towards the shop, (now) as I write this, I should of used this trick right away to move to the side of the road, or even go ahead and deliver the load. Hindsight is 20/20 sometimes, but it all **builds** character. When you got a bad clutch, broken linkage, or a hydraulic assist issue, you can still move the truck, just be careful! I'll tell you how. 🙌

Make **sure** your you have enough air pressure, 80-100 should be enough. Build air first if need be. → With the truck off, go ahead and put the truck in the lowest gear possible, either gear 1 or 2. Push your brakes in (**released**), and when you start the truck, it will **GO**! But remember, if you come to a complete stop, you'll have to repeat this process; unless your clutch pedal is good and will hold the truck back from bucking, in this case just slide it into second gear before you stop and hold the clutch the whole time until you go again. So, do what you can not to stop if you're in this position, time the traffic lights just right if your clutch pedal doesn't work at all. ✔

In this case, like I mentioned, I'm at a big intersection, there's too much going on to just wing it and I know I need a hand for what I'm about to do. I search Apple Maps for fire stations. There's one .3 miles away. Good! I call them and explain what I need to do, block traffic at the intersection so I can make a U-turn and head to **Charles'** shop. I tell them at their convenience. After that gesture, they said they were right on the way and they'll do it. When they arrive, we talk, and they flag a passing police officer down to help. I explain to her the plan and make her feel comfortable and thanked. She ends up calling state police too, and that's ok. We block the 12 lane intersection, (6 lanes on both sides), I power my motor on in 1st gear and instantly start moving.

I make big slow U-turn and head the other way. She stays with me for a couple of traffic lights, blocks traffic for me and does a lot. **Thank you**! Respect, confidence and being a problem solver goes a long way! 🚚

I'm parked here at Charles' shop now. We'll see what tomorrow has in store. The closest rental car place is 15 miles away. I need a car so I can get the parts. Then we can knock it out. Also, I let Austin, my customer/broker for this load know what was going on in an email, he'll see this first thing in the morning. I tell him I'll contact him in the morning as well. 💯

7:00 PM- Real quick I'll tell you this. I'm not too sure it was just a hole in the line though. <u>Remember</u>, the clutch wouldn't go down at all, then I smashed it down, and it hit the floor. What if this extreme pressure is what bust the line, but there was already an issue in the master or slave cylinder that caused it to get stuck in the first place? Since this line is so **difficult** to find, and there's only one in Greensboro, I think it will be wise to go a little further in the repair, and make it an investment as well. I think replacing both the master and slave cylinder and the line would be a wise move for the temporary and the long run. ✅

Because if there was a problem prior to the line busting, and I just put a new line on, I very well might bust it too. These are the **calculated** decisions you'll have to make as you go. If I bust a new line, then I'm down until mid-next week, paying for another new line, wasted money on a rental, which almost adds up to the cost it would take to do it all at once. Pick your poison I guess! But I tend to favor the side of <u>longevity</u>, and the long run. I'm guessing the master and slave cylinder will run about $300-$400 each, the line is $85, and by doing the cylinders will probably add about $150 in labor. They're pretty simple and straight forward, bolt on and go. I've never worked on the hydraulic assist myself, but I'll be watching for sure and taking notes. The main thing I need the shop for is bleeding the air out. I need to watch and learn this method. More to come tomorrow. $_zz^z$

Friday: 7:00 am- Charles comes, we check the throw out bearing, there's still a gap between the throw out bearing and the stop break. **Perfect!** The clutch is good. You can check this by looking through the inspection plate under the transmission. Look up into it and you should see a gap between the piece that moves when you touch it (stop brake) and the piece that's connected to the clutch itself (throw out bearing). He's **99%** sure the line collapsed and it has nothing to do with the master and slave cylinder. Brad from his shop is driving me to enterprise. Good! Enterprise will only rent me a 15 passenger van because of the 5 day rental policy for Labor Day. What a bad policy for the customer. Got to love corporate policy I guess (not!). I just need it for 5 hours. The van is $139 but I need something, and it will have to do. I need to deliver this load today. Austin my broker says he understands and thanks me for the update, but one of his supervisors emails over us and says it is "very" time sensitive. Yeah right, they are going to go park these hummers in the field somewhere but I'm working fast on it anyways. OK

8:30- I'm out of Enterprise and a cool young girl accommodates me further and puts me in a cheaper more fuel efficient 4 door car. Remembering people's names really helps. I called and spoke to Nehemiah before I got there and he approved my one day rental. My lady assistant corporately told me they couldn't rent for one day. I politely

12

but firmly explained to her, I already made a deal with Nehemiah and had been approved. <u>That changed everything quickly!</u> I'm leaving now for Greensboro, 140 miles one way. I called Forest at Advantage truck center to double check that he could put his hands on the part, and to write me a will call ticket so it doesn't get sold from underneath me. I got my fresh coffee I made in the truck and I'm up the road. 😎

10:45- I'm turning and burning already. I picked up the hose and worked a deal to go ahead and buy the slave cylinder and reservoir all at a discount. I decided to go ahead and buy the slave cylinder because the dealership down the road didn't have one, but they do have the master cylinder if I need. I don't want to return the car, end up needing the part, and being right back in the same boat. THINK AHEAD! The slave cylinder ended up being $220 down from the asking price of $260 and much cheaper than I anticipated. **It pays to call around and get prices over the road**, that number $220 came from the Volvo dealer in St Paul's, they didn't have it in stock though. In Greensboro I go ahead and ask to see if they have it, they do, for $260. I go in to make my deal. Parts guy don't have much authority to make deals, but if they like you, and your reasonable, usually you can <u>shave a few bucks off retail price if need be</u>. I ask, if I go ahead and buy all three, will you sell me the slave cylinder for $220? I got quoted this already on this part. Not only does he agree, he takes $10 or so off each of the other parts. **Thanks Man!** $

I get on the phone with Charles and tell him I'm coming back and it will be about two hours. I ask him will he be able to already have the line off before I get there that way when I arrive the hose can go straight on and maybe I can actually make my delivery today before 4 or 5. He agrees, and says no problem. **Take initiative, be proactive. This is your show, nobody's going to do it for you.** You're in more control of your fate then you may realize! This is why if I'm using a shop, I prefer independent shops like Charles'. <u>You just don't get this type of service and flexibility with dealers.</u> **You have to know what you want, stand your ground, be likeable and realize there's other people involved and their world doesn't exactly revolve around you**. Just be mindfully of others time, effort, and business can really help. 😁

12:00- I stop very quickly at Hardee's to get a Beyond Veggie Burger with no cheese or mayo on sourdough bread with no butter. If you know what vegan means, you'll see how I order my burger without animal products is aka vegan. This is not something I'll push in my book but I will talk about some at the end of my health book "**10 Secrets 4 Successful Health**"! A healthy body does increase the likelihood of having a healthy, happy, positive and successful mind! I've been eating like this for almost 10 years now.

1:15- I deliver the hose to **Charles**. He already has the line off and ready to go. Don't you just love when someone keeps their word and makes it happen?? 🏆

2:30- We're done bleeding the air. I get the jist of how he did it, at the least, I got experience in watching the procedure. See, even as I write this book of mine, I'm still learning. **That's what this takes**! You have to open the slave cylinder on the back with a pry bar. That opens it up where the air bubbles can come out the reservoir. Between doing this and me pumping the clutch, we finish bleeding the air within 15 minutes. <u>I pay Charles $200</u>, thank him so much, and race back 15 miles to Enterprise to go drop the rental off.

But before I leave the shop, I call Enterprise and talk with Brad. I ask him will he have a driver ready to take me back to St. Paul's. He does, now they're expecting me. ✊🏽

3:30- I get dropped back off at Charles shop And I'm **outta** here! Just in time to make my delivery at 4-4:15. They're going to wait on me. Every bit of hustling I did since yesterday has been worth it! I did not waste one minute, and I'm still delivering today, with not really one minute to spare. You **see** how that works?? Now I can look for loads still. Let's see if I can still swing another load too before the long weekend strikes. 🚛

4:15- I arrive at Fort Bragg. I get checked in, I've **already** called Lieutenant Joe, they're expecting me. I've kept him updated all day. I'm the last truck to get unloaded before their Labor Day weekend starts, they are happy to see me. The dock was right past the inspection point, I back up to it. I then jump out the truck, greet everyone, and quickly get all my chains and binders off so they don't have to wait on me no more! This whole process takes maybe 30 minutes. I get my signed BOL paperwork back and everybody leaves. I've been on **GO** all morning and day, and since yesterday, so I move the truck out of the gate, park in the staging area, pull up Truckstop.com, and mentally crash for a moment with relief. 😄

5:15- Look-e-here, I book a load with a new customer just after closing hours! I know the company, Baggett Transport, I just never hauled for them before. I fill out their carrier packet, it's digital and pretty simple. A lot of my info was pre-filled. It's not the **best** load, has a bigger deadhead, but it loads tomorrow, on a Saturday, on a Labor Day weekend. It pays right at **$2** a mile to go to Fort Worth from Huger, SC.

It's a heavy load, 44k lbs of steel beams, but no tarp. $2250 on 1128 miles. I figure I'll make right around $1830 after fuel. That plus the $3100 for Fort Bragg makes $4930. Not bad in 6 days, considering Labor Day weekend and my delay. This load will take me back through home, so why not? I'll spend Sunday afternoon and night at home I'm thinking.

10:00 pm- Recap on costs. $100 rental, $400 in parts, $200 in service. $700 total, in actuality, I didn't need the reservoir or extra slave cylinder, those were about $300 together. I'll have them for spares, backups and just in case. $

So **really**, it cost me more like $500 to quickly handle business and make my commitments. If I were run that number out of the weekly total with the next load combined, it'll still be $4230/$4430. That's why you got to make good deals and decisions. Even after my repair I'm seeing double and triple what many owner ops and lease operators are making. Just **remember**, every set back like this no matter how small, builds character, it makes you stronger. The stronger you are, the more you can handle, the more you can do and the further you can go. Do as much as you can on **your** own, be prepared, always budget your money & time right, carry tools, and always be learning. Good night! zᶻᶻ

Saturday: 5:15- I awake early only to find my 10 hour break is not ready yet. Dang! 😄 I must of counted wrong. **No sense** in going back to sleep. I'm 40 minutes early, so I decide to jump in the Petro and take a quick shower; I'm dirty from the last couple days or ripping and running.

8:00- I arrive a Nucor Steel in Hugor, SC. I usually don't come to these big steel mill operations. In my experience, they never really pay well, the loads are always heavy, and I

16

don't like the atmosphere. It's to corporate, Get treated like a number, and they put hyper safety over common sense. Be it the situation with barely getting unloaded yesterday, and booking a load after 5pm, this will do and I put my pride to the side for a sec. I **must** admit though, they got their system very automated and it works. My appointment is at 8:30. I go ahead and check in on my CB and lay my dunnage out for my load. 🌑

9:50- I'm loaded up and gone. They had a scale on sight that weighed me out by the axle. **Good**! That's a free $12 for not buying a scale ticket. I probably buy about 3 or so scale tickets a year. That's shows you how often I load this heavy.

It's an easy load to tie down, about as **simple** as it gets for flatbed. A chain in the front, a chain in the back, 4 straps, one every 10 ft, and two tie downs in the first 5ft (one is the chain). I have 3 days to run 1150 miles. Now the pace slows down **big time**, I won't go much over 60mph unless I'm going down a hill. Why speed race there? I'm not going to be dragging my feet and be irresponsible, but I will take my time. 😎

→ **Do you know** 1 mile per gallon difference in a years' time will save you about $5000 to $7000 in fuel? That's great incentive to me! 💲

Plus, I don't like being in a rush. I enjoy my time way better when I'm not in a rush. The smart thing to do if I wasn't stopping by the house would be; to still not rush, but drive average fast (60-62mph) and park as close as possible, probably TA Terrell, and make a 34 hour reset out of it. I'm not too worried about that on this one. I got 41 hours on my 70, it'll take about 23 hours to get there, that leaves me 18 hours to reload Tuesday, drive 500 miles, and to drive 300 or so miles Wednesday with full hours coming back to me every day after Wednesday night. This is not a business of luck like some may think, it's more like a 5-dimensional game of chess in which you control many of the factors. ♟

3:05- I stop at TA in Madison, GA for fuel. 382.5 miles divided by 58.97 gallons = 6.5 mpg rounded up. **Not bad** considering most of these miles are with the 44k lbs of freight I picked up. ✔

6:00- I stop for the night at Newborn Truck Stop in Tallapoosa, GA Exit 5. I really like this truck stop, because there's **always parking**, it's old school and usually attracts mostly owner operators. It's very easy to remember too, I-20, exit 5, Georgia side, right by the state line. They got a chrome shop that has odd ball stuff not easily found in other places, A cb shop, and a repair shop if need be.

When I stopped, I opened up my Keep Trucking ELOG app to go off duty. It says I have a violation! **How**?? 😄 It was my mistake, I'm still getting used to this app, this is my second time going out with it and I'm still getting myself into a new routine with using it. I got it mostly down but still have old habits that'll kick in and I'll forget to do something on it. I really like and endorse this app though. It's way better than I thought a phone app would be.

What happened was that I got carried away talking to my friend on the phone about business and I drove past my 30 minute break by ten minutes. **Jeez**! BUT. I do some digging on the new revisions to the 30-minute break and find on the fmcsa website that I actually didn't violate the rule. HA! It now states that you have to take a break before 8 hours of consecutive driving, not 8 hours after being on-duty like it used to be. Revised July 23, 2020. I screenshot it on my phone and highlight that part. I also make a shortcut on my home screen so I can quickly access it in case I get inspected in the next 7 days. Keep Trucking hasn't written the new revisions into the software yet.

https://www.fmcsa.dot.gov/regulations/hours-service/hours-service-drivers-final-rule

I got some free time now. I'll stay up for a few and wake up a bit later than I have the last couple days. I'll do something fun now, like make some happy music on my laptop and keyboard I keep in my truck! 😄

Before I do that, when walking back from inside, I spot a truck with its hood open. I have plenty of free time so I walk over there to see if he needs a hand. He has a 2012+ truck with a full emissions system on it. Dpf, doc, and def. It's a good looking truck, an all yellow Kenworth with a new Tripac evolution. **But I would not want to be doing business in this truck**! It has a Paccar motor, nothing is reachable, the wiring looks terrible, and the up to date emissions systems adds way too many potential problems. This is his issue now, a nox sensor and low def check engine light. He's looking around underneath and I search all around myself looking for obvious wire fraying or a bad ground. Looking at his truck makes me nervous! It's just not built for the owner operator. Everything under that hood is very expensive, and very annoying to work on. I saw a ground that he should consider cleaning, but he would have to take some reservoir off to even reach it. There's too much stuff in the way to reach practically anything on that motor. This is NOT a good thing when you're the owner and will be the one working on it.

Sure, you can take it to the dealer and just throw money at it. But as a one truck operation, that is not sustainable and a great way to go out of business fast! 🚛🚛

He gives up on it, and I don't really see any leads myself. He seemed like he really didn't want help, so I didn't get on the ground or anything to further look. It could be a multiple of things. Just a bad sensor, a bad sensor further up in the emissions chain that's not allowing the nox to burn right. It could be a damaged wire, but he said the wires look good from where he was. It could be a grounding issue. Maybe it's just a sensor, but he can't get one now, everything is shut down for Labor Day. <u>He said the dealer had a 3 day wait</u>. **See**, that's why you don't just throw stuff at the dealer. The dealers almost **NEVER** really care about you, your time, your money or your business either. And then, when they "fix" some stuff, and it often goes right back bad, it's tooth and nail to get them to warranty their own work and your back to wasting more time to get in and back out with another weak fix. This is why you **GOT TO** know your truck, and choose your truck wisely. I will help you do this later in my book.

11:50 pm- I stayed up a little late talking on the phone, doing music and writing this! Goodnight. Hasta LaVista. $_z{}^z{}^{\mathbf{z}}$

Sunday. 8:15- I awake early before my alarm goes off. I'm ready to go. Today I'll check the oil level since I'm on flat ground, the motor is cold, and I'm not needing to wake up and instantly power the motor on to warm up the truck and get going. The amount you will check your oil will be a little different for everybody. I know that between 8000 to 15000 miles on an oil change is where I start checking the oil at least twice a week just to be on the safe. Especially if I'm been heavy or pulling mountains. Sometimes I need a pinch of oil sometimes I don't. I usually end up using about a 1/2 gallon to a gallon of oil between oil changes. I need about 1/4 of a gallon. That's fine.

8:55- I leave out. Westbound on 20. I'll be going home today for the night. I will be adjusting my clutch when I get there to **compensate** for the adjustment done to the slave cylinder. My clutch works now but it still takes too long to go into gear from idle. I got the measurement tool, and it's an easy job. It will take about 15 minutes and I do it better than most shops will.

Most people won't buy the measurement tool. It's only **$50** and it works every time. There's a very small clearance needed between the throw out bearing and the flywheel, it's less than an inch. That's why you need this tool, it's shaped like a fork, it fits right in the gap at the perfect width. With the clutch pressed down, you just tighten the adjustment bolt until it's snug against the tool and now you're in adjustment! Many mechanics will say they can eyeball it and don't need the tool. I disagree. Out of ten people that says it maybe 2-5 get it right. But in my experience, they almost never do. So, if you ever need a clutch adjustment on the road, make sure to ask them will they be using the measurement tool, or how do you measure the gap. If they say "oh we've been doing this for 20 years, I don't need no tool." I would say ok, and just move on to somebody that does. Some people charge $50-75 for an adjustment, don't use the tool, go down there for 5 minutes, spin the adjustment bolt until they think it's right and your left not much better than you started. 🐿️

11:45- I make a quick stop at the welcome center in Mississippi, make and eat one of my salads that I like to make.

3:05 pm- I stop for fuel in TA Tallulah. 514 miles divided by 77 gallons = 6.7 mpg. Not bad! I'm still hauling 44k lbs up the road. 😁

4:15- I stop for the night at home. I made **great** time while not even driving too fast. We go ahead and adjust clutch. It's a simple 2 person job, my wife presses the clutch in while I adjust it from underneath. I adjust it to exactly 1/2 inch using my clutch fork measuring tool to check the clearance. I also spray brake cleaner to remove any extra grease that may cause the clutch brake to slip. I power back on the motor and test out how it feels. It's better, but not all the way where I want it. I may have to adjust the slave cylinder adjustment nut to get it just right. I'll do that at another time. Maybe tomorrow. It's good now to do what I need to do. Charles did say the more I use the clutch pedal the better it will get. See you tomorrow! ✌

Monday. 4:00am- I wake up early again! I can't sleep because I'm so **excited** about projects I'm working on. I figure I'll read this book I got on my night stand, "How to Control Your Mind" by Napoleon Hill. It's a big long interview with Andrew Carnegie; And Napoleon Hill is asking all the right questions! I really enjoy the tactics and techniques I read and just lay there with my eyes closed until the sun comes up. The plan was to sleep in lol so much for that! 😌

9:35- I leave by now. I usually park at home but I didn't want to bring this heavy load onto my property. I have a pretty sharp turn to make getting on to my road, it's challenging enough as it is without 44k lbs of steel sitting on top of my trailer. So, since I parked at the Truckstop, my wife now drops me back off. I load back up the fridge, log my pre trip, eat some warmed-up Coconut cauliflower chic pea curry we cooked last night, and tell her goodbye for the moment. We had a good time yesterday.

Today's pace will be very relaxed and chill because I got about **240** miles to drive and that's it. I figure I'll go ahead and park at TA Terrell. It's still 70 miles from delivery but I rather not park at the Truckstop's in Dallas. I'll get up early and have plenty of time to unload early then book my next load. Plus, the I-20 part of DFW doesn't really get too bad with traffic. I put my truck into gear and guess what? The clutch feels really good! Maybe I don't adjust the slave cylinder later like I originally thought. 😎

11:20- I go through Shreveport. I see a lot of guys **blaze** through here but I would not recommend it! The road is so messed up through Shreveport, that's there's literally 1, 2, and 3 inch drops offs in the road. If you've ever been through here, you know what I'm talking about. It's like driving down and up little stairs. I **ALWAYS** drop it down into 9th gear and go 40 to 45 miles per hour through here. It is not beneficial for me to take my truck through that much abuse just to get to the other side of Shreveport 5 minutes faster. This road will tear something up! Blow and air bag, crack a leaf spring, etc. If you slow anybody down behind you, don't worry about it, that's why there's two lanes, they can go around. You're out here to make money and be successful, not tear your truck up for the satisfaction of others **who** don't pay the bills on their truck! 👍

2:15- I stop in TA Terrell. I go ahead and fill up so when I deliver tomorrow, I'll **already** have a full tank to turn and burn. 306 miles dived by 44 gallons. 7mpg. Good! Due to my easy driving and slower acceleration, I made about $70 more on this load because I used less fuel than I estimated at 6mpg. I just made that much extra by slowing down a little bit and driving with a fuel consciousness, it was more enjoyable than driving fast too! 🙌

I'll wake up at 6am and sleep by 10pm or so. So, I have plenty of time to do what I want. I cook some Ziti with organic olive oil, basil and garlic for lunch / dinner. I update my book and kick back to do other things with all this free time. I got some other business projects that I decide to work on next. Then after that, maybe I'll watch something on amazon prime. I don't end up watching much TV when at home or over the road. Don't get me wrong! I love a good movie or show, but I am also **very self-disciplined** and I don't feel right relaxing on tv if there's more important things that I was supposed to do first... If I watch a show I'll catch up on some reading after.

9:00 pm- I make a new customer profile in my Quick Books app for Baggett Services, Inc. This is really easy to do and I'll will show you later in the book with screen shots. I really like the ease and effectiveness QuickBooks. The invoicing template is **great**, the invoice tracking is great, & the user interface is really cool to work in! And it's only $10 a month. After I make the customer profile, I generate tomorrow's invoice for this current load. I almost always make my invoices the night before I deliver. **Why**? It's speeds up the process of getting paid and it's very professional to have your invoice delivered the day of delivery. Remember, brokerages need that signed BOL so they can bill their customers or to turn it in to their factoring company. **I get it**! As soon as I deliver, I usually have my invoice and BOL submitted before I even leave the property. 😁

Tuesday: 6:05 am I awake. I get up and do my routine of making my bed and putting up my apu. I decide to make coffee in my truck, so I set that up. I go inside, do what I need to do and come back. I look over the truck and leave by 6:45.

8:05- Heidi from R&R express and I make a deal. **It's for $2450 on 1100 miles**, $2.23 a mile, 7k lb load, insulation delivering Thursday in Rock Hill, SC. I plan to make right at **$2100** on this one in two days. It's a 65 mile deadhead to Gainesville. This Gainesville plant is GAF, and like Nucor and the big steel operations, the big construction material operations like this are usually avoided by me too. As mentioned, I just don't like the hyper sensitive safety culture, long lines, and the company driver atmosphere. The deal works for me so I ignore my dislike. 🚚

8:10- I arrive to my delivery, check in, and go park behind the truck in front of me. He's taking his tarps down so I decide to get out and help him fold his tarps up. I'm already waiting on him anyways, <u>might as well help</u>! He **thanks** me. They take a couple of beams off me with a crane, then take the rest off with a big lift. I spend a little extra time preparing myself for my next pickup. I know it's insulation and insulation takes all 48ft of deck space, nothing can be on the deck.

So, instead of trying to scramble with my dunnage at the shipper I go ahead and find a way to secure them underneath my trailer above 2 crossmembers. I chain one end and strap the other with a 1" ratchet strap. It's now solid and won't go anywhere. I also get an idea for a custom dunnage rack where I can do this in the future but not need chains or straps to hold the wood. I think I can build the whole setup for about $200. I've been wanting to buy a big dunnage rack, but it just hasn't been much of a priority, I

25

rarely haul insulation or anything that takes all 48ft, and when I do, I can usually put the dunnage underneath the load. ✔

10:00am- I open up a can of Pineapples and leave out for Gainesville.

11:15- I arrive at GAF in Gainesville. I check in and go park in the dirt lot and go check in with the loaders. They tell me to back right in. **Good!** It's going better and smoother than my memory of this place last time. Attitude really counts. I back in, get loaded, they got a metal bar they hook up to the forklift that attaches to my tarps. They use this bar to lift my tarps right over this 8ft tall load. How convenient! This really speeds my process up and decreases the work involved to get this load ready. I email my Heidi and let her know that I'm loaded. She responds "awesome, thank you very much". I make one of my great salads for lunch. 🌴

1:45- I leave out south bound on 35, take quite a bit of traffic, take 80 to Terrell and eventually get back on 20. I'm straight shooting from here. I got some phone calls to make and I also start taking calls for reloading in South Carolina.

8:20- I pass right back by home so I stop for the night with 5 minutes left on my 14. I don't usually cut it that close, but I knew this was in my reach so I did. My wife picks me up and I'll enjoy some food and another night at home in my bed. Tomorrow's Wednesday, one week since I started writing this. I plan to wake at 6, and be leaving out on the toad by 6:45. See ya then. ✋

Wednesday. 6:45 am- I get dropped off and I leave by now. Me, my fresh coffee and some new ambition for the day.

7:50- I stop at TA Tallulah. 549 miles divided by 84.2 gallons = 6.5 mpg. Pretty good, pretty good! I was flying pretty fast yesterday and will be today to an extent.

9:00- Great! I Make deal with Shelia for building that I'm putting on my property. I'm **super happy** about this. 🏆

11:20- I Stop Livingston, AL at exit 17 once again for lunch at Taste of India and 30 min break. I order my usual, Channa Masala no butter no milk, and one Roti (bread) no butter. I'm running low on my hours so I decide to park early before Atlanta and drive the remaining 275 miles in the early morning.

11:55- I'm back on the road.

2:10- I book a **crazy good** load for Friday. It was just one of those "right time at the right place". I know the company and have hauled for them before, the company is ATL. You might not believe this if I told you, but I'll screenshot the rate sheet so you can see! **$3850 on 638 miles**, 25,000 lbs, 95 mile deadhead. That's **$6** a mile. I'll take it! I plan to make $3575 on this load over the weekend with a day and a half worth of driving. I thought my Fort Bragg was going to be the one that stole the show for this round, but I proved that wrong! 🎖️

It's ok, but It does go to Delaware, mid-state, about 60 miles east of Annapolis, MD. There's a $25 toll to cross the Chesapeake Bay Bridge, and that's already factored into what I plan to make. But hey, when the deal makes sense, it just makes sense! I have no problem going to Delaware on this deal. $

2:15. I book this other load I called on earlier. It picks up **15** miles away and goes 240 miles into Atlanta. This works perfect since I'm working on recap hours and wouldn't have much left to drive after delivering tomorrow. It's a new customer, their name is Best Logistics, I work with Tice. I already checked their credit score (I'll show you how I do this later) and it looked good to me, 27 days to pay which is standard out here for the most part.

We agree on **$850**. I plan to make **$765** on this one. It's a perfect use of time, the profit margin is nice, it's **5 hours'** worth of driving, and it puts me 95 miles from my Friday pickup. It does deliver right in down town Atlanta at Turner Field though lol. But it's right off the exit and shouldn't be too bad if I just take my time. I've done tricky deliveries before in Atlanta downtown for sure. I've done the Marriot hotel years ago in a van trailer, and I went underneath Emory hospital too, that was a fun one. The more specialized equipment or skill it takes to deliver the load, the more the load will ultimately pay depending on how you deal and etc. everybody can deliver to a big warehouse outside the city, but not everybody can do those loads that take fine attention to detail and high driver skill.

4:50 EST- I stop in Temple exit 19 at the Flying J. I almost always feel **goofy** at the Pilots, Loves and Flying J's. I'm surrounded by Swifts, CR England's, Primes, Werner's complaining about dispatchers and stuff lol. It's ok. But when I do park outside of TA Petro, I'd rather park at the Flying J. Their parking lots are much bigger and depending on the spot you pick, your less likely to get backed into by a new truck driver. Since I'm leaving at 3:30 am, I find a good spot that I know I won't get blocked in with in the morning. **Gotta plan ahead and take initiative**. I back in and call it day. It'll be leisure and reading for me the next few hours. Today marks a week since I first left from home and starting writing this. Since Monday was Labor Day, I'll give you one more day in my shoes then we'll move on to the specifics so you can get to streamlining **YOUR** understanding, knowledge, mindset, and ultimately your success in trucking as well! $

PS: I just watched Mercer, an owner op, driving his own loaded spread axle flatbed, making one of fastest and sharpest U-Turns I've ever seen right here in the parking lot. It was so sharp the trailer tires are jumping off the ground, made me cringe! I wonder if he remembers that he is the one paying for those $300-$500 tires?? Making U-Turns that sharp and fast especially with a loaded trailer is terrible for tires. It's even worse on spread axles, this is how you really can start flat spotting tires and at the least, you'll be taking tread off your tires fast. If you must make a U-Turn, **please** make it as wide and slow as possible. See ya early tomorrow! z^z

Thursday. 3:30 AM- I am up I am up I am up! It's **crazy** how you can be perfectly asleep and that alarm goes off and you just instantly spring out of bed because you know you got business to conduct. I put my stuff up, go inside the store, log a pre-trip, look over the truck, trailer and load and I head out! I'm assuming Atlanta will look much better as far as traffic goes compared to what it looks like in the day time.

I do some stretching too! I don't think I've been mentioning this but stretching is something that I do **every** day and it's **very** important. I do different stretches, touch my toes, then I rise into a yoga position called the table I think it's called, but basically you make a 90 degree angle with your body with arms and hands fully extended forward. This really stretches a lot, even down to the lower calf muscles, your lower back and more and yeah! ... it feels great! Doing this consistently will help keep your body limber for the long run and assist in keeping good posture. 😁 different stuff like that.

4:00- I leave

5:55- I stop at TA Commerce for fuel. 516 miles divided by 74.1 gallons = 7mpg. Good!

9:30- I arrive at my delivery.

12:30 PM- I'm still getting unloaded. My 14 hour clock is getting lower. Good thing my pick up is close. I call Heidi and tell her I've been patient but I think we should start billing for dentition time. She agrees and tells me to get it documented and they'll pay. I also call Kevin the site manager and tell him the same thing, that I've been patient but now I'm cutting it close for my next job. I ask him will he get his driver to unload me and stage it on the ground instead of going all the way around the building and loading it onto the roof. This is what's been taking so long. He agrees. **Come** on! I got stuff to do. 😐

This is why I also booked the load yesterday with a **20** mile deadhead, because my 14 would be low and just in case a slow unloading time like this. You're going to hear me say this a lot, but, gotta take initiative. This is your show! 🙌

1:15- I leave out by now. Everything moved much **quicker** once I made my calls. I only got 20 miles to deadhead but still, got to make it happen right? People will just walk right over you if you let it. This is what **separates** a business owner from an employee. Employees will just go with the flow and get pushed back. An owner will create the flow. This is your job as an owner. You create the flow; you **dictate** the outcome as much as possible. I'm not suggesting you be Super Jerk, but I do suggest you stand your ground but in a likeable way. Make it hard for others to say no. 😎

1:40- I make it to my pick up spot in Richburg, SC. I pull in and park by the other trucks that are loading. I talk with another driver for a moment, then the young woman who is in charge appears, she's good and we get started on the logistics of loading. 🏗

2:40- I leave by now. 4 concrete pieces is what I have on my trailer now. I'll deliver at 9:30 sharp in the city center of Atlanta. **Wish me luck**. I plan to stop in Augusta. It's about 20 miles longer to go this way, but it's all interstate compared to 45 miles of back roads and traffic lights, so I decide it's worth the tradeoff. 🚚

5:00. I stop down in Augusta on the 520 loop exit 9. There's 2 truck stops here. Ones $5 to park, the others free. I snag a free spot for the night. I'll wake tomorrow at 5:30, but you won't be following me then! It will be a mystery!!!! You've already got one real week and a day with me! Including my next load to Delaware; $11,370 dollars after fuel in 12 days with a repair breakdown and a Labor Day weekend. That's a **$5,685** simple NET average per week AFTER fuel. I killed it this time. I usually do good but in that $3k to $5k a week after fuel. But some weeks I just really crush it! $11,370 less $700 in repairs is $10,670 after fuel. Not bad not bad! 😎 5k to 8k $ simple profit weeks have of course happened too.

Now you get to start **getting** the knowledge it takes for you to be in this same position and better, doing what it takes to write your own story of **success**! Now that you know me much more than you did when we started, I know now your more inclined to put in motion the methods of this book. Done right, you will be the next teacher. 👍

I really, really, really wish I had all of this information when I started! I would be in a MUCH further place financially right now. **But that's ok**! I have it now, and I'm sharing it with you. **Let's do this**! <u>Are you ready</u>? I didn't sell you a get rich quick scheme, I sold you the key 🔑 and catalyst to unlock your own success in trucking. A key to unlock your inner business man, your inner business woman, your inner boss, and your inner success.

Trucking can be very challenging, but it's also **very** rewarding. You may stay in trucking forever, or maybe you use trucking only to get you forward to your next business. <u>Let me help you</u>! **Lend me your ear**! Lend me your **attention**! 🫣

Everything I've said and will say from here on, is for a reason and has purpose! **So**, for your benefit, listen close, pay attention to the punctuation, and begin to allow the rhythm of success into you. **Success starts with mentality**. That's where we will go next. If you have the self-defeating mentality, you will not catch your break and you will <u>continue to lose</u>. In order to win and use the **SPECIFIC** information I give; you must first have a <u>mentality</u> that **can accept it**, a <u>mentality</u> that **can use it**, and a <u>mentality</u> that **can process it**. 😇

DEGREE 2 - MENTALITY

"Weak desires produce weak results". This is one of my favorite quotes. Napoleon Hill wrote this back in the 1930's and it's still holding strong to this day.

Emotion as defined in this degree is emotion
= energy in motion.

GAME ALERT ✔️

Let's get straight to it. The more you want something the more you will find ways to make it real. **This is called desire**. The key is to want something so much, that desire turns into **obsession**. Obsession is the powerhouse of Creation. To the broad public, the word Obsession sometimes carries a negative reputation, but it's one of your MOST important tools! Once your obsessed with something, whether positive or negative, you're bound to make it real! Obsession is like the magnet that attracts all things universal and physical that is in harmony with that thought. 💪

Napoleon Hill, who wrote Think and Grow Rich, which most modern self-help books got inspired from, teaches that in this life man is basically only in control of one thing, his thoughts. If you will, picture your conscious mind, the one you use to think with throughout the day;

→**Picture that your conscious (thinking) mind is the gardener**.

And that your subconscious (non-thinking) mind is the garden. 🌴

Only what you plant in your sub-conscious mind with your conscious mind is what will grow. ✓

If great seeds are planted and the weeds kept out, a great garden will be had. If the weeds are not attended to, it doesn't really matter what gets planted in this garden, it won't growbecause the weeds will choke it out. $ ok?

> The weeds in our subconscious mind are;
> doubt, worry and fear.

→Doubt, worry and fear will swallow up the great ideas you seek to grow if you let it. Doubt, worry and fear carry an energy and force of their own and will destroy a garden of ideas and dreams before it even gets a chance to grow. It's pesticide to organic food.

Using your subconscious mind with doubt, worry and fear will eventually attract to you the things and or cause delays in your own plans. INITIATIVE! **Do not allow doubt and worry to crystallize into fear!...** Causing complacency... Doubt and worry <u>has the tendency to evolve </u>into mild fear or full fear. Having fear is an unstable emotion to be building any business around!

One of the biggest fears to overcome is fear of not having enough money to maintain what was built and being built on and upon. Positive self-talk helps on the mental side. Action helps on the day to day.

It is my belief and also Napoleon Hills teaching, that our subconscious minds are the translator between each 1 of us and the entirety of the universe. The more accountability you exercise of each your conscious and subconscious mind, the more likely you successful in whatever endevor! **It is said that our subconscious mind is what communicates us to Straight to God and the universe**. YUP! But how to train it, use or discipline the subconscious mind? 😑Awareness creates real change as its embraced with excitement, action and results.

Our **subconscious** mind is there, it's ancient, and it doesn't differentiate between positive or negative energy, feels or emotion. Once an emotion is attached to an ideal, the subconscious mind steps this signal up and sends it into the entire fabric of space. Like an old radio station does with voice broadcasted out through frequency strength. Once the universe gets the signal it starts to create this reality for you. Nikola Tesla figured out, when two things are vibrating on the same frequency there is no such thing as distance! Cell phone became the example of that.

When you get on the same frequency of exactly what it is that you want, the universe begins to pull the two realities closer and closer together. This is the power of the subconscious mind and knowing exactly what you want! But the reverse is true too. If your subconscious mind is focused on failure and fears, that is the frequency that you are bringing into your reality because that's whatit is being cast out in vibration. **BE CAREFUL!** 🙌

An example would be, "I don't think I can do this", or "it's going to be so hard" or "I can't get the money I want from brokers" or "I'm just cursed, my truck ALWAYS breaks down" ... once a negative feeling, doubt, worry or fear gets attached to these ideas, the subconscious mind takes that message, a vibration, a waveform of kinds, translates into the universes for further creation. The universe then gets busy attracting to you what it is you requested through your subconscious mind body vibration frequency. **THIS IS VERY REAL!** ⚡

<u>I was my own worst enemy for many years.</u> I would doubt. I would doubt when looking at how much money I owed on my truck. I would always look at the check engine light wondering when it would light up again. By attaching negative feeling to these ideas, I assisted that reality to be created against me. I hope you innerstand how important this one KEY is. 🔑 With this type of power, wouldn't you want to be more involved in creating a great life for yourself instead of just letting life happen to you???? **Yes!!!!**

→The next very important part of mentality is **knowing exactly what you want**.

Napoleon Hill teaches, You have to be very specific! You can't just be like "oh I want to be successful" or "I just want to make some money". We can have periods of re-evaualation later if you don't have this answer yet but still, specific as can get… Be careful because these desires mixed with feeling are going straight to God's "request line" of universal law. We can tell by looking at Earth, our human bodies, the stars and etc that we're dealing with a very intelligent God! I like to say that a God this intelligent probably has a very intelligent SENSE OF HUMOR too! So, for instance. If you are desiring money and weren't specific, any amount of money could fill that request. Without saying how much money you wanted and just broadly desiring money you got what you wanted and "that's the joke" so to speak. But it's not too funny if you don't understand the lesson. Being **DELIBERATE, PRECISE** and knowing exactly how much you want, and when you want it by helps ensure THE results 💲

If you were raised Christian or Catholic, you may find this hard to do in the beginning because we're kind of taught that we're supposed to just accept whatever God blesses us with and to not be greedy... But I Know, that if you're a righteous man, or a righteous woman, and your intentions are positive and whole, then whatever it is we want is righteous too and is of GODS WILL! Serious! God is just waiting on **us** to take responsibility, faith it out, take action and get our head in the game that we are allowed to want! Your future and present is waiting on you to be exact, to know exactly what you want and to have extreme faith that it will be. Vibrating there.

Now that we got the power of the subconscious mind and knowing exactly what we want.

The next part is **repetition and habit.** A method by Napoleon Hill called auto suggestion.

Using your conscious mind, you must repeat over and over what it is you want until you finally convince your subconscious mind that it's real and that it's going to happen. Once you get your subconscious mind on board, your good to go! At this point, it will just take regular maintenance of keeping the "weeds" of doubt, worry and fear out of your conscious mind. Because if it's in your conscious mind it will leak into your subconscious mind and try to take over your manifestation process **THIS DISIPLINE TAKES WORK! BUT IT IS WORTH IT FOR SURE!** 🌴

Yes, quick thoughts may come of doubt, what if I break down? & what if I don't have enough money? If thoughts come like this face them head on, deal with it and dispose. Do not allow these negative feelings or emotion to live inside of you. They will not serve you one bit; they will only attempt to overthrow your positive goals and dreams and once it hits your subconscious it's over with and these thoughts start to become real. Countering this is called discipline of the mind. Almost all successful people have mastered discipline of the mind to some degree. You can achieve this discipline too if it is this That you want. 😎

But before going to the next key point of mentality, I will show you exactly how I have achieved discipline of my mind and how I convinced my subconscious mind that it will be. I had to say this every morning and throughout the day until I finally believed it and knew it true. Feel free to alter it to make it more personalized or just repeat it like how I DID. My version has been through about 10 upgrades since I first began doing this and it will get more refined in time.

REMEMBER

saying mantra's and not believing them and knowing them True will do nothing! I repeat <u>WILL DO NOTHING</u>!!!! **You must believe what you say and Know It True**. You must attach positive feeling and emotion to it. It will be challenging at first and may even sound like your lying trying to con yourself…. Because maybe you kind of are! At first….. But you must continue your day after day so you can convince your subconscious mind! Once your subconscious mind believes and knows true, the universe is now on your side, assisting you in your desires! It takes 21 days to neurologically build a new pathway in our mind. It takes 21 days of consistency to create a new habit positive or negative.

21 days habit. 3 months lifestyle. 3 years permanent.

(the money amount will be up to you according to where you're at in your journey and what you want your current money goal to be. This could be $10,000, $20,000, $50,000, $100,000, $150,000 ETC! It's up to you. But where I write "X", replace it with an <u>exact</u> dollar amount that you want to have by *this time next year or end of year*)

→**OUT LOUD I SAY:** ✔ (out loud for vibration and frequency projection purposes)

I will have "X amount" of money in the bank, this year by December 31. I will do this by successfully delivering my customers freight, by taking initiative and by making smart decisions. I FEEL (important) as if I'm already in possession of this money! 😁

I will not let doubt or worry crystallize into fear and I will not allow my reactions or expectations of others or anything else cause me to drift, → because I have → accurate thinking, definite of purpose, I know what I want, I stand my ground in a likeable way, I make decisions quickly and I'm slow to change them, I'm very enthusiastic, I have an attractive personality, I'm highly favored, I'm highly valued, highly respected, I'm highly loved, and I'm highly appreciated, I make great deals and people love to make deals with me... ✔

I BELIEVE and KNOW I will be in possession of "X amount". I have so much faith that I can see the money, "X amount" in my bank account already, I am this money, I can see it in my online bank accounts. I feel the money transferring into my hands, I feel as if I already have it my possession... $

SAY: Faith, desire, obsession, enthusiasm, love, sex*, Hope, initiative, intuition, action, persistence, imagination, instinct, strength, accountability, responsibility, self-control, problem solver, deal maker, vessel of great health, success and true happiness... THIS is who I am, this how I think, this is how I conversate, project myself, interface and is how I'm received. And most importantly, this is how I FEEL! 😇

(*sex is one of the strongest positive emotions Napoleon Hill teaches)

thanks be to the most high, and a special shout out to earth and the people on it, to my positive ancestors, and for the love I give and receive 😁

The last part is a part I add to it. If you want to thank God in a personalized way, right here at the end is a good place to do it. It becomes a prayer, and an even stronger affirmation sealed in faith and gratitude.

Remember,
what you're doing right now is **LITERALLY** convincing an ancient subconscious mind.

You're like a salesman doing your best to convince your subconscious mind that all of what you want is real, that it's yours and that you actually already are that! ✔️

It's pretty hard to convince it and assume the feeling of the wish fulfilled.
You can say affirmations all you want but if you don't truly feel, believe and know it, it won't happen or change anything! It's not until POSITIVE feeling and emotion is mixed to an idea that it begins to work.

The emotion is energy in motion. If you want to put your ideas in motion, you have to mix positive energy into the thought. 🔑

NEXT IS ENTHUSIASM!

Enthusiasm is what gets you sold, enthusiasm is what let's others know you must be onto something, enthusiasm is contagious!! Enthusiasm is vibration instantly at work.

** I've noticed that enthusiasm and using another persons name, is one of the most highly effective methods in making deals, dealing with the part stores, repair shops, shippers and receivers, brokers, the cashier at Walmart, family and etc!!!!** just be genuine.

Do make an effort to be **authentic**, and to be genuine as possible. Nobody likes a con man. After a while the charm rubs off and the illusion becomes unattractive. Most successful people will know if you're just trying to butter them up and talk a good game. 😵 and that is very not good.

Being **enthusiastic** can be difficult if there's not something to look forward to, or something to be happy about right away. I'll tell you what Ive done. I would let my exact goal be the source of my excitement! Being excited I know is much more sustainable than always trying to be happy. When your excited about something, happiness tends to follow! And if ever you start to get down and unenthusiastic, remember your goal and <u>INCREASE YOUR DESIRE</u>!!!! Napoleon Hill really stresses this in "Think and Grow Rich". When one starts feel down or lose his drive, increase your desire. Make yourself want it more! Remind yourself this is what you want. This is what I did. Do it over and over again until you pull yourself out of the slump and get excited again. Your mental state is **YOUR** responsibility and treasure!

And still once you get your mental to the positive state, it will take maintenance and preventative maintenance to keep it there lol. The good news is, IT IS WORTH IT!!!! ok let's continue. And yes, excitement will balance and flow also.

With your subconscious mind in agreement to your conscious mind, enthusiasm will begin to lighten your load and even move mountains for you! Think back to when my clutch line broke earlier, and I had a lot riding on getting that part and line back on to make my Friday delivery... It seemed like a mountain at the time but because of enthusiasm and initiative, it moved and I not only got past it but scored heavy on the following back to back loads that came from me getting reloaded that Saturday.

Would I of made my deadlines and got reloaded if my enthusiasm was low? If I just put my hands up and said whatever happens happens? Probably **No**! I knew what I wanted. I mixed positive emotion in, namely **faith**, **desire** and **obsession**. I then worked with real people and enthusiasm as the vehicle to make it all happen. The positive side of universe & universal law is wanting to work with you, but you must be a vessel. Be a vessel that understands the mechanics of universal law. Even in the Bible it says ask and ye shall receive. It's **OKAY** to know what you want! It's OKAY to have what you're going to have! It's **OKAY** to believe and know in yourself! Like I mentioned earlier, as long as you're a righteous man or a woman and your intentions are positive and doesn't hurt anyone, then why would your desires not be God's will too?
Contrary, God has shown me that once I got a hold of my own conscious to subconscious flow that I could be the co-writer to my own destiny!

→**Now let me warn you**, Napoleon Hill also teaches this in "Outwitting the Devil", that once you make your mind up on a goal, you probably will be faced with some external and or internal resistance and or crisis. This resistance is a weapon that negativity uses to see if you will give up and join back to the negative, easy, self doubting, non-producing side. Don't let the speed bumps, detours, pauses and challenges in the beginning and along the way trick you off the path to owning your own mind and life force! You have to prove yourself to negativity that you're not going to give up and that you're not worth trying to plug back up to negativity's time.

Once you **stay** committed and dedicated without doubt long enough, negativity will leave you alone until your next level! Because at this point, you're just not worth the time! Negativity literally has no power over you once you know what you want and you take back control POWER and WILL of your subconscious mind flow. I'll make a quick book list at the end of this chapter, and this book will definitely be in it.

I remember I used to be very **loose** and **vague** in my money goals. I would say things like, "I want to do well this year, maybe I'll even get to $50k this year, if everything goes well that is" or stuff like "I'd really like to make $10k this next go around, I'm not going to promise anything, it may not happen" or whatever it was lol I can barely remember **because I just will not allow myself to think or speak out like that anymore!** It helps nothing! I used to think that I was being rude to God if I asked for too much, or if I said I'm going to have a certain amount of money by a certain day. I thought I would "jinx" or curse myself. I was still thinking in that old mentality that God would bless me with whatever I'm supposed to get. This is **superstition** and there's no place for superstition in business!

It seems righteous but really in my opinion in hind-sight, it's just self-doubt, is being timid and acting un-worthy. 🔑

"If you're a **good** person then <u>why are you worried about offending God</u>?" This is the question that took me a long time to start asking. God has built this universe on **law and order** and has also said, "my people perish because of a lack of knowledge." Knowing that you can do it, and how to jump in Gods operating system is **knowledge**. <u>Acting</u> on this knowledge is **faith**! I challenge you to study the metaphysics, ancient history, alternate history and health etc in your spare time if you have not already! 😎

But how does this all **relate** to trucking? You know; you can see, ...

Without a positive mentality you're stealing your blessings from yourself. ✔️

You can very well be <u>your own biggest roadblock</u> and **don't even know it**! You have to be real with yourself; You have to on a regular basis, do a full inventory of your thoughts, goals, emotions, energy, feeling, how you displace energy on others, your ambitions and etc.

You have to **get rid** of what doesn't serve you in positivity, and only feed your mind with the greatness, strength and faith! Nothing less is accepted, not even self-pitty for more than a moment. Negative thoughts may come and go of course but it gets easier, and don't sweep it under the rug just dispose of that thought and feeling that came with it. 🔑

→Quickly endure the negative emotion, dispose of it and **let it go**! You then get to get straight back to <u>programming yourself for greatness</u>!
Right back to keeping your "train" upright on its track to going on its great destination. 🚂

These are the <u>biggest</u> things to REMEMBER and BECOME when it comes to mentality. ✔

1. Know what you want. Exactly what you want. Put a date on when you want it by.
2. Take control of your subconscious mind flow by and through the practice of auto suggestion.
3. Affirmations don't work unless you mix in positive feeling and emotion, and that you must believe it and know it. Don't just simply repeat the words, you must believe it and know it.
4. Faith, Desire, Obsession and Enthusiasm are your best friends. Attach all your desires, ideas and goals to these positive energies in-motion.
5. Enthusiasm is contagious. Play offense with enthusiasm and watch how often it gets returned right back to you and often in a playful manner!
6. By being obsessed with what you want, the "how will I do it" part will get revealed to you the more you increase your desire and go forward.
7. This chapter on mentality is all real. There's no smoke and mirrors to it. It will take work and effort but a positive sharpened mentality is bridge you for success. Would you rather build in harmony with the universe or against it??
8. Enjoy your process. Don't be so blinded to the goal that you can't have fun along the way. A positive mind should be enjoyed and shared with others when out.

One more thing I want to share about mentality is this. ✔

Our mind, and mind space, is like **real estate**. It's prime real estate, it's like New York, New York, Manhattan 5th Ave type real estate ok! WHY? BECAUSE IT's our most special piece of real estate that we own outright and always live in.

We were born into this world with this free inherited plot of land. It's up to us to decide what we build there (in our mind), who we let live there (in our mind), and what rules and traditions we set up and how good of a place it is.
What am I saying? Well, negative emotion loves to catch a free ride. 👎ok?

There are **certain people** in your life, positive or negative, that **you** allow to live in your head, which is, inside your PRIME real estate. Now **imagine**, this is your land, you're the president, you're the bank, and you call the shots. Would you allow negativity and distracting Lulls and clicks of negativity on your prime real estate? Would you let onlookers influence or ruin your amazing creation? Especially for people that make you mad?? 🤐🤫😶🔑

When we **allow** negative emotion to be entertained, negativity gets to have a free ride in this very important mind real estate we're talking about. This negativity can be energy from a family member, a mother, a grandma, cousin, a friend, your loved one, or whomever ok? And ourself...

Even **anger** against one of these people if held in for too long will give that person and negativity an all-access pass to live in your mental real estate (in your mind!).

Even if you're not consciously or consistently thinking about this person or what they did or didn't do, IF the emotion is still lingering in your subconscious mind flow, it will **therefore** be affecting your manifestation process and ultimately your happiness and quality of life. 🎭

The sooner you realize **YOU'RE IN CONTROL** of what lives in this real estate of yours, the better. The more you take Lead charge of what lives in your head and mind flow, the more little things won't anger you as much. Why? Because you're inside the gates of This Amazing estate and this little aggravation is on the outside looking in or is even too small to notice! Everything hits you differently when in this type of awareness and safeguarding, you're not so emotionally moved by everything little thing once you get in control of this mental real estate and enjoy doing so. You just see it as it is, maybe laugh, and with your enthusiasm you just keep it moving forward without distracting yourself from your Desired state and frequency. 💲😎

My must read book list ✔️

I've read many books over the years from health to ancient history, to metaphysics, to DIY projects and etc. but these 3 books have been essential in my growth and stand out. **Especially** "Think and Grow Rich", think and grow rich was the spark and the catalyst that allowed me to use everything else that I had already learned more quickly, effectively, and intentionally.

1. **"Think and Grow Rich"** by Napoleon Hill. This is a timeless classic that MANY of the self-help books today are based off of. It was written shortly after the Great Depression. So, Napoleon Hill knows struggle,

but importantly he knows how to be a winner of one's own destiny. (I read this book constantly and over and over again) https://amzn.to/3n43Dn0

2. **"Outwitting the Devil"** by Napoleon Hill. This book is SERIOUS. It will teach in detail; all the tricks negativity will use against you. It's set up as an interview between Napoleon Hill and the devil itself. Through Hills accurate thinking and definite of purpose, he is able to make the Devil expose his tactics and mechanics of how he causes most people "drift" and not have control over their own lives. "Know thy Enemy" right???? https://amzn.to/384KiOB

3. **"Laws of Success"** by Napoleon Hill. If possible, get the original 1925 edition. It is said that the tycoons of his time demanded this edition to be took out of production because it had too much knowledge in it that would threaten their lively hoods LOL! This book is written pre–Great Depression. It's a big book and one I read throughout off and on. Hill goes in great detail about the lessons of persistence, imagination, self-control, action and MANY more!
https://amzn.to/38OaxaR

    Let's keep it moving! Don't take lightly this chapter Mentality! You will need it to really activate and use the knowledge and experience that's on the schedule to be delivered to you in this guide. I can honestly say, I didn't start to truly level up in trucking, freedom of time and making money very fast and steady until I got my mind right onto this level of awareness, positivity, being intentional and actually believing and knowing it all.

Don't get me wrong, it did well, bought my first home cash, paid 2 trucks off. But It took way longer to do those things at that time because of my mentality. I learned to finally work with universal law and not against it! <u>Make my mindset your mindset too-</u> The next chapter is "**Operation**". One of the biggest determining factors on how much gross money you can make depends on the style and type of operation you choose. Will you drive for a percentage? A set rate per mile? Lease to a fleet? Get your own authority? Let's discuss. $

DEGREE 3: OPERATION

I remember hearing a statistic that close to 90% of new solo owner trucking companies fail within one year. And the ones that make it past one year, 50% of those companies fail within 2 years. I won't sugar coat it much; and I'll show humility by calling myself out in the stories… But one of the main reasons these statistic startup companies fail to work is because they choose an operation that was not fruitful enough and usually also a Truck with the wrong motor and carried over issues that is to fast to fix the issues before the money dries. Choosing an operation that doesn't allow growth combined with Early on maintenance issues and that's the most of it. Another company done. ✗ this is what we're trying to prepare against in this Solo Owner-Operator guide.

Let's dive straight in with it, if you're not making at least $2500 a week after fuel, that's not good. If you're consistently making over $1500 to about $2000, you're not doing horrible but to make all the extra responsibility worth it and to have a more guaranteed chance of company survival→ I would consider a stable operation with growth potential to be $3000 a week net after fuel or better.

If your making at least $3000 a week after fuel and lease on take outs if you have those, and if you save your money well, buy tools, fix it yourself your truck along the way, there's a reassuring increase in constantly progressing and building up a nice juicy bank account reaching that 30k 50k 75k 100k and beyond levels!

The amount of money you actually keep is the real score keeper in this game. We'll get into budgeting and tips to lower operating cost in later chapter but there's plenty of solo owner operator companies who make close to $200k + gross per year with one truck but can't afford a set of 8 name brand tires when it's all said and done 12 months later. I was willing to sacrifice for some years in the of my solo owner operator journey. NEED THAT bank account balance there running a highly leveraged instrument like a semi truck! Parts, insurance, service, diesel, waiting for money etc… 30k cash not just credit is a nice starting point for solid financial cushion… Sacrifice now, and live like a King later! 😎

→TWO easy NEED TO KNOW TERMS IN all BUSINESS ARE; GROSS & NET.

GROSS IS THE TOTAL AMOUNT OF MONEY YOU MAKE **BEFORE** EXPENSES.

NET IS WHAT YOU MAKE **AFTER** ALL EXPENSES. ✔
-You will also hear me use the term "Simple Net". This is a term I made up for what it is you make after paying for fuel but before the rest and other smaller expenses.🚚

ANOTHER IMPORTANT TERM IS <u>PROFIT</u>! profit IS THE AMOUNT OF MONEY MADE **PAST/AFTER** THE AMOUNT MONEY YOU **SPENT**.

<u>Example:</u> IF IT TOOK YOU $50 TO MAKE $100, YOU MADE A $50 PROFIT.
-YOUR GROSS AMOUNT MADE WAS $100. Then, Minus $50 for expenses.
-PROFIT IS $50! PROFIT AND NET ARE VERY SIMILAR AND CAN BE USED mostly INTERCHANGEABLY. 😎

→ANOTHER BUSINESS WORD TO KNOW IS **OVERHEAD** OR **OVERHEAD COST**. your overhead is how much it costs you to run your business per month, per year, per week or per however you need to view it. you can measure overhead by the year, by the month, by the week or even by the day or load. I usually measure my overhead by the month and by the year.

TO FIGURE OUT YOUR OVERHEAD, SIMPLY ADD UP ALL YOUR COSTS FOR THE YEAR. **THAT'S YOUR YEARLY OVERHEAD**.   DIVIDE ÷ THAT NUMBER BY 12 TO GET YOUR MONTHY OVERHEAD.   DIVIDE ÷ THAT NUMBER BY 4 TO GET YOUR WEEKLY OVERHEAD. -ONCE YOU PASS YOUR OVERHEAD COST, YOU START TO TRULY GENERATE YOUR PROFIT! $

There's an old saying, and it's used in trucking too, "don't put the carriage before the horse" type of thing Right? Because the horse has to be first in order for the carriage to be pulled. 😶

In trucking this happens when a solo owner-operator company goes out and buys or lease a truck and doesn't first know what type of trailer they will be hauling… or what company or operation they're going to run it with. -They don't know their 1-to-5-year business plans. -They don't know how much money they'll be making at the said unknown companies that they haven't decided on yet!!
Got to know the numbers.
But it happens every day. Figuring out your numbers & your potential profits BEFORE you buy a truck, & BEFORE you choose a company will be most beneficial. This is will give you vision.
Because look at this too, the type of work you do will also have to do with what truck, engine, transmission, differential gear ratios and etc that you'll need to choose. It is this way smarter to just figure out your plan first, run the numbers on paper, see how much you'll be making on the low side and the high side at each different company and operation style. Then factor in about .15 - .20 a mile for maintenance until you work your kinks out of your truck and that number may come down some. (More on this in a later chapter!) 🔧

I was one of those guys when I first started, I got into a lease deal at 22 years old (2012). I didn't go into it completely blind; I had a mentor who was breaking down cost per mile and revenue with me and I knew basic business and math. But as far as having a great plan or really knowing the business, I was PRETTY blind. And after about 6 months, the light bulb come on in my minds eye and I asked; "Why am I paying $900 a week for a truck that I cannot keep??"..... This is the positive self-talk, audit keeping conversation, right question asking moments that's needed to be had with self or mentor. So...., $900 every week is $3600 a month. I could be buying a BRAND-NEW truck for $3600 a month if I wanted. Something about this lease deal ISN'T ADDING UP!!!! 😵 →

I made decent money there at Prime, leasing, more money than I made previously before as a company driver, but only about $1200-$2000 a week tops. I don't actually remember making more than $1800 in one week but that wasn't very common at all. The thing with this lease deal was, I could make decent money but also I could never afford to Truly come home, stay home and enjoy it. This was frustrating to me and I knew I could do better. If I stayed home 5 days, now I would come out about $1100- in the hole. That week my settlement would be about negative $1100!!!! 🤑 that's a lot of pressure for not being able to own a truck and low weekly profits.. when do you get to live type of thing? Ok.

On a good week I would make $1500. That means my next settlement covered my negative balance of last week and probably still didn't cover my fixed expenses of this week; Still leaving me $500 in the negative to somewhere around breakeven. Those 5 days at home cost me 2 weeks of catch up time with no new money, but im doing all sorts of new work and taking new risk… **Hustling like this is hustling of the self !** 🏆

Now of course there are some exceptions and some deals that make sense in the lease world but in the most part carrier sponsored lease deals are taking the bills and liability off of them, and putting them on who signs the lease deals who also typically get no ownership and low weekly profit 😵 while still assuming risk, doing the job, and covering the tax liability....

My opinion is, it's better off being a company driver and saving your money and doing something else. The treadmill and waste of time could be avoided by taking the company gig over the lease... The sad and wild to me part is, in my situation at Prime Inc, I would never be able to keep my first truck I paid off! This is common knowledge, and they let it be known, but I would have to return the truck PAID and wait until truck 2, then put like $12k down, then go through the whole process again. But I'm young and impressionable for this oppurtunity at the time... I want in!

Remember, typical fleet lease deal, I'm responsible for maintenance, on a truck I couldn't even keep! Not just oil changes of course, but anything not covered under motor and transmission warranty. I so excited to be running my own business at 22 years back in 2012 lol, that I didn't care, or it didn't become obvious to me yet that, that was a negative time consuming and energy DEAL!!!! ✖

I got back into the "lab", did a bunch of number crunching on paper and decided my next move. By leaving Prime, I would cut my overhead in 1/2. Instead of paying $3600 a month on lease notes, I would be paying $1650 a month using a truck that I *would actually own*. I wanted more control of my freight, I wanted to haul lighter loads, I wanted to go to **Landstar**! Only thing was, I had to be 23 years old to apply for Landstar. This gave me time to save more money and to work a deal out for financing. I was approved for my truck at 22, a couple weeks before I put my application in with Landstar. Just so you know, Landstar's hiring process usually takes about a month if you decide to take a stop or tenure there with them. 😎

At 23 I got my truck from Lone Mountain at their Georgia location and took it to Landstar. The total cost was $65,000.00 financed with $6200 down (or $7200 I forget!). 🤠

My very own 2009 Peterbilt 387, it was an ex-prime truck, had a metallic blue paint job, subtle chrome flames and had a trip-pac apu on it since day one (less idling). This was exciting and a cool truck but in order to make it work and make it through that ownership was often not fun….. it sure gave MANY life lessons of self-reliance ! 🥴

But the point I'm making is, before I went to Landstar, I went to online webinars for using their load board. I knew how much their fuel discounts were, I knew how to calculate their percentages, I spoke to many owner ops at Landstar. When I first started at US Xpress when I was 21, I knew I wanted to be at Landstar one day. Once I learned that they picked their own loads and had that type of control on their freight and service destiny, I just knew that's where I was supposed to be too! I didn't go to Landstar just because of that 1 sensation or emotion, I crunched the numbers, I did the math, and I made the most sense. 💲 it was a sensation at first though lol which lead me to the math.

This chapter is called Operation because after mentality, this is next most important parts that has to be in place besides choosing the right truck. In the chapter following this one, I give detailed information on exactly how I run my operation. But as it concerns the textbook at this moment, we're going to document a spread of options as foundation then go to specifics of each.

It goes like this basically:

You have to know your goals. You have to know your budget. You have to know what makes you and your family happy. $4k a week might not mean nothing to a man that's making his $2.2k a week but is only gone for one night or two doing 2 loads a week always around home with a paid for truck.

This solo owner-operator with the paid of truck, paid off house, and a light load schedule probably wouldn't want to trade that for more money. That operation has made them happy and makes him or her available to home life often. But you'll see, who runs these types of operations ARE, usually the guys having the old paid for often pre-emissions truck, they got their own tools, they do their own brake jobs, grease their own truck, do their own oil changes and etc. They offset this lower income by being very self-sufficient and not outsourcing small or medium jobs. 🌴

If you don't work on your truck at all, then you got to be making the big bucks pretty much. At least $3k or more. But even then, why pay someone $50 to put in your air filter? Pay for mudflaps? Windshield wipers? Sensors? Lights? Solenoids? Switches? Fuses? Relays? ❓ there's small things we can get in the habit of doing right away to save money and get experience. Then once your paid paid, maybe you pay for these things out of convience and morale.

These are things I think every owner operator should have the tools and know-how for. This is a great way to build confidence for bigger jobs and to keep that profit margin higher and closer to home.
I can't tell you how many times I've bought the tool to do something and later I end up using that same tool again and

again, paying for itself over and over. Then the more tools you collect, you find yourself being able to fix most of the repairs you need to make along the way. I have a pdf book called "MY TOOL LIST" with all the tools I carry and with pictures of how I organize them.

Everybody has their own style, their own method and their own approach to their operation. It's up to you as an owner to decide what will be the Best for you! It will likely take trial and error; or with enough research and from studying this textbook, you may be able to Cool get it the first time! 😎

I met solo owner-operators all the time who are content with making $1500-$2500 a week even with high equipment costs while not working on the trucks themselves or trying to know how. I could never operate like that, but hey it is free will right. Some solo owner-operators would rather pay more for a newer truck thinking that makes them clear from maintenance. But I'll tell you, new trucks need repairs too and often and usually they need MORE repairs because of the emission system and the 30 sensors that run it (exaggeration but seriously!) 🤮 ... I'm getting a little side tracked because operation does include what type of truck setup you choose, but I'll go more into WAY more detail on equipment in a following chapter. 🚚

Next, I'll cover for who doesn't know the different levels/stages and operation types. 😎

1. **LEASE OPERATOR**: Lease a truck from a carrier, lease that truck to the same carriers DOT# This is usually referred to as being a **Lease Operator**.
    Many owner operators do not consider this being an owner operator. Actually, to be in this position and

to tell people that you are an owner operator, is pretty ignorant to the game. As a lease operator in this capacity, there are many of the owner operator responsibilities that aren't had. Like… You don't book your own freight, you don't work on your own truck, you don't actually own the truck, you will never own the truck in a standard lease, you don't handle the compliance side like IRP, IFTA, UCR, INSURANCE and more.. so, Just so you know, Many guys take dislike when new young lease operators jump out telling everyone he or she is an "owner operator"! Not quite my friend, not yet! You are a business man or woman, you are leasing, but not quite an owner operator yet. This phrase is more like a company driver, with more financial responsibility, with a slightly increased pay, which is usually lower than a company driver pay once you factor in home time and maintenance and 1099 liability. (SORRY!) Just the truth over here! ✌

2. **LEASE PURCHASE**. This is much of the same type of operation as above; You lease **purchase** instead of just leasing. You still lease your truck from the same carrier you will be leased to but are working towards owning the truck. In this operation, most carriers will not let you take their truck to another company until you have paid it off first. The main difference between lease and lease purchase is, in a lease purchase, you actually get to own your truck when you finis paying for it (depending on your deal). So, if you are lease purchase, and someone calls you a lease driver, say hey! I'm a LEASE PURCHASE driver! It's more dignifying because you get to own the truck. 😄

3. **LEASED ON TO**: Buying your own truck from a bank or etc and leasing it to a company (to the carriers DOT#) This is usually referred to as an Owner Operator leased to a company. This is what I was doing when I brought my own truck to Landstar. I was LEASED TO Landstar. Not leasing from Landstar. It can sound a little confusing because the same word "leased" is being used in different way. The key word is Leased "TO" and Leasing "FROM". Leasing from is a lease purchase, or lease operator operation. Leasing TO: Is on the owner operator side of things. There are MANY real owner operators that choose to LEASE TO a company like Landstar or Mercer, and that's perfectly fine! It's all about what works for you and makes you happy and paid right! 😁

4. **OWN AUTHORITY**: Having your own truck, and leasing it to your own company. This is called having your own authority. In order to do this, you must have your own DOT#, MC#, IRP, and IFTA. You're completely in charge of all your safety, state, and federal compliance. Some say this is being a true owner operator. And I agree, but there's nothing wrong with being leased to a company if that's what works the best for you. 👍

IF YOUR NEW PLEASE READ THIS CLOSELY

Trucking in house stuff:
If you are leasing a truck FROM the same trucking company your leased to, many solo owner-operators do not consider this being an owner operator! Technically this is being a lease operator. I know the pride factor well, to get started, just keep this in mind, before any chest puffing out at the

truckstop telling everyone that you really are an owner operator now! Cool but- 😬 The guys that could really show something or give you a good lead probably will steer clear with you because they see the ignorant pride. So just be mindful and try a little patience if this becomes a thing! 🤠

Many guys with their own authority even look down on guys who have their own trucks leased to companies! They even say that they are not real owner operators. If your main goal is to make money and define your own success none of this really matters, it is mostly just part of trucking politics and culture, but is good to know. It's also good to know who's who out here. These real deal owner operators with life experience, are the guys that will be more likely to help you, help you fix stuff, help show you tips and tricks, will help you find better places to make money and etc. When you find the real deal guys out here, they almost never complain. They're too busy making money and finding solutions to everything! 😎

Just remember…. One more time….. there's a big difference between leasing a truck FROM a company and leasing your own truck TO a company. 🚚

Some people will say leasing a truck from a company is a good way to get experience before getting your own truck. I say yeah, maybe a little, but ultimately, it's an unnecessary step in my belief. As long as you do your research, study this textbook and get real first-hand advanced knowledge from the people you met, read forums and etc I don't see a real need for wasting time leasing, paying a huge overhead for low profit margins. 😕

What you would learn from leasing a truck from a company would basically be responsibility. <u>But not even great responsibility</u>, just **basic** responsibility. Like "oh jeez" my headlight is out, maybe I should fix it because nobody is going to fix it for me" or maybe it will teach you to be more responsible with your money and to save for repairs and etc. 😛

What you won't get most of the time is real experience that you actually need like; booking loads, negotiations, doing things more on your own (outside of their control state), deciding your own repair shops and fixes, choosing your own routes, planning your own fuel stops, controlling your fixed costs, even being allowed to fix your own truck. I've meet COUNTLESS lease operators that will have a simple repair to do, I suggest I'll help them do it, and they freak out and say no because the company won't let them fix on their own truck!!!! 😵 So, what type of experience are you really getting by leasing a truck FROM a company? What skills and experience are you getting besides basic money management and basic responsibility? 👻 paying taxes on a 1099 I guess

Leasing a truck from a company is a pretty nice time waster in my opinion, UNLESS it's a good deal for you. Like if the truck is $25k with a rebuilt motor and when you make the last payment you get the title with no balloon payment and then you're free to take the truck wherever you want. Those type of deals make more sense than just basically overpaying to rent a truck- to work for a company that chooses your freight and has you running around like for like horse and carrot. If you are in one of those type lease deals now, PLEASE RECONSIDER! Plot your path to an operation that will have ownership in it, one that will have a higher level of profit.

Because once you own your equipment outright, especially as a 1 truck owner operator, this is when the fun really begins. Because now your bills are low and you can afford so much more home time if you want if you do it right. 🌴

Leasing to a company with your own truck... ✔️
I think this is the route to go in the beginning. This is the route most guys start and stay on. Many solo owner-operators do not want the extra paperwork and responsibility that comes with having your own authority, which in my opinion is not much extra, but is understandable.

There is **nothing wrong** with being leased to a company. I was leased to Landstar for almost 6 years. I learned a lot when I was there. Glad I did it all in all.

The key is to find a good fit for you, and one that is profitable with good perks. 🔑

I always say this, "if you're going to be leased somewhere, tmake sure to be getting **GREAT** benefits". Here is a list of benefits / perks I would be looking for in a company.

- has to be a **percentage based company** or have a very high base rate of $2+ a mile with fuel surcharge (which almost nobody has)
- A company that offers a **good percentage** of Gross, and has a good reputation with its own direct customers, and a decent safety score.
- **Ability to book my own freight**
- Ability to use outside load boards
- **True** no forced dispatch ✔️
- No home time limits 😁

- **Great fuel discounts** (.35 cents off the pump price or better)
- Since I'm a TA / Petro guy, I'm looking to see if where their fuel discounts are
- **Massive tire discounts**. (Called national accounts or national tire accounts…)
- Free trailer rental or very affordable trailer rental fees. And if I'm paying for trailer rental, I need to get a higher percentage of the gross in my contract.
- Preferably a maintenance free trailer, one where the big company pays for the trailer maintenance. 🚛
- **Will buy my tires up front** and take interest free payments week by week until their paid off. (This can be a great way to leverage your relationship with your company. You get the tires at a great discount, then keep your cash flow active by making interest free payments until the balance is paid in full). I used to really be against credit, but if your responsible, and it's interest free, there's really no difference in finally cost to you.
- **Will issue me a loan if needed**. This is a great option to have, especially in the beginning, or if you don't want to use your own money on a larger repair or etc. At one time Landstar loaned me $7500 I think it was, at a very low interest rate. That deal came in super handy at that time. 🎱
- Do they have terminals? Where are they? Will you get discounted maintenance from their mechanics? These are not deal breakers but something to consider.
- **Company policy**. I would look hard into the culture of that company and see if you like it. I'm way more inclined to smaller companies now; 10 to 50 truck operations. Ones that I know understand trucking and will cut you more of a break when it comes to DOT

inspection violations and warnings, ones that will let you do your own thing on the load boards. Etc. Some people like the big corporate structure, but I got out of liking that a long time ago. I'd rather know the owner; I'd rather not be bothered by recent college grads in the compliance department calling me and being disrespectful and petty on the phone. So, keep this in mind too, morale is important. ✌

- **Potential for growth**. At Landstar I started as a van, went to specialized van, then I bought my own flatbed and eventually started hauling loads up to 14 foot wide. <u>There was room to grow in that company</u>. Keep that in mind too. Are there ways to advance and specialize myself within this company? 🔑
- Weekly settlements is basically a must. ✔
- It's just got to add up. Do the math on the low side of gross and profit and the high side of gross and profit. Don't just take a recruiter's word for it. Go talk to guys at the Truckstop's who work for this company that you're interested in. If it doesn't add up, it doesn't make sense. $

The two percentages I've run on was 65% at Landstar plus 7% for having my own trailer, so 72% in total. 72% of 100% of the gross amount of each load. The other percentage I ran on was at a smaller company, we made a deal for 87% of the load, but I paid my own liability and cargo insurance ($300 a week).

Let's do some math…. What I was paying for in my percentage paid to Landstar for was; To use their DOT / MC #, to use their liability, cargo insurance, to use their back office (safety Dept, compliance etc), to use their in-house load board, and basically to use them as a factoring company because they paid me every week. Is this worth the 28% I paid? Well let's see. 😗

If I were to gross $175,000 and times that by .28 (the 28 percent) I'll get $49,000. So, I paid them $49,000, (more than what many people will make in a year, to basically run on their insurance and DOT#). I'm not really trying to sell you on leasing vs own authority but **I pay $12k a year for insurance**. $49,000 - $12,000 is $37,000. I'll even be generous and take out my load board fees and fuel card membership fees which will bring it down to $34,950. And since I don't factor, I keep all of this $34,950. <u>To me that's still a lot of money</u>! I still remember in detail, not having 😄. I still consider $100 to be a lot of money 🤣. So, to keep $35,000 or more after insurance was eventually a no brainer to me. But let's stick to leasing for now. 🚛

Now, for company 2, Let's take the same $175,000 and times it by .13 and we'll get $22,750. Let's add in the insurance cost. $300 times 4 is $1200 per month times 12 is $14,400 a year. Then let's add back in the $22,750 with $14,400 and we'll get **$37,150**. So, at company 2, I actually saved $11,850 compared to Landstar. $49,000 minus $37,150. By leaving the almighty Landstar and coming to the smaller company I actually took a step in the right direction as far as bottom-line profit and cost. I lost a couple of the perks but all in all it was a good transition move for me as I'll explain a little later. 💲

It's just got to make sense ok! And I'm telling you, $1500 a week isn't making much sense! $2000 a week to me really doesn't make sense if you're really trying to run the whole week that is. The very first load I hauled in chapter I made over $3000 in two days on 1000 miles! Why would I drive 2500+ miles hauling heavy loads through whatever type terrain and weather to make way less money????

These Large Fleet companies' prey on ignorance. These companies hope we don't realize that we could make way more without them if we figured out how and did it. Just look at the guys that are "owner ops" at Swift and CR England making like $1.20 or todays rate a mile plus fuel charge, driving so much for less. but that's everyday....

 "If it was easy everyone would do it." Well, most people **do** sign up for these type of lease deals because they are easy to get into… and around they go on the carrousel that keeps spiraling down if complacent for long enough.

This is can be a tough business day to day, you don't want to be just breaking even, or barely getting by. You don't even want to be just making your truck payments. We do the job of like 5 people, so, we need to be making about the salary of about 5 people too! And it's possible! First thing first, if you're in one of these low profit lease deals, just know, if you're not clearing $2000 a week after fuel, you can be getting more with your own truck depending on maintenance and etc. Keep looking for a better opportunity. I would recommend some companies, but it's a pretty short list! They always say, the best companies aren't out here advertising often because they don't have too. Landstar or Mercer is not a bad bet though. I would seriously consider them. Or a smaller company 10 trucks or so.

Owner operator with their own authority.

To my readers who only came for the specific information, you will see the further I go into the guide, the more specific the information gets. There are readers of this book that don't have this basic information clarified yet, or is not sure if they understand right what they think they knew already. 🏆

Having your own authority is like the **pinnacle**, it's like being at the "pent house" level of independent trucking politics and culture next to owning a fleet that is. Even to the ones that won't admit it, they have extra respect for the guys who have their own authority. When you have your own authority, you are the owner, you are the safety department, you are the compliance department, you are the driver, you are the mechanic, you are the dispatcher, you're like a one-man rock band! What respect these guys should get yeah! They really get it done! 😎🏆

Having your own authority is a goal for many, a rightfully so; If you do it right you can really increase **your** cash flow and greatly improve your lifestyle 🌴. Ever since I got my own authority, I've been working less and less. All the way to the point where I work only about 6 to 3 months a year! I have a clean profit margin and I kept my home bills so low, that I could afford to take off essentially as much I wanted to! Think about it, the last time I was out (chapter 1), it was 2 weeks and 2 days, and I made $14,500 after fuel. I have no truck note, no trailer note, no house note, and my insurance costs $1200 a month or so. So really in essence, I could take the next 3 months off, it'll costs me $3600 in insurance plus my home bills like electricity, phone, car insurance and etc. Let's just say that's about $700 a month, $2100 for 3 months. We're talking $5700 for 3 months is what it will cost give or take if I wanted off. ♠

So, in less than three weeks I paid for 3 months off AND still increased my bank account by $8800! If you get my "jist" you can see why working only 6 months a year is a reality for certain guys. Some guys work even less than 6 months! And if we wanted to get really technical, I could take more **than** 6 months off and still do better than break even. Or we could say just this last going out paid for my whole years' worth of insurance and my IRP plate. So, in a sense, if were to keep separate my home expenses, I just broke even there.

I could really enjoy to stay out and drive but why would I want to drive for Werner at a flat rate? Could you really convince me that it would better for me to be at that company?
At $1500 a week, that would take me 2 and a half months of driving 2500+ miles a week, driving heavy loads up and down the mountains putting crazy wear and tear on my driveline, motor and suspension to make what I just made in 2 weeks and 2 days. it will be hard to convice you too!

Is getting your own authority worth it? **I would say get insurance quotes first**. As a new company, insurance can be pretty expensive. I've heard companies talk as high as $30,000 or more a year for liability and cargo insurance. Again, if it doesn't add up it just doesn't make sense yet. There's plenty of guys that are leased to Landstar that are way better off than someone with their own authority. If you can get your own insurance cost down in the $10,000 to $20,000 a year range, and you believe you got the will and the discipline for it, then having your own authority could for sure be a great thing for you. There are a few things that will affect your insurance cost the most. That will be...

- How old your company is (they call this active authority, how long has your authority been active for)

- domicile aka where you live (they consider this "where you garage" your truck at) states with higher auto fraud, and living in highly populated cities that have statistical crime will more than likely increase your insurance cost.
- Years of driving experience. The more years the better for you in lowering your cost. 5 years' experience give or take is probably where you'll start seeing a drop in rates.
- Your age. 25 and under I'm pretty sure are considered the higher liability risk and the insurance companies will charge accordingly. The older you are the more you'll be considered a lower risk, which drive the rates down.
- The cost of your equipment and whether you own it outright. The more money you insure your truck and trailer for Physical Damage, if you do insure it, the more your insurance will cost.

In the next chapter I will show you **EXACTLY** how I got my operation set up. But I would say, after insurance you will need to look into the cost of owning or leasing a trailer. I know a good way to transition into having your own authority is to already pay off a trailer while you're still leasing to a company. That way when you're ready to go, you already have your own trailer. That's what I did. 😎

The next thing to consider is that in the beginning, you may find it harder to get work with brokerages as a new company authority. Some brokerages will only do business with you if you've had an active authority for at least 3 months, 6 months, and for some even a year. I didn't run into this issue much because freight was really busy the season I got started. Many companies that year were making exceptions as long as I was empty and ready to go lol. But there's still great companies like ATS that will load you with an authority that's one day old. Then you got the big chain brokerages like TQL, CH Robinson, Coyote and etc. I'm proud to say I've never hauled a load for any of these companies, especially TQL. Why? Many owner ops haul for these guys, and sometimes they'll make a crazy outrageous deal with you for something that's got to go. Still not worth the **_risk_** to me. Plus, these are the brokerages that'll call you 20 times a day, inclined to talk to you like you don't know nothing, and basically just casually disrespect you. I'm not doing business with a company like this because if I'm not liking it now, I know I'm not going to like it when a problem with my company's money were to arise. 🚛💲 personal research on forums on truck stops will show you more about whos who and what the reputation is with these just mentioned companies.

Then you got the book keeping side. Which in my opinion is more of a scare tactic then anything. When I activated my authority, I stayed home for about a month and followed the checklist OOIDA gave me for the required paperwork I had to have filed. I probably could of got it done sooner, but I was feeling my way through it, took my time, and was learning as I went. ✅

You'll have to pull a driving record on yourself, fill out an application so you can hire yourself. You'll enroll in a random drug testing consortium, and give yourself a pre-employment drug test. You'll write out your company policies regarding different topics. Once you do those things, it's filed in a file cabinet, and you really don't touch it much ever again! It's there so if you ever get audited, you'll have the files. 👍

When I got my New Entrant Safety Audit, which all new carriers do within the first year and a half or so, it went really smooth. I was basically asked to just see my authority certificate, registration, insurance, and my logs. I emailed them with a picture of my truck and my company logo above it, and that was it. Passed! So, if paperwork ever becomes the roadblock to you and to having your own authority, let me tell you now, there's really not much paperwork involved. There is just paperwork involved in the beginning, but once your system is set up it's mostly simple maintenance from there. 🌴

You will be responsible for paying **UP FRONT** for your registration (license plate). It's called an IRP plate. My IRP runs me about $1600-$2000 a year. It's usually closer to $1600, the cost is usually based off miles ran in certain states. This is something you do at your DMV that handles commercial vehicles. You pre-fill your application out before arriving, have all the required documents that your state requires, and bring enough cash to do the deal! I still just put all of these documents in a folder, and come in with my cash, and knock it out. These documents are insurance, title, etc, it's a little different state to state. Their website lists what will be needed at the time of renewal.

If you were leased to a company, they usually pay this registration cost up front, and charge it back to you in small $30 increments. Even though I pay up front, I've consistently seen lower prices by buying my own plate. Another thing to consider is, there's nothing wrong with buying your own plate even when leased to a company. This gives you more freedom and flexibility of your situation. Say the company your leased to goes out of business and your stuck in Utah and you live in Florida. Now your license plate / registration is no good, so technically if you move your truck you're doing so illegally. Risking sharp points on your driving record which could in turn damage future opportunities for you. Another instance is, if you want to change companies, or maybe you get let go, you can still move your truck if you have your own base plate! It's something to think about, and as the money gets right, I recommend getting your own plate. 😄

To factor or not?

You may have heard of factoring or maybe not, but I never really knew what it was until I started pounding the pavement for info regarding having my own authority. Factoring is just basically a pay advance with a 1 to 5% fee charged by the lender. The way billing works in trucking is very similar to how CashApp works. In CashApp you can get your money off instantly, but for a fee, this is factoring. But in without factoring if you wait for your money, there's no fee. Billing cycles for my customers range from 3 days payment with no fees, all the way to about 45 days for some customers. I do not factor; I bill my customers direct and wait for my money. Every solo owner-operator has his or her own strategy on what they think is better and really, it's just up to you if you choose to factor or not. 💲

Me personally, I don't see the long term benefit in factoring. Yes, you can get your money a bit faster, but the goal is to be building a company that can run more than 30 days without needing a cash stimulus. Being **prepared** on the cash side before starting your own authority will really increase your chance of success. You should always be at least 3 months ahead on all bills, plus a juicy emergency fund in the bank (at least $10,000+) and if you get those credit card offers in the mail, hold on to a few like I would do. I would get offers all the time for 18 months 0% APR. You can leverage a big expense onto one of these 0% APR cards. You pay same as cash over a period of 18 months' time instead of spending a large amount of money too quickly. I still do this sometimes. And by 3 months ahead on bills I mean, having enough money in the bank to pay 3 months' worth of business and home expenses whether you deliver one load or not. 🗝️

Some guys will say "well if the broker doesn't pay, I have non-recourse factoring so I'll get paid". When the fine print is read on a lot of these factoring contracts, this is usually not the case. Now, there is true non-recourse factoring but those deals are usually in the 4-5% per invoice range. There's just really not need to pay that much for invoice insurance. If you do your due diligence and check brokers credit, your chances of getting stiffed on a payment are next to zero. I have some easy ways to check credit and I'll show my process later in later part of the book. That subject has its own chapter! I never had an invoice not get paid! 😎

Then it just comes to the numbers. 3% of 175,000 is $5250. That's a lot of money! You have to ask yourself, is that $5000 worth more to you in your hand, or by paying it to have a quicker cash flow? If your own cash flow is solid, if your liquid cash in the bank is solid, then why do you need to pay this $5000 to get money quicker that you're not even going to use right away? I don't factor because of this mainly. I don't knock companies that do but I don't do it. .....Which leads to the next part in this operation chapter specifically dealing with your own authority. 🤐.......

Your own money. You need to be ready.

It's my advice to be having $30,000-$40,000 in the bank before you go up this road. And preferably with a paid for truck and trailer. You can probably get by on a little less in the beginning but I wouldn't push it too far. I'd say probably no less than $20,000 in the bank to start after down payment with confidence in the maintenance of your truck. You're making an insurance down payment ($500-$xxxx) , paying for your plate ($1500-$2xxx) paying your 2290 ($550), you're paying for your own fuel, and your waiting on your money for sometimes a month or a little more. You don't want to get out here and spread yourself too thin too fast, that's where the companies that fail fall ✖.

They don't have the knowledge and the tools yet, come into the business a little too quickly, don't continue their education once in, money is spread too thin, choose a factoring company, and are one maintenance repair from being out of business. Yes, your supposed to follow your heart and your dreams 🦅, but as far as yhis trucking is concerned, please do so with this wisdom! With the wisdom of how expensive everything is, and that the truck and operation need to match.

I think back, if I would have waited one more year before getting my big blue 387 Pete, I would have been in an even better stronger position current day and wouldn't of been in certain situations I was in early on.
There was a moment one month or so after I started, that I had only had 183 dollars cash in the bank! That was it! $183. $183 to my name and I owed $65k on my truck. I didn't really know nothing at that time about mechanics and the trucking business specifics either. Don't be me back in 2013!!!!
 I didn't have enough money to buy a TIRE! Stack your companies' money, do your research, collect your tools +

know how, build your budget, choose the right truck, choose the right operation, and come out way stronger!!!! 🏆

It's okay, these trucks and freight aren't much going anywhere too quickly, there will still be a great future for you in this if you have to wait another year. I challenge you in a positive way to save up at least $20,000 in the bank after your down payment. Or even better I challenge you to save $20,000 in your bank after you pay CASH for your truck! I also challenge you to not solely rely on cash at dealers to fix your problems, learn to rely on yourself to diagnose maintenance, learn to be your own problem solver. Solo owner-operators who throw money at their problems, especially in mechanical fixes, tend to always be in a downward spiral of not finding success. If you have 5 trucks running then yes, maybe you do just throw cash at most of your problems, but as a one truck owner operator, these shops will eat us a small trucking company alive if we don't know our maintenance and how to problem solve. And do that standing of the ground in a likeable way.

You walk in with one simple emissions code, and next thing you know, they're trying to sell you a $4000 turbo, or a $3000 EGR cooler job, or $7000 DPF/DOC replacement job. 😰

BUT THE WHOLE TIME IT MIGHT JUST BE A SENSOR OR TWO! 🥴

→That's why it really pays to know what you're looking at, the terminology, and how these systems all work! And really, the goal is to not bring your truck into dealerships at all! If you must use a shop, I almost always suggest going to the independent shops. We'll talk a lot more on this in the "Shops and Part Stores" and in "Maintenance". But the point I want to make here is, **Cash is King**, and make it your goal to not come into this business cash weak. And when you do come in, don't just rely on cash to fix everything, that's a great way to exhaust your cash and find yourself exhausted stressed anxious and harder to get ahead. No problem in establishing business credit either. Business credit could turn to be critical at a certain time for the company.

PROS OF HAVING YOUR OWN AUTHORITY. ✔

- Splitting your money with no one. $
- 100% of the deals ($) you make is yours $
- True freedom of time and day to day schedule 😁
- Higher earning potential 🔑
- No annoying safety & compliance departments calling you about petty stuff
- Huge sense of pride, accomplishment & ownership 💪
- The responsibilities really expedite your process of becoming a man or woman. (My opinion!) ✊
- All the knowledge and experience you gain, and how it can be used outside the trucking world. 👍
- More respect in the Trucking World. It's hard not to show more respect to the guy who had the guts to make it on his own and became successful. 🙌
- Making your own rules for you & your company! (As long as the go along with FMCSA's rules) 😄

CONS OF HAVING YOUR OWN AUTHORITY.
✔

- higher startup cost
- Not getting regular weekly pay unless factoring
- You're responsible for your back-office record keeping
- You file your own IFTA
- No large pool of easy access trailers to use.
- No national tire discounts
- Repowering loads can be more difficult
- You will work much harder than most truckers some days.
- (I enjoy this but...) You do the jobs of driver, dispatcher, accountant, mechanic, owner, safety, compliance and etc. If you don't want to do one of these jobs, expect to see your profit margin decline a little more for each job you outsource.
- Responsible for your own fuel card / method of fueling.

Now we're getting to it! Operation is a very **IMPORTANT** part of finding your success in this business! <u>Do what you can to not settle for less or don't settle for less for too long.</u> Keep on doing your homework. Do the math. Use pen and paper to discover what your true potential earnings are weekly, monthly, yearly for each company you consider leasing to.

If you're in a company sponsored lease deal with high overhead and low profits, **PLEASE** plot your way out of it! If you're still in the process of going owner op, I advise making sure you got an operation together BEFORE you go truck shopping. Ask around at the truck stops. Make notes of the good, bad and ugly of each company you are interested on. Research on TruckersReport.com Trucking Forum | #1 CDL Truck Driver

Message Board (thetruckersreport.com). Use the search feature and type in the name of the company your researching! This is part of the due diligence… 😎

Once you make this step of getting your own truck, you will officially be a business. You must treat yourself as a business in the ways necessary. Do what you can to not Stress Yourself. Do what you can to not move off of emotion and impulse. The more work you put up in these early stages, the more you increase your potential for success throughout and later on! Find your balance between taking your time and not taking too long. If you must side on one or the other, side on taking your time. 🚛

Come into this business strong, with knowledge, and with the liquid cash. You have this textbook as resource, stripping away uncertainties and blind spots. Don't make the same mistakes that I and countless others did, don't happen to learn the hard way, which makes it way longer to make money and be having your goals! Learn here and now! By-pass a lot of it. Take the drama out. And make your time count as you continue to self-educate yourself with this text book Guide! Write notes, re-read chapters, do whatever's going to help until this trucking finally clicks and you figure out how you want to run your operation! The Homework now at this section end is, working on your plan as we continue. The next section is titled "My Operation". In this degree, you will get to see exactly how I run my operation and how its set up. This will be good insight for you because this will let you see a different extreme in how this trucking business can be ran! It will also give ideas for reverse engineering and how to run your own company too, especially if you're considering getting your own authority. Let's proceed! 😁

DEGREE 4: MY OPERATION

- I **have** my own authority. ✔
- I have my insurance cost down to around **$12k** a year. ✔
- I own and **have the title** to both my truck and trailer; which is a 2000 Volvo mid roof 64T, an all steel 1999 Fontaine Flatbed with a wood floor. ☑
- I run a **pre-emissions motor**. Which is a <u>Cummins N-14</u>, 435 HP.😄
- I run 3.73 gears. That puts me at 1450/1500 RPM's right around my cruising speed of 60-62mph. 🚚
- My house and land is paid for. I paid cash for it back in 2016 when I was 26. 🏆
- I book **95%** of my freight off <u>https://app.truckstop.com</u> the other 5% comes from DAT, and customer load boards<u>https://www.brokeredloads.com</u> like ATS's . 🍂
- I do not use a factoring company. I bill my customers with <u>https://apps.apple.com/us/app/quickbooks-accounting/id584606479</u> . This is the link for the exact **QuickBooks** app I use for invoice and billing. It's $10 a month. 💲
- I'm set up to receive my invoice payments at probably 40% ACH and 60% paper check in the mail. ✔
- I capture my BOL's / POD's with an app called **Tiny Scanner**. It's a good app that costs about $5. It will convert your bills into perfect PDF files that really impress customers. ✔
- I save the PDF BOL / POD files into "**Files**" on my iPad. If you do not use Apple products, you can use an equivalent cloud type or internal memory. Once I have

the PDF in Files, I can link it into my invoice on QuickBooks! 😎

- I do **50 to 80%** of my own maintenance. 💪
- I do my own oil changes and grease.
- I use Rotella and Fleetguard filters 💪
- My company name is a LLC. 👍
- I do taxes as a **pass through entity** (LLC), though maybe I go in the direction of getting taxed as an S-Corp later on. That's something you may want to look into. 💲
- I collect **all** my business related receipts in a 5 gallon Ziploc when I'm over the road. I come home and put them into another 5 gallon Ziploc I keep in my office. I take off the first or second week of January, spread all the receipts into categories on my bed. Add them all up on a **paper printing calculator**. Then put each category into its own folder, and then file it into my file cabinet. (More on this later in the "Taxes" chapter) 😁
- I file my own IFTA. 😎
- I go into my DMV every year with the required paperwork and **pay cash** for my IRP plate. ✔️
- I pay for tolls through **I-Pass**. This is the Illinois version of EZ Pass. It's way easier to get a commercial transponder and the website is very user friendly. 🚚
- I buy all my fuel with my **NASTC** fuel card. I'm a NASTC member, this costs around $250-$350 a year. (**GOOD FUEL DISCOUNTS**!) 💲
- I fuel almost **exclusively** with TA / Petro.
- I use **KeepTruckin** ELD and dashcam.
- I use http://www.brokercreditcheck.com and CreditStop shipper powered by Ansonia to credit check new customers. I cross reference these 2 sources and aim to have my customers down to 30-37 days to pay tops.

(More on this later in my "How I Credit Check New Customers" chapter!) 😄

- I **don't** use prepass. It's not a bad thing to use this, I just think as a new carrier, you will get pulled in for more inspections when your transponder pops up on their computer, and they see that you're a new company. 🤔
- I have **clean** organized decals on my truck and trailer that are not crooked! 🚚
- I **never** have a messy dashboard. 🏝️
- I'm **enthusiastic** and make **good** deals with brokers & who I meet and do business with. (Even though sometimes I have to amp myself up first to get into my deal making spirit lol) ✔️
- I keep my **overhead** costs low as possible. 😎
- I don't often buy stuff I don't need.
- My wife and family are **frugal**, we each make our own money, she saves money great, she doesn't blow her money, and my wife doesn't spend money irresponsibly behind my sight. This would create financial stress. She also is **very grateful** and patient, she's not driven to live over materialistic or outside our means. (We will talk later why this is important in "Home Life and Budgeting" chapter!) 🔑
- My home bills are like **$5k** a year, and my trucking bills are like **$15k** a year. (if I don't move my truck a mile it costs this) got a piece of land out in louisiana paid for with house.
- I'm a firm believer in work **SMARTER** not harder! ☀️
- I average 300-500 miles a day driving when I'm out. **1500-2500** miles a week. I'm usually at a relaxed enjoyable pace. Some days I drive 600 miles when the job really calls for it. But most of the time, it's smarter

not harder! (Why would I put more wear and tear on my equipment and stress on me if I don't have to?) 🚚

- I usually do **shorter** loads through the week (200-800 miles) and look to do $2500 + gross over the weekend on 800-1500 miles. 🚚🚚
- I always aim to make **$3-5k** simple net a week after I pay fuel (I call this simple net, my gross $ - what I paid in fuel). I aim for no less than $3k. And I always strive to do more than **$5k** a week. And many times, I do! ✓
- I drive **60-62**mph. Sometimes I driver faster if the situation calls for it. The main thing is, I ride the momentum of the hills 🚚, I work with gravity and not against it. What I mean by this is, yes, I drive 62mph but I'm not going to force my motor and driveline to maintain 62 all the way up a hill. I will slowly ease off the pedal as the incline takes over, and dropping gears to keep RPM's up at a 1400-1500 (depending on your gear ratio) in order to take **stress** off the motor and driveline. 🏆
- By driving 60-62mph I'm almost always by **myself** on the road. You won't catch me tailgating and following to close in a pack. This mentality alone probably gets me out of **95**% of the potential situations that will result in a crash or accident. 🔒
- I carry **a lot** of different tools, and spare sensors, hose, fluids and parts. 🚚
- I have the Cummins **mechanics** book for my motor. This book is specific to my motors electrical and mechanical maintenance, and will show step by step procedures and troubleshooting. This is the **same** book they use in the big shops. ✓
- I use Bridgestone R283a's 22.5 for my **steers**. I use Michelin XDN2's 22.5 on my **drives**. And for my spread axle I use Duraturn's DA-30's 24.5 if I can get

them; and then I'll use other decent tires on my last axle. But the Duraturns is what I love to use on all trailer tire positions if I can get them. It's a $200-$250 tire, but it's A SOLID tire, it's incredible! It's puts up with the abuse of spread axle far better than even higher up name brand tires have in my experience. 🚚

- I use **brake safe** visual brake stroke indicators on every position. This really helps me on staying on top of brake stroke measurements. I can put a board against my chair and brake pedal, and walk around and check all my break stroke measurements in 5 minutes or less. ✓

- I use **TST tire pressure sensors** on every tire. When you're the one paying for tires, its best to be keeping those tires within 2-5 lbs of air pressure of each other! These tire pressure sensors are a great way to do this. Also, they are great in catching weather / seasonal air pressure changes because of the drop or increase in outside air temperatures. 🔨

- I have a hogh quality mattress in my truck. When I bought it, it was the same price as Tempurpedic. You're the boss, you're the one out here making it happen, so make sure you have a great mattress that will reward your body with replenishing sleep! That way tomorrows work is that less strenuous 😴

- I mostly make my invoices the night **before** I deliver, and 95% of the time I have the proof of delivery and invoice sent in to my customer before I even leave the receiver. ✔

- I don't hang out in the Truckstop's listening to much complaining. But I **would** listen to someone if we are talking business and are trading trade secrets! 😎

- If I have time, **which I often do**, I will stop and ask if the person with their hood up needs a hand or tools.

This is <u>true trucking politics and culture</u> and just good people culture in general. Sometimes you end up getting some great tips, ideas and lessons about how to fix things, business and life in general. 🔧 I know I did.

- I keep **God (most high)** first, and what I **want** always in mind. I take <u>discipline</u> in my subconscious mind. I do not let it **drift** off into being an enemy of mine. It's so much of a <u>habit</u> now, it's like second nature, it's just automatic. 🔒

- I don't run to a **dealership** or to the shops every time I get an issue. I always see what I can do about it first. And if I do go into in a shop, very rarely will I let the shop tell me what I need done, unless I really need their help in diagnosing. And even then, they have to convince me very well. Because I know enough now, that if you don't convince me, you're probably just throwing parts at it. 🤢

- I do what I can to not **overpay** for food and drinks at the Truckstop's. I pack and store 75% of my own food. I buy spring water by the gallon. Not just to mention affordable, my food ends up being more clean and healthy than what I can get out of a truck stop. If I have plant-based food along my route, I might eat out once a day. If a good eating spot isn't convenient to me that day, I'll just wait and eat what I have in my truck. 😋

- When I drink coffee or tea, I was mostly making my own. It's **WAY** cheaper over time and I get to control the quality of it. Spring water and organic grounds are a way better alternative than **fluoridated** tap water with pesticide coffee beans in the truck stop! 👍

- I don't allow **negative** energy from life perception or from people into my mind or into my life for longer than necessary. 😎🔑

This is the <u>foundation</u> of **MY OPERATION**. I could go on and on, but then I'd be getting more into what I use and how I do certain things which is a slight deviation from what MY OPERATION is.

Many of these points on my operation will be further discussed in detail as we go further. But I wanted to give you a running list of what my real, actual operation is and what it looks like! If I knew a finely tuned machine like this early on, I would of spent **less** time "chasing my tail" so to speak and **more** time getting to it in the ways I do now! $

one method improvement that you ca pick up from <u>this text book will have paid for itself plus many times more</u>! ✓

PREACHING:
This is **10** years of dedication, a **10** year of self-education, a **10+** year of trial and error, and **10** years of feeling my way through it. It takes knowledge, common sense, and usually experience to even think about putting an operation like mine together. Am I the only one that runs like this? NO! But very **rarely** did I come across solo owner-operator companies with a more fine-tuned operation! Unless you have a successful owner operator in your family, you just don't wake up overnight knowing **all** this stuff and **how** it all **fits** and **works** <u>together</u>!! 🚚 welcome!

But now **you** can, <u>in a major way</u>, take where I took it to, from my trial and error, and directly apply it to you. Or as they say "**reverse engineer**" it. At the very least, let the **confidence** and **discipline** rub off onto you. I **love** where I'm at in life right now, learning and living, <u>and I want you to too.</u> Trucking is how I've done it. lol

You **believed** in yourself and you **believed** in how to be successful in trucking enough to press the buy button, a **deal** that I will deliver you what I **know** about trucking and being successful in it; and that you will **continue** to achieve bigger and further things with the **access** and **implementation** of this transferred knowledge. **Thank** you! And **thank** yourself for believing and knowing in yourself and **taking** action! This knowledge must continue to be put into action if you want it to benefit you! Knowledge is not power per sayy; but the implementation of knowledge is power! Knowledge + implementation. 💪

ABOUT AGE:
Your **20's** are not to be wasted logistically. If you handle business now in your **20's**, you can really start to build in your **30's**. Most of the time people we see in life who **struggles** later on and **can't** seem to find their way, are usually the same ones who in hind used their 20's working **entry level** paying jobs while going out, **overbuying** on clothes, food and partying etc, but the key thing is was **repeating** old habits from high school and not snapping out soon enough; Now they're in their **30's**, **40's**, **50's** still playing having to play **CATCH UP usually living a life that is unpleasant and they don't want to be in**! My aim is not to frighten or scare tactic you but don't let this be you please! Go out there and get it in your 20's. Go all across the country. Save money. Explore. Travel. Find love do something different. Knowledge seek. Expand your horizons! 😐

Always have **respect** for yourself. Have **faith** in yourself and faith in a greater purpose! Know you can still have **fun**! Just keep the bigger picture in mind.

Remember, you still have to pay taxes on the money that you make also right….

Remember, we all are grown now –The only person you should be trying to impress is you and your **bank** account (and your parents too if it's convenient). 🙌 (kids etc)

If you're already in your **30's** and up, then you definitely know what I'm saying! If you haven't before, it's time to <u>buckle down ok</u>! This is your sign. Just saying, the motto is "put your **needs** before your **wants**, **sacrifice** now and live like a **king** later. Have the will power and don't be so quick to choose comfort over progress. 👑 not fun I know. But you will make it.

You're about to enter into a **VERY** important chapter. The next chapter is titled "Which Truck Should I Buy". Never before have I seen a collection of **real** information on old trucks to new trucks in <u>one place</u>. I designed the book orginally to stand the test of time. It has taken me over 10 years to gather the data that I present and then MONTHS of my time to physically write it all down! And lord, the revisions. My **goal** is to Leave a **Gold Standard** in post-education for getting and **STAYING** in the trucking business. And to do it well enough to influence lease drivers and those new to the trucking industry Who heard about that age old quest of becoming an owner operator! 😇

My **goal** isn't just to get you **into** the business, **THAT'S THE EASY PART**! My goal in this textbook is to deliver you the <u>mentality</u> and keys that it **truly** takes to be <u>successful</u>. I want you to have **short** term and **long**-term success! But **you** have to continue, we're just getting started. Let this info get into you so it can become easy. 🤓

As you read through the book, continue practicing the **Auto-suggestion** I showed you in chapter 2. You need to really get your mind and spirit ready to **receive** the rewards that come from putting this knowledge into use! If your **mentality** isn't positive or accepting of good fortune, your chance of making yourself successful becomes **A LOT** more thin ok. 😐 telling you from experience.

There will be **a lot** to discuss in chapter 5. The truck you choose to run your business with is one of the single-handed **most important** factors to your **success**. 🏆 you don't want to be married to a problematic truck.

I will tell you everything I know about The different motors and trucks. I will discuss with you the **pros** and **cons** of it all. I will discuss with you about **emission** motors vs **pre-**emission motors. I will tell you my personal and business opinions and experiences as well. There will be a **ton** of info packed in here. Come back to chapter 5 as you need to, it may be a lot to take in at once.

 In order to get yourself more familiarized with all the different motor and truck possibilities. One thing we're not going to do is; buy a truck based off its **brand** name of the truck or that "because it's **newer**" or because the salesman said it was a **good** truck! **RIGHT**? Ok. Let's continue! 🚚👌

CHAPTER 5: WHICH TRUCK SHOULD I CHOOSE? (MOTOR)

The old saying is "**Nobody** sells a truck that's making money". And for the most part, that's true. But there are a few exceptions to this **rule** that I've found. ✓

Exceptions are, it's an owner-operator who did so **well** that and he's retiring himself. He's now selling his truck that got him to **retirement**! Imagine me selling my truck type of thing. The one I had for years, fixing it up....

Another exception is → sometimes an owner operator will be "upgrading" to a newer truck and doesn't fully realize what he's getting rid of. **Next** would be someone selling because of bad health or a death in the family that resulted in having to sell off the inherited truck. ☺

But besides this, the exceptions are far and few and the old saying goes back in motion "Nobody sells a truck that's making money". KEEP this in the minds Forefront.

This is 1 reason why many successful owner operators **keep** their trucks for a long time and or forever! Once they find the right truck, work the kinks out of it, and consistently make money in it, they just keep it **forever** and keep rebuilding it! 🏆.   lol

Before I go any further, I will say this chapter is more so about buying a **USED** truck. I will talk a bit at the end of this chapter on the pros and cons of buying new. Some solo owner-operators prefer the strategy of buying new, I **personally** do not like the new truck strategy.

But like mentioned, I'll explain more later and ultimately there's nothing really wrong with either way. If it works then it works!

For the **record**, if you're a fleet owner, then some of this chapter won't apply to you as much as it does for the **one truck** owner operator. There's still value for you here as a fleet owner but it's a different strategy a fleet owner must have compared to the one truck operation. In a **one** truck operation, we only have one truck <u>producing the revenue</u> and it must be **reliable**. In a 3-5 or more truck operation there's more than one truck producing revenue, though reliability is still important, but so is the driver's comfort that you're looking to retain.

It's **pretty** difficult to convince and retain a fleet of driver's rolling around in pre-emission trucks that don't look as nice and be as fresh as the **newer** trucks on the inside. With 3-5 trucks in motion, there's more incoming cash flow to justify paying dealers and etc to work on your trucks. But the single truck owner operator can't really afford to just "**throw money**" at every little problem. They need a truck that's going to be easy for them to work on. Something they can truly increase their profit margins in. something the can rely and go towork on…

In my **opinion**, probably about **90**% of the trucks out here for sale regardless of their age, are money traps that I would never want to build my business risk on! They are also usually someone's else's problem that they couldn't **afford** no more, so they got rid of it. Or maybe it's just an **over used** big fleet emission truck that got traded in at 500k miles. But neither is a truck I would <u>build my business</u> around! I knew too much to be **gambling** on trucks because some dealership armor-alled the tires, cleaned the inside, washed the motor and told me it was "fleet maintained"! 🤣

In my professional opinion, **most** trucks that hit the used truck lots are pretty much **DONE by the time they get there**! Especially if they come from a big fleet. And what I mean by this is:
Think about it 🤨, big fleets usually attract drivers of an **entry level skill** land or integrity. They're **grinding** gears, **mashing** brakes, **lugging** low RPM's while climbing hills, switching drivers, **idling** the truck ALL the time —— then you factor in that any truck after 2012 has a **full** emissions system of EGR, DOC, DPF, and DEF; This motor has almost lived its first full life by now (400k – 750k miles)! 🚛

I'll explain in more detail later in the maintenance chapter on how the emissions system hurts the motor so bad but **basically,** the recycling of used exhaust as "fresh" intake produces soot in the oil 😑. The little **soot** particles build up and produce **friction** in the moving parts of the motor, especially in the valves of the cylinder head, the cam(s), and bearings. Oil is **supposed** to lubricate right? not cause friction… this friction tears the motor internals up.

It's this friction (soot in oil) that causes resistance in the moving parts, wearing them out much faster and causing all sorts of problems in the long run. This turns a once million-mile motor into a **400k** mile to maybe a **750k** mile motor. Which means even if you're buying this truck at **500k** you could be very close if not overdue for a top end or full motor rebuild already. **BE** very **CAREFUL with these emission motors**. This is the type of stuff you really need to know! The cost of rebuilding newer post 08, post 2012 motors will be in the $15k to $25k range, or **more** depending on what add ons are selected 💲💲😕 Facing one of these early expensive emission motor rebuilds could be a pivotal moment in an early solo owner-operator company beginning, causing it to close early because the repair bill is too much cost. It's something to consider, plan, budget for and be aware of when choosing a truck…. Emissions, rebuild costs… etc

"**Which** truck should I choose" is a **very** important subject! Please do not rush this truck buying process; Because choosing the wrong truck is a real thing, and can **REALLY** put you in a disadvantage or even **out** of business. Most trucks on the used market are NOT GOOD money maker trucks to be honest with you. Ok?
    When looking for a truck, I want you to be FIRST thinking more along the lines of '**Looking for a Motor**'. 😐. What I mean by this is, instead of looking for a Peterbilt, you're more so looking for a Cummins ISX 871 or a Cummins N14, Detroit 60 series 12.7 **etc**. and then,,,,,, looking for a truck to wrap around that motor. 🏁 the motor is what counts.

All trucks are built **pretty** well but what separates them almost the most are the **motor**. I will make some motor recommendations in just a sec! But **I** made the mistake early on by buying a **brand** of truck instead of really knowing the motor and driveline. I bought a Peterbilt and **didn't even know what type of motor** I had! **So** sad! Don't be me back then! 😂

Yes, there are many things to **consider** when choosing your truck and unfortunately for a new buyer, you **may** not have the experience or the "**eye**" yet for spotting these things easily. I'll do my best in this chapter to translate my experience and 'eye' into USEABLE information for you to use in your endeavors. Plus, there are many photos "**PRE-PURCHASE INSPECTION**" E-book; Showing **exactly** what I'd be checking, and where to look and what I'd be checking for.

Your truck is a **tool**. When you're out truck buying, try **not** to get too *emotionally* attached to the **LOOKS AND COSMETICS ok**. ✔️

With that being **said**, it's <u>best</u> to know your operation first; Then you can **better** select your truck. There's no sense in buying a mid-roof truck if you're hauling a van or reefer trailer and there's no sense in getting a gear ratio to tall if you're not driving 70+ mph. A lot of starter companies **go out** and **buy** a truck **first**, and don't <u>know</u> what company they're going to lease it to; How much money they plan to make, or even what type of trailer they'll be pulling. **Do** <u>your</u> best not to be in this **situation**! Do what you can to figure all of this out first before you choose and buy a truck. 💪

What I'm looking for in a truck is **dependability**. I'm looking for the **ease** of being able to do my own maintenance. I'm looking at the **cost** of parts, and the overall attractiveness and appeal to me. I'm looking to **find** my truck off <u>craigslist</u> or from a <u>private</u> sale of some kind. **These** are where you're more likely to find the **best** trucks and the **best** deals! If you're **starting** off with low cash or financing, try a place like <u>Lone Mountain</u> (that's what I did originally); but knowing what I know now, most of those trucks at a place like Lone Mountain are not trucks that I would prefer to run my business in… and throughout this chapter I know you'll see why 🚚🚚

I want to **know** the **owner** of the truck if possible. I want to **interview** him one on one. I want to get a **feel** for his or her **character** and **personality**. I **want** to get a feel for his knowledge in mechanics. I want to **know** what he's fixed already, and what he thinks might be on the **horizon** for future **repairs** needed. I want to see if the seller is **clean cut**, and if takes care of himself physically. If he takes care of himself and is clean cut, he's more likely to have took good care of his truck too. (you see what I'm saying? 🫤) I want to know **why** he's selling the truck. I want to get a **feel** for if he's been successful in this truck. **THIS IS WHY I SAY DON'T RUSH THIS PROCESS**!!!! ✔️ I don't want to buy the misfortune, especially if I don't have or want to put the extra capital into it.

    Finding the good truck you can count on, can definitely become a process. If you **do** this right, it takes time. You might go through 5-15 trucks **until** you select the right one for you. There is also a chance **that** maybe the first truck you go look at becomes the one too! BUT the time you spend on the "**front** end" will put you in a much better financial position on the Future back end. If you **rush** this process, you can very well end up with somebody else's **issue**, a **big** bank **loan** or cash invested, and **constant** time and money spent at **shops**. Wouldn't you just rather **skip** that and just invest your time into the truck buying process?? 😁 come on.

You want to get the **vibe** of the seller. You want to **see** if he's someone who **cuts** corners and let's his equipment go without maintenance. You **want** to see if he has **integrity**, if not, you may be riding around in barely done repair work that he did or let someone else do while still driving the truck hard. You **want** to make sure he does things the right way. 🆗 . Just get a feel. Ask questions. Check the body language.

I know, this may **sound** like overkill **BUT IT ISN'T. because…..** At the end of the day, it is **you** that's going to be **spending the** $10k - $50k plus thousand dollars   right?? You will be the one that's accepting the **bank** loan or paying cash. You will be the one building your **business** around **this** truck. And…... You were the one that stayed <u>disciplined</u> long enough to save up this much **cash** in the first place!! And also, you will be the one responsible for the repair cost and maintenance of this truck. 😔

→DON'T **SHOOT** YOURSELF IN THE FOOT! GIVE YOURSELF THE BEST OPPURTUNITY! **DON'T** <u>RUSH</u> THIS PROCESS! Give yourself a little time in this process if possible.

It's ok to say NO! (right) REALLY try and GET A **FEEL** FOR WHO YOUR DOING BUSINESS WITH; **BECAUSE** YOU ARE BUYING HIS OR HER **HABITS**, WETHER those habits WERE POSITIVE OR NEGATIVE!

KNOW WHAT IT IS THAT YOU <u>WANT</u> AND WHAT IT IS THAT YOU'RE LOOKING FOR! Same theme continued.

Then we have to take <u>RESPONSIBILTY</u>!

DON'T JUST TAKE A SHOP OR A DEALER'S **WORD** FOR IT; small shop MECHANICS KNOW THE DEALERS IN CERTAIN TOWNS AND THEY WILL ALL KIND OF WORK TOGETHER TO GET YOU TO BUY, *ESPECIALLY* IF THEY assume YOU'RE A **FIRST** TIME BUYER OR A NOT SO SAVY TRUCK OWNER YET! 🚚$

With the information you're getting from me here now, and by applying this already done it **mentality**; I know you will be **much** more successful at finding and selecting the truck that will run your business with the strength count on ability you need.

LET'S GET MORE SPECIFIC! ✓

At this point, I'm **only** looking for **pre**-emission motors. That will put the age of the truck down to a 2003 or <u>older</u>. In 2004 they started with the **EGR** valve. In **2008** the Diesel Particulate Filter (**DPF**) and the Diesel Oxidation Catalyst (**DOC**) came out. These filters are **very** expensive (about $3k each), they are **fragile** to cracking, and if your emissions system isn't running spot on, these filters like to clog up and not bake the soot out fast enough. This causes you to have to go to dealers and get them to do "forced regens" on truck. Ever heard the loud truck next you that keeps **revving'** up over-night when you're trying to sleep? Chances are it's an emissions truck, trying to bake soot out of the filters by doing a regen.

Then if **that** wasn't enough, in **2012** the Selective Catalytic Reduction system (**SCR**) and the Diesel Exhaust Fluid (**DEF**) is introduced. So, by 2012, you have all of these emission systems going on at once inside your truck. Each one of these systems has **its** own sensors, parts and set of potential problems. The **sad** thing is, many of these emission sensors can **shut** you down **easy** or **derate** your motor where you can only go at very slow speeds. Buying the **DEF** fluid alone brings an additional cost to your business and MAN, are those DEF parts expensive!!!! I'm trying to tell you.

Remember how I mentioned that the **DPF** and **DOC** are about **$3k** each, well the **DEF** pump, the **DEF** sensors and etc are just as **expensive** too! Since I never owned a truck **newer** than a 2009, I can't personally speak on the exact prices of **DEF** parts but I did have a friend in a **2012** and I heard the many stories out here of how it's not cheap and I can imagine just from owning a 2008 for my first few years.

I did a lease years ago on a 2012 Pete 587 at Prime Inc for about 6 months and it had DEF, but when the trucks are that new, they do pretty decent. It isn't until they hit about 300k - 400k miles that they really start to show their true status of being undependable and being the "shop queen". **Yes**, there are exceptions to the rule! But generally speaking, when these 2008/2012 + trucks hit about 400 – 500k miles, they really start to show the abuses that an emissions system makes to a motor internal and its attached systems. ✖

So, at **300k** miles and up in a 2012 to 2017 truck, **I WOULD be very weary or not want anything TO DO WITH THAT TRUCK**! Even the new trucks under 100k miles are having issues, mostly emission related. I mean just look at how many big fleet trucks you see calling for a tow truck! It's more than these simpler built trucks im speaking on. Some solo owner-operators swear by "oh these new trucks are great, or they're not that bad". **Either** they haven't owned the truck for long, or they're in the "buy new and trade it back in every 4 years once the "warranty" runs out" crowd which is ok but misleading to new comers looking for a reliable truck. 🙄

I put **warranty** in "quotes" **because** that's pretty much what a warranty is, a so-called warranty. Here's why I say this.

These heavy-duty warranty companies are usually **no** good and will fight you tooth and nail to not **cover** the cost of the repair, it just is what it is. There's **usually** a back-and-forth game where the shop takes pictures of the failed part, and they send it to the warranty company. The warranty company then decides whether the picture is good enough and if they are going to warranty it or not. This process might take a day or 2 at times. So, now you might of wasted **2** days to get into the dealership, **another** day is gone with one of the **new** hires to poking around at it, they send the warranty claim in later that day, the warranty company might not come back with an answer until tomorrow; tomorrow comes and they actually approve it (day 4) but they don't have the parts in stock and it has to be overnighted (day 5). **You** get the part the next day, and it makes the check engine light go off just long enough for you to book your next load, hook up to your trailer and **BOOM**! The check engine light comes right back on in their parking lot because they were part changing and not problem solving! NO THANKS! 👎

They didn't know if that would fix it, **chances** are, they replaced what their diagnostic computer suggested. **NOW YOU'RE RIGHT BACK AT WAITING TO GET INTO THEIR SHOP AGAIN**! Keep in mind, you're paying for your own hotel and food every day; You're not making any new money, and your **truck payment** is still due and **so** are home responsibilities because your still away from home. $

Some people call this warranty "**SECURITY**" or "**PEACE OF MIND**" when they explain their reasoning for buying new trucks. But in this example, you just wasted one week for warranty work, and still owe $1500 to $3k a month for that truck, and you **still** really don't know if that fixed your problem. It's **my** opinion through experience, that these emission systems just add **too** many variables and **too** much unnecessary risk. 💯 avoid if possible

** now let me say this as a disclaimer ** ✔️

Newer trucks do have the potential to get **way** better fuel mileage. Some owners say this **increased** fuel mileage makes up for the **increased** maintenance cost. And mathematically speaking, this does have truth to it. Let's say at **100k** miles per year divided by **6** mpg, it would take **16,666** gallons. **16,666** gallons times let's say **$2.25** for fuel is **$37,500** in fuel.

 Now let's do the math of **100k** miles traveled at **7** mpg; That would take **14,285** gallons. **14,285** gallons multiplied by the same cost of the **$2.25** fuel is **$32,142**. So that's about a **$5k** difference. But additional maintenance costs for the **average** emissions system can **easily** be $10k a year or **more**. Sometimes it will be less. I average right around 6-7 mpg in my 1999 pre-emissions motor.

So, for that to make sense for me I would **need** to be seeing 8-9 miles a gallon to **account** for the **additional** costs in maintenance. Your average new truck these days still **aren't** getting 9 mpg consistently yet. And **remember**, that additional cost in maintenance really doesn't account for your down time of missing loads, covering your home and otr living expenses, and covering your fixed costs. 🤔

*Now of course, some guys do what's called "**A DELETE**". Technically this is illegal, so I will not suggest you do it. But with the emissions system deleted, all the emission filters are left in place and everything looks stock but they are hollowed out so exhaust can come straight through it. The emission* *sensors are turned off and usually the **EGR** will blocked in some manner. So, essentially you get the best of both worlds, you get a newer truck and better fuel milage that runs with the dependability of a pre-emission motor.* 🐵

*Like mentioned, this is **illegal**, especially in California to the California Air Research Board (CARB). They will **post** up at random spots and weigh stations like the Banning Scales on I-10 and do **emission** checks. Every now and then someone gets busted and has to pay a fine of a couple hundred dollars to a couple 10 thousand dollars. The people who **do** deletes are usually really good at blending in and usually **don't** talk about it much. The <u>people</u> that usually get caught, are the ones going around <u>telling</u> everyone that they deleted their truck. **AGAIN**, it would be **illegal** for me to suggest deleting your emissions system, but many people do go this route for a solution to their emi$$ion$ nightmare.* 😿

***2** things to take into consideration are; that **if** a <u>dealership</u> finds out by hooking their computer up to your truck that you have a **deleted** truck, they are not allowed to release your truck until it's converted back to stock ($6k in DPF and DOC filters). **SOME** SHOPS ACTUALLY TRY TO ENFORCE THIS **SO** BEWARE. And the other thing is to make sure to get the **right** "program". If you get a bad delete, with jacked up horsepower and stuff, you can really do some damage to your motor internals and or blow a turbo quick! For the record I will say again **DELETES** are not **allowed** in the USA. Getting caught with a delete can result in a HEFTY fine.* 😿

***Most** guys that run deletes do most of their own maintenance too and or go to smaller independent shops to avoid detection. Because in order to get your truck back in compliance you'll have to buy a new DPF and DOC filter* *because they got hollowed out, now you're at $6k just in parts plus labor. Even by them hooking their computer up to your truck and if a tech automatically starts updating your ECM software, you'll lose your delete file and now you're stuck in a sticky situation of trying to keep it cool that you don't have a delete and have someone reprogram your ECM at their shop ~WHICH~ could be a big challenge... or you just end paying them to put the $6k filters back on.* 😬

There are <u>some</u> exceptions of solo owner-operators **doing** great with newer motors, some guys custom tune them for even more fuel efficiency, but unfortunately, they are the exception and not the majority. Knowing what I know now, I wouldn't want those problems **just** for increased fuel mileage and some newer paint! They say 2016's / 2018's and up have gotten a lot better. But I can't really report on **that** in too much detail. Cummins has put out the **X15** series and it has a way bigger **DPF / DOC** for increased service intervals, the computer engineering has gotten better as well. But you're basically talking about buying a new truck at that point. **AND I DON'T WANT THOSE BILLS!** 👻 **if these new x15's prove reliable, then maybe go for it.**

I **already** paid off a $65k dollar truck when I was **27** and I value my home time, family and my other passions more than just having a new truck., the **newer** the truck, the **harder** it will be for you to work on it <u>yourself because of tech and added emmissions</u>; And the more you will need to own specialized tools and software to be able to plug into to it to read fault codes and etc. 😔

Some solo owner-operators love to always be on the road, and I do too, but I would not have the balanced lifestyle that I have now if I was out **chasing 100k** miles a year and having a **big** loan note to **pay** back on a Truck Like This. Especially because, once I pay the loan note off, that emissions truck will **not** be worth much of a dang; it'll probably soon need a **$20k** plus motor rebuild and I'll get stuck having to replace almost every element of that emissions system. **NO THANKS**! This is "why" many guys trade their emission trucks back in and get another new one because it just won't last much longer correctly. That's cool, but now they're right back into the hole with the bank loan and now pretty much become forced to get right back on the road. **Unless** these guys are really killin' it doing double drop low boy heavy haul type stuff, and doing over well over $5k net a week, they never get to stop much. They have to be over the road to continue to make the payments and still profit. 👻 especially in a van trailer cross country operation...

Here's **food** for thought, I drove something like **44k** miles last year and still increased my net worth by **30%** or so. I **did** this mostly by keeping my **overhead** at home **low**, making my business overhead **low** and by making **the good freight** deals. I yes, really enjoy being home! So, why would I trade that freedom for a newer, more problematic truck!?? **There** comes a time when you'll have to decide for yourself, how **much** money is enough for you and or what it is that **really** makes you happy. 😁

If you **don't** know how much money makes you happy, then you'll probably just always be on the road trying to **make** more of it; Not realizing the rat race you're in. **But** when you have discipline with your money, learn to do things on your own, **create** a low overhead operation, you can keep just **as** much money or **more** than people with the new trucks driving **100k** miles a year do but with half the work!! 🔑 ok

Let me tell you another big thing to consider too when deciding on what age of a truck to get. Another **big** thing to consider is **PARTS PRICING**. Parts on older trucks for the most part are **way** more cheaper, especially the engine parts. Let me give you a few examples. A couple years ago my old friend lost **his** turbo in his **2012** with a Cummins ISX (2350). This **turbo** <u>cost him</u> right around $**6,000** plus labor. The turbo on my N-14 costs $**750** to $**1500** tops. **AND I CAN INSTALL IT MYSELF!** I can install it fairly quick and I don't need a computer to recalibrate it. 😗

The **air** compressor on my N-14 is like $**700** compared to the upwards of $**1500** and up on my **2009** ISX (cm871). You can do this for almost every part on the motor; The oil pump, fuel pump, the head(s), the cylinders, the pistons and etc...
When I compare the **cost** of parts against **newer** motors, I see <u>consistently</u> 50% less in **cost** compared to the same part on a newer truck. 💲

Let's look a **motor** rebuild, I can do a **very** decent motor rebuild on my N-14 for about $**7500** to $**12,500**. This is compared to the well over $**20,000** I spent rebuilding my 871 ISX. I imagine rebuilding a 2012 + motor will be at least the same or even more. Especially when you get into **cutting** the counterbores, **injectors** and **etc**. 🚛

If I was out truck buying, there are 2 motors I would be looking for the most. ✔️

- Cummins N-14 435 HP (pre 2003) 🏆
- Detroit 60 Series 12.7 (pre 2003) 🏆

Some runners up would be... ✔️

- Cat 3406b (6NZ) 😎
- Cummins Big Cam (mechanical motor) 😎
- Cummins ISX 870 😎
- Cummins X15 efficiency series 😎
- Volvo D-12 (pre-emission) 😎

CUMMINS N-14 ✔️

I **really** like this motor! I **own** a 1999 N-14. This is the motor I take **all** around the country. It's a **very** straightforward design. It **has** everything it needs, and nothing else in the way. People have made **A LOT** of money with this motor. When truck drivers back in the day **were** making all that money, they **were** doing it in a **pre**-emissions motor. The N-14 was one of these motors. **Early** on in trucking I was so immersed in figuring everything out in the trucking business. I remember talking to the **older** owner operators and three motors always popped up; the N-14, the Detroit 60, and the Cat 6NZ. ✔️

Even though I already had a 2009 Pete with an ISX, I **would** always tell myself, whenever I got the opportunity to buy one of these motors, I will! 😄 And that's what **I** did. My intuition was correct! These motors are built well enough to go well past 1 **million** miles when driven easy and maintained well. If the truck is in good shape, and if the motor sounds good, I wouldn't hesitate to buy a good N-14 with 800k miles on it and put it **straight** to work. I burn **1** gallon of oil between my **15k** mile oil changes. I'm at **1.1** million miles with no piston and cylinder rebuild. In the maintenance chapter I'll describe what all's involved in a rebuild. But **yeah**, this is a great one of the best ever type motor, almost every part on it is something you can replace yourself with basic hand tools. 💪

And to rebuild this motor for pistons, cylinders and bearings is like Imentioned; about $**7500** to $**12,500** or so. Some cons on this motor are really none (lol), **but** over the years the rebuild quality of the injectors seems to have gone down, or the cores have just been reused so many times that the re-man injectors can be hit or miss and not work correctly. **Cummins** does not make new injectors anymore for the N14, but there are some 3rd party companies that do I believe. Some owners say there's a <u>conspiracy</u> to get people that have kept their trucks forever to submit to buying a new truck, and……maybe so huh? 👻

But I got a workaround for this. If you buy a N-14 and need injectors, make sure to **<u>buy the "PX" injectors</u>**. Cummins makes **RX** and **PX**. **RX** is a reman (remanufactured) injector, but the **PX** is a rebuild too, but of higher quality and they use higher quality rebuild components. The cost is a little more, but come with a longer warranty of two years instead of one. If you don't specifically request PX injectors they **will** usually try to sell you RX injectors. People are getting those hit and miss problems with the **RX** injectors more so and not px injectors. When you get the box, look at the part number on it, it will start with **PX** then the part number. These are PX injectors. **Plus**, there's a collection of videos on YouTube for how to fix on these motors. ✔️

Cummins Quickserve can be a **damn good** resource for all Cummins motors when it comes to having access to <u>step-by-step</u> procedures, wire diagrams and etc. **DON'T BE INTIMIDATED**! I got videos on YouTube adjusting valves, air compressor install, starter install, piston cooling nozzles, Oil pan install, and etc. This is a **very** straightforward motor with only a few sensors and no emissions choking it down and making the oil dirty.

In **my** opinion this is what it's all about. **Minimizing** risk, and **increasing** efficiency! A **pre**-emission motor really helps do this in many ways. Many solo owner-operators loved this motor. Please keep this motor in mind as you proceed in your truck buying!

DETROIT 60 SERIES 12.7 ✔

The **Detroit 60** Series is another **GREAT pre**-emission motor. **MANY PEOPLE** swear by this motor and love it as well! **This** motor can even be <u>cheaper</u> to rebuild than the N-14. **I've** never owned one, **but** from my research, the average cost to rebuild this motor is around $**6,000** to $**12,000** for basic Piston, Cylinders, and Rod and main bearings. **Many** solo owner-operators have told me that this is a **very** user-friendly motor to own and work on yourself. $

I've **even** heard an older owner op telling me how he used to <u>rebuild</u> this motor **over** the weekend by himself and a friend, in their own shop for $**4k. THINK ABOUT THAT**! For $4k a man was able to rebuild his own motor to last another **MILLION** miles! **THAT'S INCREDIBLE**! Now of course, if you're not doing the labor yourself, it will cost more, <u>BUT STILL</u>. $4k for pistons, cylinders and main and rod bearings is **PERFECT** news for the owner operator. Like mentioned, I've never owned **one** of these motors, **but** it still remains top 2 on my list if I were to ever go truck shopping again. ✔

There are **resources** like www.truckersreport.com where you can **search** keywords like "Detroit 60 series" and read about the **pros** and **cons** of other people's experience. I **highly** suggest doing this regardless of the motor you choose. **RESEARCH MY FREIND!** 💪

There are a **few** flaws to every motor pretty much, **one** flaw on the Detroit 60 is the bull gear. I've heard horror stories on the bull gear, but for the most part it **never** overshadows the extreme performance and durability of this motor. The bull gear is something to keep in mind and is something to ask about when you go to buy your truck. Ask them if the **bull gear** has been changed already. And if they say yes, make sure you see the receipt! 😑

To do the bull gear is probably a $2000 to $3500 job (if you catch it before it breaks loose!). The front end of the motor has to come off, the radiator usually has to come out and etc. **So**, if you can buy a Detroit 60 series with a fresh rebuild and or a new bull gear that will be a **GREAT** benefit! But don't be too concerned if it doesn't have a new bull gear, they seem to **last** almost **forever**, maybe 800k to 1.2 million miles, but when they go, they take a lot down with it. **SO JUST BE AWARE!** The Detroit 60 is a **good** motor. The motors that came out before 2004 are all pre-emission with no EGR and etc... The one's that came out from 2003 – 2007 have only an EGR...

Whether it's in a freightliner, a Peterbilt, a Volvo or whatever, it really doesn't matter. This Detroit 12.7 60 Series is another **GREAT** engine to build your business around.

RUNNER UP'S 🐢

3406 (6NZ) CAT ✓

The CAT 3406 is **another** legend. The only reason it makes my runner up list is because it has the reputation of <u>lower</u> fuel mileage. From most of my personal research this motor sees 4.5 to upper 6 mpg. **Now**, maybe if you really baby this motor, you can get 6 mpg plus. **BUT**, the <u>selling</u> point of this motor is it's **pulling power**, it's **reliability**, and it's **ease** to work on it **yourself**. This motor was out at the same time the N-14 and the Detroit 60 series was out. I've **never** owned a CAT 6NZ but if I were in the market for a new truck and the N-14 and the Detroit wasn't in market, I would **really** consider this motor! **There's** a ton of old school guys out here that have made a <u>killing</u> off this motor and swear by it. 3406 had an A model (3406a) and a B model (3406b). I think the main difference from what I've been able to tell is that the B model had a computer controlling the injectors. But many solo owner-operators liked the B model better. I may be a bit wrong on this one, so please do your own research further a bit here. I just have never really frequented CAT motors **but** I have been semi aggressive on collecting info on them over the years. 🚛

CUMMINS BIG CAM (mechanical motor) ✓

This is a **really** cool motor that I would be <u>interested</u> in! **This** motor came out right before the N-14 did. It's **completely** mechanical, and there's **no** ECM or computer controlling it. That means there's **basically** <u>no sensors</u>. There's way **less** variables when it comes to what can shut you down. Your motor basically runs or it doesn't. And this motor **has** a reputation for being a runner! Again, I never owned this motor either but I've heard many good stories from longtime owner ops who loved this motor and wished they never sold theirs! You'll hear that a lot when talking to older owner ops, **that they wish** they never sold their pre-emission motor. 🤭

Guys tell me all the time, "**That's** a good motor you got there (my N-14) … I **wish** never sold mine, now I got this <u>new emissions junk</u>!" **LOL**. Seriously though, I hear **this** often when I'm outside looking under the hood topping off oil and etc. I'll tell you another cool thing about this Big Cam Cummins motor then I'll tell you a con of this motor…. The good thing is **PARTS ARE CHEAP**! I don't know how true it is, but I was told once by an owner that injectors for the Big Cam are like $**50**! That's insane! So, for $**300** you can get all six injectors compared to about $**500** - $**600 PER** injector for mostly ever other motor. I never went and cross checked him but he didn't seem to have a reason to lie. If you find one of these motors and you're considering it, **call** your parts store and check on injector prices **first**! Don't be like <u>Andrew</u> **told me** they were $50 injectors and you **buy** the whole motor over that one statement! Just double check that one. 😁

The con and really only thing that would concern me on this motor is the fuel mileage. You're probably not going to see much more than 5 – 6 mpg in this motor. This **motor** is a dinosaur of the "yesteryears" when fuel was cheap and fuel mileage didn't matter so much. These motors are usually / often khaki in color. 🚛

CUMMINS ISX CM870 / 871

These are 2 **different** motors. The ISX 870 came out in **2002'** ish, and the 871 was introduced in **2008**. The ISX 870 replaced the N-14 and has less emission systems than the **871**. The **870** only has an **EGR** valve. In comparison, the **871** has an **EGR** valve, **EGR** cooler, Aftertreatment injector (7th injector), a **DOC** and a **DPF**. A lot of people liked the 870, even though most people thought the N-14 was **way** better, but the 870 did fine for the most part and probably saw a slight fuel mileage increase compared to the N-14. Parts on the **870** cost a bit more than parts on the N-14, and parts on the 871 cost way more than both the 870 and N-14. **WAY MORE!** $

I started off in my first truck outside of leasing in **2013** with this motor, the ISX 871. **MAN**, this motor almost **broke** me, I can't even lie. It **did** teach me a lot and **got** me prepared to enjoy more simple motor designs though. 🐌 The **871** can be a great fuel-efficient motor if it gets "tuned" or deleted like mentioned earlier, which is illegal so I'm not suggesting you do this. But many solo owner-operators did to stay competitive. And when they got the right tune, it **ran** amazing. The oil would stay yellow for 5k – 8k miles. It was a mean efficient machine then. **But** mentioned, the parts on this motor can be very expensive. A turbo is like $**3000**, the turbo actuator is another $**1000** or so. The **DPF** and **DOC** are $**3k** each, so on and so forth. 😌

You have to be very proactive with this motor (**871**) if you're going to run it with the emissions system intact. If you have this motor, I recommend going to **WWW.RAWZE.COM** and watching **RAWZE's** YouTube channel. I have met Rawze in person and he is a **good** man who helped me. He **taught** me much in my early years, directly and indirectly. Go be a member on his website (**it's free**) and just soak in the knowledge! Read other people's post's and learn from them too. And if you have an issue, **post** it up on there! If you're respectful and if you articulate yourself right, you'll more than likely get an answer back. And Rawze's whole website basically revolves around the ISX **871**, because this is the motor Rawze has and it is the motor he has figured out down to the "T". Other motor conversations are welcomed too. 🚛🚛

If it wasn't for **Rawze**, I **would** have been *for sure* out of business early on! I wouldn't have been able to learn mechanics, problem solving and the business quickly as I had to if it wasn't for him. **GRATITUDE!!!!** 🙏

But Rawze has a video called the **EGR** tune up on YouTube. If you have this motor, you **MUST** do this **EGR** tune up once or twice a year. This **EGR** tune up gets the soot out of your Venturi pipe and your differential mixing tubes, it cleans soot off your sensors or you just replace them. This is the first repair / maintenance job I decided to take on myself. It gave me the confidence boost I needed to do bigger and more repairs later on. 😎

If **one** of those **5** or so sensors that **run** the **emissions** system is carbon packed, it **can't** sense correctly!

Which therefore **gives** inaccurate data to the computer, **which** in turn makes the turbo do funny things to overcompensate for it, and or the **DPF** doesn't passive regen right and **etc**. If you're **not** hip to this knowledge, then there's a great chance the dealerships will "**EAT YOUR LUNCH**" so to speak. When they plug their computer up, it might say "**bad turbo**" or "**bad EGR cooler**" or "**DPF plugged**" and **etc**. If **you** don't know better you might agree to <u>buy</u> a turbo or an **EGR** cooler or a new **DPF** that **you** <u>didn't even need</u>! If these sensors aren't reading right because they are packed with soot, all sorts of funky things and engine codes can and will happen. 🔑

I **remember** one time early on I was in Michigan, in Detroit area. I **get** a check engine light. I didn't have the Cummins Insite software and hook-ups, so I stopped at a Peterbilt or a Cummins (I forget) to get the code read. They plug up to see what the code is. **Mind** you, I just dealt with some pretty big repairs right before this and I think I had like **$5k** to my name in the bank. I'm probably **23 – 24** years old <u>at this time</u>. The man now says I need an **EGR** cooler, and that it's going to be a **$5k** dollar job (for some reason) -by the time they get the parts and do everything they need to do. I was like ok, **NO WAY**! I got to figure something out! 🐚

Luckily, I had Rawze's number and I gave him a call. **He's** a <u>tough guy to me the young buck at the time</u>. He asks me "**Have** you **changed** your Exhaust Back Pressure Sensor yet?". I said no, I have not. He then tells me that they **go** <u>bad</u> around **500k** to **600k** miles. **Well**, that was about the mileage I had on my odometer. He tells me to go buy the sensor, change it out, and call him back. I go back in and buy the exhaust back pressure sensor, it's like $150. At this time, I'm not carrying many **or** any tools yet. **But** I was soon discovering that if I wanted to be **successful** in my business, that I was going to <u>need to collect as many tools as I needed and learn how to use them ASAP</u>. **All** I needed to do the repair was a deep socket. I didn't even have that, so sad! Don't be me back then! 👍

Lucky for me, my **enthusiasm** must have won one over one of the mechanics enough for him to step outside and pop the old sensor off and put the new one in for me. **This** was embarrassing and one of the moments I realized I need to be doing better and taking more **initiative in owning tools**. Long story short, when I keyed on my ignition the check engine light **was** already off. **Not only** was it off, it stayed off for the next couple months, which gave me plenty of time to stack more money and get in a more secured position. I called **Rawze** back and thanked him so much, it wouldn't be the last time either. 🙏

I highly suggest in addition to this book that you find a good mentor in this business when the opportunity presents itself. 💪

Make sure y'all get along first, and if it's organic, just ask for his or her number and **say you won't ask for money**! Tell em' it would be **great** to get advice and to have someone to call if things get out of your experience level and if you need help figuring something out. **Successful** people usually **love** to help those with potential who also help themselves. 👐

DON'T BE TOO PRIDEFUL TO ASK FOR HELP! 😎

It took me **MANY** years to discover that asking for help or receiving some help is OK. It's called respectfully **utilizing** your resources! 🆗 ⚡

My story I just told is an example and something to keep in mind when it comes to the emissions' system; And how it can **be** a financial disaster if you're not ready and not prepared for it. I highly suggest going to **Rawze's** website and downloading **his** book, and read the section on his breakdown of what the **EGR** system actually is. He makes good analogies to help better understand the function of this system so you can better understand how important it is to stay ahead of it and do <u>preventive</u> maintenance on it. The whole book is great for sure and helped me tremendously to get going in the **right** direction. **A lot** of the things I still do today is from the <u>knowledge, experience and tactics I picked up in his book</u>! ✔

But my honest opinion, if I were to do it again, I would **not** get another 871 lol. (Though the 871 runs great on the proper delete) The parts **are** just <u>too</u> expensive, there's <u>too</u> much **unreliable** emission components, and I never did really enjoy working on that motor. It seemed like there just wasn't enough free space to reach parts right, or I had to take too many other parts off to reach the part I was working. And plus, it's just too many sensors. **This** is my opinion but it also an opinion <u>from my experience</u>. This **CAN** be a great motor, you just got to really be involved in making it one and keeping it one, and it was Fast and responsive…. I don't have as much negative to say about the 870. Everyone seemed much more happy with it for the most part.

CUMMINS X15 EFFICENCY SERIES ✔

Cummins released this motor right around 2017-2018. It was released in two models, one for **power** and one for **efficiency**. This motor was supposed to be the redemption for the bad reputation Cummins was getting after the 871, 2250 and 2350 models. **I** first saw this motor in the Dallas Truck Show at a Cummins exhibit. I was very impressed! It seemed like they worked most of the kinks out of the emission system. **You** got to **remember**, the **EPA** and **CARB** was **making** these <u>emission standards</u> so fast, that engine manufactures originally had to cut corners and make new technology quick enough to keep production moving. ✖

Regulations were hard enough on motor companies that CAT stopping making Class 8 Diesel motors all together. The last emission rulemaking that added more parts to the motor went into effect around **2012**. That's when the **SCR / DEF** came into play. Now-a-days motor manufactures have had much more time and experience through trial and error. So, when the **X15** rolled out, they seemed to have figured out how to correct the things they previously had to rush for compliance to do. 🛠

Besides this, I can't tell you much more about this motor. The feedback I've read and heard has all been pretty positive with great fuel mileage to toot with the efficiency series. If I were to be getting a brand-new truck, it would have to be one with this motor. 🚛

VOLVO D12 (PRE-EMISSION) ✔

The Volvo **D12** has a great reputation in solo owner-operator circles too. The later Volvo motors such as the D13 and up **have** gotten a <u>not so good of a reputation</u>. I remember reading a post off truckersreport where a guy was talking about his **D12**, and at 1.7 Million miles, he still had never opened his motor up. No rebuild, same pistons, same cylinders, same cylinder head, he said he put a couple injectors in over the years and that was about it as far as major work. You'll see these D12's installed in **generation 1** Volvo's up to year 2003. This would be my 4th in line as far as what motor to pick. But it's a wildcard. If the truck was in great shape and I liked the owner, it may jump up to number 1, 2, 3 on my list. I'm just not sure on parts availability, so I would have to check on that first. And also, I would like to know if my local independent shops know how to work on them. 🚚

IN CONCLUSION ON MOTORS: ✔

THIS IS WHAT YOU WANT! A motor that **you** can take care of and that **you** can count on when you make your freight deals. You want to be able to work on it yourself, for it to be cost effective on parts, and for it to be a motor that **places** know how to work on.

Whether it's an N-14, the Detroit 60, this D12 I just mentioned or another one; Use this guide of motors to get you going in the **right** direction. Do as much research as you can on www.truckersreport.com and on www.rawze.com . Be observant. **Listen** to older solo owner-operators and **see** what has worked and hasn't worked for them. Take note of the **successful** owner ops at the truck stops, what type of motor does he have? And by successful I'm talking about the ones with the paid off trucks, financial freedom and freedom of time. There are successful people in **newer** trucks too but you have to really make sure that they're as successful as they **seem**. A lot of those guys stick their chest out like they're so bad, but are one breakdown away from being out of business as well. Instead of telling you to avoid the situation that he's in, he pretends to be making off so well... confusing the next person ✊

This is why you need to **survey** as much as **you** can as you save up money to start your business. If you've already started your business, **you still** need to be out **collecting** this real-life info... It pays to collect **first-hand** experience from others. The **more** you collect, the **better** you can make an educated decision based off everything you've collected on your own and from others. 🗝

Many make the **mistake** and listen to **one** person's opinion on something and then go make big decisions **based** off that. You can ask what **10** peoples' opinions are on the same motor and will likely get a range of answers. It's **up** to you to find the trend of truth in those answers. It's also up to you to find the **success** in those replies. 💭

A man with a habitual lack mindset and a **lack** of initiative will find a **way** to mess almost anything up. **So**, what if he's the one telling you "don't do this, and to do this"? **Be careful**, the reason why something didn't work for him **may not apply** to you; Because you actually **drive** your truck easy, you **don't** accelerate hard, you **fix** things right, you **change** your filters and oil on time, you **keep** a healthy reserve of money in the bank, and you **keep** your home bills low. 💯

Maybe it wasn't the motor, maybe it was just him! **You** can still learn valuable lessons from people that didn't quite make it, but just **be** careful. **Misery** loves company and **many** unsuccessful owner ops get in the habit of hanging around listening to **'the losers of the game'** too much and they let other people's shortcomings **become their own**. There's **power** in proximity… Be mindful of who you hang around. 🔑

If you've been doing this long enough, you know there's **always** somebody out here **complaining** about **something**. You must be the solution-oriented one. You must **be** the one that looks for **solutions** and **not** problems. As long as you're always looking for ways to improve and doing things better, **you'll** begin to naturally shy away from the dead-end conversations with the complaining parties at the different truck stops. When you're busy being **successful,** you don't have time for complain problems, only time for solutions and answers! **Success** has so much to do with your mentality. 🔒(continued trend)

WHICH MOTORS I WOULD AVOID AND SOME OTHER THINGS TO WATCH OUT FOR. ✔

I would not get a …
- Navistar N13 also known as as the MAXFORCE. ✖
- A Volvo motor after 2003. Maybe they've gotten better but I definitely wouldn't get one up to 2108. ✖
- A Paccar motor. ✖
- Cummins ISX 2250 or 2350 (in trucks 2012ish - 2018ish) ✖
- A Twin turbo CAT ✖
- Detroit motors past 2007. Some guys do well with the 2008 and up. But me personally, I wouldn't want it. ✖

The Maxforces **have** a horrible reputation for being quickly made, under tested **junk motor**. They've had many lawsuits.

And That's the reason it's so much cheaper when you see a truck with this motor in it. Nobody operating in their right mind wants it. ✖

Be very careful if you have an ISX **2250** or a **2350**. These motors have a **high-pressure fuel pump** that has a <u>bad reputation as well</u>. →The **ceramic** plungers inside the pump have broken and entered the oil. **Once** the little broken pieces enter the oil, it's <u>over with</u>. You either **have to** replace your whole motor with a brand-new crate engine, or you have to trust that every piece of those little plungers has been removed from **EVERY** little path of oil. Because if those little pieces go into a moving part, you're going to bend, break, or scar up something in your motor. <u>It's sad</u>. **A lot** of people **went down** <u>like this over this motor</u>. 😵

If you already have one of these motors, don't worry too much but **consider, consider** changing this pump **asap** if it has over **300k** miles on the pump. They have updated this pump and made the plungers out of steel now. And for the most part, it's been working better; But the plungers can still break! **If** I owned this motor, I would count on **changing** this fuel pump out for a new one every **250k** miles or so. 🚚

I would **avoid** Automatic transmission's all together if possible. They seem convenient, but the extra electronics and sensors involved make it an unnecessary variable. ☜

If you buy a **Volvo** or a **Paccar** motor, be prepared to get turned down at some shops because they don't have the software, the specialty tools or the mechanics to work on them. That's one **downside** to having a motor built from the same brand as the truck, it starts to limit you to dealerships more for service. ☜

Detroit 60 series has its famous bull gear stories of failure. But it must not happen to often enough because everyone still **loves** this old motor! Just keep this bull gear in mind when buying and asking your questions. You can research it further on www.truckersreport.com ✔

The **twin turbo CAT** has never really had a great reputation and the turbos are expensive and you need 2 of them (of course)! ☞

Don't get too **excited** about someone trying to sell you on the phrase "**Fleet maintained**". Fleets are **too** busy running their trucks to really maintain them at all! They just want those trucks to last good and long enough to trade them in after 4 years. Fleet drivers can sure tear up trucks too. Be careful if you're buying a used fleet truck. 💯

WE TALKED ABOUT MOTORS SO WHAT ABOUT TRUCKS?? ✔

Like I said earlier, most of the trucks are built well. **So**, I'll share with you some things I like and dislike for each brand. **And** for the record, **I've** only ever owned Peterbilt and Volvo. **So**, I definitely have experience in the ownership of these two brands; the shops, the parts, the people and **etc**. But I've pretty much drove every brand of truck at one point and I've collected info over the years from the **conversations** I've with **successful** owner operators. 🚚

My personal truck favorite is what they call a **Gen 1 Volvo**. Gen 1 stands for **generation one**. These were produced until 2003. This is the first real generation of Volvo trucks after transitioning from being Volvo GMC white. These Gen 1 Volvo's **are** just built plain right **in my opinion**! They came with all 4 of the popular pre-emission motors. The Detroit 60, the N-14, the CAT 6NZ and the Volvo D12. If **you** are looking for a Gen 1 Volvo, try searching Craigslist in Chicago, Atlanta, Miami, Dallas, and Houston. Type in "N14" or "Detroit 60" or "Volvo D12" and etc. They're still out here. I wouldn't hesitate to pay $20k for one in good shape. They can still be found for around $10k - $15k if someone doesn't realize its value or if it's in not so good shape or market dictates otherwise.

*If you time the year of your truck just right, you can still get a Gen 1 or another brand and **avoid** ABS regulations too. All trucks manufactured before* <u>*March 1, 1997*</u> *are not required to be in compliance with ABS regulations... Abs sensors and valves can be problematic andcome with "gotcha" tickets from DOT if your ABS is on, or because it doesn't' flash on and off at key on.*

PETERBILT ✓

Peterbilt is made by Paccar and so is Kenworth. Peterbilt **is** the first brand of truck <u>that I owned</u>. It was a **387** model with the **871 ISX** in it. It was a pretty good truck overall, it definitely looked good. I would **not** recommend getting a **587**.

That model is the newer version of the **387**. I had a close friend that owned that truck and something about the suspension just isn't right on it. He tells me even the dealers tell him about how bad the 587 goes through shocks and other suspension parts like it's nothing. ✗

If I were buying a Peterbilt I would be going for an early model **387** that has a pre-emission motor or a **379** with a N-14 or Detroit. Though the **379** are not a fuel-efficient design at all, the ease of working on a motor in one of these trucks is **DRASTICALLY** increased! With the long hood design, it allows the motor to sit **further up** in the chassis. This allows pretty much complete access to all parts of the **motor** including the **backside** of the motor. Most modern trucks today have the motor buried so deep in the "**doghouse**", that **reaching** the back cylinders, the wire harness' and hoses around the back can be such a pain. 💪

PROS
- The brand of parts **TRP** makes almost everything for Peterbilt and Kenworth trucks at a cheaper price and they're usually stocked at all the Peterbilt Kenworth dealers. This provides a good alternative to full priced OEM parts. ✓
- **American** made. The Peterbilt is kind of like America's truck. The long nose Pete's are pretty much the most depicted trucks in the movies and etc. Almost everybody seems to like a Peterbilt. The old school guys especially love the older 379's. This truck still holds its value very well to this day. It's **not** uncommon to see a decent 379 with over a million on it still going for $40k plus. ✓
- Peterbilt's in general hold their value pretty well. ✓

- Peterbilt's tend to **ride** pretty well as far as the suspension goes. ✓

CONS
- I was **not impressed** at all by the way my **387** was wired up, especially behind the dashboard and around the motor. I remember troubleshooting for a repair and going behind my dashboard to check my wiring. It looked like a kid wired it all up for fun. There were wires all over the place, stuff was disconnected, the labels were worn off, nothing was really zip-tied and organized. Basically, it was just very unorganized and that made me very unconfident in the wiring of the truck. ✗
- They **don't** have a great turning radius. I just couldn't turn as sharp if I needed to. On plenty occasions I found myself having to back up to finish making a turn. ✗
- Peterbilt name brand parts can be pretty **expensive** at times. ✗
- I didn't like the fact that **my** main fuse box was **outside** under the hood. It seemed like a **weird** place to put it. Putting it outside helps expose it to the elements, and by placing it so close to the motor, the **heat** from the motor affects the relays and wire temps. ✗

FREIGHTLINER ✓

Freightliner can be a cool truck because of its **ease** to find parts. Many of the TA Petro's are Freightliner service points and they stock freightliner parts. A truck I would consider buying second to the Gen 1 Volvo would be a **199x to 2003 model Freightliner**

Columbia or Freightliner Classic. The older Columbia's have a reputation for being loosely made on the inside. When you **look** into somebody's old Columbia, **chances** are parts of the door and cabinets will be missing **lol**. This is nothing crazy when it comes to business but I have heard many guys talk about the rattling "Freightshakers" will make going up the road. But you'll **still** see **many** old Columbia's and Classic's getting' up the roads doing just Fine. 🚚

Like I say, when a man finds his truck that makes him money, he just keeps it! 💲💲🏆😎

PROS

- Parts are **widely** available ✓
- Parts **tend** to be cheaper ✓
- **Older** Freightliners had Detroit 60's and N-14's. ✓
- Freightliners tend to be cheaper to purchase than other brands ✓

CONS

- Freightliners don't hold their re-sale value as well as other brands ✗
- Older Freightliner Columbia's tend to be more cheaply made on the inside. ✗

INTERNATIONAL ✓

International is an **OLD** company. They've been making trucks since pretty much the beginning. Not only do they make over the road class-8 Semi's, but **they** produce vehicles and trucks for the military. Even though International failed miserably with the ProStar model that had the MaxForce motor, International has made great models over the years. 👍

The International **9400 Eagle** is a popular **pre**-emissions truck in the old school owner operator crowd (If made before 2003). The **9400** models after 2003 were cool too, they just didn't have pre-emission motors. The Prostar with the 870 and 871 Cummins has been a great choice for some. This is the truck that **Rawze**, who I mentioned earlier has. He really highlights the fact that it's aerodynamic-ness is hard to beat. That Prostar can **really** put out some **good mpg** if the motor is tuned right. 🚚

PROS

- International **has** maintained an overall great reputation for putting out quality-built trucks. ✓

- The **9400** Eagle is a great pre-emissions truck. ✓

- The Prostar is very aerodynamic for those looking for ways to increase their fuel mileage. ✓

- The cost of a used International tends to be right in the middle of the used truck price market. ✓

CONS

- The **Maxforce** engine was horrible! ✗
- Not too many others I can think of actually! ✗

KENWORTH ✓

Kenworth is the sister company to Peterbilt. **Paccar** is who produces Kenworth, just like Paccar is who produces Peterbilt. What this can do is make parts **more** widely available for you. There's a **good** chance that you can find Kenworth parts at Peterbilt dealerships and vice versa. Kenworth has 2 really popular pre-emission trucks, the infamous **W-9** and the **T-600**. I was really considering a **T-600** at one time. The **T-600** still catches my attention as a **good-looking money maker**.

I would **likely** never own one though. I test drove one before and I didn't like how tall up the driving position is and how little the windshield is. It **reduced** my visibility and made me feel **too** separated from the ground; This combination made me feel more likely to hit something or that I would make a mistake while driving or turning. But that's me, guys drive **T-600's** and the newer **T-660's** everyday out here. It's just personal preference at that point. 🚛

The **W-9** is not aerodynamic at all or fuel efficient but it's the other classic long hood truck of America. You got to love em because of their place in trucking politics and culture. Many older guys still love the W-9 and drive them into their glory years of trucking. They **drive** them for the style and the pride, they made it! They're successful and they want to show it! **But** also, the pre 2003 **W-9**'s had the great pre-emission motors we've been talking about. The **new** Kenworth's are cool but as you can tell, I'm biased against anything **2004** to about **2018**. The newer Kenworth's mostly have the ISX 870, 871, 2250, 2350 or a Paccar motor. The brand-new ones are coming with X15 Cummins or Paccar motors. 🚛

PROS
- Having **access** to the **TRP** brand for aftermarket prices. ✔
- Having **access** to both the Peterbilt and Kenworth network for parts. ✔
- The **T-600** and **W-9** were very popular pre-emission trucks ✔
- Pretty good resale value ✔

CONS

- **Reduced** road visibility ✕
- Slightly **lower** fuel mileage ✕
- Since it's made by Paccar and giving my experience with Peterbilt, I would really have to check the wiring inside and out the truck to make sure it meet my "protect the wires" standard ✕

VOLVO ✓

Volvo gets a bad rep in our industry for some reason. At one time, men conspired and decided Volvo's weren't **manly** enough 😂… pretty much lol… Once this seed got planted it **grew** wild! Now you got drivers saying they don't like Volvo's and if **you** ask them why, they don't really know! **They** will say something like they don't like em' and that you should get a real truck like a Peterbilt. **But** these are also the drivers that haven't owned and maintained rigs usually! **So**, take it with a grain of salt. But on the same token; It is ok that guys have an opinion that they don't like a Volvo or another truck. We are in United States right! Freedom of speech and thought. 🚚

But over time, Volvo's have made their way into being **perceived** as the truck for the 'flip flop, foot on the dash, no tool having truck driver'; And also, Volvo's have a reputation for being the truck of the new drivers and owners that immigrated and doesn't speak much English. Though it is true to extent, so what! We're all Americans now and they are here to work too! I just think that some of the older truck drivers are doing what **they can** to preserve their old trucking politics and culture. They get bent out of shape when they see classic trucking culture changing or fading away a bit. 😬

That's where we need to all do our part to always **make** trucking culture and politics better, while carrying the **common sense** and **decency** parts of the **culture** that was already built. **Real** truckers **help** their fellow truckers if they need help, **real** truckers have operate respectfully at the truck stops and while driving, real truckers do what they can to not make messes at places and etc. 🚚

Now that that's out the way, let's talk Volvo. Volvo is a **European** brand. They do things a **little** different than its American competitors. **A lot** of Volvo parts you buy will be made in Sweden and other countries in Europe. A lot of the American made trucks parts will be made in Mexico. **I've** found higher quality and more pride (quality control and integrity) built in the parts I get from Volvo compared to Paccar. ✔️

Volvo's have the best interiors hands down, my opinion. The big full-sized sleepers sometimes have desks at the bottom. Volvo **really** build these interiors to accommodate the lifestyle of someone who stays on the road a lot and lives in their truck. The other big companies have got better over the years but they just don't seem to get it like Volvo does (Even though some of the old W-9's had studio sleepers with couch's in them!). But Volvo definitely kills it in this department. 😎

I've mentioned before the **Gen 1 Volvo** being my favorite and a choice of many owner operators '**in the know**'. I would not go for a Gen 2 Volvo or really any Volvo with a Volvo motor other than the D12 or Dertroit 12.7 60 Series. I think it's the D13 motor that has a bad reputation for leaky injector cups that cost thousands of dollars to fix and it might happen again the very next year. ☑

I **really** also like the fact that my main fuse and relay panel is **inside** my cab in my dashboard and not outside. The wiring standard is so good. All my wires are numbered and are **bundled** good and tight where it looks organized and won't rub, chafe and ground out on anything. 🔑

PROS
- **Superior** interior ✓
- **Great** turning radius ✓
- The **Gen 1 Volvo VN and VNL's** were rock solid ✓
- **Volvo's** do ride real smooth ✓

CONS
- **Volvo's** aren't "cool" to many in the trucking world. ✗
- **Prices** on Volvo parts can be ridiculous at times. ✗
- **Volvo** motors can only be fixed at Volvo dealers usually. Unless it's an older model Volvo D12 motor, some independent shops might take it in. ✗

MACK TRUCKS ✓

Mack trucks are also owned and ran by Volvo. A lot of the same things I mentioned about Volvo are true to Mack too. Mack's **tend** to be more popular in <u>local and reginal operations</u>. **You'll** see a lot of Mack dump trucks and cement mixers but not so many class 8 full sized sleeper semis. They are out here though. I don't have a **lot** of info on the older ones or the newer ones. **STUDY STUDY STUDY** - If a deal comes up for you on a Mack truck. **Check** the year, check what type of motor it has and etc. **Get** as much info as you can first. A lot of people that have Mack's that I met have loved them! But as with any truck 2004 and up, be **very** weary the condition of its emission components and the wear it may have put on the motor.

GEAR RATIOS ✓

An <u>important</u> thing to **consider** also is gear ratio. **Gear ratio** is the way your differentials are geared up. Kind of like a 10-speed bike verses a 13-speed bike. That's not really a great analogy, but with different ratios you will be at different rpms when you reach "**cruising**" speed. I ride at 60 – 62 miles per hour so I have a **3.73** gear ratio. This is **perfect** <u>for me</u> because at **3.73** that puts me into my motors "sweet spot" of about 1500 rpm. 👍 and shifting in the low gears with weight on produces less of a lug effect…

You'll have to find the **right** gear ratio that fits the speed you want to drive and the motors preferred cruising rpm range and also to the weight and terrain you intend to work. To **find** the suggested highway speed RPM, you might have to do some digging on the internet. There are resources online that will show how to do the formulas to find the right gear ratio for **your** desired speed. **Don't over-look gear ratios**. Gear ratio's play an important role in your fuel mileage, transmission health, differential health, and motor health. If your gear ratio isn't right for your speed, you may be going 62 mph but your engine is lugging down in the low 1300 rpm zone causing extra pressure on your motor. Find the math out for what ratio is best for your desired speed. 🔒

BRAND NEW TRUCKS VS MIDDLE AGED TRUCKS VS OLDER TRUCKS ✔️

This is an age-old debate in trucking. Everybody seems to have their **own** opinion. **Some** make really good points and make really good results. Others make good points but not so good results. And Others just don't make good points or good results! I'll sum it up the best I can with you from my opinion and perspective. 😁

BRAND NEW TRUCKS are nice. They smell good and look good! They got a brand-new frame and a brand-new suspension. They got a brand-new electrical system and they have a brand-new motor. They also come in at the price tag of $**100k** - $**150k+**. So, a $**100k** dollar truck will cost you around $**2k** a month for 5 years. A $**150k** truck will cost you about $**2700** a month for **5** years. **Plus**, insurance! The newer and the higher your trucks suggested value, the more you'll be paying in physical damage and gap insurance also. **Gap** insurance is the insurance you have to carry on high dollar truck loans to cover the remaining cost you owe the bank in the case the truck is a total loss. 🚚

With a new truck you're looking at anywhere from maybe $**2200** to $**3000** plus a month in just truck notes and physical damage / gap insurance. If you have your own authority, this doesn't cover the **Liability** and **Cargo** Insurance which could be another $**1k** to $**2500** a month. Between insurance and truck notes, if you had your own authority, you'd be paying anywhere from $**3000** to $**5000** a month whether you make a dollar or not! That's a **lot** of overhead. What if you got <u>home bills</u>? <u>Rent</u>? <u>Car notes</u>? <u>Insurance</u>? <u>Kids</u>? A <u>Child to support</u>? $

Most owner operators, if leased to a company, are not making much more than $**2500** a week after fuel and company deductions. As an independent with your own authority, if you're only doing $**10k** a month; That leaves maybe $**7000** to $**5000** a month. What's that, $**1750** to $**1250** a week. **SERIOUSLY**?? And your gone from home! A company driver in the right gig can do than and with benefits! As a leased operator who doesn't pay for liability and cargo insurance up front, it would be in the $**8000** to $**7000** range per month. So, $**2000** to $**1750** a week. Not bad, but still not great. And I'm being lenient on that $**2500** a week. I meet a ton of solo owner-operators out here not making more than $**1500** - $**2000**. (Many do much more to if they got into the right operation) 🚚

We have not considered in the fact that; new trucks break too and there will be things you need to pay for that isn't covered by warranty. Sometimes big things, sometimes small things. **Buying** a new truck does not <u>excuse</u> one from the world of mechanics and maintenance. **Sure**, some guys get a new truck and do fine with very little mechanical issues. And other owners get into a new truck and can't stay off the tow hook because of **crazy** emission issues. An example is, Look at all the new trucks that the big fleet companies own that are on the side of the road waiting for a tow. 🔒

Once you factor in physical damage insurance, gap insurance, truck note, and repairs, it's not a very attractive business model to me unless I had a DAM GOOD operation and wanted to be on the road 24/7 for a while with my wife or something. Those numbers of income I just ran also depend on working **EVERY** week with no time off. Not only is that **not** realistic, what if you want to **take** time off? **Go** on a trip? Or **Relax** over the winter months because the roads are so iced and crazy? All I got to say is, if you're going to get a brand-new truck you got to have a **VERY** profitable operation, know what you're doing, and or have a team driving operation to make it all worth it. 😐 being gone this long for home will affect home life to in some degree.

The sad and crazy part is, when some of these owners finish or get close to finish paying off their truck, they **go right back** in and trade it in for another, repeating the whole process again. This to me is like **being** a prisoner to my own job and business. Maybe this will fit your personality? Maybe **you** want to stay on the road non-stop? And if so, **this new truck could work for you**! Just please make sure you really **do** the math and really know the truck and motor you're getting **before** you pull the trigger. 🆗

I'm **not** trying to steer you **away** from getting a new truck if that's what you really desire. I'm just **highlighting** the fact that the large increase of overhead doesn't even necessarily mean your maintenance costs will go all the way **down**. And that the **higher** your overhead cost is, the more will be required to be on the road. And the **catch 22** is, the more your own the road, the more wear and tear you'll be putting on your equipment! 🌚

MIDDLE AGED TRUCKS are sometimes the **only way** to get into the business. If buying a truck cash is not an option yet, then you're probably not going to be able to get a new truck either; And banks don't often finance older pre-emission trucks 2003 an older. **So**, that leaves the heavily fleet used middle-aged truck.

The main problem with middle aged trucks is → the **emission** systems **usually** puts these trucks at high risk of needing expensive and confusing maintenance right away. At **400k** to **600k** on a **2008**- 2017 truck is often a nightmare waiting to happen in my opinion. 🌚

Maybe you get **off** fine for a while, maybe you drive 2 weeks and end up with a $**10k** emissions bill that still doesn't really fix the truck. As mentioned earlier, you're dealing with $**3k** filters, $**4k** turbos, increased labor costs, soot in the oil and sensors carbon packed giving false readings of whats actually wrong. It's a **tough** cookie to crack but you can still do it and be **successful** in a middle-aged truck, you just got to be hyper-sensitive to everything you do with it. My first truck was one of these. The 2009 Pete 387 mentioned earlier. The way you drive, the way you idle, the way you do preventative maintenance and etc are all things you need to be **SUPER** aware of. Things can get expensive quick when your just "throwing parts" at an emission's issue. The **crazy** thing is too, many of these **2008** + motors don't make it past **800k** miles before needing a rebuild. Truck prices go up and down according to the **demand** in the truck buying market.

Usually when freight is real strong, the used truck prices are higher because more people are buying trucks. 🚚

If you **already** have one of these trucks it's ok. But it's mandatory to <u>Buckle down</u> and **get** serious with it though! **Be consistent** in doing your **EGR** tune-up's. **Drive** slower. **Don't** idle your motor every night. **Find** a solution to idling. **Change** the emission system <u>sensors</u> out if you haven't already (**EGR** differential pressure sensor, **Intake manifold** air pressure sensor, **Exhaust** backpressure sensor, **DPF** differential pressure sensor and **etc**, there will be more if you have a **SCR / DEF** 2012 + truck). **Do** you what you can to <u>learn</u> the parts of your motor. **Know** how the systems work. **Put your destiny** <u>in your hands</u> by being **proactive! Don't** wait for <u>problems to happen</u>, **beat** the problems by <u>paying attention</u> and staying ahead of them and by **not** creating an environment for them to exist. 🗝️

I know its <u>tough</u> in the beginning if you don't have cash to buy a pre-emission's truck; But speaking from my opinion, I would not want to own one of these middle-aged trucks again. I **would not** want to own a 2008 – 2018. The **parts** are <u>too</u> expensive and the emission system makes the truck too unreliable for me. It would **throw** a huge wrench into my lifestyle and how I operate. I did it for years. I don't want to go back to paying $**3k** plus for a turbo, $**3k** for filters that clog up and <u>become unreliable</u>. I don't want to be paying all that money for parts on a motor I'm **destroying** by creating soot in my oil (emissions).never knowing when the next emission code will pop leaving with more work to do and downtime. Some owners would tell me I'm **overreacting**, and **maybe I am** 😄. **But** this is the thing about the trucking business, the freight is here for you to haul; It's up to you, how will you run your operation? 👻

OLDER TRUCKS

are an option that **many** never entertain. A lot of people get stuck in the mentality **that** if it's not new then it is <u>junk</u>. **Many** people think if a truck **doesn't** have a great paint job that it is a "junker". In many cases this couldn't be further from the truth. There's a reason why many successful solo owner-operators **keep** their old truck, **BECAUSE THE TRUCK WORKS**! I call these trucks **money-makers**. These owners <u>don't care</u> if their paint job is off a bit or whatever, they make money in these trucks! 😊

These owners drive up and down the road in a truck that's paid for itself over and over again. **Think** back to my **first** chapter, I ended up clearing a little over $**14k** in those **2** weeks and **two** days. I paid $**10k** for my truck originally. **Yes**, I put a couple **more** <u>thousand</u> into it before it was ready for me to haul freight with, but it paid for itself in just those **2** weeks.   The **real** question is, do you know how many times I've already done this?? **Maybe** not $14k in two weeks, but how times I collect $**10k** in a couple of weeks? The cost to rebuild my motor is $**10k compared to $20k plus in a middle-aged truck**. Just do the math. Tell me what operation would you rather be in if you could have one of these money-maker trucks in good shape? 🚚

Now let me give you a **reality** check to older pre-emission trucks. It's not all sunshine and riding off into the sunset yet. **Though** your motor is more than likely to hold strong and you won't have emission issues holding you back; Older trucks are **more** prone to be faced with frame and **suspension** items like leaf springs and little parts here are there that are going to need attention. The **good** thing is, once you fix these little things throughout your course, they'll be good to go for another long time. Because we're talking half-million-to-million-mile type parts This is why doing a **great pre-**purchase inspection is **mandatory**. If you can catch certain things early, you can **negotiate** your deal <u>better</u> and fix those things early on maybe before you get going. 🔑

<u>SO, IN SUMMARY TO THIS WHOLE CHAPTER</u> ✔

I did not know **ANY** of this when I first got my business started! I just knew I **wanted** a Peterbilt because "**it rode good**" **LOL**!!!! Wow lol **How NAÏVE!** (im still here) **But** that's why I know I'm doing a good thing by taking the time to write all of this and promote this book out ok! If this book is **helping** you get ahead, if this book has showed you anything you didn't already know; **Please** tell other drivers and people you meet about the info you learn; **Please** tell them about this book as a guide. **All** this **hoarding** of trucking information needed to stop! And it definitely stopped with me! **There's** a saying I like that goes like this "The **less** you know about something, the **more** of a risk it is" and it also goes to say that "The **more** you know about something, the **less** of a risk it is". **Risk** is the <u>unknown</u>. By having this **information**, you **add** way more **strength** into your strategy and help lower your risk by discovering the unknown. ✔

Just use your head, and **be** patient. The truck you choose will be the one that you spend **a lot** of time with. **Keep** researching, **keep** asking questions, **keep** investigating. **Walk** up to guys at the truck stops **who** are <u>owner operators</u> with their hoods open. **Tell** them you're still in the **research** stage on which motor and truck to choose. Get this person's **opinion** and **make** note of it. Look at the motor, pretend it was yours, would you want to work on this motor? ?

Dependability, the **cost** of parts, the **ease** to work on it yourself and fuel efficiency are the main things we're looking for. <u>There's not really a one fit all answer</u>. **There** are many variables like **how** someone took care of the tuck and how they drove it that will determine whether are not it's a good deal. ✔

Craigslist, the truck paper, the classifieds section on www.truckersreport.com and www.rawze.com ,good old word of mouth and looking for private sales in your area are the **best** places in my **opinion** to find this type of truck I'm talking about. 😎

I would almost **never** get a truck from a <u>used truck dealer</u> that **resells** big fleet trucks. **Please** stay away from recently acquired used fleet trucks at the truck dealers. **These** could be old Schneider trucks, used Swift trucks, US Xpress, USA truck, Knight trucks or <u>whatever</u>. **If** you **must** go this **route** **due** to **financing**, aim to get one that has had an **APU** on it since day one. Like a Prime Inc. truck. **Idling** an emission's motor every night <u>kills</u> these newer motors. At least with an **APU** <u>you know</u> that it probably idled **way** less than a truck without an **APU**. Plus, the **APU** is about $**10k** new, so, you're looking at increased value in the APU alone. 👍

Inspect your truck really good before buying. **Get** to know the owner. **Find** any red flags and no-go's before you do the deal. **Find** any issues, and if they're not deal breakers, ask for a lower price. <u>This</u> is where **CASH IS KING**. You can knock thousands **off** the asking price if you don't need a bank and can close on the truck with fast cash. $🔥

Important:
*DO NOT BUY A TRUCK WITH CASH OR AT ALL **UNTIL** YOU SEE THE **TITLE**. THIS IS **ESPICALLY** TRUE WHEN IT'S A <u>PRIVATE SALE</u>. THE NAME ON THE TITLE NEEDS TO MATCH THE NAME ON THE **SELLER'S DRIVERS LICENSE**! MAKE SURE TO **DRAW** UP A BILL OF SALE TOO. THE NAME ON THE BILL OF SALE <u>MUST MATCH</u> THE NAME ON THE TITLE. IF NOT, YOUR STATE **MAY REFUSE** TO LET YOU RETITLE IT. GET THE BILL OF SALE NOTORIZED TOO!* 😵

    Check to see if your state has a "**Rolling Stock**" <u>exemption</u>. **If so**, you can end up paying **no** taxes on your newly purchased truck. **I've** done this **twice** already. **This** even applies to if you were making payments and you finally get your title in the mail. **Before** you go to retitle it, **check** for a **rolling stock exemption**. <u>Search on the web</u>, if you call the DMV they will probably be unaware of this. **Once** you find it, just **print** it**, fill it out** and **take** it with you to the registration office. I like to use tag and title places for this, they're way more happy to see you and usually are **way** more helpful when it comes to these exemptions. 🔑

"**Pick your poison**" is what they <u>tend</u> to **say** when it comes to choosing a truck. I don't look at it quite this bleak, but each truck and motor I named has some quirks or disadvantages to it. **Just** make sure you're doing what you can to minimize those risks. **Make** sure you're taking an **educated** and **more conscious** approach. 🏆

GOOD LUCK AND GOOD FORTUNE TO YOU in this process! You now have a big leg up on me when I started! It won't be **easy** selecting your truck, **but** if you do it right, it will be **very** rewarding. **Keep** studying. **Keep** getting real life experience. **Stay** positive, balanced and optimistic. Try to **Ask** the right questions. **Know** what you want. And increase your desire! 🚚 ok

Next, we will discover the **simple** term "Cost Per Mile" also known as **CPM**. This is a **very** simple number to discover, but is also a **very** important number to know because it is the base line number for operations. I will show you what CPM is all about in the next chapter. Let's continue! 😄

DEGREE 6: FIGURING YOUR COST PER MILE

Figuring what your **cost per mile** is a valuable **tool** in the early stages of your business. Even as a more advanced business owner, it's still good to run your numbers again from time to time to make sure you're on track with everything. ✔

Cost per mile is also shortened to C.P.M. *Your CPM is how much it costs you to run your entire trucking business per mile*.

Essentially, it's just an easy math problem. You just got to take your total dollar amount of costs and divide it by the number of miles you plan to run per year. **With** this number, you're better able to gauge if something is a good deal for you. With this number you can **estimate** how much money you'll be **making** at the company you're interested in leasing onto. 🚚 (their number subtracted by your number.)

For the person who books their own loads, this number can help them decide what rates they should charge. An example is, if your **CPM** is **$1.10** but the company you're looking at leasing to is only pays $1.**20** per mile plus fuel surcharge of maybe .**30** or so, just do the math. $**1.50** minus your CPM of $**1.10** is .**40** cents. Though it's common sense, after doing the math you'll see that the above example is not a good deal with only 40 cents a mile left over for profit!

A **company** driver will make **more** than that, so, **KEEP LOOKING!** Let's do a simple pretend calculation for a leased driver. These numbers will be based off <u>yearly</u> cost in each category.

TRUCK NOTE: $18,000 ✓

INSURANCE: $3,000 ✓

 IRP PLATES: $1,800 ✓

FUEL: $35,000 ✓

MAINTENANCE: $15,000 (.15 X 100,000 miles) (.10-.20 per mile is a fair estimate cost for maintenance) ✓

ALL THESE NUMBERS ADDED UP EQUALL: $72,800 ✓

$72,800 DIVIDED BY 100,000 MILES (OR HOW EVER MANY MILES YOU EXPECT TO DRIVE) IS <u>.73 CENTS</u>.

In this example **CPM** is .73 cents per mile. But this was a very basic example. In reality you would add everything you can think of that has to do with your business expenses. Cell phones, ELD fees, truck washes, heavy highway tax, IFTA and **etc**. In <u>revenue</u>, I believe a **good** place to aim for making is at least **$1 - $1.50 a mile** <u>OVER</u> your **CPM**. For this example, that would be at least $1.73 needed in order to begin to be profitable in a decent way. $

Keep playing with your numbers (**costs**) until you get them **low** as **possible**. **Also**, play around with <u>different</u> scenarios.

Run the numbers if your truck note was $**1000** a month vs $**2000** a month. See what your **CPM** would be with <u>no truck note</u>. If you're **interested** in getting your own authority, then get some insurance quotes and add the insurance cost into your cost totals. 🤓

By <u>running</u> the numbers like this, **you're** able to see what will work and what will not work for you so you won't have to waste time by letting it happen. **You** should always be <u>moving</u> in a more **profitable** direction. If you're already leased to a company now and you decide to leave, you need to **really** run your numbers against what the new company is offering you and figure out if you're going forwards or backwards with this move. Aim to never to go backwards, if you must side step then side step but **always** aim to make your next move you're **best** move; And in a more profitable direction. $

YOU'RE THE ONE PUTTING IN ALL THIS HARD WORK AND PUTTING YOUR MONEY UP, SO, MAKE EACH MOVE COUNT! ✔️

For example, this was my course since I started 10 years ago; You'll see that each move I made got stronger and more profitable. I **started** at US Xpress for 8 months, **went** to Prime Inc for about a year, **went** to Landstar for 5 years, **went** to a small company where I ran my own dispatch on public load boards for **6** months, **then** I got my own authority. I ran my numbers every time before I made a move. 🔑

By knowing my cost per mile, and by making altercations or **edits** to it, I was able to tell if my next move was the right move based off the math. **Before** I got my own authority, I got my insurance quotes. I figured out how much I'd be paying for fuel since I wasn't going to have the same fuel discount anymore. I plugged all of these numbers in and started making simulations based off the math. 🤓

I figured out if the **13%** extra I was going to make was going to cover the cost of the extra insurance and allow me to profit better. After doing the math for a while and really figuring out, I was **able** to make an **educated** decision that I was advancing myself and I have been right each time! 💲💪

*THIS **CPM** FORMULA IS ONE OF THE **EASIEST** AND **BEST** WAYS TO get a **FEEL for** WHAT'S GOING ON WITH A POTENTIAL MOVE AND TO SEE IF YOU SHOULD BE*

DOING BETTER ON INCOMING REVENUE OR EXPENSES.

EVEN IF YOU DON'T WANT TO DO THE MATH ALL THE TIME THAT'S FINE, BUT definitely **RUN** THE **MATH** BEFORE YOU SWITCH COMPANIES, OPERATIONS, OR BEFORE YOU TAKE ON A NEW BIG BILL. ✔

Run the numbers and make sure everything still makes sense, run the numbers and make sure everything still adds up. **This** is with any business; **you** have to know the **cost** of your goods and services in order to know if your making money at the prices you currently charge or accept. **Trucking** is a business just like any **business**, and the more you **treat** yourself like a real deal business owner and not just a truck driver, the better it will be for you and your company. OK

Know your numbers, **know** what you need to profit, **don't** accept less just because you didn't do the math until it was too late. Go ahead and **Do it now** because a real business owner would! And you're a real business owner too! It's your responsibility to know things like your cost of doing business. **Luckily** this is a pretty easy thing to do. It's just what I call **BASIC MONEY MATH**, add up your costs and divide your cost by the total miles per year you plan to drive. ✔

So **What is YOUR** cost per mile? Anything under $1 per mile is considered **pretty** good in the industry. **With** the amount of miles I run (around **50,000** a year) I'm right around that .75 - .85 cents cost per mile myself (which will differ with the cost of fuel and etc). Knowing your **CPM** is like being in the huddle before the football play. Once you know your **CPM,** it's like knowing what play you're about to run, compared to hopping on the line of scrimmage and just winging it. 😄

Know your numbers or people will try to take advantage of you. **Do not** let people, places or entities take advantage of you! **You** are the **business owner**, not just a driver of the truck. Driving the truck is the easy part you get to do once all your business in order! **Don't** let companies or brokers tell you what's good. **You** run the math for yourself and decide for yourself. **YOU GOT THIS!** 🏆

RECAP: ADD UP ALL YOUR COSTS per year AND DIVIDE THAT NUMBER BY HOW MANY MILES YOUR DRIVE THAT YEAR. THIS NUMBER IS YOUR CPM.

The next chapter will be one **even you** might take lightly? But I **advise** you, do not take the next chapter lightly. The **next** chapter is "**How to Drive as an Owner Operator**". How you drive will have a <u>huge</u> **influence** on your truck maintenance cost, how much fuel you use, how long your tires and transmission lasts…. and **ultimately** your **success** in this business. The **GREAT** part is, how you drive is completely under control of your foot and hands! Let's continue! 💲😄

CHAPTER 7: HOW TO DRIVE AS AN OWNER OPERATOR

I won't get many **cool** points in this chapter from some, <u>but it's all good</u>! **Many** solo owner-operators get out here with their own truck **just because** they want to drive fast in a truck that has no speed governor 😵. This **driving extremely** fast habit is very counter-productive to running a profitable trucking business. Not only are you burning more fuel, but you're putting **more** wear and tear on your truck from all the hi-speed crossing bumps in the road. The excuse I've heard the most was "These trucks are built to do the speed limit" or "This is my truck and I'll drive however I want". 😞

There will always be some owners that just doesn't get it, but **make** sure you're not one of those drivers. **It's pretty simple!** The **faster** you drive, the more **VIBRATION** you create. The more **vibration** you create, the more every part of your truck and trailer gets **rattled**, **shook up** and **potentially** gets its life span cut short. Some roads are **so rough**, that doing more than 50 mph on it can break a leaf spring or blow an air bag instantly if you're not careful or rattle loose a compressor or something lol. 🚛

If you come from a **company** driver mentality, then you may really need to challenge yourself to re-learn how to drive. **How** you drive is one of the single most important parts of solo owner-operator **success** that you are in **complete** control of. I want you to think **WAY** more responsibly. I want you to drive as if **you** pay all the bills! **You** are the one that pays the repair bills, **right??** 😁

Be easy to your truck and it will be **more** inclined to be **easy** to you. **Remember** early in chapter 1 when I mentioned driving through Shreveport**? Remember** how I talked about slowing down to 9th gear all the way through the city? Those roads are very **ROUGH. There** are parts of that road that **literally** drop off and go back up a couple of inches. **Yes**, you will see people drive 60 mph + through there all the time, but that doesn't mean that they are right or that it's ok for you! 🔒

I've made deliveries in West Texas, to oil field wash board roads so rough, I had to drive **under 10 mph** for over 10 miles. It took me almost an hour to go that short distance because the road was a **COMPLETE** washboard. I couldn't get myself to drive any faster, it was just **too** painful. **But** that's because I have sense and appreciate my ride. **Why would I sabotage myself**? Other truck drivers would give me the look as if I was crazy and get out the way, but they were the ones indeed that were crazy for driving **so** fast down that washboard road! That's why a lot of those trucks that run the **oil field** look so junky, it's not because they aren't making money, it's because they drive **too** fast on those rough oil patch roads. If you drive **too** fast on rough roads long enough, all sorts of parts on your truck will start breaking, loosening and falling off or apart. ✔

Not only is it about driving slower per say, it's about not overusing your truck in any way that you can control. This means, acceleration, braking, clutch use, boost pressure, idling, how you climb mountains and etc. 🔑

I drive at about **60 to 65** mph. It just **depends** on how **heavy** I am, the **wind direction**, and **the terrain**. Another factor that comes into play is; That if I made a **dam good deal** on a load that requires I <u>drive</u> a little faster; and in that case I step it up to around a constant **65** mph but this exception doesn't get made often. Besides that, I just <u>ride</u> the **gravity** and **momentum** of the hills.

For example, I may be driving at **62** mph and I approach a hill. I will continue at **62** mph with my foot at the same place on the accelerator pedal. **Once** I reach a point on the hill where my speed starts to slow down, I **won't** press harder on my pedal to keep my speed of 62, I will **instead** start to ease off the pedal and if I end up needing to drop a gear, **I do.**

You never want your **RPM's** to get much lower than **1300 / 1200** rpms. Once you get that low in the rpm's, you start to lug the motor and that causes extreme pressure to the motor, crankshaft, U-joints, yokes, and differentials. I **wouldn't** press the pedal harder to get over the hill, I would **only maintain speed** <u>if the hill was really small and short-lived</u>, **even** then I would be careful to not let my motor lug down too low in the rpm's. In the reverse order, when going down hills, I will allow a faster speed because it is **not** <u>requiring</u> any extra diesel or force from me. This is called "Riding the Hills" … **UNDERSTAND THIS!**

If you're coming from a <u>company driver mentality</u>, you **may** have never thought about what effects lugging a motor has. **But** as an owner, **please** stay out of those **lower RPM's**. Do what you can to never drop below **1200** rpm while cruising in top gear, while climbing a hill, and especially don't lug if you're loaded heavy. **Some** newer motors and drivelines are built to better withstand the lower rpm's but 1300 RPM is still too low in my opinion. You want to be in that 1350 RPM range and up. You may find yourself dropping down a gear more often than other guys, **but that's fine!** You're driving to win. $ not to race them….

I cruise at about **1500** RPM's, which is my motors "sweet spot". **You'll** have to do some research to find your motors sweet spot, I'd do a **google** search on "recommended cruising range" for your particular motor. A lot of it will have to do with the what **gear ratio** you have, but if you **dig** enough on the internet, you should be able to find a **manufacture's recommended RPM range** for cruise speed. Sometimes your gear ratio won't allow you to do the speed you want and to be in the right RPM sweet spot at the same time. That's why I have **3.73** gears. My **62** mph puts me right at **1500** RPM's or so.

A **calculator** such as this one from **SPICER** may be able to help https://spicerparts.com/calculators/transmission-ratio-rpm-calculator . The question of **gear ratio's** is another good question to ask and to research on www.truckersreport.com . **For example**, if you're going to be heavy in the mountains a lot, you want to consider a different gear ratio than if you were only in the flat parts of the country.

Lugging your motor and driving too fast are 2 of the **biggest** mistakes I see solo owner-operators do out here, especially new owner operators. **Don't** get me wrong, it's <u>your truck</u>, you can of course decide to drive it however you will. **But** since you bought my book, I think your more interested in how to be **successful** rather than <u>appearing</u> to be cool and just driving around fast, right?? An old saying I always liked goes "It's not about who makes it to the top of the hill first, it's the one who **makes** it up with the **most money** that wins".

Don't overwork <u>your truck</u> going up these mountains, slow and steady wins the race. **Don't** overuse your brakes, slow and steady wins the race. **Don't** overuse your clutch, slow and steady wins the race.

Bobby, a great mechanic and freind at one of my local shops, expressed to me how impressed he was when he inspected my clutch. It was time for me to put a new clutch in, and when we got my old one out, he said <u>it barely looked used</u>. He asked me how long did I have that clutch for, I told him about 5 years, he was **amazed**! He brought me outside to the scrap-pile to show me a clutch he took out recently. **He** said it was only in the guy's truck for about **a year** and a half and it was **TRASHED**. He says he sees it all the time when people over-use their clutch and don't use it right. He **complemented** me and that was that. A **clutch** is about **$1000** give or take and another **$1000** - **$2000** in labor. <u>Do yourself a favor</u>, don't make this a bill you pay more often because of over using the clutch. 👍

As far as clutch use goes, you should **only** be **using** your **clutch** to get from **neutral into low gear, and when you are going into reverse**. For everything else, you should be floating gears, and bumping the accelerator pedal to pop out of high gear into neutral when you need to stop. 🚛

So, like mentioned, I'll make exceptions and drive faster from time to time, but I **DON'T LIKE** doing it. It has to really be worth it in order for me to put that extra strain on my equipment.

The thing with many owners is, when they drive fast, it's not even worth it!........

They drive for a $1 something a mile flat rate, and just speed race everywhere while trying to "rack up miles". **Most** of these guys don't make much more than $**1500** - $**2000** a week either but work full fast 600 mile days. 1500 to 2000 dollars may sound like a lot, but it's not when factoring in maintenance and etc. You know what happens when you constantly drive faster? You wear your tires out a lot faster too. As you probably already know, tires **are** expensive. A good name brand drive tire will be in that $**400** - $**600** per tire plus **FET** (sales tax on new tires and vehicles), plus mount and dismount and etc. 🙂

Between driving slower, driving less miles and by using **tire pressure sensors**, my tires usually last me a **LONG** time. I've owned the set of Michelin's I have now for over **5** years and they STILL have plenty of tread! Be careful not to drive over nails, screws and other objects that can get into your tire. **Sure**, many times you luck out and just get your tire patched for **$50**, but sometimes that nail is too close to the inner or outer wall and they will not patch it. Not only that, **but** it takes time to stop and get it patched; And that's if you catch the leak early enough. If you don't catch the leak early enough, you could do permeant damage to the tire and still be out a tire. That's one reason why I use tire pressure sensors on **EVERY ONE** of my tires. It helps me keep track of the change in **tire pressure** due to <u>seasonal temperature change;</u> And at any given moment I can check my tire air pressure in the cab. **Talk about a time saver!** It's allowed me to catch slow air leaks before they got bad or too low. <u>It also allows me to keep each tire within 3-5 psi of each other</u>.

😎

→*The **place** where you are **most** likely to **pick up** a **nail** or **some other object** is <u>on the side of the road</u>. The sides of the interstate can really collect debris over time. I **would not** stop on the shoulder of an interstate unless it's completely necessary. If you do stop, be careful and aim for a good spot that looks like it doesn't have random stuff on the ground. **Another place** you can pick up nails is in the **truck stops** and at **shippers** and **receivers**, <u>especially if your flatbed</u>. **Be careful**, **be observant**, and **minimize** this risk by <u>paying attention</u>. If you're backing up to a loading dock or to your loading spot and you see a piece of something on the ground, **don't play it lightly**, <u>go ahead</u> and get out and move whatever it is out of the way. That one little moment of can **cost** you **half a thousand dollars** after you pay for a new tire, or $50 on the low side for a patch, **but still**, <u>it's unnecessary</u>. **Even** if you don't see anything but you notice* *the place you're at seems unkept and messy, I would still get out and go look before backing in. Not only have I done this many times over the years, I still do this, and you know what? I very rarely ever pick up a nail… **I wonder why**???? 😵 luck or intention? It's both, but luck increases because intention.*

The key thing to **remember** is that this is not a **sprint**, <u>it's the real deal long term marathon</u>. **Slow** down, **enjoy** yourself, and **make smart decisions** <u>with how you drive</u>. **Some** owners say "**It's too boring** if I drive slow and I'll get tired". **Well**, if that's you, you'll have to ask yourself "**well, do I want to win**?". If you answer **yes**, <u>then you will be able to adjust your habits in order to give yourself a higher probability of success</u>. **All** that extra vibration **is not** cool, it's not necessary for your operation. That **extra** vibration is you, **aiding and abetting against yourself**. That extra vibration is **increasing** in a <u>negative</u> way how **often** you need new parts. Parts and maintenance costs are high enough as it is. **Don't** add to it just by not slowing down a bit and being more mindful to the drive. <u>Do yourself a favor</u>, and give yourself a **raise** by slowing down to save money on fuel and maintenance! 🚛

Another big one is ***BOOST PRESSURE*** (turbo boost pressure). Some trucks have a boost pressure gauge on the dash. Mine does not, but my first truck did. I learned the habits well enough that I didn't need the gauge. **Basically**, the harder you push the accelerator pedal down, the higher your boost pressure is. In other words, the less you press the pedal, the lower your is boost pressure is. **JUST BE LIGHT ON THE PEDAL!** 😬

Rawze taught me early on, if I want my turbo and motor to last, and if I want to increase my fuel mileage, that I needed to *keep my boost pressure below 20 PSI* at all times possible. Some guys actually go the complete opposite route and tune their motors and turbos to do increased boost pressure. In some applications such as heavy haul this actually makes sense, but for most of the operations, extra boost pressure is not needed and is a liability. ✔️

By keeping boost pressure low, you're putting a **minimum** pressure on your turbo and demanding less fuel for your injectors, which of course results in less fuel burned and more money saved. Quick spurts of boost pressure also relate to increased moments of torque, increased **moments** of torque under a heavy load can also put a major strain on your driveline parts such as U-joints, Yokes and drive shafts. 👉

If you have a boost pressure gauge, start practicing to drive under **20 PSI**. This even means while accelerating from low to high gear when merging onto the interstate and when climbing hills too. If **you** keep your boost pressure under **20 PSI**, it will be very obvious when you need to drop gears when climbing mountains. This may **seem** inconvenient, or like it's slowing you down, but you're really doing yourself a **HUGE** favor in the long run by producing less wear and tear to your truck. If you don't have a gauge, you can get something like the scan gauge https://www.scangauge.com/products/ to read your boost pressure. It's about $100 for this tool, **but** if you don't know what it feels like to drive under 20 PSI, then this is a worthy investment to teach yourself this skill. 🚚

By driving under **20** PSI boost, will really help you take care of the next topic which is **acceleration**. Just be easy on your acceleration, **especially** if you're loaded. To get a heavy truck from 0 mph up to highway speed creates more strain on the driveline than just coasting at top speed; Don't make it any worse by demanding it to accelerate faster. **Gradually** get up to highway speed, and be on your way! The more and more you drive like this, the more you will see the value in it and the more you'd **never** go back to another way of driving the semi.

YOU ARE THE ONE THAT PAYS THE REPAIR BILLS! SO, DRIVE LIKE YOU DON'T WANT TO CREATE NEW UNECCASRY REPAIR BILLS! 🏁

The next thing is *braking*. You'll see the theme in this chapter is "just be easy". And it's the same for braking, **just be easy**. If you do it right, you really won't need to use your brakes much. The less you use your brakes, the longer all your brake parts will last. I know you've seen those guys that will rush past you, just to stop **quickly** at the next traffic light, right? Then here you come **just** rolling up and if you time the lights right, you don't even have to come to a complete stop. **Now** your ahead of this guy and he's puffing smoke out trying to get back up to speed lol. Not only are you physically ahead at this point, but you didn't wear your brakes out at all or driveline to get back to speed and he did! If you want something to last, you **HAVE** to make it last. 😎

I'll tell you what I do with braking, starting with the interstate. **When** I need to get off on an exit, I'll put my turn signal on and put my truck into neutral. **9 times out of 10** I'll time it just right where I coast all the way to the end and use almost no brakes to stop. **Of course**, I'll use a little bit of brake right before I get to the light or stop sign but that's about it. My brakes **last** a long time. If I'm off the interstate and on a highway or city street, I'll just time the traffic lights right! If I see from the distance that the light just turned yellow, I'll go ahead and put my transmission in neutral and **lightly** use the brakes if I have too. My goal is to not come to a complete stop. Not only would I use more brakes if I didn't brake like this, but it takes a lot more fuel and driveline activity to get the whole truck and trailer moving again from a complete stop. *__Take these habits and make them your own__*, do you what can to limit the use of braking! 💲

I'll mention this again in the maintenance chapter, but if you are someone who uses very little brakes, **GOOD**! But this can throw off your automatic slack adjusters over time. Over time your brake pads start to get a little thinner and the automatic slack adjuster are supposed to **make up** for this wear. It does this of course to make sure the pad and the drum will still make good contact in order to stop. **Well**, the problem is, that it takes **HARD** brake applications in order for your automatic slack adjuster to automatically adjust right. If you're being easy on your brakes, you can sometimes end up with a slack adjuster that doesn't ratchet down enough to compensate for the wear, which may result in a brake being out of adjustment. ✔

THE FIX TO THIS IS TO PRESS YOUR BRAKES DOWN ALL THE WAY 6 TO 12 TIMES A DAY. 🗝

Sometimes referred to as a "**six pack**". I do this in the morning before I start my day off. Before I leave, with brakes **released**, I press my brake pedal **all** the way down about 6 times. This ensures that my automatic slack adjusters are getting the signal that they need to adjust if need be. **Keep** this in mind and make it part of your daily routine! 🔒

Next, I want to talk about being in tune with your truck. Over time you should be learning the sounds, smells, and vibrations of your truck. In **other** words, "**Become one with your truck**". You **need** to be able to pick up that little whiff of coolant, oil, smoke, exhaust or refrigerant. You **need** to know when something sounds or feels off. You **need** to know when a slightly new vibration shows itself. By having this state of awareness, you can catch problems early on before they become big problems.

Coolant has its own smell. It's kind of like a stinky sweet. Pay attention when you get your oil changed, the first day or two after an oil change, you can smell the smell of fresh oil really well. **Remember** this smell. **Refrigerant** smells like a weird version of rain. If you start to smell some rainy thunderstorms and its sunny outside, you might have a refrigerant leak. **If so**, stop quickly and try to find the leak. The **freon** will be greenish in color. Because finding a refrigerant leak once all the freon is gone can be a **real** challenge. By finding the leak yourself, you're able to guide your mechanic and save yourself time and money when it comes to the repair. The leak will be somewhere between your a**/c compressor** to your **air dryer**, to your **hi and low-pressure sensors**, to your **evaporator, a/c condenser and etc**. Basically, just follow your lines off your a/c compressor and go from there! 🔧

You should become **very** familiar with your motor and truck's particular sounds. The **more** you know these sounds, the **more** you can tell when the sounds are off; Then you can see what the issue is and nip it at the bud. **I'm** so in tune with my motor's sound and feel, that I can instantly tell when someone pulls up next to me at the pump and their motor is off or has a different sound. I'll hear the **difference** or feel the **whooping** vibrations and I say "I know that's not me!" and sure enough I'll move or the other truck will and the difference of sounds will go away. **Just** be in tune with your truck's normal sounds and feels; That way you can be aware enough to spot anything outside of the normal. 😊

Same thing with **vibrations**, it's very similar to the way you pay attention to sounds. By vibrations I'm mostly referring to the low end, bass like sounds such as the low end vibration I mentioned about the truck next to me with the low end "whooping". By vibrations I also mean, being able to notice extra physical vibration, or if the truck is shimmying too much. **If so**, check your wheels in the mirror quick. Make sure nothing is loose. The more in tune you are with your truck... the more you can hear, smell and feel where the problem area might be if need be. ✓

TO WRAP UP THIS SECTION ON HOW TO DRIVE AS AN OWNER OPERATOR ✓

I will leave you with a **summary** and some good tips to know. The summary goes like this, **take your time**, be careful and **drive your truck like you are the one paying the repair bills!** At the core of it, it's really that simple. If you stick to this foundation, you will start to learn new driving habits on your own that conserve your truck and your fuel. This is **your** truck and it's **your** business, you **MUST** take responsibility! ✓

Don't drive over **rough** roads, don't use shoulders on the interstate unless needed, **keep** braking to a minimum, **and make sure to not overuse** your clutch. In a successful business, you're always looking for ways to lower your overhead and increase your profit. By **improving** your driving habits, you lower your overhead with reduced fuel costs and with reduced maintenance costs so this equals extra money automatically by fuel. At this stage- **You're the boss now**, and Nobody is coming behind you to pay for your repair bills or help you out anymore! No more calling the breakdown department and a guy from Loves or TA just shows up. This is your show and it's all on you. **You got this**! Just be responsible, pay attention, and keep improving and educating yourself! Drive as if you don't want any extra repair bills. **BE EASY! BE PROFITABLE! DRIVE TO WIN!**

TIPS AND TRICKS OF THE TRADE ✓

- WHEN YOU START A NEW DAY, **ALWAYS** LET YOUR MOTOR IDLE FOR **15** MINUTES OR SO TO WARM UP BEFORE YOU TAKE OFF. ✓
- **ALWAYS** LET YOUR MOTOR IDLE FOR **5** MINUTES BEFORE POWERING DOWN. THIS IS TO **ALLOW** YOUR **TURBO** TO COOL DOWN SO IT DOESN'T GET HEAT DAMAGE! ✓
- **DO NOT** PRESS YOUR CLUTCH IN AT HIGHWAYS SPEEDS UNLESS YOU HAVE TO, PRESSING THE CLUTCH IN AT HIGHWAY SPEEDS CAN **BREAK** THE TWO TEETH THAT HOLD THE CLUTCH BRAKE IN PLACE. ✓
- DO NOT SWITCH DOWN THE HI-LO SWITCH ON THE GEAR SHIFTER UNTIL YOU HAVE REACHED SLOWER THAN 15 MPH. THIS CAN DAMAGE THE TRANSMISSION. ✓
- AT THE START OF A NEW DAY, **DON'T** ACCELERATE VERY FAST ONTO THE INTERSTATE. THE OIL IN YOUR DIFFERENTIALS TAKE TIME TO WARM UP, JUST LIKE IN THE MOTOR. **BE EASY** AND SLOWY GET THEM UP TO TEMP. ✓
- BACK UP SLOW AND DON'T BACK UP TOO SHARP UNLESS YOU HAVE TO. THE MORE YOU SPIN THE TRAILER ON A DIME, THE MORE YOU'RE TEARING YOUR TRAILER TIRES UP. ESPECIALLY ON A SPREAD AXLE TRAILER. ✓

COOL. Now that you know the tips on how to drive your truck as a profitable owner operator, let's talk about another **VERY** important topic. It will hit close to home, because we are literally about to discuss "Home Life and Budgeting"...

But **seriously**, you can make <u>all the money in the world out here in trucking</u>, but if your home life and budgeting isn't top-notch, your business really doesn't stand a chance. 💯

I **compare** it to a cup with no bottom. You can pour all the water you want to into that cup, but since there's no bottom, that cup can never hold water! **Do you see what I'm saying**? <u>The same is true for money</u>. You can make a ton of money, but if you got the big mortgage, 2 cars and a boat on bank loans, a wife or a husband who blows your money, or even if **you're** the one that's making the money go out too quick; If the money is going out quicker than it's coming in, it's like the cup that can't hold the water; You won't hold much cash either. You have to get disciplined. And **FAST!** 🔑 the sooner the beterrrrr!

People love to talk about making more money, <u>how about</u> making sure you know how to save and stretch money first so you can actually KEEP that new money when it arrives? How about making sure to do a full self-audit on yourself to make sure that you're using your money right already. As I say, "**Sacrifice now, and live like a King later but do enjoy the process**". Always keep your morale up and treat yourself, but never over indulge in a continuous way that causes your business to slide backwards for too long, this is a judgement call. because coping is coping and this is up to you to balance how you cope... just know when to draw the line...

A lot of solo owner-operators failed business' start right at home with overspending and lack of budgeting and saving practices or know how. Let's continue into chapter 8. Even if you're good at budgeting and saving, I still want you to get through this chapter. It's **very** important. And even if your great at saving, It will still benefit you. **LET'S GO!!!!** This plays a big part in the TOTAL trucking success picture.

CHAPTER 8: HOME LIFE AND BUDGETING

It really **doesn't** matter how much money we make if our home life and budgeting isn't **top notch**. The **lower and balanced** you can get your bills at home (home overhead), and the **more** you disciplined you are with money, the **quicker** you will see your bank account balance grow.

Imagine the Styrofoam cup, imagine pouring water into this cup. When the cup is in good shape, it will hold water.

On this same cup, if we were to **cut the bottom out** or poke holes in it and **pour water in**, the water will pass right through or will leak through the holes.

This is the trap of **debt**, **overspending**, **lack of discipline**, **lack of planning** and more. This is the trap that many solo owner-operators get caught into. They continue to try and make more money, but just like the cup, they can't hold on to it because of the negative money habits that are causing a **financial hole** in their operation.

This **financial hole** can comes in different shapes and sizes. And depending on the size of this "hole", it can really drain an entire operation dry. I'll list some of the top ways individuals create this financial vacuum, or financial hole. 👍

1. **NOT LIVING WITHIN MEANS**. ✔️

> It's ok to treat yourself and live your best life, but you need to <u>pace yourself</u> and **remember**, if your business doesn't have money, neither do you. 🔑

What you spend should be **proportional** to what you have in cash. When a millionaire buys a **$65,000** Ford F150, it's **not** that big of a deal. But if you buy a **$5000** car cash and you only have $ **10,000**, you just spent **50%** of your cash at once; **50**% of your net liquidated balance at once. The <u>millionaire</u> only spent **6%** of his liquid cash to buy the new F-150. It's a totally different ball-game. 🎯

In the **beginning**, it might look like you have enough money to eat out a lot, and buy full priced drinks at bars, snacks and soda at the truckstops, shoes and clothes etc; <u>But it all adds up</u>. In trucking as a solo owner-operator, one must first secure **$ 20,000 to $ 30,000** cash **FIRST**, before starting to often buy more personal stuff. A motor rebuild can hit for in that $ **20,000** to $ **30,000** range. 💰

> <u>If you don't have enough cash to rebuild your motor and you're out here using money too much, your priorities need to be straightened.</u> 🕳️

Get your business straight first <u>and your fun will be waiting on you</u> 🏆! Promise.

Wouldn't you rather build your business first, knowing that it's rock solid, than to be out here with the **illusion** that your solid? If you're not past $ **30,000** cash, you're not as solid as you might think. Make it a goal to have at least $ **30,000** cash **ASAP**! Make this your desire and your goal to have at least $30,000 cash by a date one year from now. 🤏

Then once you touch **30k**, aim for **$50k** cash. <u>Then keep building up.</u> You'll be glad you did. I call these "**financial floors**". Once you reach your next financial floor, make a commitment to yourself that you'll never go below that amount again. You may have **$55k**, but if your floor is at $50k, you really only have **$5k** to spend. <u>And even then</u>, **don't spend it too fast**. 😎💰

It's a lot quicker to spend money than it is to make it. 💯

A **good** businessman and businesswoman **is in it for the long run**. Permanent success requires discipline. But the discipline is very rewarding! The more you save, the more you take away your stress in trucking and in life in general. **When your financially strong**, <u>you don't have to rush and</u>

worry so much. **Remember** "Sacrifice now, live like a King later" 🔥🔥

2. NOT SAVING ENOUGH MONEY. ✔️

The trend in America is most people don't save their money or haven't found a way how to yet. The statistic is like **50** to **70**% of Americans do not have **more than $3000 in the bank**. 💸😵

That's crazy to me! **You have to be patient**. If you remain disciplined, keep growing and learning in this business, and getting better at what you do, you're **bound** to have the money eventually to do and have the things you want and desire the most. As a **trucking entrepreneur,** you definitely have to save your money, so you can be prepared to tackle big jobs and repairs when need be. Go out and get your good meals, but **save save save**! You should be saving almost all of the money you make. **Re-invest** of course into your business for future gains; But on the personal side, you should be saving almost everything you make until your little purchases become so small in proportion to your bank account balance, that you can hardly notice any missing money when spent. 💰

3. HOME BILLS ARE TOO EXPENSIVE. ✔️

I would **not** want the bills some of these owners out here have. They got the **new** 5-bedroom house, the **new** F150, a **new** car for the wife, a **new** boat, they pay for their kid's cars or colleges. Some owners are looking at over $3-4000 <u>a month</u> **just in home bills**. 😮😨

Then you add in the truck note, maybe a trailer note, general liability and cargo insurance, you might be looking at $**7000** a month or so. <u>That's without a lick of maintenance</u>. You tack in another $**1000** or so a month for maintenance which equals $**8k** a month in overhead. And depending on maintenance and other factors, it may be higher. **THIS IS INSANE**! 😵😵🥴😤

This means, this owner must now make over $2k a week **just to break even** with all of their expenses. **Well**, let's be real, a majority of owner-operators are not consistently netting over $**2k** a week because the wrong operations, dispatchers hired, factoring, don't have the right fuel deals, over-paying on maintenance and etc. 🤷

With this type of **high overhead** at home and business, you can't really afford to stay home. Not only can this owner not afford to stay home, they're not really able to build up their bank account balance either. I always kept my bills at home **super cheap**! And lived on the road until I could afford my land and house cash. No wonder I get looked at crazy sometimes when I mention I only drive about 6 months a year! 😌

SUCCESS STARTS IN THE HOME. ✔️

This means that if you're married or together in a relationship, <u>they better understand your sacrifice</u>, <u>they better be frugal</u>, <u>they better save money well</u>, **they need to be money conscious**, <u>and not spend money out from underneath you.</u> 💯 💰 😇 or you will be stresssssssssed chances are lol

If you're together with someone who is negative with money and is constantly blowing the money, **how can you ever get ahead**? 👻

A lot of owners think they just need to run more miles, or stay out longer and do more work; When in reality they need to fix and improve their home life. I'm not saying go breakup with whoever that you're with, but <u>do have</u> these **important** conversations. It must be understood, that the **bank account** balance <u>has to be at a certain level</u>. It has to be understood, all bigger purchases will be discussed first. It has to be understood, **that if y'all sacrifice together now**, <u>you won't have to sacrifice and settle for less later.</u> 🖊 🕐 📈 👑

You work as a team and not against each other. ✔️

I highly suggest having separate checking accounts. It almost never works when the husband and wife share the same account. When a couple shares the same account, the blame game becomes common about whose fault it is when the account balance gets low. By having **separate** accounts, you can avoid most of this potential drama. And as a business owner, you need to **KNOW**; You need to count on having your resources exactly the way you left it. No surprise thousands of dollars missing, no going to pay for a part or service and your card gets declined because of what got spent at home. **NO NO NO!** ✖

PS: <u>It is my opinion that</u>: If you're the **main one** making the money, then you should also be the main one paying all the bills too. Take care of all the big bills like insurance, car note, electricity, mortgage if you have one and etc. 👄

4. COMMITMENT TO LARGE NON-BUSINESS PURCHASES TOO SOON. ✔

Large purchases like a house, or a car can really cripple a startup trucking business. If your still in your 20's and single, or together with someone, do really need an apartment or a house yet. **WHEN ARE YOU GOING TO LIVE IN IT**?? Same thing with a car. When will you be able to drive it? **What** a couple days out of the month? 🖐

That's one of the beautiful things about our business, we have a bed and shelter everywhere we go. **Now**, if you have kids, it will be different because chances are you will need a home of some kind for them. Some companies will let you lease onto them and your kid can come too! **I think** a young kid, especially if there's two parents in the truck, would be an amazing bonding and learning experience for the young kid. Most parents don't get to spend those first **5** years together, and those are the years when the foundation of <u>who your child will be is developed</u> and you get to be there to **completely** influence it! **BUT**, if you are not having a kid yet, stay out here and stack your money up!!!! 💯

If you do it right, you'll have enough cash to buy your home outright with no bank, or only having to borrow **30** to **50**%. <u>That's what I did</u>. I told my longtime girlfriend when I was **23**, there's no sense in us paying all that extra money for a house we never get to live in and a car we never get to drive. I told her, we'll stay out here long enough until we have enough to pay **cash** for a home and **that's what we did**. We got over one acre, now we have over 2 acres, plenty of room to park my truck, it's <u>peace and quiet</u>, close to a major city but in the **country**, the house may not be the nicest, but in due time we'll upgrade again but we're in no rush. **The point is**, we really enjoy our property and privacy, and **we owe nobody anything**! In Louisiana, we don't even pay property tax. 🚚

I bought my first property when I was 26 or so. So, you **see**, the sacrifice wasn't even that long. **Just think**, many adults will **never** own land and a home, and the ones that do, usually take **30** years on a mortgage. If you be patient now, go hard in learning this business, make great deals, be disciplined and consistent, you can **really get ahead** in life. And if it's your desire to own land and a home of your own, you can make it happen. 🔒

In the **beginning** stages of a trucking business, it can be real tough to get the ball rolling and to build your bank account balance. **So**, don't make it **any harder** than you have to by taking on large purchases like houses and cars too soon. Aim to save up enough to buy these purchases in cash. Once you pay for your home, you could retire from trucking if you want and start another business or work a relaxed job of your choice. Or you can do what I do; Go trucking whenever you get ready too 😌! I usually stay out 2-3 weeks and then stay home for a month lol. In the busy seasons of summer in flatbed I may stay out for longer and go out more frequently because the money is strong in the market. <u>But that's how I can afford to live this lifestyle</u>. **Because** I didn't take on large purchases too soon, because I've created an operation in business and at home that is very cheap to run. 🐀 🔑 😊

5. GETTING INTO HIGH PERCENTAGE DEBT AND TAX ISSUES. ✔️

Be careful and pay attention to detail, when it comes to making **ANY** deal on loans and credit. <u>I use credit cards</u>, **but many are not disciplined enough for credit**. They max out their cards, only pay the minimums, get stuck paying **17 – 20**% or more in compounding interest, and they get trapped. **Don't** get trapped in high APR (annual percentage rate) bad credit deals. Some of these credit cards have **crazy** compounding interest that is just simply not in your favor. will be stuck trying to do debt consolidation…

It's **ok** to carry and use a credit card, just make sure you pay the balance off in full every month. That way you're not dealing with **interest** fees and you can get cash back points depending on your credit card provider. Another thing I like about using credit cards, from my research, is its way less liability on you if your card gets **hacked**. According to my research, you will get your **money** back much quicker and with less drama of having to prove it wasn't you spending the money compared to a debit bank card.

Another thing to note here is **taxes**. If you don't pay your taxes in time, you get stuck paying interest fees on it too; Just like with the credit cards. **Be careful here**. As a business owner, you're responsible for paying in your share of taxes, right?

YOU HAVE to be DISIPLINED. Disciplined enough to; Hold onto your money throughout the year so you pay your taxes in April in one lump sum. If you're not disciplined enough yet, you need to be making ES (estimated) tax payments into the IRS website at the end of every financial quarter.

$1500 - $3000 every quarter is a good place to start. If you end up over-paying, you'll just get your money back in the form of a refund. If you have already paid taxes before, you can take the amount that you owed last year and divide it by 4. This will give you the number that you need to pay in every quarter. **Don't** let taxes or credit cards put you into a **death spiral** of never-ending compounding interest. 👊

Be responsible, save for and pay your taxes; and if you use credit, use it **tactically** and for a **purpose**. Pay your balances off every month. The only time I won't pay my credit balance off completely at the end of the month is if I took a 0% interest offer from a credit card company to make some bigger purchase. **In this case** I will take the purchase price and divide it by the amount of months I get 0% interest for, and whatever that number equals to be is what I pay each month until it's paid in full. 👍

> **For example**, a **$10,000** purchase dived by **18** months of **0%** interest would be **$555** a month. If you paid **$555** a month for **18** months, you would have **zero** dollars extra in interest fees, and it would essentially be the same as cash, just spread out into lower payments. 😶😁

SUMMARY: ✔️

There are many **books and topics** when it comes to budgeting, but at it's core, it's pretty simple. 💭

→**Don't spend more than what you got.** 🔒

And if your extra smart, you will act as if you have no money even if you do lol. The financial floor I mentioned is real; A large portion of your money should be off-limits for spending. **If** you just take your business serious, you should have **no problem** with budgeting. You can't just go out buying everything you want because you got the money in the bank. Not yet at least…. **Yes**, get some things you want, <u>but be patient for the rest</u>.

It will come; Pace yourself. **Self-control** is a very **important** attribute to success. A lot of what smart money managing and budgeting is; To not overpay for things, do things yourself like maintenance, buy in bulk when possible, cooking for yourself more often and etc.

    Let's just take bottle water for example. A **24** pack of Crystal Geyser Spring Water is like $3. But at the grocery store 3 of those same bottles will be $3 as well. **By buying in bulk**, you get **21** more bottles for the <u>same price</u>. The same is true for many parts of life. **One thing you should notice is**, <u>convenience costs</u>! Aim to not to buy things at a convenience cost. A convenience cost is like paying $**20** for a gallon of oil when Walmart has the same gallon of Rotella for $**13**. A convenience cost is like paying $**2** for that **20oz** cold drink and you can buy a **2** liter for the same price. A convenience cost is like paying for tools at the truck stop compared to the cost of buying them at Harbor Freight or Home Depot.

If **you** have a habit of buying everything at a **convenience** cost, you will find it <u>harder</u> to come up and build up **your** bank account balance. Before you can learn the rest of what it takes to be successful, you have to first master this frugal but elegant way of living. **Common culture and politics** will have you think you're not supposed to check prices and just pay whatever the offer price; But you're not common culture, you're **going to be successful**! Think about the food deserts neighborhoods and in the country, because of this lack of competition in business, a few places charge their customers high convenience prices, which in turn plays a part in why the people living in these areas have such a hard time closing the wealth gap. It's hard to save money and build your bank account balance if you're overpaying for everything. 🗡️

MAKE SURE NOT TO BE overpaying for stuff and really pay attention to how **every** dollar is spent. 📣

I'm **not saying** you have to be **cheap** about everything, but there is a balance you must find. When you find this balance, you'll realize it's frugal but elegant in nature. You will still buy nice things, food and whatever you need, but you will do so in a frugal way. **Sometimes** this means holding off on a purchase until the price is right, **sometimes** this means buying less of the one thing you were going to buy multiples of. This also means paying attention at the register. Mistakes happen at the register and if you don't catch it, you just got overcharged. **Don't let people accidently steal your money either**! Call it out. You worked hard and smart for it. 💯

Budgeting is ultimately about self-control, common sense, and not buying off of impulse. The more you master these

three things, the **more** you will be a **master of your future too**.

Stay grounded, stay disciplined, stay vigilant, pay attention, do your basic math, know your prices and the true value of items, don't overbuy, don't rely on credit for everything, don't make bad credit interest deals, keep your home expenses low, **make finances an important value at home with your loved ones**, move as a team, **don't** buy at convenience prices often, find ways to lower what you spend, enjoy being frugal with taste, plan for your future, have faith, have faith in yourself, know what you want, set financial floors and goals, be in it for the long haul. **This is not a sprint**; this is the real-deal marathon of life. And only the strong and financially clever will survive. Pay attention. Never stop learning.

DON'T TAKE LIGHTLY THIS HOME BUDGETING AND FINANCIAL DISIPLINE! If you mess up your money at home, you're going to make it 100% harder to run your trucking business. **You need money in the bank**. You need a financial "cushion". Think about how much lower your stress and worry will be when you're rolling around out here with at least $30k cash in the bank. You got to stay down if you wish to come up. **Put in your time**, so you can get your stripes! Learn how to make more with less. A **BIG PART** of making more with less is keeping your home expenses low. If you make all these **BIG** bills for yourself at home, how can you ever come up? In due time you will get what you want. You must first put in the work and make sure **NOBODY** around you is being sloppy with the money.

Have some **self-respect** for yourself! You are out here making it happen and working 2 to 3 times harder and longer than the average person. **Don't let nobody**, <u>even yourself</u>, become a **leaky faucet** to your money. Keep your money! Stack your money! **MAKE YOUR BANK ACCOUNT BALNCE GROW!** 🔒

I hope I have put a **stern** but casual warning into you. If you do not **master** these spending habits for success, you will be spending a lot of time and energy essentially getting nowhere. <u>Don't just exist, that's too much like losing</u>. **THRIVE, STRIVE, AND GROW! BUCKLE DOWN! YOU GOT THIS!** ✔️

Let's talk about **trucking etiquette** next. Especially if your new to trucking, you need to follow me into chapter 9. Even if you've been in trucking for a while, follow me into chapter 9. See how you check out! See if you're already **putting** this etiquette into motion for your own success. <u>Trucking has a culture and politics of its own</u>. The more you **respect** and flow with this culture, the **more** people will help you along the way. Of course, be careful of shady'ness especially if you're a woman out here solo, but never be ashamed to get help, or have somebody teach you something. 😁

You can **still** say you did it on your own if you get help along the way! Because it's **YOU** that's <u>making your success happen</u>. If you sat on the couch and did nothing, your success would never come! When I was young, I would want to always say "I did it on my own"; But as a man now, yes that's cool, but it doesn't really matter. **What matters is**, were you able to make it happen? **Were you able to manifest**? By <u>sticking to your pride</u> of wanting to do everything yourself, you can **very easily** not make it to the other side. <u>Just make sure you get to the other side, whether you get help or not.</u> Let's continue! 🌩️

CHAPTER 9: TRUCKING BUSINESS ETIQUTTE

Why is this an important chapter?

Let's just start by defining **etiquette** from a dictionary. Etiquette is "the set of conventional rules of personal behavior in a polite society, usually in the form of an ethical code that outlines *the expected and accepted social behaviors* that are in accord with the conventions and norms observed by a society, a social class, or a social group." 🤓

Key thing, rules of personal behavior within a society.

Trucking culture and politics **IS** a society and a social group of its own. And it does have rules. We can easily say this. My quick explanation is, **etiquette is just doing right by yourself and others in the situations you are in**. 🐿️

Etiquette is a power in its own. Life would be so much smoother and more enjoyable for many; But we live in this programmed forced "real" world, where fear, jealousy, ego, envy and anger is still the driving force inside those programs… it's like this mostly because of perpetuated **Negative** emotion with words and action repeated that are negative etiquette alive. But In this chapter we talk about what all truckers should know and could know as an advance,, when it comes to trucking business etiquette, day to day trucking etiquette, and plain etiquette in general. **It is my belief that exercising great etiquette is an important building block to success.** 🔒 🔌

When I mention good etiquette, I don't mean being a soft-e or just letting things happen. I actually mean the opposite! ✔️

I mean operating at such a level of awareness, that you are now attracting the right for you people; People who will help you succeed and people who you will actually enjoy to be around. I also mean **operating** in a such a fashion that pushes the overall culture of natural success forward. Even if you might be young right now in your early 20's or late teens,, perfect. but if you initiate with having positive **etiquette** and **respect**, the successful elders out here will come to help you. 💯 which is basically love and respect

Challenge + Skill = Flow

Attention + Enjoyment = Flow

Balancing energy….

Do what you don't want to do….

I'll tell you something I've experienced. Successful people with time and money often actually love to help people who are on the come up. The reason is, if they see something in you, they are in a good spirit are so happy and satisfied in their own success, that they **want** other people to feel it too, appreciate, and reciprocate that respect.

It's all natural. Just be cool….

   They want other people to be able to relate to them and to respect them for their **ability** to be a success.

Sometimes a successful person just wants to be listened to and for you to find their ways valuable. They **want** to feel appreciated. And Don't we all..

Truckers that've been out here a while might be a bit or all the way stubborn and for good reason. They just want to make sure you understand the "**code**" and the blood, sweat, and tears that it really takes to be a solo owner-operator success because they know from the hardships. And yes, If these guys deem you worthy, they will be a great help to you on your path to success. See who you can flow with.

But remember, take everything with a grain of salt and come to your own conclusions based of all the information you gather.

With enough work, eventually you become a master and an "elder" in your own right; 10,000 hours later or so passing down game and it continues as you as the teacher. **It's a circle of life** and you want to make sure that you're in that circle. I can't begin to tell you how many times I've been helped out here! But I also can't tell you how many times I've helped or offered help too! With that being said, this is a perfect Segway into our particular etiquettes that we can put into motion right away as it relates to being a solo owner-operator. 🌐

1. **IF YOU SEE SOME ONE WITH THEIR HOOD UP, WITH TOOLS ON THE GROUND, OR TRYING TO FIGURE SOMETHING OUT, you could see and ask them how they're doing!** ✔️

At the very least **ask** them if they need a hand especially if they look stuck and if you got some time 15 minutes or more to spare. If you're flatbed, you could help them roll their tarps up, that's always cool. or **help** them tie down their load. If it's a mechanical issue and if you are now carrying enough tools to offer help and lend a tool, you could go ask them if they need help and let them know you got tools if they need to use them. 🔧 That's always good!!! Imagine being on the receiving end!

Even if your new to this and you don't know how to "wrench" or turn wrenches as we call it, you are still invited to get involved. **Maybe** this owner operator just needs someone to hold something while he tightens it. Be careful of course, but you just never know when you'll make a huge difference in somebody's day. This person might be **over-whelmed**, down low on their morale, we just never know. **When** you show up with your smiling face and your willingness to help, it can be such a relief. 😄

If you're ever on the other side and you're the one that needs help, you'll **know** what exactly what I'm meaning here! Even if you don't know how to fix stuff yet, this is a perfect learning opportunity to get free first-hand experience and just watch, chill, listen, observe and learn. Not only is this **good** etiquette, but this is **initiative**, this is what will separate you from the rest of the pack on your journey.

While the rest of the pack is watching cell phone videos and social media posts, numbing themselves from the day, you're out here learning **the** real life skills that will help you be more competitive in the future.

Of course, there will be days and moments in time when you won't have the time or are plain exhausted. But if you do have time, please go out and offer a hand. The old school guys love this and will respect you so much for it. will answer your questions, give you powerful advice and etc and your teaching the next generation this spirit of support.

Some Owners will even take the time to help you figure out your operation. I hear from a lot of the old school guys, that back in the day, everybody used to help each other like this. Then came the "**steering wheel holders!**", and the electronic logs, and the **CSA2010** and **etc**… After the "We got to hurry up and beat the e-log" mentality set in, big fleets kept producing more over-privileged drivers, and next thing you know; The **golden** days of trucking comradery started to fade. At least this is what I'm told and can see through my decade of observation.

But that's where real people like you and me come in! We get to write those wrongs, come back together easy, and show and prove that the etiquette we carry is what's needed out here. **WE appreciate trucking and we do what we can to HELP EACH OTHER OUT HERE!** 🪝 🔧 💯 😊 this is love, care and support manifested.

EXAMPLE:

A couple of years ago I was by Allentown, PA at the Trexler Travel Plaza. It was late winter and I caught some <u>unexpected</u> snow coming out of Dover, DE. **After** delivering my good paying sheet steel load to Pottstown, PA I noticed my trailer brake lights were **stuck** on even if I didn't have my brake pedal down. **Well**, this was pretty urgent and I had to figure it out before I could continue on loads. I go up to the Trexler plaza and park. 😣

After hours of **trouble-shooting by myself**, I **decide** it's my 7-way plug underneath my trailer; I believe it has road salt connecting the hot wire with my brake light line. (my flatbed has 2 hook up spots for electric and air, one in the normal place and one underneath). I go to Hale truck parts and get the plug and start to hook it up myself. I **put** my tool bag on my brake pedal to weigh it down so I can <u>check my trailer brake lights</u>. Everything looked good! I forgot the brake pedal was still down and I continued to install the 7-way plug. I ended up making a big spark when I let two of the wires touch. 😵

I go back into my cab and **yeah**, <u>I messed up</u>! None of my dashboard was working, and my e-log wouldn't work either. I tried new relays, new fuses, it seemed like nothing would get me right. Long story short, I gave up for a moment and I looked around the parking lot and there were two men working on their truck. I figured hell, I wasn't going to be able to fix my truck yet, so I <u>might as well</u> see if **they** needed a hand. Charlie and Carlos are their names. Father and son.

Well, they actually did need a tool or two from me and they thanked me. Come to find out Charlie, the father, was a licensed mechanic and knew mechanics very well! **Afterwards**, He came over to help me, and he found <u>exactly what my issue was</u>! He said "Did you check every fuse?", I said no but I did change all the important fuses and relays dealing with ignition. He said "**no, you must check EVERY fuse with a test light**", and sure enough he was right. I blew a fuse that I didn't change because it wasn't part of the downed circuits or so I thought. 🔧 [test every fuse anyway]

Once we replaced that fuse, my whole dashboard came back to life, I learned an important lesson; And I was back ready for business! That night I repaid them with beers and conversation at the dive bar across the road even though they refused to **let** me pay! **Imagine** that; I thought I was stuck, and because of this positive etiquette we're talking about here now, I went to see if they needed a hand, and what'd I get in return? **Talk about instant karma**! This is just one example of many. This has happened so much I probably can't even remember all the times I've either got or gave help. It's just the true trucker way. Even if it seems like no one is helping you, keep **fighting** the **good** fight and continue to be helping others. If your intentions are pure, your times of help will come to stay too. 😊😎🚚💯

2. **BE CONSIDERATE TO OTHER'S TIME AND SPACE**. ✔️

   So, this is like not leaving your truck at the fuel pump for too long if the place is busy.
   Not driving **aggressive** and cutting off trucks in the truck stops if they had the right away. This is slowing down in the truck stops and **watching** for people!
   Be careful of people's trucks when you're backing up. Get out and look if you have any uncertainty. Take your time. **If** you're blocking someone in somewhere, inch up and let them through! 😄 this is super easy stuff that adds to the positive flow for everybody.

It's the old golden rule right,, "Do unto others as you would like them to do unto you". **Trucking** culture and politics overall is really cool, special and this simple; Birds of a feather but everyone goes their own way after that brief meet up in flight.

Yes, it has been celebrated to **"take** first place" by aggression or by force, but that's not true in trucking 80 percent of the time. If you behave in that way of self-entitlement, you will quickly get boxed out by the same people who would have helped you and rooted for your victory. I found it hard to believe in the beginning **but despite environmental traumas and what society portrays,** good people really do exist and not just this dog-eat-dog culture we are led to accept.

And **remember** this, to see what we want in this world starts with self.

If **you** want this world to be a **better** place too, the starting place is to make it a better place within yourself! Even if it doesn't seem to pay off or that nobody's minding. Doesn't matter. Take **initiative** to be the one with enthusiasm, because that **enthusiasm will be contagious!** you may have to remind me one day, because yes, enthusiasm can be a tough torch to keep lit when its heavy pouring rain.

3. **HAVE STYLE AND CLASS.**

   Do your **best** to represent trucking in a stylish and classy way. Have a clean dashboard. Be professional with shipping and receiving crews.

If you must stand your ground, do so in a likeable way.

STANDARDS:

Don't litter. **No full jugs** of pee (men!) at least empty them for who's cleaning. **Don't** carry too much offensive odor. **Shower** when you need to! <u>Help be a problem solver</u> when it comes to loading freight, or dealing with situations. **Respect** the elder trucker when they're attempting to give you advice. If someone is getting old and disabled, help them throw their tarps on their flatbed. Help other people pick stuff up. **If** the fork lift driver **needs** his forks slid over and you see him struggling, <u>just help him push the forks</u>! 🖐 these are simple things that will go a long way.

Have a **positive** balanced attitude. If you're **not** in a positive mind-frame do what you can to not take it out on others and confuse them. <u>Meditate more often</u> and develop your inner-peace, and when possible block out distractions 🔇. Attempt to be grounded and smooth and to not respond emotionally to people or situations. Be patient with others. People will **understand** what they **understand**. This is a balanced lover and fighter approach. 😁

Conserve your energy when it comes to low level disrespect.

Forget it, Smile more often! **Be enthusiastic**! Give plenty of space before you pass someone on the interstate. Having a CB radio on and thanking people when they accommodate for you. Let people know on the radio if they have a brake light out or some other issue. If you see something wrong with somebody's equipment, respectfully let them know. 🚛 this is a courtesy!

4. **DON'T BE THAT GUT WHO'S ALWAYS COMPLAINING**. ✔️

I promise you, <u>complaining almost never fixes anything</u> and it really **gets** on the nerves of successful people. **Complaining** is like the nails on the chalkboard sound. **It's annoying**. <u>Successful</u> owners and people in general find solutions, we don't sit here and complain. If we do complain, it's only for a short moment to vent. You'll hear these guys at the truck stops, complaining about cheap freight, complaining about their dispatchers, complaining that there's no money in trucking. **These** <u>are the guys you should probably steer clear from</u>. 🔑 just let them have their moment.

It's this **negative** mentality and **pessimistic** attitude that makes life such a drag to live in. 😵 drag on enough like this and I promise you that you will manifest a negative reality.

Many owners and people don't understand the power their own thoughts and emotions have on their reality. ✔️

When you have an idea and attach a **negative** emotion to it, like we did in chapter 2, you in-turn <u>create</u> that negative environment for yourself over time. **It's the law of attraction**.

There are some pretty simple but unchangeable universal laws. Got to be knowing these universal laws asapppppp so that you don't end up being on the wrong side of one or more. 😊 universal law. Stoic type knowledge.

I won't spend much more time here on this chapter **but do know** that great etiquette is a valuable resource to your **success**. Make a true effort as you continue, to grow and pay attention to trucking culture and politics....

It's easy, I promise. Trucking has its unspoken rules that don't really change. Be a decent **genuine** person with **self-respect** and **enthusiasm** and ultimately people will reflect your energy and show you the support you need going forward. It really takes a winner mentality to be successful in anything in life. **Trucking as a Solo Owner-Operator is no exception**. 🔑

Move as if you've already won the fight, move as if you're already successful. **Successful** people don't let the little things get to them. They have bigger fish to **fry** in comparison to the emotional disagreements with people in truck stops, shippers, receivers and etc.

Keep your mind on your goal, feel as if you've already accomplished it, know what you want, increase your desire; And mentally accept nothing less than what you want. **Be happy**, **be enthusiastic**. **Be likeable, be highly favored, be**

highly respected, **be highly loved**, and **be highly appreciated**. ✓ you are these things if you allow it to be

The **more** you **respect** yourself and have **integrity**, the more others will have to respect you by <u>default</u>. The more you love yourself, the more others will show and give love to you by default. This is universal law. Try to cheat the universe if you want right! The **universe** made us and also made this **amazing** possibility of a reality we live in. I **choose** to be with the side of nature and the universe <u>a long time ago</u>. **Every** part of life has its own ecosystem and sets of rules.

The same thing that's accepted at a barber shop may not be accepted at a movie theater and vice versa. ✔

The key 🖋 here is to always be paying attention to **your** surroundings and to spot <u>the leaders</u>, and **learn from them**. Eventually you become a leader yourself and get to decide how you want to lead. And this is **your** chance to **improve** society through trucking and more if you choose! But before we can improve something, we must first understand it. Understand your industry, understand trucking. **Understand** yourself and **understand** the universal laws of time and space. ◪

We take initiative and <u>don't work against</u> **etiquette**. Working against the code of trucking is a great way to **delay** your success. Continue to learn from the success and failures of others; And learn to appreciate, respect. And add to the industry that your making thousands of dollars a week from. You got to give respect in order to receive it in this world and this is true in trucking as well. But do make sure you make it a habit to always be respecting yourself first! 🏆

By **implementing** the above codes, you will be much more natural in discovering how this all works. Step by step, brick by brick. Have **faith** in yourself and **pay** attention because yes, it pays to pay attention! 😄

In the next chapter we will discuss **shop etiquette**. Shop etiquette is often even more important than general trucking etiquette. You will see, **each** chapter in the book gets more into the longevity and how to really make this stuff work. Brick by brick we go! **Are you still focused? You're doing well** already, stay the course here. This **next** chapter will **assist** you into a ownership / boss mentality when it comes to navigating part stores, repair shops and dealers.. In **MANY** cases, shops are **not** our friends! These dealerships will sit around like vultures waiting to prey on the weak. **You** have to know your truck. **You** have to know mechanics to a certain degree. If they sense you don't know what you're doing, they will attempt to run up crazy big bills on you! I will show you how to get ahead of this unfortunate reality. Let's continue! ✔️

DEGREE 10: SHOPS AND PART STORES. INTERACTION AND ETTIQUTE.

Shops and part stores play a **big** part of our. **Even** for a guy that does most of his own labor, he will still need the part stores.

How we conduct ourselves in these places of business can really help make or break us. In the **beginning** of my trucking business, I got **hustled** many times by the dealerships and part stores. **Why**? Because I was green, I was new, and I **didn't** have mechanical knowledge yet nor good enough people skills to know what I can and can't do. If you don't know mechanics, and they think your young or new, these shops **will** casually attempt to take you for as much as they can get. Shops often have no heart. Know this. This is an important thing to understand if you're going to be successful in this business of ours!

→**You** need to know the difference between a dealership and an independent shop. ✓

You need to know the difference between paying full retail price or when to ask for a cheaper price on parts or labor. **You** need to know how to <u>figure out</u> what you need a repair shop to do, **instead** of having a shop diagnosis and tell you what you needs done. **You** need to **understand** that these big-time dealerships are usually not going to be your friend at first. This is a job for them, punching the clock with no emotion to your situation. They are there to **please** their corporate machine and to collect their W-2 pay check, and go home.… Not to care about our well beings or situations. 🤏

You need to <u>understand,</u> that just because you pay a "**professional**" to do the job, that won't always **mean** it will be done right. You need to <u>understand,</u> that even in these high-dollar dealerships, sometimes the mechanics that are put on the job are brand new with little to no life experience. You **need** to understand, that at dealerships some mechanics will lolly-gag around on **YOUR TIME**, making **your** <u>bill</u> **more expensive** while they make jokes and drink soda with their friends. Not here to judge, but you have to understand that dealerships are used to billing the big fleets whatever they want, **and we have to** <u>remind them some way</u>, that it's US that are the one's paying the bill, not a big fleet. 🔒

That's for shops, but you have to **understand** how to "**play the game**" at <u>parts</u> stores as well. Certain people do get priority and it's all about who you are and the time you genuinely spend with the people who run the shops and part stores. Try to make peoples life better and just listen to them and help make easy. The **goal** is to have your part store guys <u>know you by name</u>, have casual to high respect for you and for them to actually **like** you too! 😄

Why do you need to know and do all of this? You do it so that you can have a <u>competitive</u> edge. This competitive edge will allow you to **reverse** these potentially negative conditions and make them turn in **your** favor. Folks get eaten up every day out here. The more you know and the better your awareness is, the more you can avoid having this broken system of shops and part stores break down on you. Let's continue. 🙌

1. **KNOW YOUR TRUCK**. ✔️

People at shops and the mechanics know when you don't know your truck. They can sense it off you. **They know** when you don't know your pit-man arm from your drag link. They know when you just come in there throwing your truck at them like "<u>please fix it</u>!". That is asking to be an open check book for these guys lol. Do you know, many shops **will** treat you like an open check book if you come in there not knowing your stuff like this? Please do. This is real. Some shops will do it on **purpose** and run up a <u>crazy high</u> bill on you because they think they can take advantage of you (which is "good" for their business) and will try to keep your truck as payment. **Some** shops will also make up high bills on you because they just don't know what they're doing; And keep messing up or guessing wrong on what needs to be fixed, charging you part by part; Or they are just plain slow and making you pay for it. 🔍 THIS IS WHERE KNOWLEDGE and YOUR QUALITY CONTROL comes in.

Some shops will give you a hard time just because they don't like you for some judgmental reason. They don't **like** your <u>look</u>, <u>your age</u>, <u>your hair</u>, <u>your positive balanced attitude</u>, <u>your demographic, religion, spirituality</u> and **etc**. This is why you got to **KNOW YOUR STUFF**, and proceed as a business man or a business woman and not let this stuff get to you emotionally! ✔

IF you can't make an easy going deal, or if you don't get a good vibe from a shop, then <u>don't hesitate</u> to say thanks and just walk out that door. But most of the time, it won't come to that; As long as you stand your ground but still be a likeable person, most people won't mess with you too much <u>if you know your stuff</u>. 💪

ALWAYS REMEMBER THAT SECRET SHOWED EARLIER... "ALWAYS REMEMBER and USE PEOPLE'S NAMES". ✔

When you say someone's name, you make them <u>feel special</u>, you make them feel acknowledged, and as if they **are** part of your family or network. **Now yes**, this could be considered **slight** manipulation, but as long as your **intentions** are **good**, it's <u>just a tactic</u> and habit for **better** results in life and business. Use the shop foreman's name and also use the mechanics name, use your own name often enough until who's there begins to remember you by name. **Be knowledgeable** of your truck. **Stand your ground in a likeable way**. **Smile** <u>but be firm</u>. You want to be that "**force**" that nobody wants to stop.

You want to have such an <u>attractive</u> <u>personality</u> that **nobody** wants to say no to you anyways (within reason). 😊

But without knowledge, it'll just being a big front. You can be a big front, but back it up with knowledge. We will talk more in the maintenance chapter to polish you up there, but do know the components of your truck. **Understand** your drive-line. **Understand** how your emissions system works. **Understand** basic electricity, relays, fuses and etc. **Understand** data communication flow (**J1939** and **etc**). **Understand** the parts of your motor like your oil pump, oil cooler, turbo, radiator and etc. **Understand** what their purposes are. The **more** you <u>understand</u> about these important parts of your truck, the **more** you can find the problems in advance and advise the shop what you need done; And not the other way around. The more you understand about these **important** parts of your truck, the **more** people at the shops and stores will take you seriously. 👍 and it's not that complicated with experience over time.

NOW look, THIS IS THE NAME OF THE GAME. <u>YOU WANT TO BE ABLE TO GO INTO THE SHOP AND TELL THEM WHAT YOU NEED DONE</u>. *NOT VICE VERSA*. YOU SHOULD ALMOST NEVER GO INTO A SHOP AND HAVE THEM FIGURE OUT WHAT THE ISSUE IS. IF YOU DO NEED THEIR HELP IN TROUBLESHOOTING, GO TO AN INDEPENDENT SHOP YOU can TRUST, AND LET THEM KNOW ALL THE THINGS YOU ALREADY CHECKED. LET THEM KNOW WHAT YOU THINK IT IS, AND GO FROM THERE. THIS WILL SHOW THEM THAT YOUR NOT new or

A PUSH OVER AND THAT <u>YOU HAVE</u> MECHANICAL SENSE. IT ALSO SHOWS THAT YOU WILL BE MUCH HARDER TO TRICK INTO PAYING FOR A BIGGER REPAIR BILL. 🔑💯👍🔒

I **know** this may sound like not trusting anyone, but in <u>my life experience</u>, you **have to do** what you can to **set the tone** <u>for your business as a solo owner-operator</u>.

We have to separate the way we feel personally from the way business gets handled. 🔑👊 <u>Don't forget</u>, **this is a business** and you work hard for your profit. You must take influentially control your situations as much as possible. 😊

2. CREATE A HOME BASE OF SHOPS AND PART STORES THAT YOU CAN RELY ON. ✔️

If you are like me in the **beginning**, I didn't have a home base of operations. I **left** out my hometown at **21**, started leasing at **22**, and got my first truck at **23**. I didn't have a house of my own yet outside of my dad's place. And **That** was ok, **but** I always told myself; When I settle somewhere, I'm going to build a **great** network of people who know me by name, and who I can rely on. And that's exactly what I did throughout the journey. And yes, building a reliable network has <u>proved</u> to be a great improvement to my operation. 👌

I have **2 independent shops** I use for two different types of jobs. My one shop I can almost get straight in and straight out in one day. I **go** there for body work and medium suspension type work. **They** know me <u>by name</u>, <u>they know my family,</u> and <u>they know I'm a pretty decent person</u> with **common sense** who has worked hard. They make exceptions for me all the time. 😁 including with dot inspections

My next shop is one that **specializes** in <u>major engine and suspension repair</u> and **etc**. If I need to put a clutch in, this is my place to go. If I need help doing an engine job that's out of my skill or tool range, **this** is where I go. This is the place I go when I need a highly skilled job done. I **know** <u>the owner</u> and <u>all the mechanics by name</u>. I **love** the way the owner runs his shop. **Each** mechanic **specializes** in a certain style of work, so, they become **really** great at what they do. This shop is only 5 miles from my land too! 🚛

The **only** thing about this shop is, <u>other owner operators</u> have found the **value** in this shop as well! When I go to this shop of mine, I'm in no rush and already expect a week or two to get the job done. <u>Sometimes it's faster</u>, **but** again, this is ok. Waiting a week or 2 to get high quality work done with the convenience of being at home, is way different than **waiting** a **week** or **2** at a dealer over the road whose work will be over-priced, probably with low quality, and the costs for hotels and food. 🚚

Building a network of shops you can rely on is **very** important. This goes for being over-the-road as well. If you tend to travel the same routes frequently, then keep attention to the shops in the cities and towns along the way. If you ever end up needing a shop on the road, and they treat you well, **remember** this shop for next time. As you build friendships with other owners keep mindful of shops who have done them right. Just like **Charles** at Justice fleet in chapter 1. His shop is duly noted, will be recommended, and I will go out of my way if I'm in the general area and I need a shop. ☑️

I'll **tell** you one thing that I do that maybe other solo owner-operators don't do. I **highly** <u>appreciate</u> my local team of shops and my parts guys. **So,** every Christmas time I go out and buy gift cards to the most popular restaurant in town and make personal letters to each person that has been a part of my trucking company's success. This is usually about **10** to **15** people. Each person will get a $25 to $50 gift card depending on their contribution. I've even given gift cards to guys I wasn't too impressed with but who I did business with on a regular basis. I **consider** this a **sign of good faith**. Some will call this <u>bribing</u>, but I call this **true appreciation**, **profit sharing and investing into eachother**. 😄

Part of the reason I did so well this year is because of the help of my team. So, I share some of the profit as a thank you! If you keep the receipts, you can also claim this as a deduction on taxes under the category of "consultation" … But my objective every year is to say **"Thank you"**. Thank you for supporting my small trucking business, and thank you for being a part of my success this year. You will be surprised **how quickly** people start to remember you, your name and your business when you go out of your way to thank people this way and actually mean it. 👉

A couple days after Christmas is the perfect time to do this since people have already got their gifts and are already in the energy of receiving gifts, so this helps it seem like it's not bribery or whatever. I do this **EVERY** year. If your intentions are clean then it **isn't** bribery anyways, but you might as well be natural as possible with your approach of appreciation.

3. DEALERSHIPS VS INDEPENDENT. ✔

I'm going to keep this one short. **Stay away from dealerships if at all possible**. 🔒

If you **must** deal with a dealership, be **very firm** and don't let them push you around! You're almost guaranteed to have a better experience at an **independent** shop. Why? Because independent shops are small business' that rely on customer service to stay in business. **Big dealerships don't** usually **care** much about customer service. The smaller shop will have more **incentive** to do better business with you. Dealerships don't even like to help with warranty issues half of the time either. OK

If you are **under** a warranty and **must** go to the dealer, I understand. But stand your ground and be prepared to leave those dealerships in your past as you progress in your solo owner-operator journey. You're also way more likely to find **skilled** labor at independent shops. Most of the **really good** mechanics that I've met that are the ones who like working at the **low-key mom and pop** style environment compared to the corporate punch the clock style. 🔧

4. PEOPLE MAY NOT LIKE YOU. ✔

People may not like you and that's ok! Not to get too deep into psychology, but it seems like most people have some type of prejudice, self-doubt or self-hate that they **take** out on others.

You can't let these short comings of others interfere with your business. **Strive** to be the **best** man or **best** woman you can be and that's it. Keep your head high, your back straight and your chest up. By **being** knowledgeable, professional and likeable, will help you eliminate **50** to **75**% of the issues with people in these shops and part stores. You just have to be **confident** in where you're going and be **confident in what you want**. As long as your semi-respectful you should be fine. Remember to keep positive balanced etiquette as much as possible. 💯 ✓

5. MOST PART STORES HAVE WIGGLE ROOM IN THEIR PRICE. ✓

Don't be **cheap** or be a **pain**, but do know **most** part stores have wiggle room in their prices. In a certain portion of the part stores, the part guys work off commission. **So**, it's only natural that they work up the price a little bit. It pays to call around and ask for prices on parts. Once you get the lowest price on a part, go to your preferred store, and let them know the other store has it for a lower price but you would rather buy it here. If the place you're dealing with **isn't** too corporate, they will likely go down on their price. $

Don't **complain** about the price on everything, but if something seems out of place and too expensive, then call it out so you can make a better deal. I've got **many** price reductions by simply dealing with the same part guys over and over again. Sometimes I will be like "wow, this much for this part??", and after pausing for a moment, my parts guy will say, "Let me see what I can do to get this price down for you". 🌴

The **cool** part is, a lot of the time I don't even do this consciously. I'm just honestly blown away with **the** price and my supporting team will accommodate. Just know, whether at home or over the road, the price for a part likely has wiggle room to be a little bit cheaper. **Don't be afraid to push it some and make deals**. The worst they can say is no. **Also** see about getting an account set up at the places you go to often. An account with the name of your LLC, or even if it's just in your personal name, may help you in getting preferred pricing. 🚚

6. **NOT ALL PROFESSIONALS DO A PROFESSIONAL JOB.** ✔️

Just because you **hire** a professional, doesn't mean you will necessarily get a professional job done. I've had to go behind the work of "professionals" **many** times in my day. It's **always** good practice to check the work of others, even if it's someone you trust. Just casually go back over their work and make sure all the bolts are tightened, make sure the fluids are topped, that wires are covered and zip-tied in a way that doesn't cause them to rub and create a short. 🔧

Sometimes mechanics and shops will really do some sleezy, low-down stuff out here. 👎

Like charge your for changing bushings on your radiator, even though they didn't put new bushings on. That's why on certain jobs, I **always** ask for my old parts back in return. By asking for the old parts, you're keeping the mechanic and the shop honest by casually forcing them to actually do the job; Because you're asking for the old parts back in return. They **may** ask, <u>why</u> do you want your old stuff back? **Just** tell them you want to inspect it. **You don't even have to keep it**. Just take a good look at it, this lets you know that they did what you paid for, and let them throw it away at that point. This is not always necessary, but in certain jobs, you will not be able to physically see if a certain internal component was changed and etc. These are the jobs I'm always asking for the old parts back and or I require it in my deals that I **need** inspection by me at certain points of the job so I can observe when a big step is happening, to make sure it's done right. 🔑✅

Sounds like initiative, right?? It is, you are the quality control manager and the one paying the bill. <u>Everything needs to pass your standards</u>.

This is another reason I despise big dealer-ships. A lot of them will not let you onto their floor to observe your own truck. **To me**, <u>this is crazy</u>! It's my truck and I need to see what's going on. To me, it makes it seem like they're trying to hide stuff (and usually, they are!). I understand insurance requirements might say no, but they need better insurance, a clause where we can be escorted by a trained person of safety, or just let us sign a **waiver** saying that we won't sue them. They act as if walking across a shop floor is the most dangerous thing in the world. That act as if walking across they're shop floor is more dangerous than what we already do! Trucking is the 7th most dangerous job in America, I think we can get across the shop floor just fine 🤣! This is yet another reason why going to independent shops over big-dealerships makes much more practical sense! 🚚

Sometimes the mechanic on the job is not as experienced or "professional" as you may think or that he seems. The more you learn, and the more you take initiative, the more you will start to realize that you may know just as much if not more than the mechanic. **This happens to me all the time**. I get to talking to a mechanic over the road somewhere and I realize, dang, I can do just about everything this guy can do, if not better. Still respect the mechanic of course, but don't let the **title** mechanic discourage you **from** feeling equipped enough to handle issues yourself. Learn from the good mechanics and pay attention to everybody out here. Make sure you're getting your money's worth and what you paid for. **Yes**, they are the one's helping you, but you are the customer. Make sure you get your money's worth and make sure they are skilled enough to do the job.

7. ASK FOR QUOTES UP FRONT. ✓

Do what you can to **negotiate** an estimated dollar amount **before** the work ever gets started. **As you progress**, make mental or physical notes of how long it takes to do a job. Check truckers report for posts relating to yours. Start your own thread and ask around. Usually somebody will know how many hours it takes to do a certain job. Let's say an air compressor on my N-14. I wouldn't expect to pay much more than **5 hours labor** on this job. If the shop charges $100 an hour, I can have a good estimate in my head of $500 labor plus parts. $

When I'm at my local shops, I often save money by buying my own parts in advance from my trusted part stores in town. This saves me from paying a marked-up price from the parts store, and then again for the shop to mark up the prices a little as well. **Some** jobs will be harder to get an estimate on, but if you know what you need done, you should be able to get an estimated price agreed upon before start. Aim not to come across as cheap, but as a businessman. 🙌

 If you don't ask for something, and you get charged for it, make a judgement call whether or not to pay for it. ✔️

A good shop will <u>let you know</u> along the way if there's something **extra** that needs to be done before they do it. When you sign the work order at new shops or over-the-road, **write** "contact me for all approvals on parts and labor not listed" or write something of this nature! You could verbally tell them, but it is much better to put this in writing. It's something about requests like this <u>being on paper</u> to keep people and places more honest! 😁

8. PARTS STORES. ✔️

Part stores **can be** tricky especially if you're from out of town. If you're from out of town, just **do** your best to <u>use people's names</u>, <u>be likeable</u> while not being a kiss up, and <u>be sharp as a razor</u>! It's **ok** to **smile**. Have a ball park figure in mind for the price of the part that you're looking to buy. If you're in Greensboro, NC, call a store in Charlotte or Raleigh to **see** what the price is. This will give you a good gauge to what your part should cost in Greensboro. If the part price is too high in Greensboro, and you now know what the part **can** cost, tell them "This part should only be **$150**, not **$225**. **James**, I want to buy this part, but I want to pay **$150**" … Everybody's style of asking will be slightly different. But that's about how I do it. I ask for what I want **very** directly, <u>but with respect</u>! 😎👍

It just depends on the sales guy. If he's younger, I take a more **relaxed** but **firm** approach. If he's older, I take a more **calculated** but **respectful** approach. Sometimes you really need the part and there's nothing you can really do, but in moments when you know the price is wrong big-time, stand your ground, know what you're talking about, and there's a **good** possibility you can get a price reduction. 🙌

A dollar saved is a dollar earned. ✔️

Let's talk about **local** part stores. These are the places where you want the managers and the parts guys to know you by name and to know you by face! You want these people to know, that **you** do this for real! **You** want them to know that you're **a problem solver and not a burden to no one**. That you are out here fixing stuff yourself and making your business work. **Basically**, you want their respect. 👑

But as always in life, if **you** want the respect of others, you must be willing to casually **give** respect as well. If you have the time, hang out at the stores a little bit longer than you normally would. Make the time if you have to. Consider it like making a **deposit**. The genuine time you spend and deposit with others will build up a **reserve currency** that you can make withdraws out of. **Again**, if your intentions are right, this is not manipulation, **it's just natural business and networking**. You are providing something of value by listening to their stories as a friend. Almost all successful people in business do this to some extent. 🗝️

Listen to their stories, know them by name, be interested in their life, ask them if they have any ideas on how to fix what you're working on, get to know their past a little bit, **pay** attention to see if they <u>have kids</u> or what they **like** to do for fun. Pay attention to their **political** stance. <u>Don't be weird about it</u>, **just** take your time when listening to their stores and let whatever is supposed to happen, happen **organically**. 😁

Once you start to collect information, <u>make sure</u> to **remember** it. Write it down in your phone if you have to. But as you go back into their stores, causally bring up something that y'all talked about last time! This will really help your business out in the long run. It will **give** you priority over other customers, it will **get you** little discounts here and there, it will give you a more pleasurable experience when buying parts too. Even though you're buying parts, it almost **becomes** fun, it's like going in to check up on your old friends. ☺and shoot the stuff

There's been times when I'll stay in the store for 30 minutes to an hour after, just talking because we got a good conversation going on. That's why it really pays to be **knowledgeable** in **many** subjects, **the more you know** and **experience**, <u>the better you can hang with everyone in different conversations</u>! Don't dread this part of the business, it's just part of the game. Learn to love it, but remember, you don't have to kiss up to no one either! There is a **perfect** balance that you will find with enough practice. **Yes**, there will be some people that are harder to win over than others, but stay consistent. People know when you're trying to hustle or kiss up to them, it happens way to often in their line of work. As long as you keep coming in with good **energy**, <u>saying names</u>, making **them** laugh or **feel** respected, eventually they will crack and things will go more smoothly for you. You're not alone out here, people **do** want to help you and to <u>see you win</u>.

SUMMARY. ✔️

I know I've given you a good starting place and set of strategies when it comes to; How to handle yourself at shops and stores, how to present yourself at shops and stores, and what to be aware of and paying attention to in shops and stores. I've **also** given you tactics that I have developed over time and still used up until I Self-Retired.. **That's what it's all about**. It's about always getting better. **Use** these tactics and awareness that I've shared; Build and develop better strategies on top of it for yourself. I'm constantly reading books about success, self-development, mentality, and deal making. The main thing to remember in shops is,

If you don't know what you're doing, these places have a track record of eating solo owner-operators alive. 🆗

The best way to prevent this is to **really really really** learn your truck. The more you know about mechanics, the less they will try to "pull the wool over your eyes". 🔧

Understand that dealerships are not the place to go. In my 12 years now, I can count my good experiences at dealerships only on one hand lol. **Dealerships** are fine for getting parts, but the thought of letting them work on my truck almost makes me sick. 😖

> **1** - they're probably **not** going to do a great of a job at all. ✖️
> **2** – They probably have a **huge** wait time to even get into the shop. ✖️

3 – They're **going** to be charging **$150+** an hour or so. ✗

4 – the shop people at the front desk have **no enthusiasm** and don't care. ✗

5 – a lot of the mechanics just follow what the computer says instead of doing **real** troubleshooting. This is how owners end up buying a **$4k** turbo, because the computer said so, but a **real** mechanic could see the turbo was fine but you **needed** new sensors and a clean out. This is also how dealerships bills can get very outrageous very quick. They basically change parts at your expense, hoping that it will "fix" it. I'm running a finely tuned business; I don't have time or wasted capital for guess work. ✗

Understand how important person to person business relations are. Learn about the people you do business with. Take **initiative** by being a **good** person first. **Remember**, enthusiasm is contagious. Don't be overly enthusiastic, but just bring some good and positive balanced energy to the table. Make **sure** to respect yourself. The amount of money you spend on parts and labor is a **very** important part to your success long term. If you're constantly **overpaying** for everything, and people are **ripping** your wallet off on maintenance, your chances of success will go way down and very quickly.

Take this part of your business very serious. Learn as much as you can about maintenance. Go watch people work on their truck. **Pick up** tips and tricks as often as you can. **Lower** your costs and your frequency of shop visits by investing into the **tools** and **learning** to be a mechanic yourself. The more you get involved, the better. The **more** you have real experience in fixing stuff, the more the shop guys will respect you, and the better things will go for you when you present yourself. Real skills recognize real skills.

Pay attention and **keep learning**. Keep an **eye** on everything. Get the best deals at the best quality you can. Stay away from dealerships when possible and build relationships with your local vendors and service providers. **Remember**, "you're highly favored, you're highly respected, you're highly appreciated, and you have an attractive personality" … **Believe this** and Know it TRUE.

Mentality is so important. **You can do this**! Ok? Good things take time and effort. But once you **achieve** good things, **great things** can happen fast. **Believe** in yourself. Have faith that you will figure this all out when you're supposed to. Get yourself in to a routine of success. Get yourself into a routine of **always** evolving and getting better at what you do and what you have to offer. True happiness is priceless, if you're naturally a happy person, then don't **undervalue** your happiness. The **happiness** you share with others is **real**, and it is valuable. **So, don't ever think you have nothing to offer.** Each person you deal with is slightly different. Figure out how to interact with each person based off their body language, interest level, content of conversation, direction of conversation and etc. **And don't forget**, just listening sometimes too makes all the difference. Make sure that you are **approachable** enough that people will want to talk to you!

The **next** topic I want to share with you is another important one (aren't they all 😄!). This is a topic I never really got advice or teachings on. Though it's important, very rarely is it ever discussed because of it's Taboo and politically correctness. That's why I dedicated a whole chapter to it! "**How to Deal with State Police**"! These of course are the guys and women who have the authority to stop us whenever they want. They have the authority to inspect us. And they basically have the authority to do whatever they want too. ?

They can write us **bogus** tickets and **seem** to never get never get punished for it. The main problem about bogus inspection tickets is; They still go on our safety records, and companies that you lease to can **terminate** your contract if it has happened often enough. I'm going to show you my methods of how I've learned to **interact** with state police and how I **keep** all that drama down to a minimum as possible. Let's continue! 👻

CHAPTER 11: HOW TO DEAL WITH STATE POLICE

State Police has the **authority** to stop an owner and to **inspect** whenever they want. City and County police do not have the **authority** to check your logs or to do equipment inspections on you. I'd never much worry or be too **concerned** with local police that are non-state or department of transportation / public safety. As long as you don't make moving violations like changing lanes without a turn signal, local police are not much concerned about what a truck driver does. **Ultimately**, I eventually became less worried or concerned with state police as well, but I do treat them with more caution and space. As an owner, you don't want to be on the wrong side of a state police or department of public safety officer. Ever since the introduction of **CSA2010**, everything a state police officer writes down on a ticket gets recorded into your safety score. and to your companies if you have your own dot# that you run.

State police can make issues to be make or break when it comes to losing your lease onto a company, lowered safety scores and etc. They can **increase** your <u>insurance costs</u> and impact who you can book loads with. **Don't let this spook you,** but let it remind you to stay on your top game at inspections and with your outward appearing maintenance.

Little things like a marker light being out, little air leaks that you can fix yourself, looking under your truck with a creeper to inspect for wheel seal leaks and etc are all things in your power for sure to know and be keeping tabs on because not much changes once you get in a good groove with your truck...... Making sure your headlights work, making sure you're the high beams come on, making sure your windshield wipers and water squirter work. These are "**gotcha**" tickets that **DOT** and **State Police** will write. These are also the little things that could tip you off for inspection ok? The more you stay ahead of these "**gotcha**" tickets and obvious defects, the <u>better</u> it will be for your solo owner-operator success. Many if not most of these officers don't really want to do a detailed inspection unless it's really the order for the day. They just want to find a quick little issue so that they can issue you a citation. If you cover all **the** little issues, and have nothing major that is obvious, you eliminate a lot of the possible citations and trouble. ✔

When possible, make sure your brakes **are** adjusted and that you don't have any air leaks on your brake chambers. Air leaks at the brakes chambers with brakes applies is automatic out of service citation and order. There are videos on YouTube for getting a visual on brake adjustment and what that looks like. I like and used the "**BRAKE SAFE**" product for quickly inspecting brake adjustment. Here is a link to their website Overview — Spectra Products - Home of Brake Safe® . The owner's name is Andy. He is a cool and helpful guy! 😁

By using brake safe, I can release my brakes, and with a block of pre-cut wood, I can press my foot brake in, then **go** outside and check the push stroke of all my brakes by looking at the visual indicators on the brake safe product. This whole process takes about **5 to 10** minutes, and I only need to get on the ground to see my first drive axle. The rest I can check **by** leaning in and taking a look. What a game changer **Brake Safe** was for me! Old school guys will tell you, "you can just look at the brake pad gap, or look at the slack angle" and that "you don't need to buy that fancy stuff to check brakes" … And to an extent, they are right! But Brake Safe was **less** than $**200** for me to install a unit on every position, truck and trailer. **Why** would I **not** make this small investment into increasing the efficiency of my business? 👻

When I check my brakes, I **know** for a **fact** that they are in adjustment! I can't tell an officer, "oh they were good this morning when I looked at the brake pad gap" **LOL**!!!! The

DOT officer is measuring **push stoke** and does not care about methods of "it's fine". In all reality the brake probably **is** fine, but **DOT** is measuring push rod length and not "decent enough". 🚚

Another thing I **like** about Brake Safe is that if you have different size brake chambers on your truck like I did, when you set the **brackets** on your brake chambers, you make sure that the bracket size is the **legal** limit of push rod travel for that size brake chamber. What this means to me is, it helps keep **DOT** guy **honest** and to **easily** pay attention to brake chamber size. ✔️

If you have an **oddball** style brake chamber and it's a **long** stroke, maybe the **DOT** guy hasn't experienced that size often and will just treat it as a different size that has a lower accepted travel length. I know that having **Brake Safe** installed as a solo owner-operator will ease the inspection process for full inspections. When the **DOT** man sees that you have **brake safe,** and that **you** paid for it, I think at the very least, it **subconsciously** tells him that you're a cut above the rest, and that his inspection is going to be much more easy. 😁 👍

An air leak on your **brake chambers** is an automatic out of service. An out of service order looks bad on your record and if it happens enough will cause a company to **terminate** your contract (lease). **Sometimes** I really hate the amount of control **DOT** has on us, but eventually I learned to not let it bother me or make me anxious. It's **crazy** how in life, that we tend to **attract** what it is we're looking for. If you're always **looking** for **DOT** to stop you, and to find fault in their inspection, then guess what? **That's what you will**

start to attract. You **tend** to attract what you have in your heart and in your mind. 😶 kind of like mentioned in the mentality chapter….

Do not let **doubt** or **worry** <u>crystalize</u> into **fear**. Do not look for these **DOT** guys and **state police** in that negative type of way. This is the type of stuff that feeds them to you. Just go in their scales, and stay focused on getting right back onto the road. Feel as if they have no reason to check you. **Do not attract their attention**. 👣

Be **professional** and stay <u>on top</u> of your game. **Fix** minor issues right away if possible, and do what you can to not give them something easy to get you on.

Keep your dashboard clean. Be presentable. ✔️

AT ISPECTION TIME: pants fully up. up-right stance. Shirt clean and straight. **Have confidence**. <u>Look</u> like someone that goes underneath their truck and knows what's going on. A lot of this is a **mental** game. If you do get pulled in, have your permit binder ready with everything laminated or in plastic sheet protectors. Have your permit book **organized** with the **most important** stuff in the front. **Bring** in your **BOL**, be calm, and be ready to **quickly** answer all their little questions quickly and to the point.

Don't say too much, don't try an be extra nice to them, just be a pro and give them confident but slightly enthusiastic direct answers. ✔️

Questions like, "where are you coming from?", "where are you taking this load" are **very common**. **Don't** let them intimidate you or throw you off. Make some initial eye contact and head nod but then not too much eye contact. **Just** remain calm and **confident**. It's pretty much the same questions they ask every time to everybody. The main reason they ask you "where did you pick your load up, and where does it deliver", is because they want to see if it's an intra-state move. If you pick up a load in their state and deliver the load in their state, it falls under **intra**-state jurisdiction, and usually you need a special permit or authority to do so. Again, they are looking for the easy ticket. **But**, if you don't answer these questions in a smooth, short and confident way, they **may** start to think that **you're** trying to hide something or need further inspection. If they think that you're being suspicious or don't have short answers for them, you may now become a good candidate for a level 2 or level 1 inspection.

Be smooth, be bold. Be confident. Be Quick. Personable but not too much. Don't let them **see** you sweat. If they must inspect you, then guess what? It's just your time. **We** all got to get inspected time to time. Sometimes all you can really do is hope for the best and stay focused because these inspections hold weight.

I once got put **out of service** right after doing like **$5k** worth of *PREVENTATIVE* maintenance. Did I get credit for that? No….. Not really…..It was December and I figured I would put some profits into fixing things up instead of paying some of that extra money on taxes. I put on all new brake chambers truck side, all new s-cams on my truck, I put 4 new trailer tires on the spread axle, bought 4 new rims for my

<u>outside trailer tires to look better</u>. I didn't have to do these preventative maintenances, but I did. I was **good** and **confident** that I was **staying ahead** of the **DOT**.

It was **my** fault at the end of the day, but when I went to press my brake pedal down during inspection, I had an **audible** air leak at my brake chamber. **DANG!** Automatic OOS. Why did I have this leak? **Because** I let someone replace these brake chambers for me and they didn't tighten up the **7/8's** nut on my brake line all the way. It was just loose enough to **cause** an air leak. I went down there and tightened it up, and the leak was **gone**. I should have checked over his work and I did, just not **detailed** enough. You have to be careful with those air leaks that only happen when you press the break down. Aim to make a habit of checking for applied brake air pressure leaks at least once a week. Usually this requires being in a **quiet** place so you can open the door and hear the leak if there is one. ✔

So, I "**low-key**" got **punished** for doing right and for doing preventative maintenance lol. **BUT** It still was <u>my fault</u>; I could have prevented it. It made me very mad in then though. An **OOS** order looks bad on my company's safety score, and he didn't seem to care about my culture of professionalism and safety either. He completely ignored my **Michelin** tires, my **new** brakes chambers, my **clean** professional up keep, and **etc**. He could of saw my extreme effort, and gave me a moment to fix it before writing it up. Or he could of agreed to give me a citation that wasn't **OOS** and let me fix it. It took me **FIVE** minutes to fix it myself by the way and tighten that brake hose fitting. 🙄

The **crazy** part was, after I tightened it up, the state police man in Alabama didn't want to comeoutside and check over my work. He had just given me a whole **speech** about how he just want's "**his roads**" to be safe. But he wouldn't **even** come out to check my fix and see if it was "**safe**" enough for "**his**" road. **What a damm joke on me!** **SO, JUST KNOW**, I know and understand the frustrations that **DOT** and **State Police** can bring. I just don't let it get to me like I used to because I didn't want the anxiety or stress to attract that to me. I'm **too** focused on my goals, and I'm going to accomplish my goals with or without them! I would hope **that** they see the dedicated solider in me, but I'm not going to let **the** fear of what they can do discourage me either. 🚛

It's a lot better these days because I have my own authority. **So really**, I don't have to report tickets to anyone but myself. But accumulated **out-of-service** orders and inspection citations can still impact who I do business with and my insurance costs. If were **leased** to a company like **Landstar**, who is **VERY** sensitive to CSA tickets and violations; They can quickly blow stuff like this out of proportion. And terminate leases…This is actually the main reason why I left Landstar. 😔

The year **before** I left Landstar I was gifted an award for ranking in the "**Top 300 CSA score**" of the company. I was in the top **300** lowest **CSA** scores in a group of over **8,000** owner operators. The following year I get an OOS violation **5** miles from my house for a brake hose that wasn't tightened enough and had an audible air leak, and later that year I got a **WARNING**, not a violation, but a **warning**, for a wheel seal leak that was just developing. This warning set **Landstar** off into a **frenzy**. They placed me on "**safety probation**" and

218

now wanted me to get a truck and trailer DOT inspection **every** month, for **3** months. They wanted me to pay for the inspections and if I got **ONE** violation, my contract would be automatically terminated. Hold up…. **WOW!** What loyalty that had for me after 5 smooth clean years! 🤣

I was just **winning** awards, now I'm on the <u>chop block</u>, because of my errors **yes**, but also because the **strength** of the **state police**. Landstar <u>always</u> sides with the **state police by default**. In my **5** years, they never really asked me what happened they just would side with state police. Someone from a (**904**) number in the Jacksonville safety or compliance department would just call me assuming I'm wrong because it says so on the report. **Thank you** Landstar! 🤣

It **didn't** take me long to realize that I wasn't going to let Landstar terminate me. This was after **5** years of **good** partnership at Landstar with <u>no accidents</u> only a **minor** moving violation or 2 (I was still learning 😀!). I didn't want to leave but I did. And in hindsight, **I'm glad I did!**

It was the push I needed to get my own authority and to be in more control and do things the way I really wanted. ✔️

But, at the end of the day, I am very appreciative of my experience at Landstar. Amongst other things, Landstar really got the importance of **CSA** scores and maintenance drilled into me. I carry that same professionalism and standard everywhere I go now. 😁

The **sad** and crazy part is, the majority of **DOT** I experienced and **State Police** don't really seem to care about safety all in all. They don't like give when credit when credit is due. They don't like to cut slack. It takes a **ton** of money sometimes to stay ahead on compliance. Especially when it comes to fixing things that don't really need to be fixed, like a certain seal oil leak on a motor.... but you fix it anyways because it's out of the "**Accepted range**" and it's a violation.

If the **state police** just realized how much impact they have on our business, and how much stress that causes an already stressed occupation, maybe it would make them more accountable to the tickets they write. If an officer really cared about safety, they should give us the opportunity to fix it without penalty or a lesser penalty. I'm going **on** a **rant** now... A lot of these guys don't care about safety for real, they do the job and write the ticket, and this ticket goes onto your "**safety score**" which in turn can haunt us in one way or another. ⚔ the is the power they yield knowingly or not.

If you are a victim of **extortion**, **please** fight it with Data-Q. https://dataqs.fmcsa.dot.gov/Default.aspx 💀🦴🕊✓

 Data-Q **does** works when the case is presented correctly. It does **take** time to fix though, sometimes months. But it is always worth it to fight especially if you know you're not in the wrong. How to DataQ: 9 tips (overdriveonline.com)

Your personal safety score is your **PSP** (pre-employment screening program). As a carrier, if you have your own authority, it gets recorded into your **CSA** safety score as well. **There** are brokers who check your **CSA** score, and will not load you if your score is low to their standars. 🆗

But in my experience, the main thing brokers look at is the amount of accidents first, and then your overall safety score. ✓

If you have an or some **OOS** on your safety score, it shouldn't make or break as long as the rest of your profile looks good and you don't get into accidents. The carrier safety scores go like this, "Satisfactory, None, Conditional and Unsatisfactory". There **are** more things considered into a safety score than just vehicle maintenance, but vehicle maintenance is on the list for sure. The list of categories determining your carrier safety score looks like this.

1. **Unsafe Driving**
2. **Crash Indicator**
3. **Hours of Service (HOS) Compliance**
4. **Vehicle Maintenance**
5. **Controlled Substance / Alcohol**
6. **Hazardous Materials Compliance**
7. **Driver Fitness**

These are things that **can** be researched further on | FMCSA (dot.gov) but the "jist" of it is;

Don't drive crazy, give yourself plenty of space from other vehicles so you won't get into a wreck, use your turn signals, don't speed, don't get moving violations, don't drink and drive, don't fail drug tests, log the days correctly, and be serious about controlling your "gotcha" tickets from DOT. I'll cover this type of stuff in more detail in the "Own Authority" chapter. ✓

LET'S KEEP IT SIMPLE AND HIGHLIGHT SOME IMPORTANT THINGS TO REMEMBER AND WHAT TO DO

WHEN INVOLVED WITH STATE POLICE; DPS, DOT AND THE LIKES. ✓

1. Do not try to flatter the officer. ✓

People try to **flatter** the officer all day <u>every day</u>. He or she can **see** through that. It makes it look like you're hiding something. 🤐

2. Give short, direct and firm answers. ✓

I want you to <u>develop</u> the **mentality** of, "**these guys can't do nothing to me because I'm good**". This is **not** a cocky confidence; this is a **supreme** confidence. This confidence telepathically lets them know; you are not worried because you know you're not the problem they are looking for. 😁

3. Find the balance. ✓

Find the balance between being **serious** and being **enthusiastic**. If your <u>too</u> enthusiastic they might think you're on drugs or something. If your <u>too</u> serious, they might think that you are an easy punching bag because you're **too** emotionally attached to the situation. 🆗

4. Don't get emotional. ✓

This can be a hard thing to do, **but** leave your emotions out of it at inspection time. It's ok to smile a bit, but do **not** let them get you riled up. If you get riled up and start spouting at them, it will **not** end up well. <u>Stand your ground yes</u>, but don't go overboard with your tone or voice volume. One extra smart remark can turn the whole situation against you. Just remember, people only know what they know. **Have** patience with them. If they are very wrong about something, ask if they will they show you the defect before you sign the ticket. **You still** got Data-Q to fight these tickets if need be. Don't go trying to Super Man at their scale house, throwing your hands in the air, having loud volume and cussing. It **ALMOST** never works in your favor to be that guy. 📢

5. **Double check their inspection before signing.** ✔️

Before I sign any ticket and I will ask to see the defect myself before signing it. They might ask "What, do you not believe me?", **ignore** that and respond "It's business, and I have to be aware of what I sign for" … This is your opportunity to **reverse** the ticket on the spot if you can find something wrong with what they wrote. Actually, **if possible**, you need to inspect and stop them **BEFORE** the ticket is written.

Once the ticket is written, it gets way **harder** for them to get rid of it or change because it's already logged. ⚔️

A **good** example is years ago in Texas, I was getting inspected at the inspection site near Diboll, TX northbound out of town. I heard him say my trailer **ABS** light wasn't cycling on and off. I knew for a **fact**, that morning it cycled on and off just fine. Before he could write me a ticket I asked "This morning my **ABS** light cycled on and off, maybe the sun is too bright and it's hard to see, I want to inspect it myself while covering the light with my hands, and my wife can turn the key off and on so we can see." He **agreed**. And guess what? He almost wrote me a wrong ticket, because at that moment I **proved** to him, and it worked. He grumbled himself and walked off. 🖕😂

I was at Landstar then **too**, and they would of flipped to me! Do what you can to take some level of control in these situations. **Observe** the defect before signing! If you must sign and the problem is not there like the officer says, then on the ticket write, "**under duress, will collect photo and video evidence to prove no defect**", then sign your name. The officer won't like it, but they have to respect your professionalism and your heart to fight. Then proceed to collect the evidence on your phone **BEFORE** you leave. Then if you have to, have another mechanic sign off on the ticket or a work order saying "no defect found". This is the evidence you'll need to reverse this charge in Data-Q.

6. **Don't report everything to your company so quickly.** ✓

Hear me out, I'm **not** saying or advising you to be an **outlaw rebel type trucker**, I'm just saying slow your role a bit when it comes to reporting things to your safety department; Especially if you're at a super sensitive safety company like Landstar. A company with a hyper-sensitive safety department can be worse than the **DOT**. They will write stuff up internally in a different way than the **DOT** does and the way your company writes up safety infractions will follow you from company to company.

Let me give **you** an **example**, I had a friend that got into a "jack knife". **Except** he **didn't** get into a full jack knife. He jumped the gun that day and called Landstar right away to tell them what happened. I've made this **mistake** too, I would think that I'm doing the **right thing** by being <u>completely</u> transparent, but end up getting myself into **more** trouble. 📢

What actually **happened** was, he got off on an exit because the roads were getting bad with snow and ice, and right before the stop sign, he hits a patch of ice and begins to **easily** slide at about **2** mph. There was a very slight bump, and the only damage was a **glad hand** on the trailer needed to be **replaced**. He could have replaced the glad hand himself and went on as if nothing happened. <u>Because nothing really did happen</u>. It was just a moment in time that got a little dicey, and it didn't define him as a driver in my opinion. 🚛

Anyways, he calls the police just to help with traffic. My old friend finds a way to get going again and that's it. The police asks "<u>did you call your company yet</u>?" … the answer was yes. The officer then **regretted** to inform him, that "<u>since you called your company and they know now, I have to write it up</u>" … **The** officer **wasn't** even going to write it up. But guess what the end result is? **Landstar** wrote it up as a **jack knife** and **instantly terminated** his contract. Not only was he not leased to Landstar anymore, the "**jack knife**" made it <u>more</u> difficult to proceed in getting leased with a company worth leasing onto. 🆗 💯

The **moral** of the story is, <u>keep your business to yourself</u>, if you must report something, report it **only** after you've exhausted all other options and there's no way for you to fix it on your own. **Don't** be a liar, but don't be so quick to tell on yourself either. Find the balance. If you're going to be getting in trouble, you're going to be in some trouble anyways, no need to rush it. Let the situation play out first, do what you can to change it, then go from there. Because they may never have to know if you fix it first.

Do what you think is right of course, but that's what I'd do **based** off my **experience** in **these** situations. If they were to ask me why didn't I call it in. I would **say**, I was outside being **safe** in the moment and making sure nothing else could happen. I had a **situation** in front of me and I couldn't call it in until I got a **free** from securing the scene. (Because technically I wasn't free to call, I was too busy coming up with a solution!)

Again, don't lie; Just use your own judgement and maybe not be so quick to get the company in your business! 💸🤑💰

7. **Don't be so quick to call the police.** ✅

This piggy-backs off number **6**. If you find yourself **in** a situation, don't be so quick to get the police involved. **Put** your triangles out, **put** your flashers on, and do what **you** can to create some space around you. Keep working fast to figure out what your issue may be, and if traffic starts getting bad or something, call the fire department first and let them know you are in a non-emergency situation and need some help. Getting the **police** involved too early can get you in **more** trouble than the situation really calls for. Use **your** own judgment on this, but personally I don't get police involved in any of my business unless it's a last resort and I've exhausted all other options. 💭

8. **Be presentable and up-right.** ✅

Hopefully this **speaks** for itself at this point but I will elaborate a little further. When dealing with **state police**, aim to not intimidate them. **Don't move too fast**. Always keep your **hands** to where they can see them. If you go pulled over and you see the **DOT** man walking up to you, **hurry up and grab** your permit book (I keep mine in hands reach). By having your permit book and driver's license out and on your lap already, it **lowers** the **tension** between you and the officer because you won't have to quickly reach for something. **Attempt** to put yourself in the **mind** of the officer. He or she doesn't know who you are, they don't know if may be **violent**, on a **drug**, wanted for a **crime** or **etc.** The more at-ease you can make them feel, the more likely the situation will turn out better for you as a solo owner-operator. 🗝

     a. When it comes to appearance, just be yourself but do so in a **professional**-manner.

What I mean by this is, I **have** had my hair in Locs, that's **not** considered **professional** in United States America; but when I'm on the job, or at inspection, I wear my hair back in a **professional** look by putting my hair in a band or into a dread sock that keeps my hair back and out of my face. I also have a southern / country / Louisiana type accent. This **bothers** some people officers. **So**, until I figure the officer out, I will just **say less**. The less I say, the less reason I give him or her to not like me lol. It's the little things like this that you got to pay attention to. 😊

     b. **You** don't have to tuck your shirt in and wear dress clothes or safety clothes every day, **but** do find a way to be **professional** in <u>your own</u> <u>right</u>.

In the summer time I wear **short** shorts above my knees and some type of good **fitting** shirt. I got my <u>hair back</u>, a good pair shades, a good pair of **Asics or whatever** on, some **gold** on my <u>chest</u> and <u>hand</u>. I put **Shea** on my face every day for skin care and glow, I use some good beard oil. Then I top it off with some good deodorant and cologne. I like wearing some **Gold** too like I mentioned. To me, the **gold** symbolizes that, **"I've been doing this for a long time and I'm successful**, <u>I'm not the one you're looking for</u>". As you can see, my summer time apparel wouldn't be considered professional to some, but I **make** it professional by being up-right, up-beat and presentable in my own fashion. I become a person who's **not** <u>hiding anything</u>, I become a person with good fitting clothes who is about **his** business. 😊

      c.   I remember **the** first time I grew **Locs**, I got into an issue with **DOT**, and I thought to myself it **was** because of <u>my hair</u>.

I felt like he profiled me. He did. But, I decide to cut my hair for business reasons, and a **couple** of weeks later I get **the same treatment** again different state, different officer **lol**! Except this time, I was <u>overboard professional</u>. I had my **orange** safety shirt on. It was tucked in. I was super friendly saying things **like** "hey officer how can I help you" … I guess he could see through me **lol**. At that point I realized, I'm just going to be myself in the **most** professional way possible and get better at that. I grew my **locs** back, and learned how to let my actions speak louder than my words and to <u>just say</u> <u>less</u>. **Be yourself**, <u>but be presentable</u>. **Project** confidence. And exercise the grand old **common sense! RIGHT**?? The more you get into a groove a figuring this stuff out, the easier it will become to be yourself and still get respected at the same time. 🔑$🔒✓

Don't attract the state police to you. Don't make **eye** contact with them at the scales. Wear sunglasses if you have to before **you** go into the scale. Look like you got **somewhere** to go and that you're <u>not the trouble maker they are looking</u> <u>for</u>. Keep your dashboard clean. A **messy** dashboard almost always indicates to an officer that you have a messy truck underneath as well. **Slow down** when you get off the exit ramp into the scale house. <u>Pay attention</u> to each sign. If the sign says **maintain** 15 mph, **then** maintain the 15mph. If the sign says **stop** before proceeding onto the scale, <u>then make</u> <u>sure to stop</u>. **Any** little thing like this that you aren't observant to, will give them a reason to inspect you. Think of how many thousands of truckers come into their scale every day. The odds are really in your favor to not get inspected. **You must make the odds better** in your favor by <u>not giving them a</u> <u>reason to go further with you</u>. 🚛🚛

I get **bypassed** a lot on the scales **not** because of pre-pass but because I'm usually hauling **light** loads. If you're hauling loads less than **30,000** lbs, you will get the pre-pass lane in the scale house **more** often. I don't have a pre-pass actually. Every truck that has a pre-pass will show up on the computer screen inside **the** scale house office. If you haven't got **inspected** in a while, or your company has a **low amount** of inspections, or a **high OOS** rate, they will pull you in just for that. **So**, I prefer to remain anonymous when I go into the scales. They don't know anything about me before I get on their scale. **This way**, I get to control my first impression. They can **plainly** see my **DOT** number, my **MC** number, they **see** I have a good **custom** logo on my door, my **dashboard is clean**, my truck and trailer looks good, I got my **shades** and my seatbelt on, my load looks **good** and **etc.**

I get to **control** the narrative instead of a computer algorithm. **98%** of the time, they're going to take one good look at me, and be quick to give me a green light to get back me back onto the road to do my job. I almost **never** make eye contact with them. I just **roll** my window down, get onto the scale, look down out my window on the scale to make sure my steer tire is inside the scale, look up, and expect my green light. The more it looks like you know what you're doing, **the better**.

If I **do** get pulled off the scale, that's when **everything** I mentioned earlier kicks in. I got my **clean** permit book and my **BOL**, I hurry up and **certify** my logs, **make sure** my inspection reports are logged, make sure my **BOL** number is in my e-log report, I might put a little cologne on, and prepare to go **present** myself. I **rehearse** where I'm going, where I picked my load up, and what the freight is that I'm hauling. I'm **prepared** to say as little as possible. I don't take it lightly but I don't overthink it either. I don't let any of this stuff make **me** nervous any more.

I wish you the **best** when it comes to **success** in your interactions with **State Police** and **DOT**. It can really be a pain I know. **Just** like everything I keep mentioning in the book here , **keep** on practicing, **believe** in yourself, **find** ways to become **more** professional, to be **more** presentable, and to know your truck, have **faith** in your goal, know what you want, become **obsessed** with what you want and that lead you, take care of your truck and paperwork **prior** to getting inspected, if possible don't let the officers get you with "**gotcha**" tickets, be weary of what you sign and how you sign it, **fight** the bad tickets with **data-q**, do what you can to be in control of your **CSA** and **PSP** scores.

Whether you see success or not has a lot to do with your attitude, your self-control, your initiative, and your persistence. ✓

Be persistent in getting better. Just like every other topic I **show case** in the book, **knowing** how to deal with **State Police** and **DOT** is very important to your success as a solo owner-operator. Make it a goal to **not** let them produce **fear** in your mind and body. Make it a goal to not attract **DOT**. And make it a goal to put on a great performance when you do have to deal with them face to face in an inspection. **Remember**, be confident and say less. Make it a goal to also make it very hard for **DOT** to find something wrong with your truck. 🚛

Since we've been talking **State Police** and inspections, it's a perfect time to go ahead and get into the very very **IMPORTANT** make and break conversations of maintenance. I have a pretty big chapter ahead for you to study and learn. You're already been starting to **understand** the importance of doing your own maintenance and or at least knowing more about your truck and motor. You **are** already seeing the benefits in how taking a "hands on approach" to your operation and maintenance will increase your profit margins and lower your overhead. 🙌

It **can** seem tough and like an uphill battle when it comes to getting the confidence and knowledge to **mechanic** on your own equipment. I've been there and **done** that! Know that! When I first did my own **EGR** tune-up I was so scared I was going to mess something up and that I was going to be stuck in the country with no way to fix my truck 🤣! **Long gone are those days**! I'll get dirty in no time. There are still certain jobs that I won't do, or will wait until I get home do, just in case I mess something up! Because at home I have **the** benefit of having my car to go find and buy parts. 🚗

None-the-less! Maintenance is **super** important; Even if you don't end up wrenching on your own truck that much. Like mentioned in the "Shops and Part stores" chapter, if these guys think you don't know what you're doing when it comes to maintenance, they will be **WAY** more incline to run hustle on you; Even if you're a good and good looking person lol 😊. Sometimes they will hustle you and not even know it. And if you don't know it, guess what? Your hustled! Are you ready to increase your desire? Are you ready to buckle down and **do** what needs to be done? Let's continue into another **important** chapter that sets apart certain owner operators from the rest of the owner-operator pack. Let's continue into chapter 12, "**MAINTENANCE**"!

CHAPTER 12: MAINTENANCE

This one subject of maintenance **can** easily become a book on its own. I'll do what I can to sum it up in the most <u>effective</u> way possible while giving you the direct knowledge that can be hard to get and or take years to collect. 😀

Ok let's do it→ how you **maintain** your truck will have <u>A LOT</u> to do with your success. Next to fuel, maintenance is the next biggest expense typically. $

It's imperative to **develop** a keen sense of how your truck works and operates. You must be able to know and spot small issues **before** they can become <u>big issues on you out on the field</u>. Develop the confidence and skill that it takes to work on your own truck! **You** then begin to **buy** and **collect** the tools you need to work on your truck and keep yourself out of binds. It's a good time to learn when other truck drivers are working on their truck. Look and give attention to what the mechanic does when you pay someone to work on your truck. 👉

The more information, tools, and experience you gather, the better it will be for your success. ✔

<u>In my opinion</u>, **working** on a big truck is **easier** than working on a car. With a big truck, there's a lot more actual room to work in compared to **the** tight engine spaces and low clearances of a car. There are **MANY** YouTube videos up when it comes to mechanics. I have a YouTube channel up <u>(1) ANDREWS METHOD - YouTube</u> . I **have** repair videos on this channel. If you're faced with **a** mechanical issue, search YouTube and see if a video is already up. 😀

When I started my trucking business back in 2012/13, I did not have **ANY** mechanical skills. I was the **kid** who <u>wouldn't</u>

check the oil his own car, just drive it lol I 🙇. It wasn't that I didn't have sense, I just didn't really need to learn or understand the importance of mechanics yet. Fast forward to trucking, I **quickly** learned that if I wanted to stay in business, I needed to learn mechanics, and quickly! 🚚

Thankfully I **learned** under good mentors and watched a ton of YouTube videos (YouTube University!). I remember the first big repair, or what I thought was a big repair, was **Rawze's EGR** Tune up. I watched his video over and over again (1) ISX EGR Tuneup 1 6 - YouTube until I was confident enough to do it myself. I even had a **step-by-step instruction** sheet I made hand-written to keep me on track with the job! 😁

If I can come **into** trucking with **ZERO** mechanical skills and learn to do what I've done, **YOU CAN TOO** 🖐!

Some jobs I've done and taught myself over the years are; fan clutch, oil pump, starter, batteries, electrical troubleshooting, abs sensor, brakes, s-cam, overhead valve adjustment, hose repair, oil changes, grease jobs, sensor replacement, **egr** tune ups, air compressor, fuel pump, oil pan, piston cooling nozzles, shocks, lights, air dryers, coolant tank, air leaks, slack adjusters, brake hoses, relays, fuses, air solenoid, exhaust pipes, mufflers, tool boxes, step box, differential fluid checks, abs module, brake adjustment, clutch adjustment, belts and belt adjustment, tensioners, fluid leaks and more. 🚚🚚

As you can **see**, that really only leaves out internal motor work and driveline work. Those **are** the only **2** jobs **that** I would outsource. I do have direct experience in motor internals though. I spent **2** weeks every day on the job when I rebuilt my **ISX** motor on the first truck I owned. I was **completely** involved from ordering all the parts down to torquing my own head bolts! <u>That experience</u> really gave me **X-ray** vision into my motor's internals. After this experience, I understood pistons, cylinders, crankshaft, camshaft, main and rod bearings, injectors, valves, counterbores and etc. **MUCH MUCH** MORE! I really thank my shop in north Georgia at that time for that **great** learning experience and love I got. **I got to help with everything**. Which also let me know everything was getting done right too! 😁 (business)

Which leads to the next point here…... The **more** you **know** and **experience**, <u>the more you know the job you pay for is done right or that the job you did yourself, is done right</u>. As a solo owner-operator you have to make sure that the shops and people you pay are doing the job right. Trucking repair bills can be expensive. You want to make sure that you are getting your **every** dollars' worth! $

Sometimes I would **go** overboard in this department, but I'm a frugal person and I have to know I'm spending my money correctly. If you have a repair that you're about to pay somebody to do and you are uncertain of its cost, **make** sure you research it on YouTube and <u>TruckersReport.com</u> <u>Trucking Forum | #1 CDL Truck Driver Message Board</u> <u>(thetruckersreport.com)</u> **BEFORE** you even call or go into the shop. The more you know the part names and process of the repair, the **more** you can get a feel for "<u>is this the right shop</u> <u>and deal for me</u>" and you'll know the right prices and labor to see if that shop is already selling you a show…... By knowing the process of the repair, you can also present a better game; And you **get** more respect from the people inside the shop. The more respect and casual support you have, the less likely people and shops will try to "pull the quick one" one you. 🗝️

I **suggest** buying the repair manual for the motor that you own. I have the Cummins N-14, <u>so I own the N-14 repair books too</u>. The repair books are the **same** ones used for reference in the shops and dealerships, except now-a-days it's mostly all-digital, but same information, trouble-shooting trees etc.

You'll get the <u>step-by-step</u> **instructions** on how to install and un-install parts. You'll get step-by-step troubleshooting trees for engine fault codes. You'll get **important** wire diagram visuals. And you'll get torque values for jobs that require a certain torque down amounts. These books are a **must** have in my opinion. Usually, **they** can be found on **eBay** and by different places ordered online. You <u>can</u> probably buy straight from the dealer or manufacturer but it will likely cost more. 🐁

Next, I would suggest buying the computer and diagnostic hook up that your truck and motor requires if you can't access that information on the setup of your dashboard display…….. Usually, the dealers won't sell direct to the solo owner-operator, but if you look enough on the internet and eBay, you **can** find units for sale. Some of **these** units may be considered "<u>illegal</u>" because they are replica technology products, **so be careful**, and <u>use your discernment</u>. But Many owners will own these off brand but same technology products and use them to read codes and interface with their motor. Use your discernment when purchasing, I cannot advise you to buy technically "illegal" type equipment lol. But I can say, they are for sale, on the internet, and people **use** them all the time to assist in running their trucking business.

Take for example **my** first truck the 09 Peterbilt 387. When I would get **a** check engine light, I could only get the light and that's it. There were no codes to read-out or another way for me to see what the code was. THIS was a setback.

It became a source of anxiety to me for some time...... It got real **out of pocket** going to TA and Petro paying almost $**100** every time to read a fault code.

Eventually I would buy the Cummins Insite and Inline adapter direct from a Cummins dealer lol. It became a **game changer** for me right away. Having and using that gear stepped me ahead of the pack again. Now I could check my own fault codes, reset fault codes, view trouble shooting trees, do forced re-gens, change certain engine parameters, view in-depth emission data and reports and more.

If you don't have a way to read codes yet, **consider** getting a computer hook up like **NEXIQ** or **JPRO**. Search eBay. There are usually options at affordable prices like $**200**-$**1000**. Some people will sell their laptop, connector and everything already installed.... These are more expensive but an all-in-one deal...... Some devices can also scan transmissions, abs and etc. I didn't use one in my **Gen 1 Volvo because it** had already a seriously good viewable diagnostics option on the screen of my dashboard layout.

Inside this section I can visually see and read fault codes. If you have only a check engine light and **no way** to see what's going on inside, **seriously** consider buying a scan tool of some kind. It will save **you** money from not having to pay a shop $**100** just to read codes, and it will also make you more self-sufficient and allow you to rely on **yourself** more for long term success as a solo owner-operator. 😎

If you have a Cummins motor, consider setting up a Cummins Quick Serve account Publications Store (cummins.com) . They might charge, or they may allow 1 motor serial code for free. I'm still **grandfathered** in from years ago when it was free. With Cummins Quickserve you can access all the **good** stuff mentioned earlier that's in the books. Wire diagrams, troubleshooting steps, service procedures plus part numbers. Knowing part numbers can **really** help when you're shopping around to get competitive part prices. Sometimes certain stores won't give out part numbers too because they want you to buy form them 🙄. **So**, by having access to your own part numbers can help you avoid that "tango" of the part number gate keeprs. It also allows you to present yourself more professional by knowing part numbers and procedures. ✔️

Because of Cummins Quickserve, I've was able to do difficult jobs like adjusting my internal overhead valves...... That job would have been close to impossible if it wasn't for the step-by-step instructions and torque specs included in Quickserve. This is **the** same stuff the big dealership mechanics look at! You should have access to this information too as a solo owner-operator. If you don't own a Cummins, see what is available for your motor. You will need the book and or hookup software / diagnostic scanner of some kind. You want to be **able** access to this information;

you want to be able to know **what's** going on inside your own motor at all times without having to pay for outside help.

Let's continue………. → Tools, spare parts and fluids are the next important thing. Impact guns, sockets, deep sockets, big hammers, breaker bars, wrenches, pliers, filter wrenches, extra belts, extra sensors, nuts and bolts, fuses, relays, and etc. I will continue to stress this, but the more tools you carry, the more <u>potential</u> you have to get yourself out of a bind. Carry as much as you can carry. I even carry **3** 5-gallon buckets in case I need to drain my coolant to make a certain repair.

Always carry a **spare** to **each** one of your **belts**. Also, carry a spare tensioner for your main drive belt. The bearings may fail after a while and if you have a tensioner that's not normally stocked, you don't want to be waiting days to get a new one at a truck stop or wherever. Changing a tensioner is a pretty **easy** job and something you can do on the side of the road with simple hand tools if need be. Carry a spare alternator belt, main drive belt, water pump belt, ac compressor belt…. whatever belt your motor requires.

Some motors have only a main drive belt that runs everything. My belts were separate on the Gen 1 Volvo, **so** I would keep a spare for each. You don't want to be in a bind somewhere and the place doesn't have the particular belt you need and now you're waiting a day or 2 to get it.

This is **what** I mean when I repeat "You **have** more control over your destiny than you may think". Many solo owner-operators will wait for the last moment for a breakdown and wonder why life is so much <u>harder for them</u>. **By** being prepared and investing in yourself, you **raise** your

probability of <u>success</u> in a **MAJOR WAY**. Even if you don't plan to do the job yourself, at the very least, already have the parts. 🔒 come on!

Always **carry** a wide variety of fuses, relays, and important solenoids. My truck had a certain starter relay as you can see in this video <u>HOW TO: CUMMINS N14 STARTER REPLACEMENT + NO START RELAY FIX - YouTube</u> at the 4:30 mark. If this $**10** relay fails, my entire truck <u>would not start</u>! **So**, believe I kept an extra one of these on the truck at all times. It's a very quick and easy to change part, but if you don't have it, **you don't have it**. You'll have to find one, or find a way to make a jumper to bypass the relay….. Carry many different size and amperage fuses. Carry a little fuse light tester so you can check and change your own fuses if need be. Take a look into your fuse and relay panel and see what your **ignition** relays look like. When you get time, pull that relay and go match it up at the parts house and buy a couple for back up. 🚚

ALSO: A lot of maintenance issues can be **prevented** or **drastically** <u>reduced </u>due to your **driving habits**.

As mentioned in "How to Drive as an Owner Operator", the faster you drive, the more vibration you create. The more vibration you create, the more everything on your truck and trailer <u>gets</u> **rattled, loosened and beat up some**.

The more vibration and pressure that you put on your parts, the quicker they will get worn out and need replacing. ✔

You can save yourself **a lot** of trouble by driving in a more easy fashion. <u>Slow down</u>, don't drive over big pot holes, take your time for speed bumps, don't come to quick stops, don't lug your motor going up hills, don't idle your motor if you don't have to, let your motor warm up for **at** least 15 minutes before driving, **allow** your motor and turbo <u>to cool</u> down for **5** minutes before powering down. When you turn, turn easy and wide, not sharp. When you're the one paying for the trailer tires, you should also be more **conscious** of how you turn the trailer back there…. Also be more aware of how you back up and how you U-turn. You got to make your trailer tires last as long as possible for future business…

If you have an emissions truck, which is any truck **2004** and later, you have to really know how **emissions** systems even work; And what you can do to stay ahead of its problems that arise from a complicated system. As mentioned in detail in "Which Truck Should I Buy", **2004** to **2007** model motors were **not** <u>totally bad</u> when it came to emission system set-backs…. There was only an **EGR** valve. **2008** to **2011** are tricky trucks to own because of the introduction of **DPF**, **DOC** and the **dozer** injector (after-treatment injector)….. These systems were new not yet fully tested for longevity.

In **2012** motors became equipped with **SCR** systems that utilize the **DEF fluid**. By **2012** manufacturers were getting better at the **DPF** and **DOC** side of things but now had to deal with the **new** <u>regulations</u> requiring action like **DEF**. It seems that after **2018** the manufactures of emission system motor set-ups finally got sustainable enough to base a business around.

I really **despise** the emission motor. They are, in my opinion, <u>not good for a solo owner-operator business</u>. Sure, you can get up the road in an emissions truck fine at times for some time; But there's too many variables that can shut the truck down for me to invest. And if you don't know the system, the shops will eat you alive $ … and for mediocre repairs that often don't **fix** your root problem. 📣

I spent **SO MUCH** money on my **2009** Peterbilt with the **ISX**.

Partly because I didn't know what I was doing in the beginning and partly because everything emissions related is expensive and often is guess work. I had $**6k** jobs, $**5k** jobs, $**3k** jobs multiple times, all emissions related. Then to top it off, the **soot** produced in this system **drastically lowers** the life span of the motor. I did learn eventually, ways to get ahead of these issues, or to avoid them all together by a good running delete program. And using amsoil bypass oil filter….

How does the emissions system work? **Well**, traditionally, motor exhaust was sent straight out the pipe and into the air…. This is what a **pre**-emissions motor was doing. The emission regulations were created to lower the amount carbon pollution a truck can give off.

So, the idea was to lower the amount of exhaust by making the motor **reuse** some of its exhaust as a source of "**new**" air intake. 😎

Instead of putting the dirty exhaust out into the air, some of the exhaust was to be recirculated and used again as "**clean**" new for the motor to use…. This is what the **EGR** valve does. **EGR** is **Exhaust Gas Recirculation**. The **EGR** valve is a component you'll know eventually if you have an emissions system. This valve is what allows the exhaust to come **back** into the intake manifold as "clean air". By using dirty exhaust as clean air, **soot** creation in the oil becomes a common thing. **Oil** is supposed to be a <u>clean</u> **lubricant**. When hot sticky exhaust gets mixed in with it, little **particles** of soot <u>are created</u>. This soot now gets introduced to places inside the motor that requires the lubrication of oil.

Finely tuned moving parts like camshafts and valves get affected the most by the increased friction this soot brings.

There is what's called an **EGR** Cooler in this process too. The **EGR** Cooler is on the exhaust side of the motor behind the turbo and bolted to the block of the motor its self. Its purpose is to cool the exhaust down enough to be reused as "clean air".

Next is the **DPF** and **DOC**. These are the **big cylinder-shaped cans** (filters) that are usually **underneath** the truck.

In some set ups, the cans are on the passenger side step area or elsewhere. The cans are big and hard to miss. **DPF** stands for **Diesel Particulate Filter**. The **DPF** collects **soot** particles from going out into the atmosphere. **DOC** stands for **Diesel Oxidation Catalyst**.

The **DOC** sits in front of the **DPF** physically and in the order it processes the exhaust. The DOC gets the exhaust ready by running it through a **honeycomb** shaped structure coated with a **catalyst**. The honeycomb shape forces the exhaust through small but parallel passage-ways. Inside these passage-ways the exhaust is supposed to make contact with the catalyst and convert it into a carbon dioxide and water. It is "oxidizing carbon monoxide" in this process. The **DPF** then collects the oxidized remains and attempts to burn it off.

As you can see, there's a lot going on in this process and we've haven't even brought in **DEF** yet. I'm not super scientific when it comes to the emission process. But I do understand well what's going on at the core of it. **Exhaust** gas is being re-used as "**clean**" air. The **DOC** and **DPF** catch the rest of the exhaust and attempt to chemically change it and burn it off. And **what can go wrong right**?? This is what's going on in a **2008-2011** truck. It's also going on in a **2004-2007** truck, just without the **DPF** and **DOC**.

Then in **2012**, the **SCR** and **DEF** systems step onto the scene. **SCR** stands for **Selective Catalytic Reduction**. This came in to overcomplicate a system that was still not yet sustainable for the solo owner-operator. It took our already challenging business and made it that much harder. Not to get into the politics of it; But **I've** spoken to owners with deleted emissions that will have lower NOx level reading at emission check stations than the motors that have all the emissions gear on it. 🐦😄

Then, when a truck does a forced regen because the **DPF** is **clogged** up, look at all the smoke it puts in the air. It may not put out as much NOx **along the way**, but it sure does let it all out in **HIGH** concentrations at once. As an owner, you have to take special precautions to make sure these emission systems don't put you into a financial ruin. 🆗

I'm not going to get into the science of the **SCR** and **DEF**, because I don't know enough about it by experience…. I've never owned a 2012+ truck, but basically, the system uses **DEF** fluid to react with **NOx** (nitrogen oxide) to convert exhaust into nitrogen, water, and CO2. 📑

Let's talk about ways to **stay ahead** of <u>emission issues</u>.

If I owned an emissions truck, I would do an **EGR** tune up once a year or once every year and a half to 2 years tops. <u>(1) ISX EGR Tuneup 1 6 - YouTube</u> .

RAWZE IS THE <u>INVENTOR</u> OF THE EGR TUNE UP. HE IS THE MAN! A LOT OF US WOULD HAVE BEEN OUT OF BUSINESS IF IT WASN'T FOR HIM. HE'S A LEGEND! 🙌

I've had the honor of meeting **Rawze** in person multiple times, and he's is cool, smart, real, family oriented, and clever Sir! We ate falafels' and had a time, as I got schooled and a hand up….. He is talented in many different niche's in life. Give thanks 4 **Rawze** 🙏😊

To do the whole tune up costs about $**300** or so. By doing this **EGR** tune up often, you keep the emission <u>demons</u> at bay and away... The **EGR** tune-up focuses on getting **soot** out of the **intake manifold**, **venturi pipe**, **venturi mixing pipe** and the **exhaust side cross-over tubes**. It focuses on changing the **Intake Manifold Air Pressure sensor**, the **EGR differential pressure sensor**, and the **EGR temp sensor**. These sensors get carbon packed by soot and cannot read correctly.

If these sensors don't read right, you can start to get and experience issues from clogged **DPF's**, false alarm bad turbos, or even get an actual bad turbo if sensors or a key sensor has been allowing the turbo to over-spool. 📢

Every **250k** miles or so, it is **good** to clean off the tip sprayer, or to change out the Aftertreatment Injector. It's a tricky DIY, you have to drain the coolant and etc but is possible. It's not very labor intensive of a job in a shop to outsource. 🚚 the doser valve is what keeps the diesel fuel spraying to the DPF to burn for the soot… when the tip of this sprayer gets packed or doesn't perform well, it'll stop up the emission chain from not allowing the dpf can to burn right…

Every **600k** miles or so the **Exhaust Backpressure sensor** can start to not read right. It costs around $**200** and can be changed with simple hand tools, a deep socket. If you are a new owner to an emissions truck, that's ok, but do an **EGR** tune up right away please! **Change** out this Exhaust Backpressure sensor right away for good measure and peace of mind. ✔

There is a **DPF differential pressure** down on the **DPF** itself, and also an **inlet temperature sensor** on the **DPF / DOC** area. These two sensors are good to change right away if you're a new owner to your truck, then from that point on, I would change these sensors out every **200k** miles or so. These sensors are fairly easy to change and can be changed with basic hand tools. 🛠

The **SCR** system can be a tricky one too. But since I haven't owned the **2012** or newer truck I would suggest making an account at Rawze.com: Rawze's ISX Technical Discussion and more and at TruckersReport.com Trucking Forum | #1 CDL Truck Driver Message Board (thetruckersreport.com) . But I **assume**, the same precautions need to be made. **Change the sensors out** that are **DEF** and **SCR** related every year or two. If you just got your truck, consider changing these sensors for good measure. I would look into the websites above and study your unique **SCR** and **DEF** system. Study what you need to do **preventively** to stay ahead of unnecessary breakdowns. 🚚

It may sound like overboard to change these sensors every year or two, but in the long run, you are playing a **very** important **proactive** part in keeping your emission issues away and your motor running cleanly and efficient as possible. The $**500** to $**1000** spent in parts every year or two will pay off if you even prevent **only** one emission breakdown; Especially if there was a tow truck involved. It's always good to be proactive, especially if you have an emissions motor. 🔒

IF YOU OWN ONE OF AN EMISSION MOTOR, SERIOUSLY CONSIDER BUYING AND INSTALLING A HIGH QUALITY BY-PASS FILTER SUCH AS THE BMK30 SETUP AMSOIL SELLS. Heavy-Duty Bypass System BMK30 - AMSOIL . ✔

THIS WILL HELP **DRASTICALLY** CUT DOWN THE AMOUNT OF SOOT IN YOUR OIL. THE FILTER LAST into the **80K** MILE RANGE. YOU MAY NEED SOME HELP GETTING THIS INSTALLED AS IT USUALLY REQUIRES SOME FRAME HOLE DRILLING AND PLUGGING INTO THE OIL PAN. BUT THIS **BY-PASS FILTER** WOULD BE A MUST FOR ME IF I WAS RUNNING AN **EMISSIONS** MOTOR. I HAD ONE INSTALLED ON MY PETERBILT AND IT HELPED A LOT. MANY OWNERS HAVE PROVED THIS BY GETTING repeat OIL ANYALISIS DONE. 🔑

If you own a **2012** + Cummins **ISX** motor (**2012 – 2017**), the models right before the **X15 (2018+)** → Be very cautious of the **high-pressure fuel pump**. This pump has **ceramic** plungers that operate under **VERY** high pressure. This high pressure actually <u>does</u> help with burning **less** fuel **but** these plungers <u>can and will break</u>. When the plunger **breaks**, <u>tiny pieces of ceramic</u> get put into the oil. Once the pieces are in the oil, the motor is basically over with. The pieces can get into every small galley way and **scar** up cams, crank, bearings and more and etc. The pieces can get lodged in quickly moving parts like valves. ✖

If you own a **CM2250** or **CM2350 ISX** motor, make sure to change this pump out or get it rebuilt with the upgraded <u>steel plungers</u> every **250k** to **300k**. Rebuild it at a place that knows what they're doing like Haggai Automotive & Diesel in Griffin, GA. If you are the **new** owner of a truck with a **CM2250** or **CM2350**, <u>consider upgrading the fuel pump to steel plungers asap</u> because you **may** be on borrowed time already. Once this fuel pump blows it plungers, there's really no hope for that motor. You can't just rebuild it so easy; you have to make sure **EVERY** bit of ceramic is flushed out of **EVERY** oil passage-way. This is **almost** <u>impossible</u> to do or guarantee; That would mean taking whole block out, completely disassemble it, and submerge it in some steam cleaning of some kind and put it back together with all new parts that oil runs through and hope the best. At this point your better **off** getting a whole new crate motor. **BUT NOW THAT YOU KNOW**, jif you have this motor take precaution and stay ahead of this well-known issue. 🚛or don't buy this motor

A STRONG TIP IS: Don't shut your motor off <u>right away</u> after you've been driving at highway speed. You'll see it all the time… A driver or owner will go to the fuel pump straight after coming off the interstate and shut their motor **right down as soon as they stop**. Let me tell you what's happening at this point, the turbo is **PIPING** hot and needs coolant to cool it down. ☃

What happens when you power the motor down? You **stop** coolant flow to the turbo. The turbos' lifespan gets shortened more and more overtime if this happens too often. **Sure**, you might pull up to a guard shack and the guard says "shut your truck off" (as if he's the one paying the bills!), and you shut your truck off. <u>Doing this from time to time</u> is **not** that big of a deal, but having the habit of shutting your truck right off is not a good habit. **Please** wait for about **5** minutes **before** <u>you decide to power down your motor</u>. Give your turbo and everything else some time to cool off. ☃

   Just as important, make sure to **warm** up your motor before starting off for the day 🌀. **15** minutes or so is good. When you jump out onto the interstate to start your day off, <u>ease up to full speed also</u>. **Just** like the motor needing to be warmed up, the differential oil needs a warm up **time** as well. **So**, just take your time getting onto the interstate if you're coming off a 10-hour break. 🔑…

When you make repairs yourself, make sure to do it with good quality control… **Don't** take the half done and barely done route when possible. This means using **high quality** electrical tape and using plenty of it on electric work.

This means using **wire loom** to <u>protect wires</u>. This means using **zip ties** to keep wires from rubbing around on stuff. This means making sure every nut and bolt is tight when you do the repair. This means making sure specs of dirt don't get **into** your fuel or oil when changing filters when changing them.

This means fixing things even when you don't want to. This **means** making sure clamps aren't too tight or too loose. (always use smooth inside clamps when possible, they lower the chance of digging into the coolant hose and creating a leak) 🔧

This means overall integrity. If you get that feeling inside that you should probably do it better, or re-do something, then **you** should probably do it!

Your gut feeling **is** more than likely right. You want to **get** things done right **the first time**. If you do it right the first **you** dramatically lower your chances of having to redo with that same issue any time soon. This is also what being a **man** and **grown up** is about, just doing things right the first time around. **Plus**, this is your business, you shouldn't want to do half done jobs on yourself. ✔

This is also **true** when you pay someone to work on your truck. Keep your presence **felt** when they are working on it, but go behind his work before you leave and make sure everything's **right**. Make sure the wires are not zip tied to tight and that they are zip tied out of the way. Make sure the wires are **covered** and not resting on top of something hot that will **eventually burn through the wire**. Make **sure** the part you paid for is now on the truck. Make sure the belts are tight. Make sure the new part is completely bolted down right. If there is a certain procedure that needs to be done, make sure they call you in to witness the important part (something like torqueing down head bolts). 🤚

I will keep on saying this but THIS IS YOUR SHOW, YOU'RE THE BOSS, you make sure things are done right. ✔

And if you don't know what right is, ask around and do your research until you do! This book **Heavy Duty Truck Systems** by Sean Bennett https://amzn.to/36l0JQc is a great start to learning part names and functions. It's actually a book still used in some colleges to train new mechanics. I keep one of these in a hardback copy in my truck along with my Cummins Books. <u>Do yourself the favor and invest into knowing the particulars in your business</u>. The **more** you know, the **less** people can fool you, the **more** people will respect you, and the **more** you can do on your own. 😁

     Preventive maintenance is almost always going to be better than just waiting until you have issues. Many solo owner-operators think **preventative** maintenance only means changing your **oil** and **greasing** your truck. **Yes**, this is <u>preventative</u> maintenance but it doesn't go far enough. People that are successful out here stay on top of their maintenance. They look for little things before it turns big. They **know** when certain parts are getting close to expiring and they change them out before a breakdown is to occur. **10** years + in business, and I've **NEVER** been hooked to a tow truck. A lot of this has to do with my **intense** preventative maintenance, my **driving** habits, and by keeping **many** tools and parts with me on my truck. 🔧 🔩 ⚙️

Here's a list of basic things you can do or have done to stay ahead of maintenance. This list doesn't include things like buying new parts in advance or buying a new set of batteries every **3** years or so; But the **more** experience you get, the more you'll start to know the <u>expiration</u> date on parts.

    1. Change your oil every **15,000** miles or longer depending on your motor setup and whether or not

you use synthetic. I change my oil every **15k** miles. I usually do it myself. ✓

2. **Stick** with the <u>same</u> brand of oil. The motor doesn't like it when you   constantly change brands of oil. It gets used to the formula and becomes accustomed to it. I personally use **Rotella** 15W-40 non-synthetic. ✓

3. Drain your air tanks down some **EVERYDAY** once you've stopped for the day. This helps get **moisture** out of the <u>air system</u>. It also can show you if your air compressor is failing and passing oil. If your air compressor is passing oil, you may get a little oil residue on your hand when draining your tanks. ✓

4. **Change** your big air filter at least **2** or **3** times a year. They are about $**50** and easy to change yourself with simple hand tools. This filter will help assure that your turbo is always bringing in clean air. ✓

5. Change your coolant filter every **50k** miles or so. This one is not super important to change right on time, but also don't go <u>too</u> long without changing it. Most setups that I've seen will have a shutoff valve that you can close in order to change the filter yourself without wasting a ton of coolant. ✓

6. If you plan to <u>park</u> your truck for more than **3 days**, make sure your tanks are at least **75%** full. If your tanks are low, <u>algae</u> can grow in your tanks. **Especially** if it's summer time and you're in a humid environment. You don't want this algae to grow in your tanks! This is bad stuff, can wreck your injectors, cause slow or no starts and can be a major pain to get out. If you do find yourself in this pickle, I recommend using this product by **FPPM** called Killem Biocide https://amzn.to/33KOYX2 . I always keep a bottle of this stuff in my truck just in case. ✔

7. **Protect** your motor by buying <u>locking fuel caps</u>. Do you know **$3** worth of sugar can destroy your **$20k** motor? All it takes is for one person to take **spite** or **revenge** on <u>you</u> for **whatever** reason and now your motor is toast. It could even just be a random act of stupidness. Protect yourself by going to your **OEM** dealer and buying locking fuel caps. They are not cheap but you'll be glad you did. The other clear advantage of course is that will help stop the theft of fuel from your tanks. ✔

8. Buy only **high quality** <u>fuel</u>. Even if you have to pay a little more. You are in this to make money, right? You're in it for the long haul, right? Then **please** don't cheap out on fuel. Don't buy that fuel from that random truck stop that looks like nobody's been there in the last 20 years just because it's a few cents cheaper! The same issue I just mentioned

above about algae is true to the big diesel **holding** tanks too. If it's not algae, other issues with the fuel can arise because the fuel is not "turning over" enough at that location. A busy truck stop constantly has new fuel coming in; This rotation of new fuel almost always makes sure there's not enough old stale fuel laying around that's prone to contamination. 🛢️

If you're an independent, get with a good fuel card with a company like **NASTC**, Home | NASTC - The National Association of Small Trucking Companies , and get your fuel for great deals at TA Petro. If you despise TA Petro for some reason, you can go with a company like **RTS**, that partners with Pilot Flying J; Though the discounts will probably not be as good. If you ever hear an ownersaying they got bad fuel, it almost always happens at these truck stops **that** don't turn over their fuel quick enough, or **just** source their fuel with less integrity. ✔️

9. Make sure to **grease** your truck often. Either pay somebody or do it yourself. I do it myself. That way I can have much more control and make sure that every grease point gets hit and it's not over greased. Greasing your truck will insure **you** everything is lubricated and parts won't wear out too fast. If you do decide to do it yourself, there's a bit of a learning curve. But **once** you find all the grease fittings, you'll start to understand your truck so much better and how it all works and how it's all connected. 🔧

It feels **great** hitting the road knowing that everything is greased and you're sure of it because you did it yourself. I recommend greasing at least once every oil change and maybe once in between oil changes if need be or you took a **lot** of home time. Make sure you get a good electric grease gun like this **Milwaukee M18 grease gun** https://amzn.to/3qt6LvG . This is the gun I have and use. It's makes doing this job so much quicker and more enjoyable. The link above is for the tool only. The **M18** series from **Milwaukee** has **MANY** great tools that all use this **M18** battery. So, it is worth it in my opinion to invest into this brand and battery. I'm a big time Milwaukee fan. Ever since they sold me a cordless impact gun that could take my lug nuts off, I was sold. I own many **Milwaukee** products now. The impact gun I mentioned also runs off the **M18** battery. The best thing to do is buy a bundle pack from home depot or somewhere that comes with two big batteries like 5.0ah and a battery charger. Then you can buy the tools by themselves at that point. ✓

10.   Make sure to **check** your oil pretty often. At least **twice** a week. If you are burning through oil quickly (more than a gallon a week), you should check it more often to make sure it's not low. When you check your oil be careful to not break of any rubber grommets into your oil (if your dipstick has a rubber grommet on it). **Make** sure to check your oil level on **flat ground**, and with a **cold motor**. This is best

done first thing in the morning if you haven't idled. If you have idled, try to wait at least 5 to 10 minutes for the remaining oil in the head to come back down into the pan for a more **accurate** reading. Be **careful** to not overfill oil either. Too much oil can cause a bearing to fail and spin. Spinning a main or rod bearing is not something you want! ✔

11.   **Don't** press your clutch in at high speed if possible! If you go down and look into your clutch inspection plate, you'll see what's called a clutch brake. It's a <u>little piece</u> that you can move and spin by hand. This clutch brake is what helps create the **friction** needed to stop the input shaft. **Well**, this shaft is spinning very fast at highway speed. There are only a few small tabs that hold the clutch brake together. If the clutch pedal is pressed down at highway speed, <u>you can snap those tabs right off</u>, and now your clutch brake is just freely spinning and not reliable enough for smooth shifting into low gears. 😶

The clutch brake is only $**50** or so, but it can be a pain in labor to change out, and if it's not a **2-piece** clutch brake it can even require the whole transmission to be pulled in order to reach it. When buying a new clutch brake during a clutch job, make sure to get a **2-piece** clutch brake, just in case you need to change it prematurely in the future. The friction plates on them can wear out over time too, and in that case, you'll have a <u>better chance</u> of **not**

having to drop the transmission to get the new clutch brake in. 😄

So, just do what you can to save yourself from the trouble of this; And make it a habit to **not** use your clutch at <u>highway speeds</u>. We all know the trick, right? Just bump the accelerator pedal a little while pushing the gear shifter towards neutral and it should pop out of gear pretty easily. **Forgot all of that "double-clutching" non sense they taught us in school**. That's the best way to overuse and tear up not only your clutch brake but your clutch itself. ✔

12.   Don't switch the **hi-lo** switch on your gear shifter from high back down to low until you've reached <u>lower than 15mph</u>. ✔

13.   Don't **lug** your motor going up hills. **AIM** to keep your **RPM's** always <u>above</u> that **1300 RPM** mark or higher. If you do drop down to 1300 or 1200 RPM's don't stay there for long, drop a gear! ✔

14.   Run an overhead valve adjustment every **200k** to **300k**. If everything is still running good and you haven't noticed an **MPG** drop, then play it by ear, maybe you don't need to do the adjustment yet. I do mine about every **300k**. Sometimes longer. There's an old wives-tale with N-14's which goes like "If it's running good, then don't adjust the valves" lol. Maybe this is said about other motors, and has it

ever been proved? I don't know. But I don't get into too much of a rush to do it unless I notice a drop in fuel mileage. ✓

15.   **Don't** use your lights if you don't have to. As soon as it gets bright enough outside, I turn my lights off. My logic behind this is, the less you use something, the longer it will last. There's no real sense in driving all day with your lights on. There's no real sense in idling all night with your marker lights on either in my opinion. The more you run your lights, the more you are using up the life span on each light. ✓

16.   Keep your **tires** <u>level with air</u>. What I mean by this is, if one tire is **100** psi, make sure the tire right next to it is within **3** psi of **100** psi. If your tires are more than **3** to **5** psi in difference from each other, they can start to create irregular grove patterns that will be almost impossible to stop. I suggest eventually getting a digital air pressure system like **TST** Truck's brand. <u>507 Series 6 RV Cap Sensor TPMS System Grayscale Display and Repeater (tsttruck.com)</u> . I have a YouTube video speaking about TST Truck tire sensors in detail <u>WHY I LOVE TST TIRE PRESSURE SENSORS IN MY TRUCKING BUSINESS!! - YouTube</u> .

These sensors will really up your game when it comes to staying on top of your tire pressures and doing quickly! The whole system cost me about

$1000. That's because I eventually got a pressure sensor for all **18** of my tires. Don't overlook the importance of keeping your tire pressures right. Tires can **get** <u>expensive</u> quick if you don't stay on top of it. **Also**, be very mindful of the big temperature changes when we go into summer or go into winter. When winter comes, the air pressure in your tires decrease. In summer time your air pressure will increase. If your tire is **100 PSI** cold in the summer time, be mindful that in the winter time that same tire will probably decrease to about **90 PSI**. In the winter time I almost always end up adding about **10** PSI in all my tires. And when mid spring and summer comes, I'll have to let those **10** PSIs back out. ✔

17.   You want to keep an **eye** on your shocks. Remember, shocks are what keeps your cab suspension and overall suspension cushioned from heavy vibration. This **cushion** helps to protect everything from your interior, to the parts on your motor. I change my shocks out every couple of years, but I only drive about **50k** miles a year. <u>So</u>, make sure to check the manufacturer recommendation for when to change your shocks. They should have some type of mile limit range on them. Aim to change them before that time is up. With a good impact gun like the Milwaukee M18 ½ 2767-20 <u>https://amzn.to/2JvnxKa</u> , doing shocks is a **breeze**. ✔

18.   I don't mean disrespect by this one, but don't drive low on fluids! Coolant or oil. 😁✓

19.   Make sure to change your **air dryer filter** once or twice a year. If you find that your air compressor is passing a little bit of oil, it will collect in this filter, and in this case, change your filter more often, maybe once every 3 months or so. I usually change mine out twice a year. It's about $**50** and with the right filter wrench only takes 5 minutes or so to change. Changing this filter will help ensure your air system is being filtered right and **excess** moisture is being captured and discharged ✓

20.   **Batteries**. Make sure the nuts that hold down your battery cables are tight. If you ever have a moment when your truck won't try to crank, make sure your battery cables are tight down to your batteries. If these cables get loose, they can **prevent** your truck from starting. This again only requires simple hand tools. Also make sure that inside your battery box, that the cables inside your box aren't **fraying** or **rubbing** against anything that will cut into the wire and cause a short of some kind. Be careful of course! Electricity can be dangerous if you don't take the necessary precautions 👍✓

21.   **Starter**. Maybe twice a year you should disconnect the connections to your starter and

clean them. First, disconnect the main positive or ground form your batteries, this will **ensure** there's no active current or electricity going to your starter. **Then** disconnect just the positive leads on your starter. Clean the wire terminals really good with a wire brush and some electrical cleaner in can. **Multi-purpose** electrical cleaner like Truck Lite Multi-Purpose spray works really great for this https://amzn.to/3lNGzYZ . Make sure to clean it very well. Knock off any corrosion with the wire brush. Clean it **further** with the spray. And put some type of sealant on it for further protection. The Truck Lite brand is a good **2** in **1** because it helps with the cleaning and will also act as a barrier from further corrosion.

Corrosion is one thing that will completely tear up a wire and therefore tear up an electrical system. If the corrosion is bad enough, the truck won't even start because there's too much resistance in the wire that signals power to the ecm. This is especially true in a Cummins motor because the **ecm** is **powered** directly from a cable that comes from the battery. If this wire is corroded all the way through from winter time road chemicals and snow, the truck will not start. You will have to run a new cable from the battery and splice it into the **OEM** harness that goes to the ECM.

After you clean the positive side, put those cables back onto the starter, then take off the negative side and clean those. The reason we clean them one at a time is so that everything gets put back together right. If you take the positive and negative wires off at the **same** time, there's a chance you might make a mistake when hooking it all back up; Unless you develop a method like zip tying the positive and negative leads separate with different color zip ties. But just skip all that drama by doing the negative and positive one at a time. 😁

Then after you clean the positive and negative, make sure to clean the big main ground cable from the starter to the frame rail. This is a **VERY** important ground on every truck. Clean the wire terminal ends very good with a wire brush and the above-mentioned chemicals or a good alternative. **IF** you ever have any serious electrical issues and you think it might be grounding related, just go ahead and replace this entire cable with a new one. They are like **$25** or so, but **VERY** important to how your whole electrical system works. I've had an electrical issue before that by changing this main grounding cable fixed the issue right away. It's a very important grounding cable. **Clean** it good and keep an eye on it. If you ever have electrical issues, don't count this cable out for inspection or replacement. ✔

22.   Keep a **spare** to every light on your truck and trailer. That way, if you have a light out, you can change it quick, fast, and in a hurry to avoid issues with DOT. ✔

23.   Check for wheel seal leaks at least once a leak. This is one reason why I carry a creeper in my truck. I got a cool red creeper from harbor freight for like **$30** that does well! 250 lb. Capacity Heavy Duty Creeper With Adjustable Headrest (harborfreight.com) . The **creeper** will allow you to roll right under and roll back out while staying clean for the most part. If a wheel seal leak is bad enough, usually your abs light will come on. But at that point it's probably real bad and out of oil. If a torque nut / jam nut is not installed right, it may begin to back off, causing the wheel end to get loose. 😨

When this wheel end gets loose it should throw an abs light because of the "**air gap**" between the tone ring and the abs sensor. You can see for reference in this video I made (1) HOW TO: SEMI TRUCK ABS SENSOR - YouTube at the **10** minute mark.

To check the wheel seal, shine a flash light **beyond** the brake pad and **at the** wheel seal / tone ring area. You can get a good visual of the tone ring in my above video. If this area is wet with oil, your wheel seal is not sealing. This is can very serious. I never take wheel seal leaks lightly. If your hub loses all of its oil, the wheel bearings will more than likely fail and come disassembled, then at that point, your hub that holds your wheels can come straight off the spindle and run away, start a fire and all that good stuff. **BE CAREFUL WITH WHEEL SEALS**. Do what you can to get familiar with the torque procedures so you can <u>observe</u> the mechanic you pay to put the wheel seal on. ⚒

Observe to make sure they are "<u>going by the book</u>" when it comes to torqueing down, backing back, re-torqueing down and etc. There's a couple of different torque nuts available and they have different torque procedures. I've been using the ProTorque Nut with the orange clip that holds the torque in place. They have worked very good for me.

ONE <u>VERY</u> OBVIOUS WAY TO KNOW YOUR WHEEL SEAL IS BAD IS IF YOU HAVE OIL ALL OVER YOUR BRAKE PADS. ✓

This is a "tell-tale" sign that your wheel seal has failed. Get it into a shop **ASAP**. A TA Petro or a Loves will be fine. They know how to do wheel seals. ✓

24.   **Spindles**. Just to add to the wheel seal information, your spindle is the end piece that your hub slides onto. This is what they call a **wheel-end** <u>assembly</u>. You got the <u>spindle</u>, which holds the <u>hub</u>. And the <u>hub</u> which holds your <u>brake</u> <u>drum</u>, <u>rim</u> and <u>tires</u>. The **spindle** has **threads** at the end of it, and this is where the hub gets **secured** to the **spindle** by a **torque nut**. ⚒

Inside the **hub** is where the **wheel bearings** are. The **wheel bearings** are what allows the wheels to spin freely on the spindle. The **wheel seal** is what holds the **oil** inside the hub. The **seal** creates a closed in space between the **seal** and the **spindle** to the other wall of the hub. Lubricating the **wheel bearings** is the main purpose of having a **wheel seal** and oil in the **hub**. If the **spindle** gets worn down over time from different conditions like regular wear, overloading, low oil and etc, it may get to a point where it won't **allow** a **wheel seal** to seal properly, therefore always leaking oil. 🔧

At this point you will need who's called the **spindle doctor**. Each state **only** has a few licensed spindle doctors. It may take days, or it might only take hours to get one to come to you; It just depends on the spindle doctor's workload. The cost of doing a spindle will be about **$1400**. That's how much I paid on my last one. The whole spindle gets cut off, and a brand new one gets welded on. 🔧

Be careful though, some places might try to hustle you into getting a new spindle put on when you don't really need it. Ask to inspect the spindle yourself. At the **lip** of the **spindle** where the **seal closes**, **check it** for smoothness. The **spindle** it's self should be very smooth with no knicks, scratches or purple'ish heat discoloration. **One nick**, if deep enough, can allow oil to get past the seal. But if you don't see anything to bad, you may be able to talk the mechanic into buffing / sanding the spindle down a little bit with a drill attachment that buffs with low grit or with an Emory cloth. ✔️

Then you can put on what's called a **2-piece seal** on to help cover any blemishes on the spindle and extend its life for a while. Here's a good video on YouTube by **Timken** to get a good visual of what the spindle and wear ring of a 2-piece seal looks like (2) Timken Tricks of the Trade: Removing a 2-Piece Seal Wear Ring - YouTube . The wear ring is the part of the 2 piece seal that helps compensate for **wear** on the spindle. Then the seal itself would seal onto the wear ring. Just make sure you really need a new spindle before going through that whole process of getting the spindle doctor out there. A **2-piece seal** can be an effective solution for easy to moderate wear on a spindle. ✔

25.   I mentioned this in "What Truck Should I Buy", but if you have an N-14 motor, make sure to only buy the **PX** injectors and not the **RX**. The **PX** cost a little more, but have a way better rebuild quality. ✔

26.   **Crankshaft** damper also called a harmonic balancer. This is big **counterweight** on the front of your motor. This counterweight helps to balance and dampen your motor from the activity of the crankshaft. This counter weight starts to lose its effectiveness at around **500k** to **600k** miles. It is suggested that you replace your harmonic balancer every **600k** miles or so. There is great benefit in doing so. 📢

This big weight is what keeps all your other engine components from getting shook up. This damper will help to make sure motor vibration is at a minimum and everything is running smooth as possible. I'm sure you can imagine all the parts that can begin to suffer because of **excessive** and **extreme** engine vibration. The dampers cost around $**450** to $**800** depending if what model motor and if you buy OEM or not. I've been using a damper from Vibratech for the last 3 years now. I think I paid right around $**500** for it and probably an additional $**300** or so for labor. Here's some more information from Vibratech regarding vibration dampers and how they work Vibratech TVD-Torsional Damper Design & Development .

Make sure you put a **couple** coats of paint on it first before installing. This will help make sure that it doesn't rust. I've used high quality spray paint that has primer + paint and rust protection, finished off with a clear enamel for shine and extra protection. ✓

27. Having a good electrical tool like **Power Probe 3** https://amzn.to/2VKe1Fj really helps. With **2** additional extensions https://amzn.to/39RducX you can reach **any** part of your truck or trailer. **Yes**, a multimeter is great for measuring resistance, but one thing I love about the **Power Probe 3** is that I always have a good ground when I'm checking for voltage. The reason I always have a good ground is because the **Power Probe** hooks up directly to my batteries with alligator clips. You'll see me using my **Power Probe** for testing voltage and for sending

12v to my relay to see if it would click in this video HOW TO: CUMMINS N14 STARTER REPLACEMENT + NO START RELAY FIX - YouTube at the 4 minute mark.

This tool is good to have. You can **quickly** check lights by pulling out the one that doesn't work and giving it a ground with the built-in alligator clip, then simply pressing the switch up on **Power Probe** to give it **12v** power. If the light comes on, then you know the issue is not in the light but maybe the wiring. If the light doesn't come on, you know you just got a bad light. 😁

I just used mine recently to give power to my ac blower motor. I was very close to just ordering a new blower motor because I tested for power going to the plug and there was power. **So**, I assumed my blower motor was bad. I decided to hook up to it with my **Power Probe** first and send it some power. Sure enough, the blower motor was perfect. Come to find out, I had an intermittent power supply issue because one of the pins in my 6-way jumper plug was bent and not making good contact. I fixed the pin, and good to go! **Power Probe** helped me do this. Love this tool! ✓

28. Having a good heat gun like this https://amzn.to/2JQl4ts really helps too. If it's cold and windy outside, or even just windy, it can be a real pain to **seal** heat shrink butt connectors. I had a marker light wire in a hard-to-reach area that I

had to repair in the winter time. **There** was snow and slush all under my trailer and the wind was constant. I did the repair, **now** I just had to <u>heat down the heat shrink on the butt connectors</u>. All I had was a lighter that day. The truck stop I was at in Springfield, MO did not have a butane torch or anything. After going through that struggle, I decided to always keep a butane torch and a heat gun in my truck. They are cheap and come in their own box and can be stored away easy. **Make** sure you got enough extension cords too and a way to power it like; an inverter or generator! ✔️

29.   I don't want to go **too** far off into talking about tools, because I have a **whole book** on this, but I <u>will mention</u> getting a multi-purpose oscillating tool like this one from harbor freight <u>Oscillating Multi-Tool (harborfreight.com)</u> . You can get the steel cutting attachments that will really put some work in when it comes to cutting stuck bolts off and etc in tight places. **Again**, you will need extension cords. I have a generator in a box on my truck that I use to power my home made apu but it works **PERFECT** for supplying power to my power tools as well. If you don't have a generator, you might be able to get by using a high amperage / wattage power inverter from inside your cab; Just make sure to have your truck on of course so you don't drain your batteries. 😁

As you can **see**, the list of topics when it comes to maintenance can be quite expansive. I pulled the most important topics and discussed them in detail. A lot of your success **rides** on how well you handle this day to day maintenance. ✔️

A lot of your **success** rides on how well you pick up on the techniques and procedures. A lot of your success **rides** on whether you will get up, get out, and get a little dirty for yourself. The more maintenance you do for yourself, the cheaper your overhead will be and the more profit you will show. Not only will you save money, you will do the job the right way. Having each little job done the right way is one of the biggest boosts you can give to your success. We can't be out here shucking our money to the big-time dealerships that do **low quality** work who could care less about us and our business. Take these matters into your own hands when it comes to maintenance. Learn as much as you can, **do as much as you can**. In the long run you will be proud and glad you did! 💯 🗼 💰 🤑

If you **lead** the charge long enough in your business, eventually you will break through to the other side; And then you can take 6 months off a year like I do! And or not work much in the winter conditions 😁. Or maybe you just want to stay out here and **stack as much money up as you want too**! That's perfectly cool also! I'm slightly lazy and I really value time. I love to be able to take the time off that I want while still remaining profitable and always increasing my net worth and bank account. **But I promise you this**, if I was a push over when it came to maintenance, I would not be able to afford my lifestyle.

This book of mine will help streamline you to the place mentally and physically, that most solo owner-operators will never get to. I **can** honestly say, it's not very often I come across another owner operator on the field who knows as much as I do and **can** produce the type of numbers I produce. Just saying. Take heed to this books content.

Take this information and mentality, and make it your own! ✔

Don't be afraid **to** get dirty. **Don't** wait on anyone to come **save** you. Get out here an make it happen! Keep learning. Keep growing. Increase your desire and know exactly what it is that you want. Do you want **$50k** in the bank? Well, set the goal, and everyday throughout the day, say "I will have **$50k** in the bank by **Dec 31**, I will do this by successfully delivering my customers freight, and by making smart decisions… "I feel as if I already have this money in the bank". Refer to chapter 1 "**Mentality**" when it comes to the necessary reprogramming of your subconscious mind. 😄

Be amped up! Your future is bright! If you put your foot down and continue to put the work in, it's only a matter of time until you start to break through and claim what's yours. Not to get **too** religious, but they say God blesses people. This is true. But it is also true that **God** helps those who help themselves! Take the initiative, learn the knowledge, get dirty, have the tools, have fun, take the precautions, always learn, then you can begin to experience success for yourself! 🔒

The next chapter is "**Technology**". We have <u>many</u> digital tools that our trucking elders never got to have. We have google maps, we have apps to find truck stops, we can see what weigh stations are open, we check weather and wind direction, we can book loads without dispatchers, we bill our customers without sending physical BOL's, and much more. Let's take journey **into** the <u>exact technology</u> that I use in my day-to-day operations! Some of these apps you may recognize like truckers path of course, but the other apps are a combination of ones that I've collected over the years and have found to be the best for what I do. None-the-less, **check it out** and <u>see if you find something new to use</u>! Let's continue! 🚚🚚

CHAPTER 13: TECHNOLOGY

Let's talk about technology. **Technology** has improved a lot even in the 10 years that I was in the trucking business. From load boards to weather apps, we have quite a bit. I will <u>share</u> with you the apps and technology that I use on a daily basis. The apps that I'm about to share are in no particular order.

It's important to utilize the technology we have in front of us in order to run the most efficient business possible. ✔️

1. I think it's **always** important to be a member of <u>TruckersReport.com Trucking Forum | #1 CDL Truck Driver Message Board (thetruckersreport.com)</u> . This is pretty much the number one forum for all truck drivers. **There** are <u>successful</u> owner operators and fleet

owners who frequent this forum. There are sections for mechanics, owner operators, and more. This website has been a **valuable** resource for me over the years. Many times, we don't have that super trucker uncle to ask our questions to, so Truckers Report helps to fill that void by connecting truck drivers of all backgrounds together.

If you have a **mechanical** question, ask it here. If you have a question about a company that you're looking to lease onto, ask it here. Let me give you one tip of advice. The people on this website may not be as friendly as me. When you ask **your** questions, make sure that you do some research first. There's a search bar on the website where you can type in topics and keywords to pull up all previous conversations related to what you typed in. It's kind of a trucker thing that nobody wants to give away their hard-earned information to quickly or to easily. You'll understand too one day; It was hard to get to where you are, and you may feel compelled to not give away your information so easily either.

So, with that in mind, just be **respectful** of other people's time and make sure your ask your question in a respectful way if you actually want a good answer in return! A lot of the guys on here are willing to help, but they will not "spoon-feed" you and make it too easy. Just ask your question right, in a knowledgeable and respectful way, and you should get a decent reply. I have got a **TON** of help on here over the years. Find me on here, my handle is @ANDREWS_METHOD.

2. Rawze.com: Rawze's ISX Technical Discussion and more is another **great** place to be a member, especially if you have a Cummins ISX motor. The guys on **rawze.com** are way more experienced for the most part when it comes to technical mechanics. These **guys** can fix anything! These are the type of guys you want to have on your team! **Go** in there, watch, and show some respect. You have to request an invite to be a member. Once welcomed on, remember, **Rawze** owns the server and website, and will kick somebody off his site quick if their being rude and disrespectful.

If you have a mechanical issue, search around on his site to see if there's an answer. If not, then **present** your question in a clear way; Show that you already took the initiative to fix it, show pictures, and be thankful for the people who take the time out to respond. You're dealing with a lot of **experts** on this website, so tread lightly and don't ruin your reputation.

They understand if you're a new owner operator learning the business but they don't always take kindly to people who post a lot, "crying wolf" for every little problem they got. My username on here is **Kid Rock**. This is a great place to be as an owner operator.

On your free time, develop a habit of checking places like rawze.com for info. ✓

Treat it like the news. Watch what other people **are** talking about and what they're going through. This is <u>another form</u> of **research** and **preventive maintenance**. The more you learn about potential issues and how other people resolve them, the more prepared you will be to handle issues of your own. 🔒

3. <u>Truckstop.com – Load Board and Freight Management</u> is my go-to load board. I will talk about them further in "How I Book My Freight". But I really **love** truckstop.com. I first met them at the truck show in Dallas, TX back in 2016. I was **really** impressed with their booth and presentation. They are by far <u>the best</u> in my opinion; Especially when it comes to flat bed and step deck freight. I have a **subscription** to **DAT** as well, and I find that there are way more loads with posted rates on truckstop.com. I like this a lot, because it <u>speeds</u> up my **booking** process; And gives me a better idea of what a broker is working with as far as money on load. I either agree to the posted rate, or use their base rate as negotiations and ask for a couple hundred dollars more. 🚚

I like their **user interface** <u>better</u> than DAT. I use the website version on safari instead of the app version. I pay **$150 a month for the PRO VERSION**. If you're not using direct customers, you need the Pro version in my opinion. How else will you compete with somebody like me, who always has the newest iPhone with the fastest connection running live load board updates on truckstop.com? We'll talk more about all of that in a few! 💰📢

4. **DAT** is basically the most popular, well known public load board. I like to use **DAT** for certain things, but mainly, I only use **DAT** <u>in a pinch</u>. I don't like their app, and their desktop page doesn't work well on mobile. I have noticed, it seems that **DAT** will have more posted loads than truckstop.com, especially in dead areas like <u>West Texas</u> and **etc**. **DAT** may be better for van and reefer freight; Many guys who pull those types of trailers tend to speak highly of **DAT**. **DAT** is also more of a "wild wild west", no posted rate, come and negotiate your deal type of place. 🖼️

I have no problem, and actually **enjoy** to make great deals, but there are many days that I would rather skip the tango of phone calls and just **book on sight** <u>with a posted rate that I agree to</u>. To each his own, we'll discuss way further in "How I Book My Freight". I do use **DAT** to find **LTL** (partial) loads sometimes. <u>Sometimes</u> there will be posting on **DAT** that's not on truckstop.com, it only takes **one good** load per year that wasn't on your main load board, and the subscription has paid itself off for the year. 🚚

5. **Broker specific load boards**. If you have your own authority, you'll notice that brokerages have their own load boards. Many of them aren't worth the time but there are a few that I will keep on my iPhone's homepage. <u>Usually</u>, the freight that gets posted on

these boards are the super heavy and super cheap general commodity freight like lumber, rebar and etc. But every now and then you might **find** a decent load in a pinch, especially in a dead area. The only ones I really use at this point is **ATS** logistics Brokered Loads - Available Load List . And JB Hunts Carrier 360 app Carrier 360 (jbhunt.com)

This link is just an info link, but if you search **JB Hunt carrier 360** on your app store, you'll see the app. JB Hunt requires **6** months active authority give or take to do business with them. I also have the **Uber Freight** and **Convoy** app which I don't use very much since they're not too much into flatbed yet. But I have heard a lot of success stories on the van and reefer side when it comes to **Convoy** and **Uber freight**. ✓

6. **Google Maps**. This is a given of course but I must put it on my list! Google Maps is the superior map app in my opinion. I use Google Maps often to double check my GPS, to **study** delivery location the night before delivery and etc. If I'm working on a deal and the delivery is in New York City or some other tricky major city to deliver to, I **ask** the broker for the delivery address and I **plug** it into to Google Maps to see how far off the interstate is it. I use the data I collect by viewing the maps in Google Maps to decide if I want to do the load or not, and how much I'll charge if I decide to do the load. 🚚

7. I prefer **Gmail** for all things email related. Google just kind of has the market cornered when it comes to email. Their **Gmail** app is the most responsive and

quickest of all email apps that I've used over the years. You'll need a good email app especially if you're under your own authority. ✔️

8. The KeepTruckin | Fleet Management Software, ELD, Dash Cams, GPS app. I eventually got the **Keep Truckin ELD** movement. I was resistant at first, I was on **VDO Road log** and eventually **VDO** decided to close down their operation. That only left Omnitracs, Keep Truckin, and a couple of other not so appealing brands. I had **experience** with Qualcomm Omnitracs at Landstar and I wasn't impressed. The hardware would freeze often and the system was too bulky in my opinion. Maybe I just had an older model and now they are much better. 👻

But, I decided to go with Keep Truckin and I've been impressed! They have a great user interface, they remind you to log inspections, they let you see your full **14**-hour clock and drive time while you're driving, checking your recap hours is **easy** to see, it remembers your on-duty notations like "fueling", you can log yourself off-duty if you go into a restaurant for lunch and forget to log off duty and etc.

Overall, I'm very impressed with the system and I'm very surprised that I actually endorse a cell phone based **ELD**! They also have it set up very easy to interface with state police if they request access to your logs. They have an online portal that makes it **VERY** easy to run reports on all the miles traveled in each state. This comes in handy when it's time to file your **IFTA** reports If you do them yourself. ✔️

9. **The Weather Channel app**. The weather channel app
    has got really advertised on lately and it's probably
    better to just buy an annual subscription, but the
    weather channel app is still the classic for looking a
    Doppler radar and wind direction. As <u>owner operators</u>
    and truck drivers in general, it's really important we
    keep up with the weather in certain times of the year
    like winter. ❄

If you book your own freight, you should be using this app or
a similar one to determine if certain loads **are** <u>worth taking in
the winter</u>.

 **If the blizzard is coming through and you have the
choice to go in another direction, it might be wise to just
avoid the whole storm all together and not book the load**.
✓

One thing I **like** the weather channel app for is telling wind
direction. Sometimes I'm going up the road and I feel like I'm
mashing the accelerator pedal down further than normal. I
feel as if **there's** some extra friction going on. I check my app
to see if I'm driving into a head wind; And sure enough,
almost **every** time I get that feeling, I'm driving straight into
some wind. If you're driving east on I-20 and the app say
winds are W **10mph**. Then you got winds <u>from the east
blowing</u> west at **10** mph. That means you have an additional
10mph worth of force working against you. It's good to know

these things so you know there's no real issue, it's just the wind pushing against you a bit.

10.   **NASTC** app. I have the **NASTC** app on my phone because that's who I am partnered up with as my fuel card provider. Their app shows all the **NASTC** <u>fuel stops</u> and what the **current** price is after our member discount. It has some other nice features like a route planner and direct phone numbers to all the NASTC services.

11.   <u>Find Truck Service | Semi Towing, Truck Repair, Truck Tires, Truck Parts</u> is another **great** app to have on your phone. They have a **HUGE** directory of repair shops, mobile repair shops, part stores and more. These are my go-to guys when it comes to looking for independent shops when on the road. Google maps just can't give the results that **Find Truck Service** <u>can</u>. I met these guys also at the Dallas, TX truck show. Do yourself a favor, and keep this app download in your phone just in case.

12.   **QuickBooks** is another app I keep on all my devices. I will talk about this later in "How I Bill my Customers", but this is the app I do all my direct invoicing and billing on. I really **like** their interface, their accounts receivable, and the professional look <u>it gives my invoices</u>. Their fee is **$10** a month, which in my opinion is a great deal.

13.   **Macropoint**. You might as well download Macropoint. There will be brokerages along the way that **prefer** to track their loads with Macropoint. It is just an app that takes your location data and gives it to the brokerage **so** that they can have a <u>live update</u> of your progress **so** that they can update their customers and etc. 😶😁🚚🚛

14.   **Google Street View**. I don't use this app often, but I will use it to get a 3d view of a pick up or delivery in a busy city. Let's say I have a pickup in <u>Baltimore</u>. I run the address in **Google Maps** and I see that the address is right in the middle of downtown. If I'm not familiar with the area, I may use Google Street View to get a better look at what I'm getting into, where's the loading dock and etc. ✔️

15.   Tiny Scanner. <u>Tiny Scanner - PDF Scanner App - Apps on Google Play</u> . I use Apple products, but here's the link to Tiny Scanner on google play. I use this **app** the most on <u>my iPad pro</u>. I like this app for making **PDF** files out of pictures. I use this app to **take** pictures of my <u>Bill of Lading's</u>; I turn them into good **PDF** files, I then save them to "**files**" on my iCloud, then in **QuickBooks** app, I can easily attach them to my invoice. I've been using this program for years! I use the **$5** version.

16.   **YouTube app**. This is self-explanatory, but the YouTube app is a great place to get help on repairs

and learn new tips and tricks about business. You can even **subscribe** to me on there!

ANDREWS METHOD - YouTube

17. <u>TruckSmart® Mobile App - Make life on the road easier | TravelCenters of America (ta-petro.com)</u> This is the app for TA Petro. I don't use this app very often, but I **use** it to **reserve** spots at TA Petro. It's the fastest and most direct way to check availability and book reserved spots at their truck stops.

18. <u>Trucker Tools: Digital Load Tracking & Freight Matching</u> is another digital load **tracking** platform like **Macropoint**. You might as well have this downloaded too in case your certain customer uses this platform to track their loads.

19. <u>MyRadar | Keeping You Ahead of the Storm</u> . I really enjoy using this map for getting free, **visual** <u>wind direction</u> radar activity. Once you download the app, you can go into your settings and select to see the **wind direction**. Once you enable wind direction, you can literally see the wind on their radar! This is a <u>really cool tool</u> when it comes to understanding the wind reality in your situation. Like just mentioned, sometimes it feels like a brake is dragging, or that you're pushing the pedal down too hard, when really, it's just the wind. **This** app really helps get to the bottom of those "<u>is it the wind or is it me</u>" feelings.

SUMMARY: ✔️

For years I've ran the same strategy when it **comes** to phones. I always get the new iPhone, but sometimes I'll skip a new release and go for the next one. I think this is more important to do when **you're** booking your own freight. When you're booking your own freight, you need to have the fastest and best internet speed so that **YOU** will be the first to see the load when it pops up. Time is critical when it comes to good freight, especially **great** freight with posted rates. Having the ability to see your freight pop up 30 seconds, even 15 seconds faster is a **HUGE** advantage. It gives you more time to read the load details and make a decision. It gives you more of a lead time to strike; Especially if you don't need to read the load details and will ask for them once on the phone call. 💰🚛💨

If you **have** your own authority, I really suggest you get an **iPad Pro** with its own cell signal under your cell phone plan! I like the one with the biggest screen. It's a tad expensive but is really a **powerhouse** when it comes to rate sheets, billing, and file management. I guess any tablet would work but the **iPad Pro** is a top-notch and flexible product in my opinion. 🔒

Once you get the **iPad Pro**, make sure to get an **Apple Pencil** to go along with it https://amzn.to/3owEWRr or the original which is still good https://amzn.to/3qAznDb . I'd say that **brokerages** are about **50 / 50** when it comes to needing a real signature for rate sheets. Many brokerages have moved to a digital signature for rate sheets which is nice too. But for all other brokerages, its super good to have the **iPad Pro** and the **Apple Pencil** to go along with it. It's like having a digital sheet of paper in front of you that you can sign.

There are brokerages that will still send you **20-page carrier packs** that require a <u>hand written response</u>. That's where the iPad Pro and Apple Pencil really shines! (**THANK ME LATER** 😄)

If you have your own authority; Another element to the iPad pro is, through the use of Tiny Scanner is, you can digitally **collect** all your **important** information for the year such as <u>Insurance Certificate, Authority, a pre-filled W-9,</u> <u>Occupational accident insurance or workman's comp proof,</u> <u>your medical certificate, etc</u>.

You can have all of these documents saved in "Files". Once in Files, you can put them into a group. ✔️

This makes filling out carrier packets much <u>quicker and</u> <u>convenient</u>. All the papers they are going to request (minus being a certificate holder) will pretty much be in this **group** you created. With this group, you can easily access them and attach them to an email, <u>all within your iPad</u>. I will cover this in more detail in "**Carrier Packs**". 🚛

The **iPad Pro** in combination with the Tiny Scanner app is a great combo for creating <u>crystal clear</u> **PDF's** for billing your customers or sending in to a factoring company. **Yes**, there are other ways to do this, but this is my preferred route. I will discuss this further "How I Bill my Customers"!

These are the exact set ups that I have and use over the road! I love the flexibility of an iPad Pro with its own cell signal. What's cool about the "**Files**" app too is; Everything that you save to files on your iPad can be pulled up in your iPhone and vice versa. This is a **handy** addition to have. **Say** you're walking around at a shopping mall, or inside Walmart, and a customer calls requesting a certificate of some kind or a **BOL**. Now you **don't** have to rush back to your truck to access it. All you have to do is pull up "**Files**" and there it is, at that point you just find the file and select to email it to your customer. 🏍

Whatever technology you decide to use, **just make sure it works**. Make sure that its efficient. The technology a solo owner-operator with his own authority needs is a little different than the technology an owner operator leased to a company needs. None the less, the set of apps I recommended are good regardless of your operation (minus **QuickBooks** and **NASTC** and other **authority specific** apps). Make sure that you're using technology that makes your life easier and your business run **more** efficient and look more professional. ✓

Some guys like **Excel** spreadsheets for tracking invoices (I do not), some guys like excel for generating invoices (I do not 😊). Some guys will try to convince you that you don't need to spend $**10** a month on **QuickBooks**. Some owner operators despise electronics and tracking, and I understand. This is where the new solo owner-operator comes in and **levels** the **playing field** with his or her understanding of technology, apps, load boards, emails, marketing, maps, and etc. 🚛🚛

Many of the **older** owner operators are behind when it comes to technology. Some are still sending in their **BOLS** through the mail, some are still using the **fax machine** for carrier packs, some are having a difficult time using load boards. **This is where you get to shine**. This stuff is easy for the most part when it comes to technology. You just have to match the technology side with the "**Get it Done Grit**" of the elders.

To "Get it Done" takes a **grit** that many young people don't seem to be equipped with. Allow yourself the room to grow. **Keep** improving. **Learn** mechanics as you go. **Collect** tools. **Learn** from the older owner operators out here. **There** are many life experience things that knowing technology will not help you on. Luckily, you're getting a ton of that life experience in this book if you really pay attention to all the little and major experiences I share with you 😄

Don't be afraid **to** learn from the older guys out here, they might need to learn what you know about **iPhones** and **iPads lol**! I refuse to struggle when it comes to this department of technology. There's **too** many tools, apps and ways to streamline the whole digital process of Trucking. I've took different strategies from different guys along the way and **made** the improvements and investments into the systems I thought would be the best. It's **pretty** hard to beat the iPhone, iPad Pro with its own cell signal, and the Apple Pencil combo, tack in all the other apps mentioned and yeah! It's hard to beat! 💯✂️🎯

If you have your own authority and don't want to spend on an **iPad Pro** set up yet, that's fine. Just keep it in mind as **you** progress. The setup will cost about $**1000** if you pay up front for it. But I'll tell you, I'm **super** pleased with my investment and the level of ease and convivence it has added to my operation!

Use my set up as a template, either copy it exactly, or take bits and pieces from it and improve it to make it perfect for you!

Just like many things I've taught on so far, technology is also **very** important! The way you choose your technology setup will play a **big** part in your ability to capitalize on loads, do paperwork, bill customers and ultimately it will play a big part in your success… It will also play a role in your overall day-to-day flow and morale. **Choose wisely**, and create an ecosystem that you like and that works great for you! ✓

In the **next** chapter I want to give you a running list of brands that I use and endorse! As you **progress** and get **more experience**, you will find the brands that you like and the ones that **work** the best for you. In the **meantime**, you will have this list of established brands that I created that have met my standard of business. **Use** this list as you grow and develop your own! Let's Continue! 💰✓👊✊

CHAPTER 14: BRANDS I ENDORSE

This chapter **will** be short and sweet. I will quickly discuss and highlight different brands and products that I endorse, used, and suggest. This is not an end all be all list, and **don't** worry if something you use is not on this list. That doesn't mean that it's not a good product, it's just not a brand or product I personally use or endorse (or maybe I just don't know about it!). And there's also the small factor that I may leave something out unintentionally. Let's go! 🚛

1. **TST Truck tire sensors**. Home (tsttruck.com) I **really** like this product and brand! I've had my sensors for about 3 years now and they are still going

strong! The sensors have saved me a lot of time and money over the years. ✔

2. **Brake Safe by SpectraProducts**. Overview — Spectra Products - Home of Brake Safe® .If you are an **OOIDA** member, make sure to let that be known at checkout and you will get a further discount. I like this product because of the accuracy and ease it brings to checking my own brake push stroke travel aka brake adjustment. It's a **great** idea and a **great** design. The components are made of high-quality material and looks great. It lets the **DOT** know you mean business when they come to check your brakes. They will be very impressed of your initiative when it comes to paying attention and **keeping** your brakes in adjustment. ✔

3. **Anti-seize cotter pin by SpectraProducts**. Overview — Spectra Products - Home of Brake Safe® . These pins are about **$5** each and can be a little tricky to put on; but man are they the better alternative to regular cotter pins! If you **are** going to being doing your own work like changing slack adjusters, you may run into a clevis pin that is **completely** seized and stuck. You have to heat it up and do who knows what to get it free. 🛠

This **product** makes sure that doesn't happen. This product allows the clevis pin to roll inside the clevis has the brakes are pressed. This makes sure that corrosion and **etc** never has a chance to pile up and bind the clevis pin to the clevis. And also, A **seized** clevis pin forces automatic slack adjusters to work harder with underperforming brake force. You don't want your slack adjusters working harder because of a seized clevis pin. The harder the slack adjuster has to work, the higher the chance the slack adjuster **will** stop performing over time. You may have to go to a third-party site like Let's Truck Store to buy these. 🚛

4. **Eco Flaps** of Brentwood, TN. EcoFlaps . These guys are the **original** real deal when it comes to aero mud flaps. Unlike the **gimmicks** and the **imitators**, Eco Flap actually is deigned to let air pass through in an intentional way. I have four of these on my flatbed trailer. I have had them for close to **5** years now. They perform great and are tough. They can handle snow and road slush **very** well and they look great. I know I give off positive impressions when other owner operators look at my trailer.

Sure, it's not the same as a fresh paint job and freshly polished wheels, but it is just another example of initiative. **Real** solo owner-operators embrace **initiative**. Just look how big and heavy flatbed mudflaps are. Have you ever tried to carry **2** flatbed mudflaps in your arms? I have when I was walking to the dumpster with my old ones. And at that point, I **realized** how heavy, bulky and how much wind they must stop when going up the road. The wind my old mudflaps would **block** is called wind drag. Every little thing that produces wind drag is slowing you down just a bit, and that requires more power from the motor which equals more fuel needed. **Eco Flaps** are the real deal and the original when it comes to aero dynamic mudflaps. Give them a go! 👍

5. **Fumoto drain valve**. Buy Fumoto® Valve Online | Replace Oil Drain Plug (fumotooildrainvalve.com) It is my understanding that these drain valves are made in Japan. They are granted "genuine parts" status in **Japan** by Toyota, Nissan, Mazda and more. I've been using one for years now. I really **love** the quality compared to other brands sold at the truck stops. The quality feels very solid and dependable. Mine has never dropped a bit of oil that I didn't direct it to. 🛠

For a **few** additional dollars you can buy a clip that keeps it locked and a hose that you can attach to the valve itself to so you can direct the flow of oil into a **5** gallon bucket or a container of your choice. In order to use the **hose**, you have to have a valve that has the hose hook up on it. That's the type that I have. 👍

I love the **flexibility** it gives me, and I've been changing my oil myself ever since I got my Fumoto drain valve on. **Another** great thing about this valve is, you don't have to deal with someone at the truck stop accidently **over torquing** your drain plug and cracking your oil pan! It's happened before, not to me but to others. I've heard stories. **Also**, if you happened to get overfilled with oil during an oil change, you can drain a little out from your **valve** so you don't spin a bearing from having too much oil. Here's a video of me changing my oil and showing my Fumoto drain valve <u>HOW I CHANGE OIL ON MY SEMI TRUCK - YouTube</u> .

6. **KeepTruckin Eld's and dash cams**. <u>KeepTruckin | Fleet Management Software, ELD, Dash Cams, GPS</u> Like I mentioned earlier, I was hesitant to partner with **KeepTruckin**, but they have really impressed me. And for the record, I'm not very easy to impress 😁. I **love** the software on the computer side, it makes getting info for **IFTA** very quick and simple. The app performs very well. I haven't had any real performance issues with the app. The app is very responsive and user friendly. I also use their **Dash Cam** as well! It seems to do very well and has already out performed previous Dash Cams that I've owned. The cost is about $**600 a year**, so about $**50** per month. My **VDO** Road-log was free after the initial purchase, but yeah, this **KeepTruckin** performs very well and is way more user friendly than my **VDO** Road-log was. As long as they keep their performance up and making the app even better, I will stick around with KeepTruckin for the long haul. 📱

7. **Truckers Path**. <u>Trucker Path | Technology Built for the Trucking Industry</u> I think we all know **Truckers Path** by now! I <u>still</u> use this app, and have been using it for years. It does a great job of finding truck stops along the way and for trip planning. The parking status feature works pretty good for **the** most part but is only as **reliable** as the information users <u>put into it</u>.

When I'm trip planning, and going to stage close to a major city, I will check the parking history to get a feel for when the average time certain truck stops fill up.
🔲

8. **Southern Tire Mart**. Main (stmtires.com) Southern Tire Mart is my **go-to** place for tires. If I can't get a southern tire mart, I <u>will</u> use TA Petro as a backup. In **my** experience, they have the best prices on the tires that I'm looking for. They have <u>very</u> reasonable mount and dismount prices and are usually very fast at getting the job done. 🚚🚚

9. **SpeedCo.** If I'm changing my oil over the road, I **prefer SpeedCo** over the rest. TA Petro is a **close** second though. I <u>used</u> to really love SpeedCo before Loves bought them out. After Loves bought them, the prices increased and the structure got more corporate. I used to be able to get in and out of SpeedCo's **fast**, and the guys always seemed to know what they were doing. When Loves bought SpeedCo, it just **seemed** to go a <u>little downhill</u> in my opinion. 😕

They are still the most premier nationwide brand to get an oil change done no doubt, but they used to be better. And maybe they will improve **more** along the way, I don't know. Maybe it's because I'm **so** used to the savings and assurance of changing my oil myself now. SpeedCo checks your differentials during your oil change, and will let you watch usually. That's one thing I've always liked about them.

If I'm paying someone to do the work, I want to watch and make sure the oil drops, and everything is done right. 😅

10.   **TA PETRO**. I definitely recommend TA Petro for fueling and parking. Their fuel has always been good for me and I **love** the environment much better at their truck stops. The parking lots are usually **much** bigger than the standard truck stops; This makes backing in so much easier and lowers the risk somebody will back into you at night. 🚛

Their truck stops tend to **attract** more <u>experienced</u> drivers and owner operators. This could be a big deal if you're <u>fixing</u> on something in their parking lot. You're **more** likely to get help; And access to tools from one of these experienced guys at a TA Petro compared to a Loves or Pilot. **Also**, if you stay the night a TA Petro, and you have an issue that morning with like a dead battery or a relay or something, you **can** just <u>walk over to the shop and get the part</u>! At most Pilots and Flying J's, you just don't have access to these types of parts. Loves is a step up of from Pilot when it comes to parts, but you still won't have access to as many parts at Loves like you would at TA Petro. 🚛🚛

11.   **TRP brand parts**. If you own a Paccar truck such as Peterbilt or Kenworth then **you** may <u>already</u> know this brand **TRP**. **TRP** makes high quality aftermarket parts for Paccar Trucks and they are sold at most dealerships, especially the Rush Truck Centers. I've never had a problem with any of the **TRP** parts that I bought over the years. ✔️

12.   **Cummins motors**. As far as motors go, my opinion is pretty biased because I've only owned Cummins motors over the years; But I would consider buying a **pre-emission Detroit** motor if I was in the market for a truck. I'm sure other motor brands are pretty great too; I just can't really endorse them because I've never owned them myself. In "Which Truck Should I Choose" motors are discussed in detail. 😄

13.   **QuickBooks**. I really love the QuickBooks platform. I will talk more about them in the chapter titled "How I Bill my Customers" ✔

14.   **Tiny Scanner**. I really like the Tiny Scanner product as mentioned in the previous chapter "Technology"! 😁

15.   **Milwaukee**. I love the Milwaukee brand of tools. They work great, look good, and feel good as far as quality goes. All my tools are not Milwaukee but my many of my important tools are. 🔧

16.   **Harbor Freight**. Harbor Freight has <u>saved</u> me so much money over the years. They have tools that are of enough quality to get the job done but at **great** prices. From wrenches to jack stands, they almost have it all when it comes to the <u>basic most used</u>

tools. I really like the harbor freight brand heat shrink butt connectors and the harbor freight brand wire loom. I've used them for years and the prices are great. 😄👍

17.   **Pittsburgh brand tools** at Harbor Freight. I still have a ton of Pittsburgh deep sockets, regular sockets, and wrenches. They are guaranteed for life, and if you happen to break one of their sockets or tools, Harbor Freight will refund you for another. This brand will help you get **your** tool collection started for cheap. Still to this day, I check Harbor Freight for certain tools depending on the job I'm doing. 🙌

18.   As far as trucks, I like the **Volvo** brand, the **Freightliner** brand, and the **International** brand with **Western Star** being a runner up. Truck brands are covered with detail in "Which Truck Should I choose" ✔

19.   **CRC's Sta-Lube GL4 85W90 multi-purpose gear oil** https://amzn.to/3mVnrK3 . I love this product! I was first introduced to it by Rawze over at Rawze.com: Rawze's ISX Technical Discussion and more . He explained to me that **using** this sta-lube gl4 gear oil in my oil changes will add back the minerals like Zinc that was recently taken out of the regular oils like Rotella. A lot of us from **Rawze**.com use 1 gallon per oil change during the **warmer** times of the year, and we add ½ a gallon during the **colder** times of the year. Not only does this gear oil bring

back good minerals the motor needs, it makes the oil a little thicker giving it even more lubrication protection on the moving parts of your motor, but at a not too thick consistency! 📢

20.   **Trux**. I like the Trux brand for lights and different accessories. Truck Accessories and Products | Trux Accessories

21.   **Trucklite** is another pretty good brand that makes a range of products. Truck Lite Home Page (truck-lite.com) You will be more likely to find these brands at the family-owned parts stores and the Fleetprides and Truck Pros. ✓

22.   FleetPride | Heavy Duty Truck and Trailer Parts Fleetpride is a good place to get parts when on the road. I don't have one here locally, but if I did, I would probably **shop** there more often. It's definitely a better alternative to the dealerships for parts that aren't dealership specific. ✓

23.   Home - TruckPro Truck Pro is another parts store that's a great alternative to the big dealerships. ✓

24.   4 State Trucks of Joplin, MO. These guys really have their stuff together! If you find yourself with a little time, and you're passing through Joplin, **take exit 4**, go park your truck in front of their store and

check em' out! They have an <u>awesome</u> **supply** of what <u>seems like everything</u>. They sell everything from headache racks to fuel tanks to fenders to chrome to clothing to lights to replacement motor parts, you name it! They also have an **install** team there that will <u>help</u> load up and install things like headache racks, or even help you install lights and etc (for a fee of course!) 🌴

They run promotions and sales <u>all the time</u>. Don't hesitate to order online from them either. They have a **great** sales team and **great** customer service! Everything that I've ordered from them has been delivered fast and I was communicated to by email through the whole shipping process. **4 State Trucks is top notch in my book**! 🚛

25.   I like **Bridgestone Tires for my steers**. They make a tire called the R283 Ecopia 22r. I love this tire for my steer position. I've been buying this tire without fail for many years. I get about **2 to 4** years of a set, sometimes longer when I'm not out driving many miles. **It looks like at the time I'm writing this, the R283 may be discontinued. I see the new R284 tire is on the market and being advertised now. I'm assuming this R284 is the successor of the R283, and if that's the case, I **bet** the R284 will be a great tire too!" 👍

26.   I like the **Michelin XDN2** for my driver tires. If you take care of them, they seem to last forever! I'm still on the same pair I put on about **5** years ago and I

still have a **TON** of tread left on them 😁. These are an expensive tire if you're paying <u>full</u> price like I do these days. If you can buy these on a big fleet's National Tire Discount that would be great! 😎

27.   When it comes to trailer tires on my spread axle, believe it or not, I prefer this brand **DuraTurn**, to even the bigger name brands. **They** make an awesome all-position tire called the **DA20**. It's not just because they're way cheaper, it's because they handle the abuse of my spread axle way better! On a **spread** axle the first axle gets dragged pretty hard, even on simple turns. The only problem is now, they've got a little harder to find which is driving the price up on them. 🤷

They've also recently had some container issues at the ports out west. They had problems with containers of this tire **getting** <u>held up</u> at customs for months without being released. Southern Tire Mart stocked them for a while and the price per tire was right around $**225**. I'm working on finding a replacement brand and model that can perform as good as the **DA20** at a competitive price.

So far, I haven't really found one. I'm trying out a tire from **Road One** and they've been done pretty good, I just **haven't** used them on my spread axle yet. When I find the **DA20** on sale at <u>Buy Automotive Tires Online for Less | SimpleTire</u> or somewhere on line for a good deal, I try to go ahead and get a couple for back up. I really love the performance of this tire as a trailer tire! It has **deep** treads too, unlike some of the trailer tires that are brand new with low tread. 🚛🚛

28. I used Monroe shocks for a while but I recently switched to the **Sachs brand**. My local parts house stocks them and I was convinced of their quality. I was told that these are actually **OEM** replacements and also being used as **OEM** on many of the new trucks being produced. I think there's like a **3**-year warranty on them. I recently about **6** months ago replaced all my truck shocks with the Sachs brand. The ride has improved for sure. I'm very impressed with this brand so far. 👍

29. **NASTC** of Gallatin, TN. Home | NASTC - The National Association of Small Trucking Companies If you have your **own** authority I definitely recommend and endorse **NASTC** hands down as your fuel card partner / provider. They have the best discounts that I've found; And I love their whole culture of how they run their business and treat solo owner-operators. ✓

They are a breath of fresh air to us in the truck ownership side of trucking. Their **app** works really good for finding fuel stops. The discounts I get with them are very comparable if not more than I was getting with Landstar. It's cool because David Owens, the owner, leverages all 10,000 of us or so members to compete with the big fleets when it comes to providing guaranteed business to a certain brand of truck stop, in our case TA Petro. That's how he's able to get those huge **discounts** for us because we are just as big collectively as the biggest fleets are. Check these guys out! I will talk more about them in the chapter titled "Fuel Card"

30. **OOIDA**. One Voice For Truckers Everywhere | Join the OOIDA Family I've been a member with **OOIDA** for many years now. I have also had my General Liability and Cargo Insurance with them for many years. I'm sure you probably know about **OOIDA** or have heard about them already. They go to the courts in **DC** and represent us owner operators. They seem to be very passionate about our rights and not letting the big trucking alliances push us around. It's **$40** or so a year to be a member and they'll give you a cool raised decal you can put on your truck to represent the Owner Operator Independent Driver Association. If you are leased onto a company, they **offer** other insurances for pretty competitive rates; Insurances like occupational accident insurance and more. ✔ my opinion on ooida on what they choose to fight and how good they are at it is an off air conversation lol

31. **Vibratech dampers**. Vibratech TVD - Torsional Viscous Damper Design, Development & Mfg. I've been very impressed with the harmonic balancer I bought from Vibratech. They seem to make a really good product. ✔

32. **AMSOIL BMK-30**. Heavy-Duty Bypass System BMK30 - AMSOIL The Amsoil BMK-30 is a must in

my book if you have an emissions motor. This **oil bypass filter** is the best or one of the best when it comes to keeping soot out of your oil. The filters last about **80k** miles, and the whole setup isn't a very costly investment compared to the huge benefit you get from protecting your oil and motor. The whole set up costs about $350 plus labor for the install.

33. **TRUCKSTOP.COM.** Truckstop.com – Load Board and Freight Management I will talk about them more in "How I Book My Freight", but these guys are **exceptional**. I love their layout, their interface, and the ability to look at their load board in so many ways while still being on a mobile device.

34. **Leece - Neville Alternators.** https://www.bing.com/Prestolite - Leece Neville I really like the price and performance of these alternators. They are **much** cheaper than the **OEM** alternators and perform great. If you are ever faced with the decision to get a Leece – Neville alternator or not, just know it's **not** a no name knock off, they make a great product. I have one on my truck now.

35. **Conmet.** Genuine OEM Brake Drums by ConMet Conmet makes a great product at aftermarket prices. They make brake drums and more. Don't hesitate to buy a Conmet brake drum. They do awesome.

36.   **Meritor.** Automatic Slack Adjusters™ for Commercial Brakes | Meritor I only use Meritor slack adjusters when possible. I have a Meritor transmission and I've been a fan of pretty much anything Meritor for a long time. **They** make quality products that stand the test of time. They have a great reputation in the trucking business. ✔

37.   **SPICER.** Spicer Life Series® Commercial Vehicle U-Joints - Driveshaft | Spicer Parts EMEAR I only use Spicer parts when possible when it comes to U-joints and driveline. **Spicer** is a brand you can trust. They've had a great reputation in trucking since forever it seems. 👍

38.   **Bussmann/Eaton Fuller fuses.** I prefer Bussmann / Eaton fuses, but will use other brands.

39.   **Grote** from Canada. They make some of the best electrical components on the market. They are the superior brand in electrical components in my opinion! 😄

40.   **Delco-Remy.** Heavy Duty Starter and Heavy Duty Alternator | Delco Remy Delco-Remy starters are **great** and are pretty much the industry standard. They have a solid reputation in the trucking business.

41.   **Fleetguard filters.** Fleetguard Filters – shopcummins.com Fleetguard filters are what I use. I use the Fleetguard oil, air, and coolant filters. It's up to you which brand of filters you use, just make sure you do some research **before** you make your selection. One reason I choose **Fleetguard** is because they are produced by Cummins. It always made sense to me, to use Cummins filters on a Cummins motor. 😁

42.   **Ancra.** Heavy Duty Cargo Control - Ancra Cargo - Ancra Cargo Ancra makes a high-quality strap for flatbed use. They also make other high-quality products when it comes **to** load securement flatbed or van. They have an excellent reputation in our trucking business as well. They have become an industry standard over the years. ✔️

43.   **Kinedyne.** Kinedyne - The Cargo Control People - Kinedyne Kinedyne is the industry standard opponent of **Ancra**. **Kinedyne** also makes **great** securement products and has a great reputation. ✔️

44.   **Dayco.** Dayco E-Catalog - United States & Canada (daycoproducts.com) Dayco makes great belt tensioners and belts. You will find Dayco products at local part houses, fleetprides, truck pros, and maybe TA Petro and etc. They may be in the big dealerships but I don't know! I rarely go to the dealerships anymore lol. 😇

45.   **Stemco.** Seals | Wheel End Products | STEMCO® Stemco is my go-to brand for wheel seals. ✔

46.   **Timken.** Timken is the industry standard when it comes to wheel bearings. I buy Timken wheel bearings whenever I buy wheel bearings. ✔

47.   **Eaton Fuller clutches.** Vehicle clutches | Commercial | Heavy duty | Eaton Eaton Fuller is an industry standard when it comes to clutches. Eaton makes some of the **best** clutches on the market. I like the 2 piece EZ adjust models. ✔

48.   **Minimizer.** Half Fender Sets | Categories | Minimizer I have a set of their half fenders on my truck and I **can** personally vouch for their quality. They make some stylish great product! 😎✔🚛

49.   **Merritt.** Saddle Boxes & Step Boxes for Semi Trucks | Merritt Aluminum Products (merrittproducts.com) Merritt makes some really good headache racks and step boxes. They have great reputation in our industry and cool points. I own a **Merritt** step box, and I've been very impressed with its build and quality. They also make a great product called EZ Mount brackets. These brackets come as a

kit where you can mount the L-brackets without having to drill holes in your frame. ✔

……It takes time to **develop** this type of experience and list of things that work and that don't work. This a <u>good</u> running list of brands that I trust and that have proved to me that they are worth buying and using. It's hard to be successful when you're running your business off <u>low-quality</u> parts and services that are over-priced. As you go, continue to build a mental and or physical list of what products and brands work for you and which ones don't. ☑

It's always about **learning** and **growing**. <u>Continue to learn and grow</u>! Learn from the mechanic at TA. Learn from the older owner operator at the truck stop with his hood open. But also, be mindful to separate information from facts. And to separate **facts** into the categories of **relevant** and **irrelevant**. 🔑

Much of **what** people talk is <u>just information</u>. When facts get spoken, do your own research, and just remember, just because it's a fact **doesn't'** mean its <u>relevant</u> to **you** and **your** goals. If we allow ourselves to get bogged down with irrelevant facts or information, we get in our own way when it comes to success. We **slow** ourselves down; And fill ourselves up with all sorts of unnecessary information. We need to be like a **fast-running** <u>computer</u> so to speak. The more data that's on a computer, the slower it runs. That's why retaining only **relevant** facts is <u>key</u>. Don't slow yourself down! Keep your spirits up! Keep your back straight and up! You got some money to make! 😁 😁 💰 ✔

At this point in my book, we are about to split off into the realm of having your own authority! Even if you **don't** plan on having your own authority yet, there is still valuable information for you in the "How I Book My Freight", "Taxes", "LLC or Not" and "Morale" chapters. Continue your journey with me for another **15** chapters. **We are about to break it all down**! The information I'm about to deliver you is great to **know** whether you get your own authority or not. Maybe you end up getting your own authority later and don't even realize that that's what you want to do yet! 😊 here's a seed.

If getting **your** own authority is something that's on your horizon, then the next **15** chapters are **definitely** for you! This can be a **challenging** process, and become overwhelming if you don't have someone to guide you through the process. Getting your authority is the **easy** part, but **building** and **developing** your system is what will keep you in the business or not. Things like; **How** do I bill my customers? **Should** I factor? **What** is factoring? **How** do I do credit checks on brokers? **What** about getting a fuel card? **What** are carrier packs, and **how** do I fill them out? **What** about rate cons? **Should** I get an LLC? **How** do I really manage taxes like a boss? **What** load boards should I use? **What** tactics should I use when I book loads? **ALL THIS AND MORE** is what you will learn in my 15 chapters! Let's continue into chapter 15, "Own Authority"! 🚛

CHAPTER 15: OWN AUTORITY

Ahh, the **pinnacle** of trucking <u>you say</u>? The top of the top? The **cool** kids club? Well, it kind of is.

To have your **own** authority in trucking **is** a special thing. You leave the dispatchers behind; you leave the <u>pesky</u> safety department behind; **you** leave the always in your business compliance department behind, and you now **split** your money <u>with no one</u>! But with **more** opportunity comes more responsibility. Having **your** own authority can be great! I've had my own authority for years now, and I would **never** want to go back to leasing onto a company. I'm the type of person who naturally finds ways to improve almost any business I go into, even when I'm not trying. I can hardly go into a restaurant without noticing a picture that isn't straight, a bathroom that needs better cleaning or a better way they can represent their menu, or obvious lack of customer service and etc. **So**, it's only natural for somebody like me to eventually have his own authority too. 😊

What **does** having your own authority mean? Having your own carrier authority means you have permission (<u>authority</u>) from the federal government, to be your own trucking company hauling freight across state lines. Operating Authority is issued through the Federal Motor Carrier Safety Administration (FMCSA) in the form of a Motor Carrier (MC) number. 🚚

For years I learned under Landstar and eventually a small outfit from Missouri. Throughout **the** process I would see little flaws in their operations, and things I could do better myself. **The** time came when I decided to leave Landstar, and after a **6** month stay at the smaller company, I decided to leave them too (on good terms!). I left **to** embark on my own journey. One where I'm the safety department and the compliance department. One where I'm the dispatcher and the negotiator. I **wanted** these responsibilities' because **I knew** I would do them better! I wanted more **control** of my success and more control of my freedom. I had gotten real good at trucking by this point and definitely loved trucking more than ever 😄

Many **solo owner-operators** get their own authority and **fail**. Many solo owner-operators get their own authority and do great! Getting your own authority is the easy part, anybody can really do that. What you do to stay in business and stay profitable **will** be your legacy and the challenge! Having your own authority can be such a great experience. I can honestly say, having my own authority has improved my lifestyle by a truckload. And what I mean by improved my lifestyle is; **improved** financially, **improved** my freedom of time and schedule, **lowered** my overall stress level, and **improved** my experience and morale while trucking and at home. 👍

The approach to getting your own authority can be confusing, daunting, and even seem discouraging. It does take work and some money to get started. I **highly** recommend studying everything I'm about to write and to study from other resources too, like **OOIDA** and **truckersreport.com**. Take the time to really run your numbers. Know on paper how much you will save by activating your own authority and by leaving the company your leased with.

I suggest having at least $20k to $40k cash in the bank before starting. ✔️

It really helps if your truck and trailer is <u>paid</u> for too already before getting in. If your truck and trailer is paid for, and you come into having your own authority financially strong, you **increase** your **probability** of success by a **TON!** 🚚 and pretty much, can't fail.....

Don't be in such a rush to get to this point. **Take** your time, **learn** the business, **get** your truck in <u>great mechanical shape</u>, **learn** your mechanics, **save** your money and **make** the <u>transition strong</u>. **If** you make the transition into having your own authority strong, and continue to be smart and grow, you may never have to go back to being leased with another company again. My aim is not to bash being leased to a company, and I don't look down on owners that are leased. **What** I am saying is, some owners like myself, after experiencing the other side, we never want to go back to being **in** those types of corporate structures again. 🌴

Some owners find a small company to lease onto with like 20 trucks, the owner has a shop and tools, maybe some mechanics, they get along great with the owner, the percentage they pay the company is fair, the insurance is affordable, the trailer rent is free or cheap and etc. <u>These</u> types of deals make sense and are **great**, the problem is finding these companies 😁! If you can find a deal like this, and **you** really **enjoy** being there and don't mind paying the 13% or so to the company, then <u>more power to ya</u>! **There's** nothing wrong with that! 👍

13% can really add up quickly! The small outfit I was leased to for those **6** months charged **13%**. Some weeks I was paying $**800**, $**500**, $**900** and **etc**. <u>Yearly</u>, that would be in the range of $**5000** to $**10,000** or more that I would pay in to be leased to this company. In this company I also paid $**300** a week for **Liability** insurance and **cargo** insurance. Then on top of this, I had the so called "<u>freedom</u>" to book my own loads, but the owner would book loads behind my back and make commitments without my consent.

These are loads that I would <u>never</u> haul. **Loads** that didn't pay the rates I require to go to certain areas. **Loads** that were way too heavy for the terrain. I had to literally be like "don't book loads for me" lol, but his dispatch still would. I just came from **5** years at Landstar, booking every one of my loads myself. This was super frustrating to me. This is the main reason I stayed only **6** months. They were just too used to booking for their lease operators. I came in there and broke the mold I guess 😄 (**P.S.**) I already had my own flatbed trailer paid off before I got to this company. 🚚

But I did get some valuable experience. I learned how the real world of owner operating works. I learned about **carrier** packs, I learned about **public load boards**, I learned about **credit** checking brokers, I **learned** about factoring vs not factoring, I **learned** how brokerages work, I **learned** about fuel cards, I **learned** billing techniques, and I **learned** about insurance. ✔

I learned that I had the ability to do this myself and have a real shot at it. ✔

I <u>didn't</u> have a family member or a mentor close by that I could ask. None of them had crossed this bridge yet. They were all playing it safe **on** the other side, and that's ok. The point I'm making is, my future was getting more clear and I decided to blaze a trail and that's what I did. Now **you** get to have this information early because you invested in yourself by buying my book! The things I had to "feel my way through" you get to already know; **Study** and **analyze** before you jump in. Talk about a game changer! Lend me your patience as we dive deeper into having your own authority.

I decided to call around and get insurance quotes. I told myself, "If I can get an insurance quote that's close enough or cheaper than what I'm paying now, I will go for having my own authority". I will leave the "**safety nest**" of a larger company. And sure enough, I get my quote back from **OOIDA** and it was exactly what I was paying for at the company I was leased to! After that moment, it was on!

I started calling around all over the place and seeing what all I needed to get started. **OOIDA** is a great resource when it comes to this. I will make a list in this chapter of all the things you will need to be an active motor carrier, **but** I actually suggest letting OOIDA do it. I know that my sound funny because I'm always talking about do everything yourself, but in the beginning, it may be overwhelming and by **using** their service, you don't end up paying much more than if you were to do it yourself.

A man in the **OOIDA** compliance department was telling me everything I need to do over the phone; I had a big pad and a pen, and I was writing down everything I needed! I was just **so** foreign to some of the terms, I had him repeat himself **many** times, and ultimately, I decided on their service. Their service is about **$800** if I remember right. Plus **$750** refundable deposit to **OOIDA** for insurance. 🚛

But since you have **my** book, you'll have all the required filings, documents, and etc that you need in plain and clear English. **So**, if you have time, and you want to save a few bucks, you can for sure go to the .gov sites and to the state sites and get <u>everything</u> started yourself. **Now-a-days** I don't pay anyone to do any of that stuff. Even down to the simple stuff like renewing my **LLC**, I am my own registered agent and I renew it myself on the state website for **$30** compared to a couple hundred dollars to let as service provider do it. A lot of this stuff is very easy. The key is just knowing <u>what all you are required to do</u>. 👍

Some of it is quite a bit of "<u>smoke and mirrors</u>" but it's not that bad. I did take off for about a month during the transition time. Not because my **DOT #** wasn't active. I just wanted to get all my back office paper work straight, and set up. You will get what's called a "<u>New Entrant Safety Audit</u>" within a year and a half from activating your authority. Don't let this audit **scare** you, but do have your stuff together! I passed mine easily! The work I put in during that first month made sure that all my required stuff was in order, from driver files to company policy. 😄

The **strange** thing was, when I got my new entrant audit, I <u>really</u> **didn't** get asked for much. It happened over email with an assigned state trooper acting on behalf of the FMCSA. He asked **for** my logs, **my** insurance, **my** active authority paper, **my** drug testing consortium enrollment, a picture of my **CDL** and my medical certificate. I don't remember <u>him</u> asking for much more than that. This is the **authority** <u>basics</u>! I had so much more prepared, but that's all he wanted to see. Hey, fine by me! But none the less, I still think it's a good idea to have all the back-office paperwork in order and according to code. It's not that difficult, it just takes a little bit of time. The **good** news is, once it's set up, you never really have to deal with it again. You just do <u>little</u> updates like re-enroll in your drug testing consortium and etc. **Maintaining** your authority is nothing like the beginning hurdle that it takes to get started. 💯😄😄✓

Before I get into the particulars of what's needed, I must say again, getting your own authority isn't for everyone. If you decide against it, that <u>doesn't</u> make you a loser or anything crazy like that. Some people find their happiness in leasing, and some find their happiness in having their own authority. There are plenty of successful solo **owner**-operators at Landstar, Mercer, and etc. They have extended cab trucks, they haul government explosives, and they <u>make a killing</u>! It's all about finding what works for you; And what delivers you the most profit in the lifestyle and schedule you prefer. 😄

My **normal** schedule throughout the year is; I go out for **2** to **4** weeks, then come home for about **3** to **6** weeks. I **take off** pretty much <u>all off winter</u>. When I do go out into the winter, it's only for a <u>couple</u> weeks and I **rarely** see snow. This was not always the case, but eventually I made it like this. **We** all know the challenges of winter, the cold, the road chemicals that eat up our trucks and etc. If **you** make **smart** decisions through the year and **save** your money right, **maybe** you will decide to take it easy every winter too! 😄

There's nothing wrong with working winter, but the point I'm making is, you have to work towards the type of lifestyle you are the most **happy** in while increasing your bank account balance. I could make more money, but my lifestyle is amazing, and my bank account is steady growing. **So**, why should I drive **100,000** miles a year? Why should I put myself and my truck through the harsh winter conditions? I've **been** there and I've done that, I've put my time in! **Now**, that I've set the mood for what's going on in this realm of having your own authority, let's begin to **discuss** the necessary requirements to having your own authority, and ways you can do it for yourself if you choose.

One more thing to notice is, make sure you have a solid plan before jumping out here with your own authority. **It's sink or swim**. Make sure you have a trailer and you know where you're going to get your freight from. Make sure you know whether you're going to factor or not. **Make** sure you have **3** to **6** months operating capital in hand. Make sure you already have insurance quotes. Make sure this is what you want! Like I keep saying, having your own authority can be very rewarding. And on the flip side, it can be a major frustration and failure for people who aren't prepared and are **not** willing to take the extra responsibilities having this extra freedom brings. I can honestly say, I make your more money and way more profit than I did leasing onto to a company. I also have way more **freedom** and **happiness** too. With that being said, let's go!

STUFF YOU WILL NEED TO HAVE ACTIVE AUTHORITY AND BE A MOTOR CARRIER ✓

1. An LLC or DBA in your home state ✓
2. Federal Tax ID # or (**EIN #**) ✓
3. Submit **OP**-1 application. ✓

4. **MCS-150** (Motor Carrier Identification Report) ✓
5. A **DOT** # (department of transportation number) ✓
6. An **MC** # (motor carrier number) ✓
7. BOC-3 ✓
8. **INSURANCE**. $1,000,000 primary liability insurance and At least $75,000 in cargo insurance but $100,000 is preferred. ✓
9. **UCR** (Unified Carrier Registration, this renews once a year) ✓
10. A paid **2290** (before you can activate your IRP account, you have to have a paid **2290** heavy highway tax for the year) ✓
11. **IRP** (this is your truck registration that you file and pay within your state, this is your license plate, your cab card, base plates and etc) (**IRP** stands for International Registration Plan) ✓
12. Be enrolled in a **Drug Testing Consortium** ✓
13. Be enrolled in the **Drug Testing Clearinghouse** ✓
14. An **IFTA** account (International Fuel Tax Agreement) (you will need an IRP account number before getting approved for an IFTA account) ✓
15. **Weight distance permits** for the states of New York, New Mexico, Kentucky. Oregon requires a permit and a bond if you decide to operate in their state. (you must have an **IRP** account before being able to apply for these permits) ✓
16. **NYHUT** sticker if you're going to operate in New York. ✓
17. **1** to **2** months of time to process all paperwork and filings. ✓

Before continuing I will share this link **OOIDA** has for public information regarding getting your own authority Microsoft Word - Authority Book revision 11-2-15 (2).docx (ooida.com) .

It has a good checklist to follow through as well. I went through **OOIDA** to file my **BOC**-3, start my **UCR**, file my **MCS-150**, **DOT #**, **MC #**, for **drug testing**, and to get set up in **KY**, **NY**, and **NM**. I also have my insurance through OOIDA. **OOIDA** has been a pleasure to work with and I have no plans to get my insurance through anyone else. **OOIDA** will help guide you through this process if you're a member, I think they may even **offer** some advice if you're not a member.

But if you decide to hire them to help you in the startup process, they will give you a **ton** of great info, pdf files and etc to make sure you get started right. **That** alone made it worth it to me. I think the fee is right around **$700**. ✓

I now update my own **UCR**, **MCS-150** and **etc**. But in the beginning, **OOIDA** was a good help. I highly recommend them! Applying for Authority - OOIDA . Not only will they make sure you get started right; They have a helpful compliance department that **will** continue to assist you in getting your paper work right and answering your questions even after your start up. This is a good link straight from the **FMCSA** to get yourself more familiar with the process FMCSA Form OP-1 (dot.gov)

1. **Have an LLC or DBA**. ✓

Having an **LLC** or **DBA** will make this whole process much smoother and much more professional. You to have at least a **DBA**. Having an **LLC** or **DBA** will let you apply for an **EIN** number. (I think you can actually get an EIN # with just a social security #). But this **EIN** number is what you'll give brokerages in the form of a **W-9** for tax purposes. Having an **EIN** number means you <u>don't</u> have to give everybody your social security number on your **W-9**. If you value privacy and your identity like I do, having an **EIN** number is the way to go. ✓

If you go the **LLC** route, you'll need to get and keep a copy of what's called the (your) "Articles of Organization" which will show your states official seal, recognizing you as a business. **Despite** popular belief, having an **LLC** will not completely <u>protect your assets</u>. Before I go on to sounding like I'm talking down on having an **LLC**, I will say that <u>I have</u> an **LLC**, and operate as an **LLC**. I've had an **LLC** for over **10** years now. The **LLC** protects the business but not the driver. In the case of a law suit, you can be sued as a company <u>and</u> as a driver.

The only way an **LLC** will really protect your personal assets is if you hired on drivers or owner operators. In this case the company and your driver would be sued, but not you personally. **SO BE CAREFUL OUT HERE**! Remember like mentioned in "How to Drive as an Owner Operator" chapter, take your time, don't be in a rush, slow down and create your bubble! 😄

2. **EIN number** ✓

(Employer identification number). After establishing your **LLC** or **DBA** in your home (domiciled) state, you can apply here for your **EIN** number <u>Apply for an Employer Identification Number (EIN) Online | Internal Revenue Service (irs.gov)</u>

There is no need to pay anyone to do this step. This is about as easy as it gets. Just log in, fill out the form, and now you get an instant **PDF** file that you can save that will have your **EIN** number on it. This PDF file is the same form banks will want to see to prove your standing with the IRS.

3. OP-1 application. ✓

This is also known as the **authority application**. This is a basic application that you can do yourself or will be filed by **OOIDA** if you buy their service. Here is the link FMCSA Form OP-1 (dot.gov) The application itself is at the bottom. If you are filing yourself, this will be the place where you pay your $**300** for your **DOT** #.

There is a mandatory 10-business day dispute period that occurs after your application is posted to the Federal Register in which anyone can protest your authority. ✓

*Once the 10 days are up, you'll need to post **proof** of insurance and your **BOC-3** form which assigns an agent or business in all 50 states to receive and forward legal documents on your behalf. After this **10** day period of "contesting", you'll be good to go with proceeding in the process.*

4. MCS-150. ✓

This will be covered if you pay someone like **OOIDA** to file for you. This is what the **FMCSA** says about the **MCS-150** Form MCS-150 and Instructions - Motor Carrier Identification Report | FMCSA (dot.gov) .They say this form can only be used to update a carrier and not for initial registration, and that the UCS system (Registration | FMCSA (dot.gov)) must be used. **OOIDA** will know if you give them a call. The <u>MCS-150</u> is just basically a form that **updates** the FMCSA of your address and phone number. It's kind of a **scam** in my opinion. It costs like $**100** to <u>convenience them</u> with an update. 🫥

But I digress! None the less, it's a necessary part of having your own authority. This **MCS-150** is also what they call the **Biennial update** (Bi-annual, every 2 years 👍).

Everybody has a different time that they are supposed to update depending on their **DOT #**. If your second to last digit on your **DOT #** is <u>odd</u>, then you file on <u>odd</u> years, if it's <u>even</u>, you file on <u>even</u> numbered years. Whatever your last number is on your **DOT #**, that's the month in which you file. For example, if your DOT # is 3098 6<u>0</u><u>8</u> you will file on even numbered years (<u>0</u>) in August (<u>8</u>). Pretty simple right?? 🚛🚛

5. A DOT #. ✔

Your **DOT** number will be issued to you after your OP-1 is accepted.

6. A MC #. ✔

Your MC number will be issued to you after your OP-1 is accepted.

7. BOC-3. ✔

(**Designation of Agents for Service of Process**) (blanket of coverage) Once your 10 days of contesting are up, you **must** show your **BOC-3**. <u>BOC-3</u> is just a form that shows your processing agents from each state who will forward you legal documents if the situation requires it. If you are an **OOIDA** member, they will file it for <u>free</u> for you. This is also part of the **OOIDA** authority package.

8. INSURANCE. 1 Million Dollar Primary Liability Insurance & $100k cargo insurance. ✓

This level of **primary liability insurance** is required of all carriers! Getting competitive prices on insurance is a <u>big part</u> of making the transition into having your own authority. Some of the popular insurance companies include OOIDA, Progressive, Northland, Berkshire Hathaway, and Great West. I personally use **OOIDA** (as you know by now lol 😑).

There are a **lot** of factors that go into how much your insurance will cost. **Your** age, **your** years of driving experience, **your** company's address (truck garaged / domiciled location is what they call it), the **radius** of how far you go out, the list of commodities that you're hauling and etc. I'm not advising you to lie, but don't talk **too** much when it comes to insurance. You want to instill confidence in your insurance agent. You want to **present** yourself as a <u>low liability</u>.

That's what this is all about, people who are considered a lower liability pay less in insurance because they are considered less of a risk. ✓

That's why something as little as your **LLC's** -address, can add or take away thousands of dollars <u>from your yearly bill</u>. A guy with his company address in New York City is going to have a higher premium than someone in Tupelo, MS. The insurance company will consider the **MS** address <u>a lower risk</u>, even if the truck is over the road **90**% of the time. 🤑😬

When it comes to **commodities**, don't claim weird things like oilfield equipment if you're not hauling straight out into the oil fields. The more commodities you claim the more your rate could go up. **But do** claim what you're going to haul, just keep this in mind. ✔

The more you owe on your truck and trailer, the more you will pay in the physical damage insurance side of things. ✔

The **newer** your authority is, chances are, the more you'll pay in insurance. Prepare to see numbers in the **$10k** to **$25k** a year range for your insurance needs. It pays to shop around. If your **very** young (21-27) and your company is based in a state that has high claims **AND** you're a new company, there's not much you can do to get that insurance cost down. You'll have to make a decision; do you bite the bullet and pay higher insurance costs or do you just stay leased onto a good company? These questions will best be answered not my emotion, but by doing the math. ⚖

Take your quoted insurance cost and divide it by 12. This is how much your insurance will cost you every month. **Divide** that monthly number by 4 to see what it would cost you per week. Now, take the **gross** number you make now when leasing, and multiply it by your company's percentage. At Landstar it was **35%**. **So**, times the gross number by **.35** (make sure to put the decimal first then the percentage like this .35).

<u>Example</u>; Let's say **$2000** gross times **.35** is **$700**. That means you're giving up **$700** to be leased onto that company for all of its perks. You could almost say that's the same as paying **$2800** a month and **$33,600** a year if you multiple **$700** by **4** (4 weeks in a month) then by **12** (12 months in a year). **So**, even if your insurance was **$20k** a year; You hypothetically save **$13k** a year compared to paying the company your leased to, to use their authority. (**33,600** of percentage payment to the lease company − **20,000** for your independent insurance)

But there are factors like trailer rental; Is it free at your company? If it is, then that's an expense you'll have to tack onto the $13k you're saving. Add up the perks and make sure you don't leave anything out. You don't want to run out here and <u>realize</u> you're not saving as much money as you thought; Because you forgot to add things like trailer rental, paid tolls, fuel discounts, national tire discounts, and etc into the math.

I pay right in that **$12k** a year range or **$1000** a month for my insurance. I think anything in that **$7k** to **$12k** per year is great. **$12k** to **$15k** is decent. **$15k** to **$20k** is pushing it but is doable. **$20k** to **$25k** is really pushing it. And anything past **$25k** a year is really costly and hard to sustain unless you're really out here on the road **24/7** and don't have big truck notes, house notes and etc.

If you're in the early stages of plotting out how to get your own authority, start now by having a great driving record. Stay out of trouble, don't speed, don't get moving violations, and consider setting up your **LLC** in a state that carries lowers premiums. Here's an interesting article on Progressives

average per year insurance rates per state for a new start up company Which States have the Best Rates for Truck Insurance - Trucking Blogs - ExpeditersOnline.com . I don't know how true it is, but maybe there's something to it. There's definitely something to there being different rates for different states and address'.

Another thing to remember is, **just** carry the insurances you need. If your state **doesn't** require workman's comp, then go for **occupational accident insurance** instead, it's **WAY** cheaper. If you've paid down your truck from **$60k** to **$30k**, reinsure the physical damage for **$30k**, don't pay physical damage on **$60k** anymore, pay on only what you owe.

If you **own** your truck outright, you don't have to carry physical damage at all if you don't want to. You'll just have to weigh the risk vs the reward . If you have an old pre-emissions truck, chances are in a complete loss, the insurance company won't pay more than **$10k** or so (probably LESS!). They are going to pay out on the market value of the truck. If the **99** Kenworth **T2000** you have is going for **$15k** on the market, they'll probably only pay out about **$10k** for it.

So, why insure it for more than they are willing to pay out in the case of a total loss? It doesn't make sense! **Right**?? Here's another thing to consider, if your physical damage costs **$200** a month, in **4** years you will have paid out **$10k**. Every dollar you spend past that **4**-year mark, you are actually paying more money than you will **ever get back** (if you own a truck with a **10k** market value in this example).

When you look at it from this perspective, it almost makes more sense to not carry physical damage and to self-insure. If you make past **4** years you broke even and have kept more money in your pocket than the insurance company would have ever paid out anyways. You're in the green from that point on. **Just** save your money right and **invest** your money right. I'm not telling you to do this, but just to be aware of this. ✓

A lot of people are paying in more money than they will **ever** get back in the case of a claim. **Many** people also don't readjust their trucks value as they pay it down, **so** they continue to pay physical damage on a rate that the insurance company wouldn't even pay in the case of a claim (if it's beyond market value). If you're still making payments on your truck, make sure to only pay **physical damage** on what you owe my friend! All right?? This is all the bank or lending company wants. Every **3** to **6** months, call back your insurance company and lower the value amount that you're paying on for **physical damage**. If you now owe only $**35,000**; then tell them you want to lower your physical damage coverage to $**35,000**! You will be fine with your lender; they just want you to have coverage on the amount that you owe! It should save you a few bucks each time you lower it down. 🆗 ✒ 😬 ✓

Commercial General Liability is an insurance not necessary, but a few customers may require it. I have a 1 million dollar commercial general liability plan that costs about $**50** a month. I think it might even be a little less. But that's how cheap it is, that I really don't keep up with it. The reason some brokerages want it, is because their shipper requires it. This insurance is to help cover the costs if something on the shipper's property was damaged in the trucking process. **OOIDA** offers this coverage and it's easy to add if you decide later that you need it. 👍

Another insurance is **Passenger Accident Insurance**. This is optional, but like **$17** a month or so. If you ride with a passenger then maybe this is something you can consider. **OOIDA** offers this coverage even if your leased onto a company.

9. **UCR**. ✔

Your **UCR** can be filed here <u>UCR</u> . <u>What is the Unified Carrier Registration (UCR) system and how do I sign up? | Federal Motor Carrier Safety Administration (dot.gov)</u> . The **UCR** is just basically a registration system and a money grab the **FMCSA** has set up to keep track of who's registered or not for each new coming year. You <u>must</u> renew it every year around the December to January time. Some years you can renew earlier, some years you **have** to <u>wait</u> until they decide on what this year's price is going to be. 🤷

Just be <u>aware</u> that towards the **end** of the year that you need to renew soon. Go to the website above and see if they've set the price yet. If they have, you can go ahead and buy. **After** you pay, save and print the new **UCR** form and keep it in your <u>permit</u> book in case of inspection. There's no need to hire a company to do this for you. **Maybe** in the beginning its ok if you go through **OOIDA** or someone, <u>but to renew it is easy</u>. You just go onto their website, fill in your information, and pay the fee. The fee is usually in that **$75** price range give or take. Every year the cost is going up or down a little. 🚚

10. **A paid 2290 (Heavy Highway Tax)**. ✔

If you've already been leased to a company, you should already know what this is. This is the **$550** we graciously pay the government to drive on the interstates. I guess this money is supposed to get redistributed to the states for infrastructure and interstate repair. You have to have a current a **2290** in order to file for your **IRP** base plates. Once you have your **2290**, make sure you print out the stamped version and keep it in your permit book. I like to use the company / app ExpressTruckTax: E-file Form 2290 & Get Schedule 1 in Minutes . I've used this company for years you fast and great results. 😄

11. **IRP.** ✔

(this is your truck registration that you file and pay within your state, this is your license plate, your cab card, base plates and etc) (IRP stands for International Registration Plan). **This** will be something you **do** at the state level. This process can be **pretty** annoying and you have to repeat it every year to renew. When you go to renew, it won't be as annoying as the initial set up. To make sure this process goes smoothly, **go** to your **states** website and follow their checklist. 🖲

Make sure you **get** everything in this checklist ready to present. **Come prepared**. Have everything inside a folder, and **bring** your cash to the **DMV**. Choose a **DMV** that is familiar with commercial vehicles and **IRP**. Your original startup cost will be in the $**1200** to $**2200** dollar range give or take. This plate / registration will be good for one year. Having your own plate is a nice deal tough. There's a **pride factor** in this lol 😄. **Even** if your leased onto a company, having your own plate can give you more assurance when it comes to always being able to move even if the company goes under or there's a termination of lease. I pay right around **$1600** to **$2000** a year to renew my plates. Here's an example of the checklist here in Louisiana 6782140pdf-new-account-checklistdocx-07202020pdf-2.pdf (la-trucks-online.org)

12. **Be enrolled in a drug testing consortium.** ✔️

Every solo owner-operator who operates a truck over **26,001** pounds must be enrolled in a random drug testing consortium. This service will cost about **$125** a year give or take. I use **CMCI** which is a branch of **OOIDA**. Here is their website Drug & Alcohol Testing - OOIDA . **NASTC** also offers a good drug testing program. Be careful to not let your membership expire, there can be step fines, as much as **$1000** a day for not being enrolled. **So**, combat this by making a notification in your phone a month before your bill is due, or see if your provider will enroll you in an auto pay to ensure your coverage doesn't lapse. The **FMCSA** takes drug testing very serious. You will have to run a pre-employment drug test on yourself and store it in your "**driver file**" (more on this driver file later) 🌀

13. **Be enrolled in the FMCSA's Drug Testing Clearinghouse.** ✔️

It is mandatory to be enrolled in this government database from the year 2021 and on. **This** is just a database to keep up with failed drug tests. The failed drug test will follow the driver from company to company. Even as an independent carrier, you still have to register unfortunately. It's like $1.25 to run a report on yourself. 😐😄

14.   An IFTA account (International Fuel Tax Agreement) ✔

 (you will need an **IRP** account number before getting approved for an **IFTA** account) This is another step that will be done at the state level. Go to your state's website, the one that runs their **IFTA** program. **Inside** this website see what the checklist of things you'll need to apply. You <u>should</u> be able to apply straight through their website. This **IFTA** account is what you'll be using to keep up with state fuel taxes. You must file before the end of the month following each **3**-month quarter. For example, after <u>March</u> ends, you'll send in your **IFTA** report by the end of **April**. Filing **IFTA** is fairly easy and quick, there's no real reason to pay someone to do this now-a-days; Because most states have digital filing that does the math for you. I will have a chapter on filing **IFTA** later in my book!

15.   Weight distance permits. ✔

Separate weight distance permits will be needed for the states of New York, New Mexico, Kentucky. Oregon requires a permit and a bond if you decide to operate in their state. (you must have an **IRP** account before being able to apply for these permits). <u>Each</u> of these states require their own account and quarterly filings. They each charge an **additional** fee per mile for traveling through their state. How nice! (not). The **KY** tax ends up costing me the most. Here's the link to each state's website.

KY - https://drive.ky.gov/motor-carriers/Pages/KYU.aspx

NM - https://tap.state.nm.us/Tap/_/

NY - https://www.tax.ny.gov

Make sure you keep all of your passwords in a place where you can access them. You can also save the password in your phone's memory, like how the iPhone lets you. 👍

16. **NYHUT sticker**. ✓

This **is** the sticker you'll need on your truck to legally go in and out of New York. You have to get your **NYHUT** on **New York's OSCAR** website. Here's the link OSCAR Home Page (ny.gov) . Create an account on here to apply and pay your fee. It's not much money is less than $**50** if I remember right. I haven't been renewing mine lately because I don't really go to New York anymore. But the stickers are good for like **3** years or so.

17. **Just be aware. This whole process will take about 1 to 2 months give or take**. ✓

You got the **10**-day contest period, securing insurance, getting your **IRP**, getting your **IFTA** decals, getting your pre-employment drug test, setting up your drug testing consortium and getting the required paper work back, setting up your accounts with **NM**, **NY**, and **KY** if you need to, getting your electronic log system going, setting up your driver's file, and writing up your company policies and etc. 😄

During the beginning of this time, you can still work for another carrier, but eventually you will need to come off the road to do your driver file, company policy, **IRP**, drug testing and **etc**. This part took about a month for me. I followed to the "T" the checklist **OOIDA** gave me. You have to write your company policies on a few topics like safety, drug and alcohol and etc. **You** have to pull your own driving record. You have to **show** and **make** proof of contact to your previous employers for getting your driving history and etc. There's a lot of little things like this that can be quite time consuming. 😊

That's why it took me a month. There **may** be services available that will write your name in on their templates for this. I am not sure because I didn't go this route. I went ahead and did it myself. I probably could of skipped some of this or did it faster, but I wanted to be "one and done". I wanted to make sure that I did it right the first time so I would pass my **New Entrant** audit with ease, which I did. 😄

It can seem and **feel** a little daunting in the beginning, but the good news is, once you set this stuff up and file it in your office, your basically done with it! You may get called up on some of it during a **New Entrant Safety Audit**, but pretty much your done with it. You still want to do everything that's on **OOIDA's** checklist though, just in case, in the worst-case scenario, you have to go to court over an accident lawsuit, they're probably going to review all your books and make sure you were up to code. Better to be safe than sorry. Expect the best but plan for the worst right! 👍🤞😊✔️

Basically, the only paperwork you will be doing after the startup is; ---->Filing IFTA every quarter, Filing NY NM and KY every quarter, renewing your UCR once a year, paying your 2290 once a year, renewing your IRP once a year, getting a tractor trailer DOT inspection once a year, filing a MCS-150 once every 2 years, renewing your insurance once a year, renewing your IFTA decals once a year, keeping a simple on-going maintenance log, renewing your drug testing consortium once a year, and paying taxes to the state and IRS, that's about it.

It sounds like a long list of things, but 75% of it you only do once a year. The only thing you will do often is file IFTA reports and weight distance with KY, NM, and NY. And You only do this once every 3 months. 🚛🚛

So, now the <u>myth</u> of having your own authority means "you have to do all this paper work" **has** <u>just been broken</u>! **The** "paperwork" is really not that serious once you get over the **initial** hurdle. Once you get over the startup process and paper work, it's pretty much smooth sailing from there. From there it's just you, your truck, your customers, your money, the open road, maintenance, taxes and a little bit of working with the **state** and **FMCSA**. ✔

A lot of people will say, I <u>would</u> get my own authority, but there's too much paperwork. These are usually the same owners that fall **behind** on taxes leased **because** of not keeping **organized** records.

This is a business, and business requires paperwork to some degree. ✔

Don't be intimidated or scared of paper work. The **expression** "<u>paper work</u>" makes it seem like there's this **never-ending** stream of paper work to do, but in our case of trucking, it's just not true. 👉

I've given up $**10k** a year upwards of $**30k** plus a year in my percentage paid to a carrier just to be leased onto to them. This money was to operate under their authority and for **them** to do "all of this paperwork". Do these once-a-year **updates** and **IFTA** filings seem like it's worth $**10k** to $**30k** or more a year to you? Even if you include paid for insurance at Landstar, $**30k** - $**12k** for insurance is STILL $**18k** I paid them to do this simple paperwork. That's a year's salary working in food or retail!

If it does seem worth it to you, then that's fine too; Just know **this** math <u>exists</u> and that this paperwork is not as hard **as** it may seem! **But** I'll tell you what, once I realized and learned how simple this stuff really is, there was no way I could justify paying upwards of $**30k** plus a year to do maybe **10** hours' worth of work a year! To do the IFTA filing takes about one hour. To knock out NM, NY and KY takes about 30 minutes. To renew your IRP takes about 1 to 2 hours at the **DMV**. Everything else is done online or over the phone in minutes! It's really not that complicated. People just make it complicated because of the unknown. People just make it complicated because they don't have good habits of organization!

In order to <u>really make it</u> with your own authority you got to be organized. ✔️

Be organized in <u>everything</u> from the way you keep track of your receipts to the way you store your tools. **Keep** all your permits organized in your permit book. **Make** it look good with page dividers and plastic paper protectors. **Put** your logo on the front of your book. <u>Keep</u> the inside of your truck clean so you can find everything when you need it. **Keep** the inside of your truck clean so you don't feel cluttered. If you build an environment that feels cluttered, this can lead to **business anxiety** and <u>feeling overwhelmed</u>. **Keep** your stuff clean. **Organize** your tools. **Bill** your customers with an app that keeps you organized. **Keep** track of all your receipts in an organized way. **Organize** your business email separate from your personal. **Organize** your important documents inside subfolders in "files" if you use Apple products. **Keep** a book with all the part numbers from off your truck as you get them, and write down when you changed your filters and other important jobs. **Organize** the apps on your phone so that only the important business apps are on the homepage for quick access. **Organize** your thoughts, **focusing** on what you want and disregard **the** negative thoughts. **Organize** facts from information. Then **organize** facts into what's relevant and irrelevant to what you want. **Organize** the way you look at the load board. **Organize** the way your store clothes and food in the truck. **Keep** your wire harness' and etc organized on your truck. **Keep** your permit book organized with the most requested documents in the front.

The more **organized** you are, the more efficient you are. The more organized you are, the less cluttered you feel. The **less** cluttered you feel, the more free you feel. **The** more free you feel, the more clear you will see things. The more clear you see things, the **less** likely you are to make a mistake. The less mistakes you make, the **more** money and profit you keep. The **more** money and profit you keep; the more time you will have to do what you love. The **more** you do what you love, the **more you will** enjoy life. The more you enjoy life, the higher your quality of life is. The higher your quality of life is, the more you live in positivity and leave the negative behind. **The** more you live in positivity, the more **value** you bring to yourself and to the people of this world. I can go on and on, but see how in a sense, this **starts** with being organized?

In science they say **2** things can't exist in the same space. There's also an old saying that goes "If you want new and better things in life, you have to make room for it". **The** concept is, out with the old, in with the new. If you have too much clutter in life, physically or mentally, you're not allowing any space for the new and improved to come into your life. 🔑

Do a self-audit on yourself on a <u>constant</u> basis. If you're holding onto to items, thoughts, negative emotions or **anything** that no longer serves you, <u>let it go</u>! Let it go so you can make room for the good stuff! Let it go so can welcome in a better reality. **Holding** <u>onto</u> negative emotion is a very **toxic** trait and can get you into a world of trouble out here in trucking and in life in general. **You** have to find your inner peace. **You** have to block out the distractions. **You** have to love yourself and respect yourself first before others will even consider it. 👍🖤✨✔️

Practice self-love and self-respect. It takes **21** days to start a <u>new habit</u>. If you don't get **the** results you want in a couple of days, **so what**! <u>Keep pushing</u>! It takes time. You're going to need to **be in** good mental and physical shape to be competitive and successful in this business. <u>If not</u>, this business **can** and **will** wear you out fast; And you may start to not like life as much anymore. Just **look** at some of the older drivers out here who let themselves go, either mentally, physically or both. 😶

Practice these good habits now! I am <u>constantly</u> running a **self**-audit on myself to see what I need to **improve** on, what I need to let go, and to make sure I'm not <u>holding</u> onto negative emotion and **etc**. You want to **be** successful financially and be happy! Each man and woman gets to define what happiness means to them, but yeah, don't let this business beat you up mentally and spiritually.

Don't let this business beat down <u>your morale</u>. The same **zeal**, and **optimism** that you started with should only **increase** with time. But you must take responsibility for your own mind and emotion. It's **very** important. **Be organized.** <u>Mentally</u>, <u>physically</u>, <u>spiritually</u> and **etc.** 😊

Don't forget, **OOIDA** is always here to help. Become a member and give their compliance team a call whenever. **Don't** forget, we have the internet and the "<u>University of YouTube</u>" as I call it. This book is the best VAULT of extremely <u>useable</u> and important information when it comes to our business. This is the most complete source of information when it comes to the trucking business and the mentality and tactics that it takes to be successful. Be confident in the experience you receive from me! I'm giving you the game. I'm giving it to you straight up! 🚛🚛

Actually, Rawze's book is REALLY GOOD too. He is super smart and talented when it comes to **complete engine repair**, **ECM technology** and more. I still do my **taxes** the way he suggested! His book plus my book will take you very far if you implement the material we give you! (<u>www.rawze.com</u> Click the "my book" tab) 😄

I made it very far off the help of **Rawze's** book. I look back at pictures of myself when I got my first truck back at **23** years old, and I tell my old self "<u>Only if you knew what you knew now lol</u>". Between **Rawze** and **I**, nobody is really giving away this much information and at this quality. That's been a problem in trucking since forever, **nobody** wants to give out their true tactics and trade secrets. And for good reason. These trade secrets are blood, sweat and tears. These trade secrets took **initiative** to create. These **trade secrets** don't

335

come easy! I understand why many elders in trucking don't give away their trade secrets, or if they do, they only give you just a little. And that's what I've done over the years, I've collected so many little trade secrets from everybody I could get. And through trial and error, I even developed many of my own trade secrets along the way! 💰 💰 🚛✔️

I don't know your age, but if you are **very** young like I was when I started, **you**, get to be the one that has all this information early on. **Don't** sleep on this info. **Use it**! **Implement it**! Catapult **your**self into greatness! Don't make the same mistakes that I did. **Choose** the right truck. **Save** your money up before getting started. **Learn** mechanics early on. **Invest** into tools right away. **Develop** a winner's mentality. **Know** what you want. **Increase** your desire. **Become** obsessed. **Become** the master of your own time. **Become** successful. Read my favorite book "Think and Grow Rich" https://amzn.to/3gBD6vZ .

Believe in yourself and keep pushing! **Don't** give up and keep on growing! If you've made it this far in my book then I'm very proud and happy for you! I'm sure it has **took** some dedication! You've done the right thing by investing in yourself with this text. You're doing the right thing by taking the **initiative** to **self-educate** yourself! I really do this. Keep it going! You too, will get to where you want to be soon enough. 🚛🚛

I'm still working on myself to get to where I want to be always! It's always a process of **self-education** and **implementation**. It's always a process of keeping the negative weeds out of your mind. The more you do something the easier it gets, whether it be positive or negative. **Keep** reaching up, **keep** controlling your thoughts, **keep** the positive self-talk conversation going in your head, always know what you want and <u>be thankful</u>. Be thankful that your alive. Be thankful you have this information. Be thankful for the big things. Be thankful for the little things. **Show your gratitude by having a great attitude**!

In the following chapters **we** will discuss <u>in detail</u>, some of the questions you may have on the particulars of running your own authority. **We** will discuss load boards and how I use them. **We** will discuss carrier packets and what that's all about. **We** will discuss factoring vs not factoring. **We** will discuss how I bill my customers. **We** will talk about fuel cards and what fuel card I use. **We** will discuss tolls and my preferred toll payment provider, and **we** will discuss taxes. After taxes and morale, Are you ready? Let's continue into some more of my trucking trade secrets!

CHAPTER 16: LOAD BOARDS

There are a number of load boards and ways to get freight. The 2 <u>main</u> ways to get freight is through load boards and through direct shippers (also known as direct customers and direct freight). ✔️

Some people prefer one way <u>over</u> the other, and many will say you can't make money if you don't do it their way 😄. The people who **say** this usually have direct customers. They say that if you run brokered freight that you "can't make no money in this business". I <u>disagree</u> with that statement, but if you got **direct customers**, <u>that's great</u>! Having direct shippers can really be a tactic to boost revenue, cut **out** the middle man, and work closer to home. 👆

The reason I didn't like direct customers is because it's **too** much like a **job** <u>for me</u> 😄. I enjoy having **complete** control of my time. If I have direct shippers, a majority of them will want scheduled runs, certain pick-up times, <u>consistent</u> weekly pick-ups and etc. That's fine for some. But at that age I would like to take weeks and sometimes months **off** at a time **so** having direct shippers won't work for me. **Sure,** I could just have good relationships with local places and call them when I need a load, though I do have great relationships with my local shippers, I did so well off the load boards and with my broker customers that this is almost **never** necessary to call direct. 💰✅

Many direct shippers ship high volumes of freight and need carriers with multiple trucks and trailers. This is **not** <u>always</u> the case though. If you keep your eyes out, you may find a small business in town that ships out twice a month and you make a deal that pays you enough money to deliver the load **and** drive back <u>empty</u> still averaging **$2** a mile both ways. **This is up to you**. How you run your operation is all up to you! That's the <u>beautiful</u> thing about this trucking business and business in general. **Nobody** gets to decide for you, the way **you** want to run your business! The same way nobody could make me work with direct shippers; nobody can make you work off load boards either!

Some owners don't like to negotiate rates and look at load boards. Some owners like to work a smaller radius and stay close to home; And they find a direct shipper that can do this.

If rates go down across the country, guys **with** <u>direct shippers</u> are usually able to keep their rates the same. Many times, the rates are in a contract **so** they <u>have</u> to stay the same. **But** on the flip side; When outside rates are booming, they can be stuck in their direct shipper contract rates as well! **See**, it's all about weighing out the pro's and cons to each . It seems that **most** owner operators with their own authority **run** off the **load boards**, <u>as do I</u>. **Which** is kind of weird because usually I do what most people aren't doing but, in this case, **I'm** on load boards too! But your mentality and how you use the load boards and your customer service is what separates you from your competition.

    Let's talk about the main load board providers and my opinions on them. There are **2** main load boards. The rest are broker load boards and smaller competitors of **DAT** and **Truckstop**.

1. Truckstop.com – Load Board and Freight Management
2. DAT Freight & Analytics - DAT

3. Load Board To Find Available Truck Loads and Post Freight | 123Loadboard
4. Shipper - Freight Shipping with Instant Freight Quotes | Uber Freight
5. https://convoy.com
6. Free Load Board | Truckloads (truckerpath.com)
7. In – house broker load boards.

1. Truckstop.com – Load Board and Freight Management ✓

I've used all of the load boards mentioned above and Truckstop.com is by far my favorite.

They say **Truckstop** is better for flatbed, step-deck and RGN; and that **DAT** is better for vans and reefer. I would say that's pretty accurate. It does seem that **Truckstop.com** is more geared towards open deck, LTL's (less than truckloads) and etc. I use both **Truckstop** and **DAT** and I get **95**% of my freight from **Truckstop**. Maybe that's because I'm flatbed. But I like the website and user interface so much more than **DAT**. ▤

On my iPhone, I can pull up the safari version and work it just like I was on a desktop. I can **organize** my view by newly posted, rate, rate per mile, dead head miles, length of the load for LTL and **etc**. This allows me to work the board much faster than I can with **DAT's** basic phone app. **Truckstop** has an app too, and it's just as basic as **DATs**. You have to just keep scrolling up until you see something you want to call on. You can rearrange search results in the app, but it's nothing like using the desk top version. You can only see like **5** loads at a time on the apps. ▤

I need a bird's eye view. I need vision. I need to be able to quickly move through the board and make quick decisions. ✔️

I use the **PRO $150** version with live load postings. 🔑

Another feature that I love on **Truckstop** is Ansonia credit reporting. When you click on the **D2P** (days to pay), and click on the **detailed** report, you can see how many companies are reporting to Ansonia and what their average days to pay is. I like to **cross reference** this with Welcome To Broker Credit Check (brokercreditchecks.com) . Ansonia is a factoring company that factors for many people. **We** get to see all of their data through this feature on **Truckstop**.**com**. If the days to pay are within **40** and there are more than **50** carriers reporting to **Ansonia**, it makes me feel confident doing business with this a new to me brokerage. We will discuss this more in my chapter "**Factoring vs not Factoring**" and "**How I Credit Check my New Customers**" 😁

Another thing I like about **truckstop** is they seem to have **more** posted rates. I like to book off posted rates compared to loads that have no posted rates. It seems like **80**% or so of loads on **DAT** have no posted rates. Don't get me wrong, I have no problem with negotiating my rate, but I waste way less time calling on posted rates that work for me. 🚛

Check out this video I got up on Truckstop.com TRUCKSTOP.COM EP.1 LIVE LOADBOARD ACTION - YouTube You will see in the video what I'm talking about when it comes to flipping the load board around and making it work for you! Check out around the 25-minute mark.

2. DAT Freight & Analytics - DAT ✔

DAT is pretty much the industry standard and has been around a long time.

DAT seems to be a better tool if you are hauling a <u>van or reefer</u>. I do have a subscription to **DAT**. I use **DAT** as my back up load board and use the members edge version. I don't really enjoy their app and their desktop version doesn't work very well on my iPhone (or iPad). Their app only allows you to see about **5** loads at a time and you have to keep scrolling up to see the next loads 😵. **One** thing that I really enjoy about **DAT** is that they tend to have more loads posted; **Especially** when I get into dead areas like <u>West Texas, Colorado</u> and **etc**.

They tend to have these loads posted that just don't make it onto **truckstop.com**. **DAT** does seem to have **way** more basic commodity loads posted as well. The lumber, the steel, and etc. These are the loads nobody wants to do because they are so cheap and heavy. That's not to say you can't get great paying loads off lumber and steel, but the general reality is, they are usually cheap and heavy loads.

Between DAT and Truckstop.com, it's really comes down to personal preference I guess. Take time with both of these load boards and see what fits your style the most!

3. Load Board To Find Available Truck Loads and Post Freight | 123Loadboard . ✔

123 Load board is one I used briefly for about a month. I **wasn't** very impressed, but I was able to find loads that weren't on **truckstop** or **DAT**. 123 Load board is still new, and has room to grow. They have some nice features too.

There just doesn't seem to be enough participating brokers on this platform yet. I do not use this load board anymore. It's on the cheaper side, maybe $**50** a month. Maybe give it a try and see if you like it. That's what this is all about, developing your style and what works for you. I would definitely <u>not</u> rely on this load board as my main load board. **Don't cheap out when it comes to load boards!**

4. <u>Shipper - Freight Shipping with Instant Freight Quotes | Uber Freight</u> .

Uber Freight has been out for a while now. I've booked a few loads with them off truckstop.com. They have their own app. They are still primarily **van** and **reefer** freight based, but has slowly but surely began to move into open-deck freight. Many people **like** <u>their app</u> because there is little to no negotiations involved. If you see a load you want, you just click "book", and it's yours. Some people prefer this style of load booking. As long as all the load info is posted, I don't mind this style of booking; **But** I still like to call so I get all the load info and to know who I'm dealing with. **Uber Freight** does pay very quickly 💵🤑! They are great on that end. I believe the **Uber Freight App** is free to use as well. **So**, there's no real reason to not have this app on your phone just in case for back up and extra opportunities. 🚚

5. https://convoy.com ✔️

I <u>don't</u> have much personal experience with **Convoy**. People over in the van and reefer side seem to like Convoy quite well. From what I hear they have a set up very similar to Uber Freight. I did use the app a couple of times, but the flatbed freight just was not there, so I decided to move on. I **check** back with **Convoy** from time to time to see if they got the flatbed freight yet. <u>So far</u>, it's a no go for me. But who knows? Maybe they will become a great value to my business at some point. I believe it is free for carriers to use. As I said, the van and reefer guys seem to like this platform and don't have much to say bad about it. From what I've been able to gather at least 😁

6. <u>Free Load Board | Truckloads (truckerpath.com)</u> ✔

I can't tell you a whole lot about this one. I've been on the platform a few times and never really saw anything that interested me. It just looked like a bunch of heavy left-over general freight. **But** then again that was on the flatbed side. Maybe there's more going on over in the van and reefer side. **Use at your own discretion**! I did see some brokerages I recognize from other places. Just not a ton of freight.

7. **In – house broker load boards** ✔

This is the category most of the other load boards fall into. In my "**Technology**" chapter I mentioned the main ones that I use.

I use the **JB Hunt Carrier 360** <u>Carrier 360 (jbhunt.com)</u> . This is actually a real nice app. You can do your check calls / updates through the app. You can book loads, and place bids on loads too. ✔

I use **ATS's** in house load board <u>Brokered Loads - Available Load List</u> . I don't use this one much, but I use it as a backup plan to my back up plan. Every now and then **I'll** snag something off of here. But they mostly only post their overflow cheap and heavy general commodity on here.

But if you are flatbed, **do make** a shortcut for this on your phone. You just never know when a good one might be posted on here! I wouldn't waste too much time on this site, but if **Truckstop** and **DAT** aren't hitting, then I would come see what's going on here. ✔️

And to be honest, these are really the only **2** in house load boards I use. I find the other ones difficult to use, they **are** not fast enough, the desktop version doesn't work good on the phone and etc. I **stick** with my **Truckstop.com Pro** account first, **DAT** members edge second, and everything else just fits in where it fits in. 🚚🚚

Let's get into talking tactics, negotiations, and how I book my freight. There are **many** different tactics that people use; And there are **many** different tactics that I've experimented with along the years. I will share with you exactly how I book my freight. It's took me many years to develop the strategies and tactics that I use. I had many years of practice and experience at Landstar, and many **years** out here on the public load boards. ✔️

I will share with you my methods, and choose to make them your own if you wish! At the **very** least, I'm sure my methods will give you a **great foundation** on to which to build your own methods. **Let** my experience streamline your process into developing your own style of load booking and deal making. How you use the load boards, how you dispatch yourself, and how you make your deals will have a BIG influence into your success! Let's continue! 🚚🚚

CHAPTER 17: HOW I BOOK MY FREIGHT

DEFINITIONS:

1. Freight Lane-

Freight Lane means different things to different people. But in general, a freight lane is a route between two places that is a common route. Freight lane also means a route that a carrier does often. In this sense, my freight lanes can be different than yours, depending on what routes I do the most. But in the general sense, loads coming out of Atlanta to the north east usually pay a certain amount, loads from Atlanta to Texas usually pay less and etc. By getting familiar with freight lanes and the freight rates of those lanes, you will have more of a solid ground when it comes to negotiations and knowing what's a good deal and what isn't.

2. Deadhead-

The amount of miles you drive empty to get your next load.

3. RPM-

RPM is an acronym that stands for "Rate Per Mile". To get your rate per mile you take the Gross rate of the load and divide it by the total loaded miles. Truckstop.com already does this math for you. It's in the column "RPM".

4. Gross rate "ALL IN"-

Whenever you hear a broker say "all in", this just means the total revenue of that load. The all-in rate in the total gross. The gross is what the load pays before fuel, factoring, quick pay, costs and etc. The total gross and all in is the same thing. The total of gross is the total amount the load pays.

5. "All I got in it"-

Is a common thing you'll hear from a broker. This is in my experience is **50**% truth and **50**% lie. Many brokers will **say** "this is all they got in it" as a <u>pity</u> tactic, or just to see if you will **budge** first. That's why all of that mess can be avoided by saying what you want early in the negotiation. Do what you can to listen to the tone and character of your broker. Some actually tell the truth when they say "that's all I got in it". Use discretion. But usually, it's a bluff! 😬

6. Macropoint & Trucker Tools-

These are 2 different apps that some brokers will require for tracking while doing their loads.

7. Broker Credit-

This is the credit of a broker. Very similar to a personal credit score. There **are** a few standards for determining broker's credit. I use these different standards together; And then decide what the brokers credit is to me. Even if you factor, your factoring company will look at the credit of a brokerage. If you factor, you could still end up responsible if your customer doesn't pay. Broker credit plays a big factor in who I book my loads with and who I don't. I will speak about this in more detail in "How I Credit Check New Customers" chapter.

8. **Trailer Type-**

You will see this option when you do load searches and when you post your truck. This is just simply the type of trailer that you haul. Make sure to select all variations of your trailer that fits what you haul. Sometimes brokers will post one style of flatbed and not the other and vice versa. For example, I select; (F) "Flatbed" (FA) "Flatbed Air ride" (FO) "Flatbed over-dimensional". If a load only gets posted to a (F) trailer type and I only have (FA) selected, I may not see that load on my load board. Make sure to make multiple selections that fit your type of trailer and the freight you can haul. If you're a van make sure to select (VF), even though these loads are usually cheap, these are loads that can go on a Van or a Flatbed.

9. **Truckload-**

Just like it sounds, is a full load, for one customer. Unless you make the deal with your broker, a load booked as a truckload is considered a full load and an **LTL** freight cannot be added to it. Even if it's a **20ft** piece that weighs **5k** lbs. If you and your customer book it as a truckload, you **can** get

<u>yourself into bad</u> standings quick with that company if you choose to **LTL** it and get caught. Use discretion ⚖ .

People do this all the time though, adding **LTL's** to loads booked as a **truckload**; But when brokers find out, they very well might put them on their "no haul list". If you think you could **LTL** their piece, make sure to make the deal in advance. Tell them you got another load that you want to load with theirs, but that **their load** <u>will take priority</u>. As long as you're upfront like this, maybe the broker will not care, or ask you to unload your **2nd** load first, so that the receiver of their load won't know it was on the trailer. ✔

And basically, that's what this **whole tango** <u>is about</u>; When a broker charges their customer for a truckload, it's looks unprofessional on them when a truck shows up with another piece. This is how brokers usually find out their freight was **LTL'd**! They will get a call from their customer asking "Why did you **LTL** my freight? I paid for a truck load". This makes the broker look bad, and there's good chance that broker will never want to load you again; And may even write a bad carrier report for you on 411. Just ask! 👍

10.   **LTL-**

LTL stands for Less Than Truckload. This is a common term that I think we all know! But when it comes to how I book my freight; I definitely book **LTL's** when the time calls for it.

11.   D2P-

D2P stands for "Days to Pay" in **Truckstop** and on **DAT**. This is the average amount of days it will take a brokerage to pay you according to their data.

12.   Origin city-

This is the city where the load picks up.

13.   Radius-

The surrounding area of a selected location. For example, when you do a load search, it will ask you for the search radius. All this is means is if you select a **150**-mile radius, the computer will search for all loads in a **150** miles circle around you. It will search to all points **150** miles around your search location.

14.   Distance-

This is a load board term. This is the amount in miles from your search city to a load origin city. This can also be the distance between a selected destination city and the loads destination.

15.   **Dead Area-**

Dead areas are places we call that have very little out bound freight. What's a dead area for a **flatbed** might not be that dead for a **reefer** and <u>vice versa</u>. You just have to pay attention as you go to see what areas are dead for you. Examples of dead areas for me are West Texas, New Mexico, Arizona, Colorado, Utah, The North West, anything Connecticut and above, middle to south Florida, Far south Texas in the valley and etc.

16.   **Out-bound freight-**

The amount and quality of freight that comes out of a particular area. Ex. Chicago has great out-bound freight for me in flatbed. West Texas has weak out-bound freight for me in flat bed.

17.   **Hot loads-**

Loads that are in urgent need of getting covered by a broker. These are the type of loads that if **you** catch them, can be <u>super profitable</u>. I once hauled a truckload of salt on my flatbed in what we call "super sacks". This load went **130** miles or so, and I got the load for **$1500**. This was a very **HOT LOAD**! Mars bars was holding on production until they could get this salt delivered. Someone made a mistake with inventory I guess and they couldn't get back to producing until this salt arrived. It was probably worth way more than **$1500** to them. They probably would of paid double that to get their production line going again. But I made like **$15** a mile, I wasn't too worried about that. I got what I wanted. I profited like **$1400** for a couple good hours' worth of work. Nice! This is a **HOT LOAD** example. 😄

18.   Cheap freight-

People have fought for **years** to define what cheap freight is. Everybody tends to have a <u>different</u> **definition** based off how much it costs to run their business.

Some people say anything less than **$2** a mile is cheap freight, some say **$1** is cheap freight, some say anything less than **$3** a mile is cheap freight. And for the guy hauling a double drop RGN, he may say anything less than **$4** a mile is cheap freight. It kind of all depends **on** <u>what trailer type</u> your hauling and what your overhead costs are.

I'm in the school of thought that anything under **$1.80** a mile is cheap freight. To me, really anything under **$2** a mile is cheap freight. But at **$1.80** is ok if I went into the area strong enough on my rate. But if you keep taking **$1.80** freight and below, it will get more and more difficult to show good profit. The general commodity freight like lumber, steel, dog food and **etc** that's 48k lbs paying $1.30 a mile or less is **DEFINITLETY** cheap freight. ✅

19.   Good reload area-

A good reload area to me is; A place that I know there's going to be high load volume in the area that I'm looking to deliver at. This area will be a good place to deliver to because the freight volume is up and the rates are competitive. Aim to deliver to good reload areas as often as possible.

20. Load volume-

The amount of loads currently posted in the radius of a selected city.

21. Commodity-

The type of freight. What the freight is, for example, lumber is a commodity, steel is a commodity, machinery is a commodity, general freight is a commodity and **Etc**

22. General freight-

This is your everyday type of freight that is in no real rush to ship and is usually the cheapest and heaviest of the freight.

23. Specialized freight-

This is the type of freight that require something extra. Either extra skill, or extra equipment. Maybe its over-dimensional, maybe it needs 8 load locks, maybe it needs 8ft tarps, maybe it has 5 drops, maybe it needs a double drop trailer and etc. Specialized freight will almost always pay more than regular freight, and especially more than general freight.

Everybody has their own tactics, tricks and methods when it comes to booking freight. Some of those tactics work great and some do not. What works for one person might not work as well for another. ✔️

A lot of it will **depend** on your personality type, your **level** of natural confidence, **your** likeability, **knowing** what you want, **your** experience level, **your** ability to stand your ground in a likeable way, **your** knowledge of freight lanes and **etc**.

It's up to you to <u>develop</u> your own style that works and that is profitable. I will share with you exactly how I would do it; **From** the way I <u>look at</u> and <u>use</u> the load board, all the way down to the **exact** <u>negotiation tactics I used</u>. I can't promise you the same results as me, but I can promise you these are the exact tactics I use to consistently clear **$3k, $4k, and $5k** a week <u>after fuel</u>. 🚛

Once you get the knowledge and the practice, what separates you from your competition is; your **initiative**, your <u>willingness</u> to **out-work them**, and your **customer service**. Focus on these **3** aspects as you continue to sharpen your conversation skills with your customers, otherwise known as brokers. Don't view them as big bad brokers per say. **These** are <u>your customers</u>. They are just a little more sharky than your average customer! This is a business for them too! Don't get caught in the mentality of the "big ol bad broker is taking all of our money" which, in certain seasons they really do,,, but: That will kill your morale quick and your broker customers will smell the blood of lacking capital and eat you up quyick if they can. It's not as important to what the broker gets if you get what it is you want and need. 🔑

That's what this is all about, you getting what you want and need and that's it. ✔️

You and your potential customer either make a deal or you don't. Aim to not make it personal in a weird way, as if you asking for more money is a rude, or bad thing. **And also**, do not think that this broker is trying to hurt you personally with a lower rate either. **This is business everyday type stuff!**

You tell the broker what it is you want rate wise and conditions, he or she either agrees or not! It's really that simple. ✔️ (at the core of it)

Some people **are** born with this natural ability to separate business and personal. Everybody else will have to develop it! I was one who was always ahead of the curve at business but still, I had to learn to separate business from personal myself because it's the emotions of it…

The fear of rejection and the cycle of no's. → Don't let either one crack or destroy your enthusiasm. Remember, **enthusiasm** is contagious right? **Enthusiasm** mixed with **confidence**, **knowledge** and **customer service** is what's going to get you these loads!

You have to keep your **enthusiasm** and **confidence** high and practical regardless of how you feel. **Yes**, you will get rejected, **yes** you will get told no, you may even get laughed off the phone as the broker hangs up without a saying goodbye. **So what!** because This is where not letting business affect you personally comes in. If you were to let every no or rejection get to you, there would be no fight or spirit left in you. 🔑🔑😄 especially after all the other work we do to run the business.

You must **guard** your <u>enthusiasm</u>. You must not let the last rejection leave you with low energy for the next phone call and deal. Brokers make **100's** of phone calls a day. They can pick up on it when your energy is low. If they sense your energy is low and at a feeble state, they will do what they can to push the rate down on you and increase their profits. ✔

Just like we brag with our friends sometimes about the **great** deal we just pulled off, <u>so do they</u>. But just like we have overhead costs and take loads for less sometimes; They have customers that need their freight moved yesterday. 🚚 it's up to us to check the pulse of the situation and to see how urgent this load really is for them. The more urgent the load, the less the leverage they have because they need it gone and can't afford to waste too much time playing hardball on rates.

Just stand your ground in a likeable wayin these phone calls, have enthusiasm, and make them feel as if your good whether you book this load with them or not. ✔

There are **tactics** to this. **These** brokers aren't as bad or difficult <u>as they may seem or get taloked up to be</u>. You just need to find your **leverage**, <u>whatever that is</u>, and make it work for you! My leverage was, my financial stability, **My** leverage is that my truck and trailer was paid for and the Land and house that I parked my Truck and trailer at...

I didn't have **to** make a bad deal; I can truly afford to <u>pass</u> on a bad deal. **My leverage** is also my **enthusiasm**, I make the broker feel good and happy to work with me because I sell confidence in the job I'm about to do. My **leverage** is also my <u>customer service</u>, they know I'm going to do a Top Tier Job even if they've never worked with me before.

My **confidence**, **experience** and **customer service** is felt through the phone! Lol. **Seriously**!

When you know you do a good job, you **communicate** with your broker customers and shippers, you make them feel good, you help them solve problems and **etc**;....... Your Level of Service will be Felt through the phone too. 😄

It takes time, but if you really want it, you'll get there. If your truck is not paid off and etc, you can still tap into the leverage that I use. **THEY** don't know that you're not positioned like that yet but they recognize that calm. **Find** your leverage, use mine, develop your own, mix it up, and practice different styles. **Sometimes** your leverage is as simple as; You're empty now, you are **30** miles from pick up, and it's **3pm** and they need the load picked up today before 5pm.... Who else could they call in this moment, your PRIME TIME ✔

Also, listen to who you're dealing with it on the phone. If it's a **young** kid broker before the age 30, maybe you approach him different than you do the **older** more seasoned broker 40 years and older. You might be more **loose** and **fun** with the younger guy, and a little more **reserved** and **respectful** with the older broker. These are your customers, it's key to figure them out, right! Be flexible in your approach, don't show too much negative emotion, and don't be too respectful too quick also because that often gets took advantage of; And also don't put the cards you got in your hand on the table too quick either by telling them too much or offering too much first.

We're going to get in to <u>specifics</u> here in just a second, but I'm going to discuss with you **mentality** for a bit longer. **If** your <u>mentality</u> happens to be **lacking** or is not **sharp** enough in this department, it will be much harder or impossible to put the specifics in motion, especially if you haven't done your own self dispatching before. 💰

1. **Know** what you want **before** you make the call to deal. Know <u>exactly</u> how much money you want and what your stop loss is (money market term!). All I mean by stop is loss is; Know what's the lowest amount of money you'll take for the load **BEFORE** you call. 💲

2. **Be happy**. Not overly happy. But make them feel like it's a great day in your neighborhood! This feeling of enthusiasm will help ease the tension of the phone call and **may** even make you <u>the leader</u> in the conversation. The **enthusiasm** also helps project strength and confidence from your position. 💪😄

3. **Use** the names of the brokers in your phone calls; <u>Then</u> use **your name**. This is more of a tactic than a mentality. I will talk about what this does in detail in just a moment. But using peoples name is also a mentality thing because it's a habit. This habit should be used often. 👍 casually of course

4. **Before** you make the call, remind yourself that **you** make <u>great deals</u> and that people **love** <u>to make</u>

deals with you. This is especially helpful if your **new** to negotiations or if it's been a slow day on the boards and you need to keep your **enthusiasm** up. I would still say this with myself, not on every phone call because it's so rooted into who I am now, but I would still say it and remind myself. The key is, when you say it, **you must believe and know it true**. If you don't believe it, saying it does no good. 😇

5. **Remind yourself** that you have an attractive personality and that people like you 😄. **Even** you don't feel like this is true at the current moment, keep on telling yourself this until you believe it and know it true. And watch how when you start to believe and know it true, so do other people! **Come on!** This is like being a hacker into your own psychology and the anatomy of yourself . It can be done! I know! I've done it myself, and continue to do so in order to make myself greater in time! **Thanks** to Napoleon Hill's Think and Grow Rich https://amzn.to/37bfOcV . This was the book that got me into having the skills to reprogram my own subconscious mind. 🔑

6. **Despite** popular belief, don't think that you always have to be loaded and moving to make money.

I'm only interested in profitable moves. ✔️

I would rather spend a little more time on the load board and making calls than driving **200** or **300** extra miles to make the same money.

I'm always looking to work smarter, not harder. ✓

This puts less <u>wear and tear</u> on my equipment and gives a much **more** pleasurable experience on the road because I'm not always rushing to make deadlines. **Why** drive 500 miles when I can make the same amount of profit in **300** miles? Why drive **1200** miles to make only $**200** more than I would on an **800**-mile load? I'd rather make $**200** less, <u>with less work</u>, and be ready to reload a day earlier that will <u>more than make up</u> the $**200** I "<u>sacrificed</u>". **Start** to think more like this if you aren't already. Work smarter and not harder!!!! 🚚

TACTICS AND METHODS

<u>TRUCKSTOP.COM EP.1 LIVE LOADBOARD ACTION -</u>
<u>YouTube</u>

1. **Be enthusiastic**. ✓

<u>THIS KEEPS BEING HIGHLIGHTED FOR A REASON.</u>
Enthusiasm displays **confidence**. Almost everybody loves to be happy right? What about when you were feeling a little down? And the cashier just **had** this big smile on her face, she <u>treated</u> you good like a person, and had **an** upbeat personality. **Didn't** it rub off on you? Wasn't it a pleasant experience? This person was **naturally** <u>enthusiastic</u> and she treated you so well, that now you feel better and more **enthusiastic** too. It's **contagious**. 😁

That's how this stuff works! Carry a high level of natural enthusiasm into **all** your deals and interactions. Whether it's brokers, shippers and receivers, or even at the state police. This high level of natural enthusiasm **displays** greatness, it showcases **strength** and **confidence**. It makes people more inclined to work with you, and not against you. 🔑

Think about it, you're giving something of **value**, which is **enthusiasm**. Many people are not very happy and you're investing happiness into them for free! In marketing this is called value posting. Posting something of value for free. In our world it's called the "Law of Increasing Returns" which Napoleon Hill talks about in fine detail in his "**Laws of Success**" book https://amzn.to/2KnSyPZ .

The Laws of Success book is where I learned the law of increasing returns. But basically, the law of increasing returns is **very similar** to what we all know as karma. The more positive things you do or say for others, the more you will eventually get back in return. It's also true with negative actions and deeds. The **more** of which you put in, the more of that is what you get back. This also goes for attitudes. If you're putting a negative attitude out, then negative attitude is what you will get back from others. If you're putting out positive attitudes of enthusiasm, then according to the universal law of increasing returns, you will get these same enthusiastic returns from others in due time. 😁

Think of it like a bank. The more deposits you make, the more that will be there for you to withdraw. **Think** about it like investments. **If** you invest your time, energy, and enthusiasm in the right places, you will have an increasing return. **GIVE IT A GO**! When messaging a friend, family, or broker, just put an exclamation point at the end of a sentence and watch the tone of their response change! Put a **smiley** emoji on your return email or text message and watch the mood get lightened! 😁

This goes right back to **initiative**. **Take** the **initiative** to be the first one with enthusiasm. It won't always work but what if it does?? **It works a lot for me**. And what if it doesn't work? **SO WHAT**! You got to be happy in the process, you didn't lose anything from being enthusiastic first. 😎✔

We have to stop thinking in that **animalistic** way; That we are being weak when we show our happiness and good nature. Of course, in certain environments you have to tone it down a bit but this type of mentality really stems from fear.

If you can handle your own as a man, or a woman, what is there to fear? ✔

If you are not afraid, then **you** have nothing to lose by being **enthusiastic**! It will make your life so much more enjoyable and it will rub off on others! And once others get the boost from your enthusiasm, you make them stronger and they get to return the favor to you! This **rotation** of **happiness** can be started by you! It will take initiative and sticking your neck out so to speak, but if you stay **persistent** and **consistent,** it will always be worth it! I know it has been worth it for me. The people in my life vibrate much higher and stronger now because of my enthusiasm; And it makes my life much more enjoyable! **APPLY THESE SAME TACTICS IN BUSINESS!!!!** 💰💰

2. **Move quickly on the load board**. ✓

 When you're out here in the "wild wild west" of load boards like **truckstop.com** and **DAT**, you're competing not only with other owner operators; But with dispatchers who sit in front of a computer that's hooked up to fiber optic internet. 👆

These dispatchers do have a technological and time advantage over you. This means that you have to be <u>even quicker</u> than them somehow. The way you **compete** with these dispatchers is by making decisions quickly. To make decisions quickly and effectively you **need to be** <u>knowledgeable</u>. You need to get familiar with the locations of cities, the distances apart they are from each other, the reputation of the brokerage, whether a rate is a good rate or not and etc. This is the type of knowledge and experience **you** need to <u>quickly</u> make good decisions. 🚚🚚

(This goes for loads <u>with</u> posted rates and loads <u>without</u> posted rates, but more so for loads with posted rates) **Good loads don't last long on the load board**. **Great** loads are gone within **15** seconds to **2** minutes. **Good** loads last **1** minute to **5** minutes. **Decent** loads last **2** minutes to **15** minutes. **Below** average loads last **15** minutes to an **hour** or so (below average loads may last hours). **Horrible loads** last **hours** to **days**. 👆

Keep this in mind when it comes to speed. If you want those great loads like the ones I haul; you don't have much time to look up where the city is, run credit checks, view the load details, run the loaded miles on google maps and etc. **You have to be ready to pounce**! That's why you should always be paying attention to everything you do along the way. ✓

Pay attention to where the cities are. **Pay** attention to the average distances between major cities. **Develop** very good estimation skills. You don't have to be super precise when it comes to working on the fly, **but** you have to be great at estimation. If you pay enough attention to what's going on, you will get better with time. 😄

You can even call on the load as soon as it's posted, and **click** on the details while you're waiting for someone to pick up. This will ensure that you're the first caller or close to the first caller in line. **But** it also means you must be really good at multi-tasking if they pick up the phone quick. You don't want to lose the load, but you don't want to make a bad deal either because you didn't run the miles and the load was actually not a good load but you booked it anyway because of the fear of losing out.

Find the balance in your approach, but do know, you **must move fast** and make decisions quickly if you plan to out-work your competitors. It's **mainly** the dispatchers that will be your competition, most of the solo owner-operators are too busy driving, or they are older and don't use technology quickly and etc. That's one **big advantage** the younger owner operators have over the elder owner operators, is the gap between **who** can use technology **quicker** and more efficiently. This has to do with what type of phone you use, and how you choose to flip and look at the load board. 🎯 💰

3. When you are actively looking for a load, stay glued to that board! ✔️

You just never know when the load you want will be posted. That **30**-minute break you take to go back to sleep or something might be the exact moment your load gets posted!

It can get rough and slow some days, but you have to stay on it! If you **go** inside to get a lunch or a coffee, take your phone or tablet in with you and keep an eye on the board. **Some** owners even drive with their load board open on their tablet or their phone. If you do this, **be careful of course**. Driving while using your phone is considered a 'serious' violation and will look very bad on your record. 👉

The **point** is, stay aware of what's happening, **check** the load board often. There are some days that I've spent all day on the load board without booking a load. **Those** days may happen sometimes. **You'll** have to decide that night on deadheading to a better location, or taking cheaper freight the next day. I won't spend more than a day and a half in the same location. Unless it's a place that I like. That has my type of restaurants around; And if I've already been super profitable throughout the week already. In this case I may spend **2** days there and make a **34** hour restart off it. 😇

If you're in a **bad** or **dead area**, and you know the loads aren't going to be hitting; Don't be afraid on day one to be looking for loads in a **300-500** miles radius for tomorrow. This will only cost you a **$150** in fuel. **Yes**, you will lose one days' worth of money; But if you were only going to break even on super cheap freight, you didn't lose on much. **Plus**, I hope if you're going into these dead areas, you charged at least **$3.50** to **$4.00** a mile to cover your deadhead out. When I go into slow and dead areas, I make sure I do great going in. That way I can deadhead out, or take a light load that doesn't pay great to relocate **500** miles or so in the right direction.

If you go into a dead area at $3.50 a mile on **500** miles, and take $**1.20** a mile coming back out for **500** miles, you grossed $**2,350** which is an average of $**2.35** a mile both ways. Always aim to do better than that $**1.20** coming out, **but** if you went in strong enough on the rate, $1.20 will average out fine. I **VERY RARELY TAKE A LOAD UNDER** $**1.80** to be honest. But then again, I don't go into dead areas very often either. ✔️

Looking at the map, I usually operate in a square shape from **Houston**, **TX** to **Jacksonville**, **FL** to **Harrisburg**, **PA** to **Chicago**, **IL**. As long as I stay in this square, I'm good for the most part on **inbound** rates and **out bound** rates. 🔑

I'd rather chase consistent profit on short to medium hauls; Than to make cross country hauls at $**2** to $**2.50** a mile with horrible back hauls. The time you **use** up doing those cross-country hauls to get back into the populated areas is just **too much time wasted** for the reward in my opinion. 🚚

If you do **cross country** hauls at $**3** + a mile, that makes more sense; Because you can still backhaul at $**1** a mile and average $**2** a mile. **Don't** be trapped into the big gross revenue numbers going cross country will get going out there! You may spend **weeks** hauling cheap freight to get yourself back into a better market. Why do that when I can stay in populated areas making **profitable** deals on loads in the **200**-to-700-mile range? The money you get on the front end of those slightly above average long hauls, I will crush those numbers when you look at how much each of us profited in a 2-week span. 🔑

4. **Strategically position yourself**. ✔

Always **strategically** position yourself, but do this especially on a **Friday** when the weekend approaches. Aim to position yourself to **be** in a great area on Friday. I like to do **short** to **medium** hauls through the week and get myself into a good area by Friday **so** I can catch my big load for the weekend. I aim to gross $**2500** to $**4000** every weekend. If I can get even more cool! If the big gross loads aren't there, I settle for a shorter load that I can still profit $**1500** to $**2000** on. If you use your weekend right, all you need is **2** or **3** profitable short hauls through the week and your good. You should be clearing $3k a week after fuel using this method if you do it right.

When Friday comes, I want to be somewhere on **one** side of the map that has high load volume; And that can get **me** to the other side of the map into an **area** that I can **get back** to crushing it on Monday!

For example, on a Friday I want to be in; **Chicago**, IL. **Raleigh**, NC area. **Atlanta**, GA area. **Cleveland**, OH area. **Houston**, TX area. Etc. I want to be in one of these major hubs, that will have freight volume; Freight volume will help ensure **the** rates will be **competitive** and **strong**. Each one of these hubs are on different corners of the map. Being in one of these corners will raise the probability that a **700** to **1200** mile will pop up paying in the $**2** a mile to $**4** a mile range.

I'm then looking for a load that will go from one of these "hub areas" to another hub area that will get me right back in the action on Monday. ✔

I had a load recently that I picked up on a Friday. I was in **Keenly**, NC because on <u>Thursday</u> the roads flooded out and I couldn't leave the truck stop after I made my delivery in Smithfield, NC. The loads were slow due to the flooding I assume, and it was starting to get late in the day. It was about **12pm** and I **decided** to book a short but <u>profitable</u> load; Because there were no longer loads going in the right direction that had great profit on it. They were all going to New Hampshire, Mass, Maine and etc.

I book **$2,075** on **437** miles. It wasn't my first choice but a <u>profitable</u> move none the less. I needed about **$150** in fuel plus **$50** in fuel to deadhead. **$200** in fuel out of **$2075** leaves **$1875** dollars in profit for one days' worth of work.

This load was military freight of dead practice missiles going back to depo in Chambersburg, PA. **There** was nice profit on this load, plus I like Chambersburg for a layover area. I'll either park in **Hagerstown** at the **AC&T**, the one by the big shopping mall or I'll stay behind **Giant Eagle** in Chambersburg on the Walker Road exit. Both places have a ton of stuff to eat like **Chipotle**, **Noodles** and **Company**, **Pie5**, and **etc**. <u>Plus</u>, Giant Eagle is a great place to find my type of groceries. **So,** it became a win win for me. **I'll** profit almost **2 thousand dollars** in <u>one day</u> worth of driving and hang out around great places to eat!

But this is what I'm saying. On Friday's, either take you a **long haul** that pays <u>north</u> of $**2.25** a mile going to a **great** to **good** reload area, or take a **short haul** around **500** miles that pays <u>north</u> of $**3.50** to $**4.00** a mile that you will make great profit on. Even more bonus if this short load gets you into a better market for Monday!

USE YOUR WEEKEND WISELY! THIS IS WHEN YOU LAY THE FOUNDATION FOR A SUCCESSFUL NEXT WEEK! ✔

5. POST YOUR TRUCK. ✔

Many people prefer this <u>method</u> when it comes to booking freight. On **Truckstop**.com and on **DAT** you can <u>post your truck</u> available on a certain day in a certain location. Posting your truck can be very helpful if you know you won't have time to look at the load board. You can just set up your posted truck and **have** your Bluetooth on and <u>take phone calls</u>. **Brokers** will call you with loads that they are looking to cover. 🖐

I don't often post my truck but I do if things are looking slow on the load board. At this point I'll **go** ahead and post. I've **noticed** that in dead areas or in slow markets, brokers may <u>prefer</u> to call on posted trucks rather than to post the load an get **100** phone calls all at once. If I'm going into a **slow** or **dead** area, I will almost <u>always</u> post my truck in advance to catch these types of opportunities. ▯

There is a <u>comment box</u> you can fill out when you post your truck. Make **sure** to write something that will make you stand out from other carriers. I usually write something like "**$2.50** a mile, will be empty at xx:xx (what time I will be empty), **great customer service**! <u>Talk to you soon!</u>". I've had brokers call me just because this message I write lol. I read some literature from DAT recently that said to make sure and put a destination city on your posted truck. They say this will help brokers find your post easier. I don't know for sure, but that's what I read! **Also**, make sure to also put what rate per mile you want. 👉

I used to not put this in, but now I do. Why not? You might lose a couple bucks on negotiations, but when you get those phone calls, they are going to be phone calls of people **willing** to <u>pay what you want</u>. It's not a bad habit to always have your truck posted. Usually I find loads very fast, and my next load is usually booked too. But if **I'm** having a little trouble getting freight or if I'm going into a dead area, <u>I will post my truck</u>. If you want to have your truck posted all the time, there's nothing wrong with this.

6. **Book in advance.** ✓

You will **have** <u>some people say</u> that you will get **more** money if you **wait** until the day of to book your loads. Some will even **say** you're supposed to wait until the last second to book loads so you can leverage the fact that the loads gotta go.

For some this may work, but I **don't** include it in my strategy. I would **rather** get what I want in <u>advance</u>! If I have **the** <u>opportunity</u> to book tomorrow's load today at a rate that I like, I will **definitely** go ahead and <u>book it</u>!

I want to deliver my freight in the morning and already know where I'm going for my next pick up. ✓

I do not like to deliver in the morning, and sit there for hours or drive to the truck stop to figure out what my next plan is. ✓

If you deliver in the <u>morning</u>, and **spend** the next couple of hours looking for a load, you just used up half the day! Your 14-hour clock is ticking down. There will probably be a <u>dead end</u> of some kind involved. By the time you **get** loaded, it's probably **2'oclock**. Now you still have **500** miles to drive with not that much time on your 14-hour clock. Now you're waking up **early** as possible so you can drive the remaining **250** miles and make delivery at a decent time. **Now your behind again!** 👻

Maybe you get empty by **12pm** and half of your day is gone again. Avoid this nonsense by booking your next load a day or two in advance! It's really that simple. If you like the rate, **take it**! If it's $**2.50** a mile and you know the boards are a little slow, why are you waiting for tomorrow?? Get your load! 😁

A lot about finding success out here has to do with time management. ✔️

80% of the time, before I deliver my load, I already have my next load booked.

I call this "turning and burning". ✔️

I like to turn and burn my loads. Especially if my next load is **500** miles loaded, I want to empty asap in the morning, go straight to my pickup, and get to it! **TIME MANAGEMENT**! This is one of the most important parts to your success when it comes to the logistical side of trucking. 🚚

Manage your time, use your weekend wisely, get up when your **10**-hour break is over and get your show on the road. The sooner you can **get** your load off, the sooner you can be reloaded. Most days I'm done by **5** to **8** pm and I have plenty of time to hang out and do whatever it is that I want to do. 😁

Yes, sleep is very important; And I always get **7** to **8** hours a sleep a night if not more. But when my **10**-hour break is up, I'm gone! I wake right up, power my motor on, and get ready for the day. I'm out of that truck stop within **20** to **30** minutes of waking up. On loads that I have more time on, or over the weekend, maybe I will sleep in more and just run a more relaxed schedule but in the weekdays I'm on it! 🕐

But the crazy thing is, though I'm on it, <u>I am not rushing</u>. **Therefore**, my day to day runs a lot smoother. If I was sleeping-in everyday, doing late pickups and etc, I would have to trade that **temporary** luxury for <u>constant rushing</u>. Constant rushing is where the mistakes happen, and the profitability goes down. Choose your poison I guess, but in my book, getting the load delivered **early** as possible is <u>priority</u>. There will be times where I'll wake up and deliver a little later because my next pick up doesn't pick up until **11am** or something. In this case I would show up to deliver at **8am** and get to my next pick up a little early. The **better** you manage time, the more opportunities you will give yourself. **You're the boss**! <u>Make smart decisions with your time</u>. Take initiative.

7. KNOW YOUR ROUTES AND DON'T BOOK TOO HEAVY. ✓

Leave all that **top** 'dawg'in' stuff to the <u>locals</u> who live in the mountains. When you're dealing with **West Virginia**, parts of **Pennsylvania**, **out west**, and different parts of the **Appalachian** and **Rocky** Mountains, do what you can to <u>not</u> be the guy hauling **42,000** lbs or better up and down these crazy off interstate routes! You're going to **burn** a ton of fuel, and it's going to **be** very hard on your truck. Leave this type of activity to the local guys who want to be home every night. ⛰️

They are the ones with trucks that are more <u>speced</u> for this type of work. Always look to **book** the **lightest** loads possible. This is a marathon not a sprint. I would rather take a load that pays **15%** less because the weight is much lower. People will try to convince you all the time "these trucks are built to haul this type of weight" **well**, let them do it then! 😄

I-68 across the panhandle of Maryland; This route has so many ups and downs. If I'm in New Jersey and the only decent load that pops up is **44k** lbs going through I-68, I don't want it. I've been there and done that many too many times. I'm over with **tugging** this <u>extremely heavy</u> freight through the harsh terrain. Not only does it put way more wear and tear the driveline and motor, it adds a ton of time to transit when you're creeping up every hill at 15 mph. And we're not even talking about some of the wicked roads **that** exist beyond the interstate in these areas. If you are going to veer off the beaten path in these mountainous areas, do it with a light load please! 🚛🚛

8. Limit your deadheads. ✔️

When at all possible, <u>limit</u> your deadheads. This is self-explanatory, but do what you can to always book freight that's close, but be practical. If there's a load that's 50 miles deadhead paying $1000 on 500 miles and a load that's 125 miles deadhead that pays $1200 on 430 miles, I'm going for the bigger deadhead every time. It's all about what's the most profitable overall. But the closer the load picks up the better is the general rule. 👍

9. STAY OUT OF DEAD AREAS: ✔️

This is a rule of thumb and **can** be broken from time to time when the situation makes sense. But don't get caught up in the **hype** of that <u>big gross dollar amount</u> to go to Washington state when it's only **$2.25** a mile. **Yes**, you will make some decent money going in, but it may take a week or longer of hauling cheap freight to get back into a good reload area. ⚖️

If you're going to go to the West Coast, to Miami, or to the far North East, make sure you get close to **$4** a mile to go there. That way you can afford to deadhead out if need be and still average close to **$2** a mile. Like mentioned earlier, you can take that "**big**" load to the West coast, and profit well since there's so many miles on the load, but when week **2** comes up, and you compare your numbers to mine, my numbers will likely crush yours, in terms of total profit. I probably won't have any **$5**k loads that I hauled, but I will have consistent **$1**k to **$3**k loads with lower miles. I won't have much more than **4000** miles driven in those 2 weeks compared to your close to **6**k miles with less gross, and less profit. 🤑💰

Be careful and mindful before you get to chasing those **cross-country** loads that look like they pay a lot. The outbound rates are **just** terrible in some of these places. Super heavy freight for a like a buck a mile. You got to go in for at least **$3** a mile to average out right. But even then, now your averaging **$2** a mile, but you're pulling heavy freight through **tough** and **windy** terrain out west. This puts more wear and tear on your truck. Just think about it. Slow and steady wins the race. 😁

If you **live** out west, you will have to figure out a solution that works for you. Either haul a load out **east** of the **Mississippi**, and stay out there for a couple of weeks and come back, or work the **I-5** up and down like many guys do out there. **One** of your main money maker loads will be the one that gets you home.

When you're out in **Georgia** or **North Carolina** and that load pops up going to Cali for like **$2.50** to **$3** a mile, that's your load! The **gross amount** will be crazy on that load since there's so many miles on it. Since you're already going home you don't have to get that close to **$4** a mile load. But still don't take it for cheap either. Since you probably left out the west coast at a lower rate, you need to really make this load going home count! This is your leverage; Most people do not want to go to **California**. Aim to get at least **$2.30** to **$3.00+** on your long hauls going back home. 🚚

Sometimes this is unrealistic <u>depending</u> on your trailer type and where you are loading at. Some brokers try to **justify** long hauls at a <u>lower rate per mile</u> since there's so many miles on the load. But I don't play that game, especially when the load goes to a dead area. And for flatbed, I consider All of the west coast a dead area. I literally **do not go** to the west coast at all anymore. The furthest I'll go is **Colorado**, **New Mexico**, **South Dakota** and etc. But I don't really go to the western parts of these states either. I've already been there and done that in my early years.

I've drove all around this country chasing loads. And what I do now, is a reflection of my experience that **90%** of the time, it's just better if I stay in my **square** where the most <u>concentrated areas of population are</u>. **More** people equal more business and industry, more business and industry equal more loads. More loads equal **higher** freight volume. **Higher** freight volume equals more competitive rates. **SIMPLE RIGHT!** ✔️

Don't get me wrong, I love the west, the west is extremely beautiful! I love the orange's and red's in Moab, UT. I love riding across the Columbia River on **I-84** in Oregon. But when it comes to business, I'm good! I'll let whoever wants to deal with that do it. **Especially** when winter comes, forget that! Let the company drivers handle the west. There's too many opportunities and easier terrain and better weather in the **South**, **South East**, **East**, and **Mid-West**. But again, this is my opinion and what I've found to work for me. Each man and woman must develop their own style! Just make sure your style is **PROFITABLE**! Make sure your style allows you to work smarter and not harder. 💰

10.   Money maker load.

This is something that I say about the **best load** you have going for the current week or time out that you're on. Since I stay home for weeks at a time, I can "cherry pick" my loads coming from home. I make sure to make my load from home a money maker. This load will pick up within **150** miles and pay north of $**2.75** a mile for a long haul and north of $**3.25** on a shorter haul. Once you book your money maker load, you are set up for a nice week of big profit. All you need is a couple more short loads and you're good. If you live out west, then you know your money maker probably won't be the load you haul from home. 👉

For **me** it's the opposite. When it's time for me to start getting back home, chances are, I've already crushed it! **So**, I'm not too much worried about my load home. **Of course**, I will look to do great on that one too. But if there's not much going on, I'll come home for a $**1.80** or even deadhead home if I have to. There's no rule against having multiple money makers either! 😁

Shoot, aim to make every load of yours money maker, that's what I do! Any load that has a good profit on it can be considered a **money maker load**. But, the real money maker load is the load that becomes the anchor or foundation for the rest of your loads to stack on top of. Like in chapter 1, the load I hauled from home was $**3500** on **1000** miles. This was my money maker until I ended up booking that load later in the week for $**4075** on **600** or so miles. They were both money makers, but the $**4075** load became the all-star money maker while **Mr.** $**3500** took a back seat. Still a great load, but no longer the main money maker load. This is good when it happens. All that means is you beat what you thought was your money maker. This is great! 💰

11.   Stay in good reload areas-

This is already kind of been explained some in the above conversation, but non the less, **STAY IN GOOD RELOAD AREAS**! The more you stay in good reload areas, the more consistent profit you will show on less miles if you book the right freight. The right freight is freight that's profitable, has terrain and load weight that's not too bad and keeps putting you in good reload areas. A load like **Jackson**, MS to **Decatur**, AL for $**1000**. This is the right load, it's over $3 a mile and will put you in a **great** reload area for flatbed. Now once I get empty in Decatur, I'll repeat the process looking for upper $2 a mile and over $3 a mile to another good reload area.

Good reload areas will have a lot to do with what type of trailer you have, who you know and what you know. If you know these loads are always shipping out of **Mobile**, AL and you know the broker; Then you might be more inclined to call

Mobile a **good** reload area while I say Mobile is a **decent** reload area.

I put reload areas into about 5 categories; VERY GOOD, GOOD, DECENT, BAD, VERY BAD. ✓

I'll give you an **example** of each for the type of freight that I haul.

VERY GOOD- **Chicago**, IL.

GOOD- **Cincinnati**, OH.

DECENT- **Dallas**, TX

BAD- **Hartford**, CT

VERY BAD- **Rawlins**, WY.

The **lower** on this scale <u>the more the load should pay</u>. I will take **less** for a load that goes into a **VERY GOOD** or **GOOD** reload area. I won't take dramatically less but I will take a little less. I will also book a load for less money going to a **VERY GOOD** or **GOOD** reload area compared to a load paying a little more going to a **DECENT** or **BAD** reload zone. Because I know the little money I lose out on, will quickly be made back once I reload from this good reload area.

Also, when you're in a VERY GOOD or GOOD reload area, make sure that you know it, and capitalize on it. ✓

Don't leave that area with a below average load of $2 a mile when you know this area is <u>capable</u> of producing **$2.50** to $3 a mile and up. The same is true when you're in a **DECENT**, **BAD**, or **VERY BAD** reload area. Don't wait all day in Hartford, CT for the $3 a mile load going south. It's probably not going to happen. As soon as you see that load for **$2** a mile that goes in the right direction and is not extremely heavy, <u>jump on it</u>! Call em up and book it fast before somebody else does. 🚛

12.   **STRIKE!** ✔️

Don't let too many decent loads pass you up while you wait on that one gold mine. **Yes**, we all want every load we haul to be **$3** a mile and up, but the reality of it is, probably not every load will be. I've had weeks when I've stayed above this **$3** mark **but** also I understand to just make every load be profitable as possible; And sometimes the reload area you are in makes it where you have to lower your prices a bit and go! It's all **supply** and **demand**. 🤝

If there's **800** loads on the board and only **200** trucks, the rates are probably great, you are in a **VERY GOOD** reload area. If there's **100** loads on the board and there's 300 or so trucks, you are in a VERY BAD reload area like Rawlins, WY, or maybe the outbound freight is just slow that day. 🚚

Regardless, you got to know the area you're in and don't hesitate to strike on a load that is a little cheaper than what you're looking for. This goes for every type of reload area. If you're in a **VERY GOOD** reload area and you're expecting a **$4** a mile load, and it's already **10** am, and a **$3.50** load pops up, **STRIKE**! Go ahead and <u>claim</u> that one so you can **be** on your way and <u>still profitable</u>. If you are in a **BAD** reload area and you know there's not much being posted over $2 a mile, and a load pops up that's close to you and it pays **$1.80** a mile, go ahead and **STRIKE**! There's no sense in waiting all day for that one load that's probably not there. 🔑

I AM NOT SAYING TO HAUL CHEAP FREIGHT, I am just saying to not be too passive and to strike and get something on your plate according to the area that you're in. Plenty of times I have turned down a decent load for like **$2.50** a mile because of the area that I'm in, and end up not seeing another load that paid that well the whole day. **Know** your thresholds and what you're willing to go for, but at the same time, get what you can out of the area you're in! If you're in **Chicago** with a flatbed, you know you shouldn't be leaving for anything much less than **$2.50** a mile. But even Chicago has its slow days. Find the balance in this and be ready to strike! 🐎

I saw a short video meme once that showed **this lion** who kept waiting and waiting to strike a passing antelope. Then **another lion** came next to this lion, waited only a quick moment and didn't hesitate to strike and get what it wanted! The morale of the story was to strike for what you want. **Don't** wait too long for the perfect opportunity. Find the balance in this when it comes to booking freight.

Just because you're good at striking doesn't mean you're striking at the right stuff! 😄

Anybody can strike at cheap **$1.50** freight all day. This is where the mentality of, "you always got to be loaded and turning the wheels come from 😶". Some owners have the fear of missing out, so they book cheap freight, and **yes**, these guys must always have the wheels turning **because** they are not making profitable deals. They have to make it up for bad deals with more revenue that has less profit on it. 🪓

Find the balance in this. You need to strike when an opportunity comes up that will be <u>healthy for you</u>; **Even** if it's a little less than what you wanted, as long as it's good for the area and it's still a respectable rate. Striking also means just <u>moving fast</u> in general when it comes to making decisions on the load board. Don't waste too much time researching the load and etc. **STRIKE!** Before somebody like me does. <u>And I strike fast</u>, because my competitors like dispatchers and etc strike fast too. Like mentioned above, for those really good loads, get the brokerage on the phone and research the google maps and credit while on the phone if you have to. **STRIKE!** 💰

13.   BE MINDFUL OF TOLLS:

This is just a <u>basic</u> thing to keep in mind. I will talk more about tolls in a following chapter but tolls do impact your profit. When you're going to **Hartford**, Connecticut from **Richmond**, VA, you are paying quite a bit in tolls. You are paying for the <u>Baltimore</u> <u>Tunnel</u>, the <u>Harve De Grace Tydings bridge toll</u>, <u>Delaware tolls, New Jersey tolls, and the George Washington Bridge toll</u>. **Yes**, the load is only **447** miles but will cost you about $**200** in tolls if you have an EZ-PASS device. With fuel and tolls you're already looking at $**375** or so in cost. Now that $**1000** load doesn't look so good does it? 👻

Yeah it was $**2** a mile, but that little $**2** a miles does not cover the tolls, fuels and the fact that is it's delivering to a **BAD** reload area. The turnpike across **Pennsylvania** is an expensive one too. It's like $**250** to go all the way across if you have EZ-PASS. There is nothing wrong with taking toll roads, just make sure you work it into the rate. <u>Keep a good</u>

mental memory of how much tolls costs in certain areas. Use the online toll calculators to check prices. I will touch on this more in a following chapter.

14.   SPECIALIZE! ✔

Do what you can to specialize. The **more** specialized the load is, chance are, the more that load will pay. There's a reason that flatbed freight tends to pay more than van. It's because flatbed is more specialized than van. There's a reason that double drop **RGN's** pay more than flatbed, because they are more specialized. Same thing with Reefers; Reefers are more specialized equipment than vans, and are even considered <u>more</u> specialized than flatbeds sometimes depending on the situation or who you ask!

If you drive a flatbed, make sure to have **15** to **20** straps (and winches!). Make sure to have at least **10** chains and binders. Make sure to have a set of **6ft** tarps. I have **4** and 8ft tarps but I rarely use the **8** footers. Make sure you have **dunnage**, **pipe stakes** and etc. Each of these things you prepare yourself with will increase your value when it comes to specialization. Many guys just want to carry the bare minimum; And that's where you come in, prepared to take almost any load! 😁

If you drive a **Van**, make sure to have at least **10** straps and maybe **4** to **8** load locks. I've been out of van for a while, so I don't know if this is overkill, but the point is, **carry stuff** <u>that your competition doesn't</u>. You have to find a way to specialize in an oversaturated market. If you haul a van, **seriously** consider going flatbed, step deck, or reefer. There's **a lot** of <u>competition</u> in the van market. That's what tends to drive the rates down.

There's nothing really specialized about a van trailer, or the skill it takes to deliver a van trailer. **Yes**, in the cities there can be some tough places to back into with a van; But the way they see it, it doesn't take the skill and equipment that a flatbed trailer requires to tie down a load. There's <u>nothing wrong</u> with hauling a van; And when winter time comes around, sometimes I wish I was hauling a van 😊, **but** do what can to find ways to specialize. 👉

Do the loads that <u>everybody else</u> **doesn't** want to do, or **can't** do because they don't have the equipment. Equipment like a lift gate can and a pallet jack can make a big difference in the rates of loads you haul. A lift gate is valuable because not many owners have them, if you do, you get to charge pretty much whatever you want. And if there's no other trucks in the area with a lift gate, the load is yours.

<u>For years</u> I would deliver to **JFK** airport in **Jamaica Queens**. <u>Why</u>? Because no else wanted too, and I knew the airport was literally **RIGHT** off the interstate exit. I would usually go to the same terminal every time, **Lufthansa**. ✈

At **Lufthansa** I knew I could sleep overnight in the cargo staging area. That's a <u>big deal</u> when it comes to **NYC** since there's nowhere really to park besides the Vince Lombardi that's always full.

By being a **pro** at going to **JFK**, I was able to reassure my customers that their freight will be great with me. Since nobody else really wanted to fool with **NYC**, I was pretty much able to charge whatever I wanted. And bonus points for me if I was able to <u>reload</u> at **JFK** or somewhere on the island without having to pay the New York toll since I was already there overnight at Lufthansa.

This is part of **specializing**. Doing what others won't or can't. In flatbed, I get to **specialize** when it comes to <u>oversize loads</u>. I don't haul a lot of oversize loads anymore but you'll be surprised how that load that's only **9**ft wide will sit there on the load board for hours because nobody wants to do it. The more you stay focused on <u>specialized</u> freight the **better**. Anybody can haul that **regular** general commodity stuff; And that's why a lot of those guys on get **regular** <u>results</u> when it comes to money, profit and success. Do what you can to specialize yourself and increase your value, then charge more for it!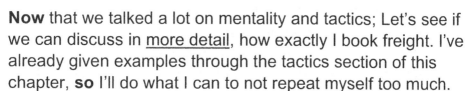

EXAMPLES: 🔒

Now that we talked a lot on mentality and tactics; Let's see if we can discuss in <u>more detail</u>, how exactly I book freight. I've already given examples through the tactics section of this chapter, **so** I'll do what I can to not repeat myself too much. Then I'll give some example negotiation skits! 😀

The number one thing I'm looking for when I book loads is <u>profit</u>, and <u>getting more for less</u>. I average about **50,000** miles a year **TOTAL**. Loaded and empty. This should tell you a lot. <u>I don't chase miles, I chase freedom</u>. I **chase** profitability. I **chase** good deals. If you come from the mentality of miles, miles, miles, it's time to rewrite that now! **Start** thinking in the terms of **rate per mile** and a **net** amount of money you want to clear each week after fuel. I think a respectable amount per week after fuel is $3k and up. $**2500** a week after fuel isn't so bad either. But in order to get these types of numbers you almost have to break away from a company who's only paying a fixed rate per mile. 🔑

Don't be worried about paying for tolls, base plates, buying a trailer and the other perks they try to convince you to stay with them for. If you run your operation right, you will **more** than make up the costs you spend on these things. ✔️

The sad part is, on those low rate per mile lease operations, they don't even pay for your plates, they just finance it for you! **They** don't even pay for your E-log, they bill it to you! Lol. Somethings got to give! 👉

If you are going to own the truck, pay all the bills, and get told where to go by a dispatcher for a fixed rate per mile, you **better** be getting all the perks in the world!!!! Free base plates, paid for tolls, best fuel prices, discounted shop labor, cheapest tire pricing, loans and advances when you want them, the best office personal and dispatchers who are all respectful and etc. **Even** then, that wouldn't be enough for me if the base rate was **$1.10** a mile plus fuel surcharge. If you're not clearing at least **$2**k a week, you are not in the right operation. I clear **$2**k many times in 2 or days on 1000 miles or less. 🫤

If you don't want to get your own authority, find an operation where you can book your own freight at a good percentage of **87**% if you pay the insurance, or **70**% or so if they pay the insurance. Or just make sure their **dispatchers** are awesome, and that they take you places you don't mind going. I've got so used to dispatching myself that I could never let anyone book my freight for me again! 😁 But that's me. I **know** what I want, I **know** how to get loads, I **know** what reload areas to put myself in, I know what weights I like to haul and etc. It's **too** complicated for a dispatcher to remember all this stuff and get it right for me lol!

An **operation** like Landstar or a smaller carrier, if you have your own trailer, can be a pretty good deal while you learn and decide if want to get your own authority or not.

A downside at Landstar is; You can't really use the public load boards like Truckstop.com **so,** you don't get that type of practice per say, but their inhouse load board is one of the best and will still give you great experience and practice! I love their "load alert" system. You set the pick-up city, radius, rate per mile and etc, and as soon as a load is posted that fits your standard, you will get an email notification with load basic load info and a hyperlink to the brokers phone number.

I hustled like this **FOR YEARS**! I would always have the **newest** and **fastest** phone **so** I would be the first to get my emails. This system is nice because you don't have to constantly look at the load board and every load on Landstar has a posted rate. That means I could be walking around Walmart, and soon as my email notification went off, **I'm** instantly pulling out my phone and booking my load with **15** to **45** seconds. Straight 'Billy the Kid' style like the old westerns when they pull their gun out on a draw! I'd stay very competitive like this for years. The older guys just weren't able to move that fast on the technology or only looked at the load board on their computer and etc.

I want **short** loads I can pick up today and deliver tomorrow. Then when Thursday and Friday come, I want to get my longer haul load. My average load that I haul in the week is about **250** miles to **500** miles loaded. Usually pays close or past $3 a mile. I will accept **700**-to-900-mile loads in the week as long as they go to **DECENT** or better reload areas.

I want loads that I can deliver early in the morning so I can go pick up my next one. I like to **already** be booked with my next load a day or two before I drop the one I have. I like for my next load to pick up close as possible to where I deliver my first load. I want loads that are **30,000** lbs or less in weight. Will I book heavier loads? Yes. But not often, and not if there a good reason not to, like very rough steep terrain and etc. I very rarely haul over **42,000** lbs, **but** I won't hesitate to haul **40,000** if the rate and the terrain are right. Hopefully that's **not** confusing to you! I'm very firm but flexible when it comes to booking my freight. There are many things that I don't regularly do, that I will do if the price and situation calls for it.

Maybe it's **3pm** on a Friday and I've exhausted all my other options, and a load pops up weighing **43k** lbs and barely pays **$2** a mile, but it goes in a favorable direction. I'll go ahead and strike on that load. It **wasn't** my first pick, but the situation called for it; I needed to hurry and get a load before I sit all weekend doing nothing! But I still didn't haul **for** a crazy bad rate either, I just adjusted my standards due to the situation. I didn't completely throw away my standards.

If the load requires tarp, that's fine, as long as it pays right. If the load looks decent at **$2.20** a mile but needs **8ft** tarps, chances are, I'm not hauling that load. Putting those big tarps on and off require labor, time, and about **$800** worth of tarps. If it's a load like machinery that needs tarps, I must know how will these machines be covered. Machinery moves that are from one factory to another are often the biggest tarp killers. **Yes**, I got felt and moving blankets, but it's usually never enough for these types of loads. I'm not going to haul a load for **$1200** that could ruin over **$500** worth of tarps. I'm also not going to tarp an **$800** dollar load unless it's only going like 100 miles lol. 🚛

That would make sense because of the profit margin, but if the load went **400** miles and tarp for $800, I don't think so, unless I was in a bad reload area going to a good one. I would want $**1000** at least. And that's for **4ft** tarps.

Don't let these people waste your time and equipment.
✔️

You **work** hard to be out here. All the **compliance** and **maintenance** you deal with, the time away from friends and family, the **time** and **effort** it took you to save up the money to get started and etc. **Don't** let them play with you like that. **Tell** them what you want. If you make a deal, **great**! If not, cool, keep it moving. When freight is slow you'll have to adjust your prices a little bit lower sometimes, but don't disrespect yourself. This business is a tough business that most people are not cut out for. Stand your ground in a likeable way, know what your services are worth! 👍😎✔️

Like I said, I want that $**2500** + load over the weekend. I really want to see $**3000** + on **1000** miles or so every weekend. I don't always hit, but this is how I look to use my weekend. Now, this doesn't mean that from **Charlotte**, NC I'll book a load to **Phoenix** for $4500 just because it's over $3000. It has to make sense and or put me in a **GOOD** reload area. 🌴

Why doesn't the **Phoenix** load not make sense? It only pays $**2.20** a mile and it will take days of running cheap freight to get back to **DECENT** reload areas. **Yes**, that $**3,750** after fuel looks tempting. But it won't be until Tuesday that you get empty. Next is probably a cheap load to Texas that still takes **2** days to do, at close to **$1** a mile which is **$760** after fuel. So far, you averaged **$750** a day for 6 days. Not too bad. The only problem is now you've driven **3250** miles and probably don't have any time left on your clock to haul over the next weekend and you drove a **TON** of miles. This <u>one decision</u> to go to **Arizona** cost a total of about **9** days. In those **9** days you could have been averaging close to **$750** to **$1000** gross a day on way less miles. And still got a 34-hour restart in.

Work smarter and not harder is what I always aim to do. ✔️

Many owners <u>never graduate</u> from the **company** driver mentality of "I have to get more miles". 😶

I guess it was a good thing I was only a company driver for about 1 year 😄! It wasn't that hard of a habit to break for me. I love my **350**-mile days that I'm profiting what a company driver makes in a week, or what other owner operators profit on a **600**-to-**700**-mile run. **Why** would I drive <u>more</u> and <u>work harder</u> when I can make great deals for less miles and make my equipment **last longer** than my competitors? When my competitors keep taking **500**-mile loads for **$1.50** to **$1.80** they are <u>driving more and keeping less</u>. They are **tearing** up their trucks <u>way quicker</u> than me, with less profit to even fix their truck with. **Now**, that just doesn't make much sense does it?? Luckily you are learning from me now! And let me tell you, don't run like that if you can help it!

I want loads where the brokerage pays within **30** days. Bonus points for brokerages like **ATS** who pay in **3** to **5** days **ACH** <u>with no extra fee</u>. I don't like working with brokerages who take **45** days or more to pay. I did the job, I sent in my invoice and **POD** the day of delivery, <u>I want my money</u>! I still do haul for **King of Freight** sometimes, and my experience with them is about **45** days to pay, but I know they are good for it, they will pay every time. I just make sure I have a healthy rotation of quicker paying customers during that period of time that I'm over the road. 🚚

I want **open window** <u>appointments</u>. I don't often haul loads that have strict appointments 🕐. I will be more **inclined** to take loads that have strict <u>cut off</u> times <u>but not appointments</u>. I will take loads with appointments but I have to be sure, that there's more than enough time on the load where I won't have to rush. I so much more prefer loads that are like "deliver on <u>Monday</u> **first come first serve** by <u>4pm</u>". Those are my type of loads. It takes the **rush** factor out and allows me to enjoy the job <u>much more</u>. It also makes sure that I won't get into funny business with the brokerage for trying to hold my pay, or <u>reduce</u> my rate because of a missed appointment. **If** you're going to take loads with appointment times, <u>make sure</u> you can make the appointment for sure before you say yes and sign that rate confirmation. It's **very important** you **don't** <u>deviate</u> from what your contract says; It's very important you make good on your word. There are places like carrier 411 Carrier411 - Carrier Safety Ratings, SMS BASIC Scores, Insurance and Authority Monitoring where brokers can **write** about you for other brokers to see. <u>Make sure they can only write great things about you</u>! 👍

I want to make a quick note on customer service.

Remember, brokers are your customers, and the shippers and receivers are their customers. <u>Always be on point</u> with both the **broker** and the **shippers** and **receivers**. Don't **bad**

mouth them, don't **cuss** at them, if you must stand your ground, <u>do so in a likeable way</u>. Give your broker **courtesy** emails when you are loaded. If it's a tight pick-up time, <u>go ahead</u> and email them when you get on site. Just let them know you're on site for pickup and you will let them know when you're loaded. ✓

This is what **customer service** <u>is all about</u>. **Communicate** with your customers, let them know what's going on. It won't take long for them to see that you are **responsible** and are <u>someone</u> who takes care of business. Once this is established, they will give you much more lee-way and will probably not even call or do check calls on you. ✓

Put a good face on at the shippers and receivers. You are a **reflection** of your customer, the broker. If you put a good show on at the shipper, the shipper may contact the broker and let them know. The same is true if you put on a bad show. **Don't** throw your broker '<u>under the bus</u>' if something is not right at the shipper. Don't be like "**my broker didn't tell me** about this" or whatever the case may be. Though the **broker** <u>may be wrong</u>, be **professional** and call your broker and discuss it with him or her first. Do business as if you are going to see and talk to these people again. Be **professional**, stand your ground in a likeable way, be enthusiastic, communicate and be professional at the shippers and receivers! 😄

Ultimately, <u>I want loads that make me happy</u>. I want loads that don't go to the big steel and lumber yards. I want loads that are practical in nature. I want loads on mostly flat routes. If I'm in the mountainous areas, I only want **30,000** lbs or less. I want loads **that** have quick on and offs. I want loads that go through routes where I have stuff to eat. I want loads I don't have to rush on. I want loads the put me in **GOOD** or **VERY GOOD** reload areas. I want loads that I make a clean profit off of! 💰💰😊✔

THE HOW:

I just <u>realized</u> I did all of this talking but I didn't really explain **HOW** I book my freight yet! I explained the what, and the why, but not much on the **HOW**. This is a **very important** part of my book and I want to make sure that I explain this topic very clearly. I need to explain it for the beginner that has never seen a load board all the way to the guys that already do this and are looking to improve their skills or see if they are missing anything.

My YouTube video <u>TRUCKSTOP.COM EP.1 LIVE LOADBOARD ACTION - YouTube</u> shows some of the "**HOW**" in live fashion. I have a series of this show. The more you watch these episodes, the **more** <u>exposure</u> you will get to how this all works! Let's continue as I break down **HOW** I book my freight. Or in other words, **HOW** I use the load board. Everybody uses the load board in a slightly different or completely different way. Here's how I do it. Real, raw, and uncut! I run a **hybrid** "**Gypsy**" style. I'm not completely all over the place, but I'm not dedicated to any one customer or any one route. **Gypsy style** is just running all over chasing the money pretty much. But I run a **more organized** <u>Gypsy style</u> that has boundaries and limits. 😊👍

I use mainly **Truckstop.com** as my go to load board. I do not post my truck unless things are slow or I'm going into a dead area. The first thing I'm going to be looking at is **RPM**, which is rate per mile, right 🫢😄?? I will **flip** the load board around to where I only see loads with posted rates, organized by highest **rate per mile** down to lowest. This is where I find **my** most profitable loads. I prefer to get my loads based off the **RPM's**. Probably **90**% or so of my booked loads will have posted rates. Very rarely do I call on loads that don't have posted rates. Usually there's enough loads with posted rates that I like, that I won't take the time to fool around with unposted rates. **But** if the area is slow, I have no problem calling on loads with unposted rates. I just go in knowing what I want, and either make a deal or I don't. 🚛

Inside the **RPM** perspective, I'm looking for loads that make sense. Loads the are over **$3** a mile are always nice, especially if they are over **300** miles loaded. That would be about **$900** all in. I don't often haul for anything less than **$750** gross in a day. Unless it's just too good to pass up like **$600** on **75** miles and there's nothing else going on. I once hauled a load **.7** miles for **$300** lol. Why not lol? It was kind of slow that day, and I had a day in between when my next load was booked. I loaded it and **went** a few buildings down on the same road and delivered it less than a mile away! **No turns** lol except out the shipper's driveway and into the receiver's driveway! 😄

Let me clarify though. **$3** a mile is not enough money when the load only goes **100** miles. A **$300** dollar is not worth it. Even though the load is **100** miles, it will take most of the day to load it and unload it. It will take about **$50** in fuel. No way am I out here for **$250** a day! 💯🌴

Inside **RPM** I'm looking for $3 and up per mile. If $3 is not there, I go all the way down to where $2 a mile starts. I will keep searching up from here until I find something. **If** I don't find anything <u>my next option</u> is to **flip** the load board to make it show me which loads are closest to my current location. To do this just press the **'distance'** tab on **truckstop**.com until the board flips and shows the loads that are closest to your search city. **This** is when I'll start calling on loads without posted rates. If I see a load that picks up close to me, and goes to reload area I like, with a decent weight; I will call on it!

First, I'll do the math on my iPhone calculator before I call. **Depending** on where I am, I will check the total miles on Google Maps, then multiply the miles by **$2.30** or so and also by **$1.80** to **$2.00**. These numbers will give me the "<u>what I want</u>" before I even call.

I call, get the load information, and on these types of loads usually the brokers will <u>try</u> to beat you with a rate that they'll do it for. Usually, it's a **bottom** of the barrel rate and that's why I don't often use this method. But if the rates too low, I will just tell them "Hey Josie (whatever the brokers name is), I'm empty now, and I want to do this load. But I want (insert the **$2.30** a mile calculation), pull back wait to see what the broker says, usually there's money on these types of loads. **So**, she will probably try to counter you or just laugh and hang up (<u>but that's ok</u>), this is where your bottom dollar rate comes in (in this example it's the total loaded miles multiplied by **$1.80** per mile). If I really want this load for some reason, and we agree to a number at or above my **$1.80** number, I'll do the load.

In-between looking at RPM and the loads that are closest to me, I will flip the board to show me what loads are currently being posted. ✔️

This is done by hitting the "**AGE**" tab on **truckstop**.com. I recommend, whatever load board you decide to use as your main board, to buy the **PRO** version of it for $**150** so that you can see the live feed as loads are posted in real-time. This will give you an edge **over** your competitors and also allow you see the freshest of loads as they pop up. I will then leave the load board like this for about **1** to **5** minutes. After **3** to **5** minutes, I will switch the board around to either look at **RPM**, **distance**, or I will look at **total gross** amount. **This** is why I use **truck stop** desktop version on the safari of my phone. It's just way more responsive and I can move like an **Octopus** so to speak! I can see the board from **8** different ways at the click of a button. This is the type of **speed** and **flexibility** that I depend on. 🚛🚛

I will also flip the board to show me gross amount. **Starting** from **high** to **low**, I will see which load pay the most in gross. Be careful to not get tricked into thinking a load is good because it pays a lot of money. If the **RPM** is not at least $**1.80** that load is not really good, even if it "pays" $**7000**. Remember, once you get to the other side of the country, especially if you go west, to the north east, or to Miami, the freight will more than likely be weak on the way back out. I **flip** to see gross to **see** if I missed something when looking at **RPM**, **AGE**, and **DISTANCE**. Or if it's a Thursday or Friday, I will look to see what loads will get me over the $**2500** to $**3000** dollar gross I want to be at. ✔️

But remember, I will not be booking a load just because the **gross amount** is over that number, the **RPM** and other factors need to pass the standard I've been mentioning too. By looking at gross amount, I can more quickly find my weekend load though. If I don't find what I want from looking at the board by gross, I **switch** back to **AGE** and start the process over again. age is the main way to view the board to watch as live load postings come in for all to see.

Owners will often find a way to leave the load board up while they drive, and leave the live load board set on **AGE**. That way when a new load pops up they can see it. They find a way to do this "hands free". I **cannot** recommend this, as it's technically illegal and distracted driving. **So**, if you go this method be careful and don't wreck into anyone by keeping a total birds eye view on everything. Another alternative to this is to **post** your truck and take calls via Bluetooth. This would be the proper and legal way. But as some say, it's not illegal if you don't get caught! **Lol**. Use your own discretion. I hereby say **DON'T DO IT**. For legal purposes.

Every time I check **RPM**, then **distance**, then **Gross**, I make sure to switch back to **AGE** very often. I will even refresh my browser if it's been over **5** minutes. I don't want to miss the **live** action by spending so much time looking at the board from different angles. Keeping an eye on the board by **AGE** is where I spend most of my time. If **AGE** isn't producing results quick enough, then I will start to make my rounds of **RPM**, **DISTANCE**, and **GROSS**.

If I'm just getting on the load board, I will probably look at the first **25** results on **AGE** to see how many loads are getting posted and to see if I can catch something good quick. After I quickly do this, I go straight to looking at **RPM**, **DISTANCE**, and **GROSS**. After I make my rounds, I go straight back to **AGE**. This is pretty much my secret tactic that I do. It doesn't sound like much, but once you team it up with everything else taught in this chapter, you will see that if done right **will** <u>produce great results</u>. This strategy ensures that you move fast and see everything from every angle in real time, as quick as possible. 💰 ✓

TO do this well is to: You have to move fast, you have to **make** <u>decisions quick</u>, you have to go to **GOOD**, **VERY GOOD**, and **DECENT** reload areas. You have to keep <u>looking</u> at the load board in these <u>different angles</u>. You have to **strike** when you see a load that makes sense. You have to **limit** your deadhead. You have to stay **out** of dead areas. Get your **money maker** for the week and build off that. Aim to book one load in advance. Haul your big load **over** the weekend if possible. Always aim for **$2.20** a mile and up. Shoot for **$3** a mile and up. <u>Know your worth</u>. **Stand** your ground in a likeable way. **Say** less in negotiations. **Give** great customer service. **Study** freight lanes and load volumes. **Learn** from experience what each area should be paying to go to another area and make deals accordingly.

Aim to haul light loads. Do what you can to specialize. It's harder to get these types of rates in a regular van trailer with nothing else to offer. **Know** what you want. **Move**, **talk** and **make deals** as if you're already the <u>Man</u>, already the <u>Woman</u>. **Be** as if you have already made it. **Don't** let the rejection and "no's" get your spirit down. **Stay enthusiastic!** <u>Make great deals</u>, and **remember**, that people love to make deals with you too! 😄 sounds cliché, but there's something to it.

Half of this game of life and business is MENTAL and mentality of overall endurance. ✔

The one who has **more** <u>control</u> over his or her thoughts has **more** <u>control</u> over his or her life. **Be** smart, **be** vigilant, have faith that you will get what you want. Put the work in, stay focused, and always learn. 🚚 this business requires morale is why these mental ringings keep getting repeated.

<u>NEGOTIATION EXAMPLES</u>:

<u>FIRST LOAD</u>: ASKING FOR MORE THAN THE POSTED RATE! ✔

The board is **slow** and I <u>find</u> a load from a brokerage I know. **Texarkana**, TX to **Nashville**, TN. **487** miles with a posted rate of $**900**. I want it for $**1000** dollars which will make it a pinch over $**2** a mile.

BROKER: Hey this is **Chad** with DOUBLE UP Logistics.

ME: Hey **Chad**! My name is **Andrew**. <u>I'm with XYZ Trucking</u>.

BROKER: Hey Andrew.

ME: I'm calling about this load you have posted in **Texarkana**, TX going to **Nashville**, TN. (<u>At this point, I take a step back to listen about the load, and listen to who I'm dealing with. Personality type and etc</u>)

BROKER: Yes, this load is a one pick one drop, **no tarp**, crated machinery paying $**900** to the truck.

ME: What time are the pickup and delivery times? (This is info I need to know, but it also shows the broker that I **am interested** about his load, it buys me a little more time for him or her to like me or my bid as well 😄)

BROKER: It can pick up any time before 4pm Monday and delivers Tuesday by 1pm.

ME: Ok sounds great! I am empty now, and I **want** to do this load, **but I want to do it for $1050.**

(I fall back **hard** at this point, I don't care if there is an awkward silence, most brokers aren't used to this style of straight up negotiation. I'll now let the broker figure out what he or she wants to do. What happens next is you either make a deal or you don't. But you "came to the table" **strong** and **confident** in asking for what you want, but in a **likeable** way.)

He or she will either agree, bump your bidded rate down $50 to a couple hundred dollars, or say "that's all I got in it". If he or she says that's all I got in it, you will have to decide if you want to keep standing your ground or fold your hand. Usually, I will say. "**Ok**, I will, lower my price to $**1000,** and my price will be good to go for the next **5** minutes." This puts **urgency** on the matter. When they hang up the phone they will have to decide "Should I go ahead and get this **covered**, or wait to see if I can get more". Your confidence is what sells this process. Practice asking for what you want. **Do not ask** "will" you do this much, or "can" you do it for this, or "do you have any more money in it"

These are **power giving words and** negotiation positions

often times. **Ask for what you want**! IT's all part of the process lol. You can do it! But in a likeable way! **Remember**, learn to separate personal emotion from business. You are doing nothing wrong by asking for what it is you want and need!... especially if the prices are good ballpark prices. Make it hard for them to say no. If you ask "**can** you do it for $**1050**?" of course his answer will be "oh I wish I could, but that's all I got in it", **why**? Because you made it too easy for him to say no! Say things like "I'm ready to go get the load now"; Or if you are prebooking in advance, tell them what time you'll be empty, and ask for what you want! This puts **urgency** on the load and lets them know in their mind, that they can get this load covered now if they deal! It's really this simple. You either make a deal or you don't. **Have confidence**, take initiative and make this customer feel confident in your ability to take care of his or her load. Try to speak in a consistent clear tone of rhythm.

BROKER: $**1050**? but this load has no tarp. It's a light load. (now he's on the defense (good!))

ME: I understand. I'll gladly do this load. My price to go is good for another 5 minutes.

BROKER: Will you do it for $**1000**?

ME: **Yes** I will, I can do that.

BOOM. Another deal made. Got a little extra than the posted rate. The load goes to a **DECENT** reload area, and I'm good to go. ✔ 😁

NEXT LOAD: NO POSTED RATE! ✔

La Vergne, TN to **Columbus**, OH. I might like this load. **395** loaded miles. It picks up close and goes to a **GOOD** reload area. There's no posted rate, but I know the brokerage and the load weighs 34,000 lbs, not so bad!

BROKER: Hey this is **Jessica** with RE-UP Logistics.

ME: Hi **Jessica**! My name is **Andrew**. I'm with XYZ Trucking.

BROKER: Hey Andrew. (with no enthusiasm lol)

ME: I'm calling about your load **La Vergne**, TN to **Columbus**, OH.

BROKER: Yes, this load picks tomorrow before **2pm** delivers Wednesday by **12** noon. Pays **$600** to the truck. No tarp.

ME: 😑 (WHAT THE WORLD! $600 on 400 miles) (I'll ask another quick little question to show interest even though I think we are way too far apart on the rate) **What is the commodity?**

BROKER: Dumpsters.

ME: What type of dumpsters are they? Are they the roll back type? (the roll back type requires more work to secure, and consist of me crawling on my stomach to run chain and binders)

BROKER: Yes. They are the roll back type.

ME: (attempting to keep from laughing or cussing) I am empty now, and can be there in 1 hour to load. (I always say this type of stuff, it lets them know you're ready and their load will soon be covered if they say yes) but I want to be at **$800** dollars for it. (this is barely **$2** a mile but she's lowballing so low that anything higher than this will scare her off)

BROKER: I move these every day for $**600** dollars. $**800** is outrageous to go to Columbus.

ME: Ok, well my price will be good for another **5** minutes just let me know thank you. (This is Nashville, I'm not fixin to do all that work for $**1.50** a mile, I **WILL** get something better)

BROKER: Ok, well thanks for your call.

In this scenario, **she** never calls back and I book another load for better anyway. Sometimes, you just don't make a deal and keep it movin! At least they won't be making notes in their company computer on how easy it is to push over on rates on your dispatch.

AS YOU CAN SEE, THE TREND HERE IS TO ASK FOR WHAT YOU WANT IN A LIKEABLE WAY, HOLD TO IT then access the offers given back to you. ✓

NEXT LOAD: NO POSTED RATE AGAIN and "LET ME ASK MY SUPERVISOR" ✓

The next load is **Murfreesboro**, TN to **Charlotte**, NC. One thing I don't like about this load is that is goes across I-40 mountain pass into NC, but the load only weighs **25,000** lbs and I am going east down the mountain and not up so that's not too bad. There's no posted rate, but I'm **15** miles from pick up and it loads for a familiar broker. **410** loaded miles.

BROKER: Hi this is **Samantha** at Straight Up logistics; how can I help you??

ME: (I like her upbeat attitude already) Hi **Samantha**, my name is **Andrew**, <u>I'm with XYZ Trucking.</u>

BROKER: Oh, hi Andrew, how are you today?

ME: I'm doing great! How are you?

BROKER: I'm doing fine, thanks for asking.

ME: I'm calling on your load **Murfreesboro**, TN to **Charlotte**, NC.

BROKER: Yes, this load is still available, it picks today by **12** pm, can you make this pick up? (<u>It's **10am** and I'm **15** miles away. The fact that this load has to go within **2** hours, lets me know I have some leverage on it</u>)

ME: Yes, I can have it picked up within the hour actually.

BROKER: GREAT! How much will you do the load for?

ME: I want $**1200** for it.

BROKER: Hmm, I think I can do that, this load has to go. Let me talk to my supervisor and I'll call you right back, or you can stay on hold. (<u>always stay on hold if possible</u>) (30 seconds goes by) Hey Andrew, are you there?

ME: Yes, I'm still here.

BROKER: I got the **$1200** for you, what's a good email address I can send you the rate con?

BOOM! Right at **$3** a mile, going to a **GOOD** reload area. Another ANDREWS_METHOD! 😄

NEXT LOAD: POSTED RATE THAT I LIKE! ✔

Rock Hill, SC to Birmingham, AL. 382 loaded miles. Posted rate of $1050. No tarp. I like the load so I book it. Small deadhead, $2.70 a mile, nice route, good reload area. No negotiations needed.

NEXT LOAD: WEEKEND LOAD. POSTED RATE. ASKING FOR MORE! ✔

Gadsden, AL to **Harrisburg**, PA. **740** miles loaded straight up **I-81**. They have a posted rate of **$1850**, but it's Friday, the load has low interest on it on truckstop.com and the load has been posted for 2 hours. It just got reposted from **$1750** to **$1850**. I want **$2300** for it. **That's only** **$3.10**. I need my weekend load to have some more "**meat**" on it. Plus, it should pay more to go back north to **PA**.

BROKER: Hey this is **Steve** at Moonshine logistics. (he's young, I can hear it in his voice)

ME: Hey **Steve**! What's up! my name **Andrew**, I'm with XYZ Trucking…

BROKER: Hey what's up man.

ME: Oh, just calling on this **Gadsden** Alabama to **Harrisburg** load.

BROKER: Yeah, I still got that lettme pull it up... It's one pick one drop, light load, military miscellaneous pallets and it does need a **4ft** tarp. It pays **$1850** to truck.

ME: Hmm, you said 4ft tarps, right? Delivers Monday, right?

BROKER: Yes. 4ft tarps and it delivers Monday.

ME: If it was a weekday, this **$1850** would be a perfect for me. But since it's the weekend I want to be at **$2300** for it.

BROKER: That's a little steep, did you say you are already empty? When can you be there for pick up?

ME: yup! I'm empty now and am 45 miles from pick up. After the rate sheet, should be 1 hour give or take a few to be on site.

BROKER: Can you hold, let me see what I can do... (30 seconds goes by) Hey Andrew, my boss said he can't do the **$2300**, but he asked if you would do it for **$2200**.

BOOM! Still got almost **$400** more than the posted rate. The posted rate was decent, but would have been better for a weekday load. **Plus**, Harrisburg can really be hit or miss for flatbed freight. $3 a mile and up is the right price for this load.

SUMMARY:

As **easy** as some of this sounds, it can really take **years** to master the flow of the back and forth and even to know when the load volume will even allow certain price increase negotiation; By having all of this type of info, **you** can shave time off the trial-and-error process. Like mentioned, one of the biggest problems we've had to face in the trucking business up until recent 2020's and beyond was; **There's** just wasn't enough information like this book collection going around. That's a **big** reason why I had to assemble this book. I'm a teacher by nature who teaches through wisdom, listening and understanding....

I **hope** you value these tactics and trade secrets of mine collect throughout this text. They are the **same trade secrets** that have allowed me to **go** from owing **$65,000** on my truck with **$180** in the bank, to paying off multiple trucks, multiple properties, and having **financial freedom** and freedom of time. It's been a **long** journey but I'm rested and cool now! **I've** put in a lot of time and sacrifice over the years. I'm was happy to share this information with you! I had to learn all of this **the long** and **the hard** way. Luckily for me, a lot of being successful was common sense, but a lot of it is also particular experience too. ✔

In addition to this book, do what you can to find **real life mentors** who are successful. If a successful owner operator is speaking with you, **listen** and **politely ask** him what his tactics are at booking freight and what not. Figure out how he or she does it. That's what I've done over and over again throughout the years until I formulated the perfect recipe for me. **To this day**, I <u>still</u> fine tune and tweak my recipe to make it even better. I never stop learning! 😄

I realized a long time ago; THIS IS MY SHOW. ✔️

I **must** take **responsibility** and <u>learn everything I can</u>.

I **must** buy the tools.

I **must** get a little dirty.

I **must** talk with the elders.

I **must** run my numbers.

I **must** sacrifice.

I **must** take initiative.

I **must** attempt different negotiation styles.

I **must** get myself a little out of my comfort zone.

I **must** have faith and confidence in myself and my goals.

I **must** believe that I can.

I **must** put forth superior effort.

I **must** go the extra mile.

I **must** profit.

I **must** make my goal.

And I **must** stand my ground with a big smile on my face!

Dig your heels in. <u>Are you ready to make the moves</u>? Are you ready to stand your ground? Do you see the value in enthusiasm yet? Do you see the power in knowing and asking for what you want? You can do this too! Meditate and picture yourself already doing these things. Practice practice practice! If you truly study the methods and implement them into your life and operation, I am confident you will experience a higher plane of living, success and happiness. In the next chapter I will discuss with you my opinion in the Factoring vs not factoring debate. Let's keep it movin.

<u>YOU GOT THIS! I WANT TO SEE YOU WIN with this information!</u>

CHAPTER 18: FACTORING VS NOT FACTORING

This is a **debate** you will here amongst owner operators and small fleets. **Some** will say factoring is **good**, and owners like me will say "keep your money, why are you paying a factoring company". **I do not factor**. I never have. From day one, I chose against factoring. The main reason that got me was that, non-re-course factoring wasn't really non-recourse and **there** was a termination fee for each broker that you want to cancel with if you decide later on not to factor.

The fee for the company I was looking at was **$25** per customer. Well, I have over **100** brokerages as customers. That's a **$2500** fee just to terminate my contract with the factoring company! 🫥 when and if I were to leave the factoring company…

If **you** plan to run multiple trucks, factoring may not be a bad idea. **Since** this book is more so focused on the **solo owner operator**, I'm not going to discuss much about that. But the idea is, if you run like **5** trucks, you will be paying for **fuel up front**, and weekly settlements. This might be $**10k** to $**20k** a week or more if you're paying owner operators that are leased to you. That's upwards of $**80k** give or take a month in necessary cash flow. If you aren't sitting on at least $**120k** + cash, then factoring might be a good option to keep cash flow active. But for the **solo owner-operator**, I don't see a real reason to factor. If you don't have at least $20k to $40k saved up, maybe you should wait a little longer so you can come into this much stronger. 💵💵💵

Let's do some math. If you gross $**150,000** and pay a factoring company **3**% to factor every invoice, that will cost you $**4500**. If you gross $**175,000** that will cost $**5,250**. At $**200,000** that will cost you $**6000**.

You have to ask yourself, is getting your money in 24 hours worth the $4500 to $6000 you will pay in per year?
✓

To me, the answer was always no. Getting my money that fast was not worth it for me. I can do a lot with that type of money. $**4500** - $**6000**? That type of money pays half of my insurance cost for the year. By not factoring, I can afford to take off my whole winter if I want.

Let me ask you question, because this is how I see it. If you aren't going to need to spend this money within **30** days, why do you need to pay **3**% on money you're just going to put in the bank? **I have never got stiffed on any broker payment**. Every load that I've ever booked, I got paid for. If you already have your own authority and you are a little strapped on cash, if you're in that $**5k** to $**10k** range, an alternative to factoring as you may know, is to use a brokerages "quick pay". At least with **quick pay** you can cancel at any time without all the red tape that's involved with a factoring company.

What I do is keep an alternating group of customers. Some of my customers pay in **3** days no fee, some pay in **15** days no fee, and most pay in **30** and some pay within **45** days. As long as I haul a little bit from different brokerages, I have a **healthy rotation** of checks coming in. The more **successful** you get at this, you will **be** so far ahead on the money, that waiting for your money is not even a concern! I do my loads, bill my customers, and by the time I get home, my checks are almost already in my mailbox. That's why **business budgeting**, **home budgeting** and saving is so important! It's really true when they say "the rich get richer". By having money in the bank, I'm able to make an additional $**5000** or so a year because I don't need a factoring company to advance me the money. 💰

I'm not saying you're a horrible person or a failed business if you choose to factor. This is a **personal** decision that is ultimately up to you. Many successful companies all around the world factor. **Many of the brokerages themselves factor to get their money.** Many solo owner-operators and small fleets factor and do fine. What I'm doing is giving you my version of the story. **So**, you can weigh out what I'm saying and your own research to see what's right for you!

But it is my opinion, if you come into this with at least $**20k** to $**40k** (which is highly advised), **then** there should be no real reason to factor. Many people factor because they **don't** budget their money right, they **spend** their money too quick, they are **afraid** of not getting paid, they **don't** want to bill their customers, or because they are **not** in a strong enough financial position. ✔️

After paying all my fees, down payment on insurance, base plate and etc I had just under $**40k** in the bank. And my **truck** and **trailer** was already paid for. **So was my land and home**. I was going to factor because I still a little nervous that I didn't have enough money saved. I have a very unique operation in the sense that my overhead is so low. Minus business expenses, my home bills only cost $**5000** a year because I practiced what I teach! 😁

When I mention get your home bills down low, and don't get into bad debt deals, I lived it the whole course of my trucking business! ✓

This is what allows me <u>so much freedom</u> on the road, and at home. I don't have these huge bills lingering over my head at every corner. I've sacrificed long enough that now-a-days I pretty much eat whatever I want to eat, I go on a couple good trips per year, I take a lot of time off, drink beer, and enjoy the fruits of my labor! 😄👍

The cool thing, I <u>still</u> enjoy to truck too!

If it wasn't for all my sacrificing and home budgeting, I wouldn't have had the time that it has taken to write this book! ✓

I got the original idea to write this book **4** months ago. I've writing for almost **4 months straight**. I trucked about a total of **1** month in these last **4** months. <u>And even then</u>, I was writing and doing all the research to develop my online presence and to get this book out to you! On this most recent stretch, I've been writing everyday non-stop for the last **3** weeks. I would not be able to do this if I was hauling $**1.30** a mile freight, paying someone to work on my truck every time, making bad deals, factoring, having high home bills and etc. ✊🙏✓

You might be asking, **Andrew**, what if I already have high home bills and a truck note and I'm leased to a company that doesn't pay well?

Well, <u>I think you now know the answers</u>. **It's time to buckle up and start sacrificing!** ✓

It's time to start skipping a few eat out meals. It's time to **hold out** on buying things you want. **It's** time to start buying tools and working on your own truck. It's time to **move** your operation to a place like Landstar or a small fleet where you can book your own freight. It's time to get **serious** about saving. It's **time** to implement everything you've been learning in this book thus far. It's **time** to find a successful mentor. It's **time** to slow your truck down and ride easy! It's **time** to take charge! It's **time** to take full responsibility! Find places your you can lower your overhead and increase revenue. This is the key. 🔑

FIND WAYS TO LOWER YOUR COSTS BOTH IN BUSINESS AND HOME! FIND WAYS TO INCREASE YOUR REVENUE! ✔️

It can be done. **And if you increase your self-discipline, desire and initiative you will figure it out.** After reading this book, do yourself a huge favor a read Napoleon Hill's "Think and Grow Rich" https://amzn.to/2JXmrXP . This book will really help you lock down and develop the mentality that it takes to find, create and own success for yourself. 😁

→**NON-RECOURSE** is a term that attracts a lot of people. It's supposed to mean that if a brokerage doesn't pay, that you will still get paid. This service usually comes at a higher rate of **5%** or so. Every time that I've read the fine print on non-recourse deals, I see where it says you still have to pay the factoring company the money **back** that they factored you in the case of a non-payment.

Maybe owners have found true non-recourse deals where this is not the case but I never have. Then again, I only researched about **4** factoring companies when I started.

There were too many stipulations, rules, charge backs, fees and etc for me. Reading those contracts almost made me sick. 😬

I decided, "yeah I'm good, I don't need these guys". **5%** of **$175,000** is **$8750! NO THANKS**!!!! I will pass on that. **There's** no real reason to need a non-recourse factoring deal in my opinion, unless you decide to deal with shady brokerages. And there enough tools out here now to do good credit checks. Give up that **$9000** dollars if you want to! **I will not lol**. I can go on multiple cruise's or something for that. I could invest that into stocks. Trade option contracts. Rebuild my motor. Buy new tires. Take your pick! 🚛🚛

This **non-recourse** factoring just gives people a good feeling, I guess. **It's** like having health insurance if you're a **vegetarian**, **non-smoker** and **non-drinker** who works out because the insurance guy convinced you "well what if you get into an accident, it can happen to anyone". 😕

Now this person is paying **$400** a month for a hospital they never go to. That's **$5k** a year! But the thing with health insurance is kind of the same with non-recourse factoring. **Yes**, you pay for health insurance, but there's still **co-pay** and certain treatments and medication that they won't cover. **Same** thing with **non-recourse**, except in the contracts that I've read they don't non-recourse nothing in actuality, they charge you back for every bounced check or non-payment! 👻

I'm **not** saying don't have health care, I personally don't because I manage my own health without medication through diet and lifestyle choices. **If** you want to have healthcare, have at! **But** let me inspire you to take more responsibility in caring for your own health, **yea**?? <u>We don't put bad diesel into our trucks, so why would we put bad fuel into our bodies?</u> **I'm** slightly a hypocrite because I still drink beer, wine and smoke on and off. **But** what I eat and drink outside of that is **super healthy** and **conscious**. <u>I drink no soda</u>. I eat almost **no** fried food. And implement some very important secrets that doctors won't tell you but can be found in my book "**10 Secrets 4 Successful Health**" 😄! It's about 100 pages and loaded with great info. 🔒

Maybe the doctors know this stuff or maybe they don't. But most "doctors" I see don't look too healthy 😄. **It's common sense right**? You wouldn't have bought this book if I didn't seem successful but was attempting to sell you on success, would you? But for some reason, people **trust** doctors who don't look very healthy. <u>Whatever they're selling must not work</u>! **I've** figured out what causes type 2 diabetes, what causes the body's calibration system to be off, why most vitamins don't really work and more! I write about the 10 most important secrets that I've found in my health book! 😄👍

The same thing is true with **non-recourse** factoring. If you do your homework on who you're doing business with, there should almost never be a need for non-recourse factoring. That's we get to talk about next! How I credit check my new customers. This whole process of having your own authority is not that complicated! That's what I'm here for! To simplify things and break it down into little bite-sized pieces. You got this! Let's keep it movin.

CHAPTER 19: HOW I CREDIT CHECK NEW CUSTOMERS

This is a **very** easy process. Let me walk you through it! When I do my homework on a new customer, I want to establish if this brokerage will pay me within 40 days. **The** lower the days to pay the better of course. I do this using a few methods. I also check to see **how many** carriers are reporting this type of data. This data comes from factoring companies. The **more** factoring customers that are reporting, the more accurate the data is in my opinion.

I have never not been paid for a load that I've hauled. ✓

I think this is due to my methods of credit checking, and the fact that I send professional Quick Books invoices as soon as I get the signed **BOL**.

Truckstop.com allows you to have access to **Ansonia** credit reporting. As mentioned in my YouTube video (1) TRUCKSTOP.COM EP.1 LIVE LOADBOARD ACTION - YouTube , this is a very valuable resource when it comes to credit checking. **DAT** has some decent reporting too, but we will talk about them in a moment. **Ansonia** is a factoring company themselves and collects a ton of data on who's paying at what times and who's not. 💰

To access the **Ansonia** detailed report of a brokerage, first log into the desktop version on your phone, tablet or computer. Pull up an active load search. Scroll over until you see the column "**D2P**". There will be a number of **Days 2 Pay** in this column on the same row as the load you're looking at. Click the **D2P** number that matches the row of the load you're looking at. This will pull up another window with more detailed information. 📱

At this point, I will look at their insurance date and their company start date. The older the better. The **longer** the company's been in business, the more that proves to me that they have proved their reliability. I will take a risk on a newer company, as long as the load doesn't pay over what I feel comfortable losing; And if there's already companies reporting to **Ansonia** with good success.

Next there will be a hyperlink in the first section of the report that says "**Get the CreditStop Shipper report for Broker MC Number**". If you are on your phone, Click and **hold** the blue hyper link, which will be the underlined part. **This** will pull up an option to "**Open In New Tab**", select this option. This will now pull up the real, detailed Ansonia report. ✔

It will **show** a traffic light with green, yellow and red. **Green** meaning good, **yellow** meaning be cautious, and **red** meaning no go. I will only book with green light brokerages. But more important than the light colors, is the data. 🚦

My favorite part to look at is "Companies Reporting". I want to see at least **30** or more companies reporting. If this number is in the **100's** then great! That just makes the data even more accurate. 🌴

Next, I look at the "**Average Days-to-Pay**". It's interesting because in many cases, the days-to-pay in this detailed report will be different than the days-to-pay on the load board itself. Like I said, for **days-to-pay**, I'm looking for a number below **37-45**. I don't care to book with brokerages that are **45** days out. But one must **remember**, not every carrier sends their bills in on time. 😶‍🌫️

This counts against this days-to-pay score. A lot of times these companies that are **45** days out on **Ansonia** are really only **30** to **35** days out. But anything past **45** I will not work with, **period**! Even if the load is great. It's just too much risk for me. There are way more brokers in the ocean.

You have to **set** your own limits when it comes to what you're willing to risk, and what you're not.

→**By using this tool on Truckstop.com, you can get a very good idea about what's going on with the credit worthiness of a particular broker.** ✔

Remember also, a brokerage may be good, but only work with select trucks that do not factor. You may view their profile and there's only **7** companies reporting, but their days-to-pay looks good and so does their overall credit score. This is one of those deals when you'll have to call them up for yourself and see if you get a good vibe from them. If they are talking **sharky**, and being **dismissive**, I would probably stay clear of them. But if they are **respectful**, and explain why only a few companies are reporting because they are a trucking company and don't broker much freight out, you will just have to decide if you trust them or not.

I've met a couple small brokerages like this that have been great. One brokerage even told me, the day I deliver, she will put my check in the mail; And she sure did. I got a call from home about **3** days after delivery saying my check from her already came in. Use discretion, **trust your gut**, if you are unsure of the data, don't book for more money than you're willing to lose. If the data **looks** unsure, and the brokers are **rude** and **dismissive**; I wouldn't book with them. ✗

If your data is **unsure**, you have to really convince me and make me **comfortable** that you're a legit business. Give me some **incentive** like paying me quick at no charge. Give me some carrier references. Show me that you've been in business **10** years. Something along these lines. I've never lost out on payment by being careful using these methods. What I like to do next to be even more sure, is cross reference **Ansonia** with another free but valuable tool! ✔️

This tool is Welcome To Broker Credit Check . Go ahead and click this link and save it to the first page on your phone for quick access. This is a free service that is pretty accurate and one that I've used a **ton** over the years. **80**% of the time the numbers on broker credit check will match up or are very close to Ansonia. Before **Ansonia** I would use **RTS** factoring companies' data. I had a **RTS** fuel card at the time which gave me access to their credit checking data. **Before** I left **RTS**, I ran a side by side with broker credit check and their **RTS** data, and it was like **80**% or higher spot on with each other. This is what gave me the confidence in this website early on. 😄

One thing I like about Welcome To Broker Credit Check is that they will straight up tell you **"NO BUY"** if a company is too much of a risk to work with. This data may not always be accurate. **But** often times when I cross reference a company off **DAT** with real bad reviews, it will be a **"NO BUY"** in broker credit check.

Use broker credit check as a tool to cross reference Ansonia and DAT. ✔️

That way you're not going into these deals **blind** with just one set of data. If broker credit check supports what you find in **Ansonia** or **DAT**, <u>you should be good to go for the most part</u>. **This is what I do**. Of course, I have a lot of experience now and I can spot trends easier than someone who's new, but it's not that complicated. 😁

The more <u>you use these tools</u>, the more you will find **trends** and a <u>develop gut feeling</u> of your own. I almost never work with someone I get a bad vibe from them on the phone. **Think about it**, if they are already rude and dismissive now, how will they be if they are running late on their payments? Will they even pick up the phone? 🤥

DAT has some pretty good credit checking features. After doing some research, it looks like **DAT's** credit scores and **Days to Pay** is powered by **Ansonia** as well. To pull up credit checks on **DAT**, simply <u>pull up</u> the load, and on the app, it will show just under the company name. It will show "**CREDIT SCORE**", and on the next line down, it will show "**DAYS TO PAY**". ✔️

One nice feature that **DAT** has that **truckstop** doesn't have is a section called "**REVIEWS**". In this section you will see what other carriers have reported about this brokerage. If the brokerage wants to, they can dispute the claim. Some of these reports can be misleading because the carrier wasn't doing right and they won't to blame it all on the brokerage. But if there's many bad reviews, all saying the same thing, chances are they might be right. 🤔

Carriers will report things like "this company still hasn't paid me, all the way to, these brokers are rude". **Some** of it will just be basic complaints, but it all adds up! If the company is not paying, and has rude dismissive brokers, you probably want to steer clear of them. ✔️

Do everyone a favor too, if you have a great experience with a brokerage, write a review so we can all see it. <u>That's how we help each other by having each other's back when it comes to sharing good and bad experiences with brokers</u>. **This** helps other owner operators make informed decisions. If you get along good with your broker, and do a good job, they may even write a good review for your company if you ask them! 😁

A lot of this will get **easier** with experience and from paying attention to <u>days to pay trends</u>. It's a very good habit to look at the number of people reporting to decide how serious you want to take the days to pay number. 100 companies reporting will mean much more than 20 companies reporting.. **Double check** the <u>data</u> you get from **Ansonia** with <u>Welcome To Broker Credit Check</u> and you should be good to go. <u>Pay attention</u> to the attitude and demeanor of the broker you're working with especially if the company has **unsure** data. Use common sense, and trust your gut. If you are unsure of the data on **Ansonia** and broker credit check, either don't book the load or tread very lightly. In these situations, don't book a load for more than you're willing to lose. If the company looks new on their startup date, and the credit doesn't look too good, maybe you should pass on them. You have to decide when and where to draw the line. **There's a ton of great brokerages out here that pay on or around 30 days.** Do what you can to not get mixed up with the bad ones. Pay attention, and use these tips and methods and you should be fine! 😁

CHAPTER 20: MY CUSTOMER LIST

These are all <u>real customers</u> of mine imported from my Quick Books account. When I mention my over **100** customers all paying me, these are who they are. These are all **good** brokerages. Most of these companies pay within **30** days. Some pay sooner, some pay a little bit past 30 days.

BUT ALL OF THESE COMPANIES ARE ONES THAT I'VE WORKED WITH AND HAVE PAID THEIR BILLS! ✔

Have a look! I aimed to be very transparent in the production of my book. If you are on the boards and see any of these companies, <u>rest assured</u>, they're pretty good ones. **These** are the guys I deal with a constant basis. I will still be adding to this list too. If you don't see a company on this list, it doesn't mean that they are a bad company per say, it just means that didn't pass my standard, or I just haven't worked with them yet. **Be careful**, if you call some of these numbers. Some of these numbers go straight to individual brokers. When I make my customer profiles I look for the main number to save; But if I don't see a main number, I will fill in the phone number of the broker I booked the load with. This list isn't really for connections, its more so to give you a running list of brokerages I trust, and have done business with. 😁👍

Customer	City	State	Phone
Acme Supply Chain Solutions	Gretna	LA	(337) 873-8660

American Transport, Inc	Pittsburgh	PA	(770) 506-3329
Amino Transport	Southlake	TX	(888) 992-6466
Anderson Transportation & Logistics LLC	Anderson	SC	(888) 258-4088
Anthony's Transport Broker Services L.L.C.	Amite	LA	(985) 747-9011
Aok Freight	Olathe	KS	(816) 301-6226
ARI Logistics, LLC	Birmingham	AL	(205) 271-4400
Armstrong Transport Group, INC	Charlotte	NC	(877) 240-1181
ATS Logistics Services, Inc	St Cloud	MN	(844) 792-2082
Avenger Logistics	Chattanooga	TN	(423) 708-3700
Aztec LLC	Mantua	OH	(330) 274-2959
Baggett Services, Inc.	Birmingham	AL	(254) 278-0675
Bennett International Group, LLC	McDonough	GA	(205) 216-5830
Best Dedicated Solutions, LLC	Libertyville	IL	(217) 645-6342
Best Logistics	Kernersville	NC	(704) 869-2174
BNSF Logistics	Versailles	OH	(813) 440-2250

Bounce Logistics	South Bend	In	(574) 243-1550
Buchanan Logistics, Inc	Fort Wayne	IN	(260) 471-1877
Business Transportation Solutions Inc.	Stoughton	WI	(608) 205-1877
Cheetah Logistics	Houston	TX	(281) 388-5122
Citation Logistics, LLC	Slidell	LA	(985) 641-8233
CMT Transportation LLC	West Fargo	ND	(903) 200-1222
Coast 2 Coast Logistics, LLC	Medford	OR	541-646-7070
Cornerstone Systems	Memphis	TN	(833) 286-9251
CR Logistics	Coal City	IL	(800) 327-8661
Custom Transport, Inc	Brookville	IN	(800) 338-6288
D & L Transport, LLC	Overland Park	Ks	(913) 608-8700
Dagen Logistics, Inc.	Newtonville	NY	(518) 427-9624
Dalko Resorces	Sharpsville	PA	(866) 707-4286
DeCarteret Transport	Houston	TX	(701) 770-9895
Epes Logistics Services, Inc	Greensboro	NC	(336) 665-1553

Eventix Logistics LLC	Houston	Tx	(281) 616-5859
Expedited Transport, LLC	Vestavia	AL	(205) 994-8349
EZ Transportation, Inc	Clearwater	FL	(978) 621-4156
Fastmore Logistics	Elk Grove Village	IL	(630) 568-9068
Fitzmark	Indianapolis	IN	(205) 661-2889
Fourshore Transportation Company	Laurel	MS	(228) 206-1759
Fracht Trucking Solutions LLC	Houston	TX	(281) 221-1700
Freight Tec	Bountiful	UT	(435) 714-7016
Fremont Express	Elkhorn	NE	(866) 753-1066
Giltner Logistc Services, Inc	Twin Falls	ID	(208) 324-7826
Greentree Transportation Company	Pittsburgh	PA	(205) 484-9131
Hazel's Logistics	Dallas	TX	(972) 685-0863
Inland Transport, Inc.	Orlando	FL	(407) 858-3039
Integrity Express Logistics	Cincinnati	OH	(937) 329-9125

Intercity Direct Llc	Lenexa	KS	(913) 754-0303
IRay Logistics Inc.	Janesville	WI	(608) 314-2639
J.B. Hunt Transport, Inc.	Lowell	AR	
JJT Transportation & Logistics	Wathena	KS	(531) 365-3555
JLE Logistics	Homestead	PA	(724) 300-8049
Jones Motor Group	Limerick	PA	(484) 369-5526
JRC Transportation Services LLC	Thomaston	CT	(866) 665-6645
King Of Freight	Wichita	KS	(888) 924-0686
Knight Logistics LLC	Phoenix	AZ	(866) 500-5623
Listo Services LLC	Medford	OR	(888) 382-5316
Logikor LLC	Cincinnati	OH	(866) 773-8400
Logistic Dynamics, Inc.	Amherst	NY	(319) 731-1311
Logistics Made Simple, INC.	Chattanooga	TN	(423) 893-5115
Material Logistics Management, Inc	Pittsburgh	PA	(412) 331-8200
Maverick Transport, Inc.	Easton	MD	(410) 820-5500

Meadow Lark Agency, Inc	Billings	MT	(406) 281-8953
Mercer Transportation Co., Inc	Louisville	KY	(502) 584-2301
MK Logistics	Diberville	MS	(228) 285-1599
Nolan Transportation Group, LLC	Atlanta	GA	(972) 823-9250
NT Logistics, Inc.	Frisco	TX	(405) 378-0567
One Point Logistics	Charleston	SC	(843) 628-4462
Paladin Freight Solutions Inc.	Memphis	TN	(888) 490-7030
Percision Transport, Inc	Titusville	PA	(814) 827-0613
Perimeter Global Logistics	Irving	TX	(877) 701-1919
PLS Logistics Services	Cranberry Township	PA	(724) 814-5100
R&R Express Logistics, Inc.	Pittsburgh	PA	(800) 223-8973
RDX Brokerage LLC	Barlett	TN	(901) 308-1364
Roadrunner Truckload Plus	Batesville	AR	(205) 832-1290
Rockhill Transport, Inc	Stilwell	KS	(913) 897-4462
Rowe Transport, Inc.	Indianapolis	IN	(317) 787-9437

Ryan Transportation Service, INC	Overland Park	KS	(913) 335-9342
SFadvance Transportation Services, Inc	South St. Paul	MN	(651) 451-2977
SSTC Logistics, LLC	Montgomery	TX	(936) 588-8558
Standard Freight LLC	Hockley	TX	(601) 794-8817
Stephen Frederick Logistics Inc.	Brantford	ON	(519) 759-6042
Sunteck Transport Co., Inc.	Frisco	TX	(615) 553-4697
Superior Nationwide Logistics LTD	Houston	TX	
System Transport	Spokane	WA	(514) 401-9978
Taimen Transport LLC	Chattanooga	TN	(423) 693-0280
Talbert Logistics LLC	Mineral Wells	TX	(940) 325-3300
Tennessee Steel Haulers, Inc	Nashville	TN	(615) 271-2400
TJR Logistics, LLC	Marion	IN	(765) 734-4534
TMC Logistics	Des Moines	IA	(888) 858-6956
Tortorigi Transport	Trussville	AL	(205) 438-7300
Total Logistics Solutions LLC	Johnson City	TN	(423) 391-0505

Traffic Tech, Inc	Chicago	IL	(770) 772-0614
Transcorr National Logistics	Louisville	Ky	(616) 284-6103
Transfix	New York	NY	(929) 293-0360
Transplace Southeast, LLC	Louisville	KY	(412) 893-4812
Trinity Logistics	Seaford	DE	(866) 874-6489
Tucker Company Worldwide, Inc.	Haddonfield	NJ	(856) 317-9600
Uber Freight LLC	San Fransico	Ca	(628) 207-0610
UCW Logistics, LLC	Winston-Salem	NC	(336) 608-3655
United Visions Logistics	Lafayette	LA	(800) 564-7973
Universal Truckload Inc	Warren	MI	(586) 920-0100
US Expedited LLC	Kansas City	MO	(918) 559-7588
Virginia Transport LLC	Chicago	IL	(773) 516-4602
WFX Logistics, LLC	Oklahoma City	OK	(405) 946-7289
Worldwide Express	Dallas	TX	(888) 956-7447
Worldwide Iscs	Urbandale	IA	(877) 685-3737

**Zmac Transportation
Solutions**   Racine   WI   (262) 664-4151

CHAPTER 21: HOW I BILL MY CUSTOMERS

Before I got my own authority, this was one question that I needed to know. I asked whoever I could when the opportunity presented itself. The answer I got the most is, "oh I'm leased to this company I don't know" or "I factor all my loads, I just send them to the factoring company and let them do it". I went onto the truckers report forum and asked there, I got a **couple** decent responses, but mostly the answer was to make Microsoft Excel spreadsheets and send those out. I wanted something a more professional and organized. I wanted something more automated.

About a month or two before I filed for my authority, I got to meet an owner operator in VA with his own authority. We were both loading a load of crane parts going to a building in downtown Charlotte by the Panthers stadium. He had a good looking **pre-emission** mid roof Kenworth T600 I believe it was. It looked like it just got a fresh candy red paint job. His flatbed looked great, and I could tell by the **letters** on the side of his door and by his truck selection; That he had his own authority or is leased to a small company. My guess was right, he had his own authority.

I asked him a bunch of questions in the **15** minutes we got to talk. I asked him about factoring, he didn't factor. I asked him about booking loads with a new authority. And the best question I got to ask him was, "**since** you don't factor, how do you bill your customers, and how long does it take to get paid, and have you ever not got paid?" This is when is got my introduction to **Quick Books**. He whipped out his new iPhone and pulled up **Quick Books** so he could show me as he explained. 📱

I was <u>amazed</u> at how clean the interface was. **It looked good**! He was super confident. He showed me his customer list, what the invoices look like, and how the program keeps up with all the outstanding invoices (accounts receivable). We **didn't** have much that time that day to talk, but he gave me the boost of insight that I needed! And you want to know the kicker? This **Quick Books** app he showed me is only **$12** a month!

Thank you Sir! I still use Quick Books today because of him. ✔

As you can see, I like **Quick Books lol**. People still try to argue me that I don't need that, and I can just do it in Microsoft Excel, and they are right! I could, but I don't want too 😄! <u>Come on</u>, it's **$12** bucks a month to almost completely automate my billing process. Every time I send an invoice out, it looks great. It has my logo on the top right. My invoices look like "**You got to PAY ME!**". My invoices <u>look like I take my business serious</u>, **because I do**! I love the invoice tracking feature. As soon as I send an invoice out, all I have to do is check my "**SALES**" section (on iPhone) or "**INVOICES**" section (on iPad) and it will show me everybody that owes me money. It will organize them from who's owed me money for the longest down to who's owed me money for the least amount of time. 💰

This feature takes no work for me. All I have to do is quickly check my app to see if someone is about to be overdue or is overdue. Then I can click on their customer detail to pull up their phone number, talk to accounts payable, and make sure they got my bills and invoice. **SIMPLE**. We have a lot of responsibilities as an owner operator, why not pay **$12** a month for a personal billing assistant that will make your life more easy. It's not like it's **$75** a month. The amount of time I make up by using **Quick Books** instead of pulling out my laptop to do billing makes it worth it on its own. **Plus**, it's a tax write off.

Let me show you how this works. When I book a load with a new customer, the night before I deliver, I pull up **Quick books** on my iPad (this can be done on the phone too).

1. **First**, I make a customer profile. I go onto **Google** and find a logo for the company and I save the image to my "photos". Inside the "**New Customer Profile**" section, I upload the photo. This gives their profile more flair and realism to me. ✓

2. After I do this, I fill in their "**Display Name**" with the name of the brokerage, then I copy and paste it to the "**Company**" name. ✓

3. I put their accounting departments email (or the email they request to send invoices to) in the "**Email**" section. ✓

4. I fill in their phone number with the main line phone number (so it's easier to reach the accounting department), if for some reason I don't have immediate access to this number and the google search doesn't pull anything; I'll use the brokers phone number in this

slot. Most rate contracts will have their main number somewhere on it. ✔

5. I continue by filling in their complete address. You will need to have this filled in, so it auto-populates onto your invoice. ✔

6. Terms: For terms I always put "Due on Receipt" ✔

That's it for setting up a customer profile. Easy right?? **So**, once the customer profile is built, I will continue to make the invoice itself. I have made it a habit to already make the invoice the night before I deliver. I do this so all I have to do after delivery is snap a photo of the BOL using the Tiny Scanner App Tiny Scanner - PDF Scanner App - Apps on Google Play and save it to my files.

Once the **BOL / POD** (proof of delivery) is in my files, I can pull up my **Quick Book** App, pull up my invoice that I made the night before, and attach my **BOL / PROOF OF DELIVERY**, then email it off! 🔒

If you set up your invoice the night before, this whole process of taking the pdf photo, to linking it to your invoice, and emailing it off, takes **less than 5 minutes**. For me it takes less than **3** minutes. I almost always send my invoices off the **moment** I get the BOL. That way my **30** days for payment starts now, rather than later. Brokerages will pay **30** days **AFTER** the paperwork has been received, not after the load was delivered. So, stay on top of your game and get those invoices and proof of deliveries sent out **ASAP!** 😄

The **Tiny Scanner** App Tiny Scanner - PDF Scanner App - Apps on Google Play makes **GREAT PDF** files! I've never had a customer complain that they can't read my files.

Texting your proof of delivery is **VERY** unprofessional. Sending anything other than a **PDF** file is pretty unprofessional. **PDF's** have become the **GOLD STANDARD** in trucking accounting departments nationwide. Make sure you <u>utilize</u> an app like **Tiny Scanner** to make your **PDF's**. I paid like **$5** for the **PRO VERSION**. It has been a great investment for sure.

Another thing I do to make sure I get paid on time is; <u>Include the original signed rate confirmation attached to my invoice</u>. **This** is simple to do if you're on an apple product like iPad.

I just go to my Gmail outbox (sent), I open up the **PDF** file where I signed, I then click on the top right-hand corner (may be different for your application) and "<u>save to files</u>". Once this signed rate con file is in my files, I can easily attach it to my invoice. By attaching the rate con to your invoice; **You** are helping to ensure that the person on the other side will have access to all the <u>in-house numbers</u> he or she will need to locate the load in their system. This really helps any problems that **may** arise about "<u>incorrect</u>" **PRO** numbers, Load numbers and etc. Plus, it just looks more professional. The more professional you carry yourself; the more people tend to treat you professionally!

This is the step-by-step process to create your own invoice. (It's super EASY!) I prefer to do this on my iPad.

1. Go to your "Customer List"

2. Press the + button. (this may say "add" or "create")

3. Select "Invoice"

4. Select the date to the day you will deliver the load.

5. On the phone you will click on "+ Add product or service"

6. Press whichever one you want, I choose "sales"

7. Once inside this section, click on "**Rate**" and type in the amount the you made the deal for. The same amount that is on the rate confirmation.

8. In the "Enter a Comment" section I will do the following; (FILL IN THE SPECFIC LOAD DETAILS AS WRITTEN IN THE RATE CON)
   LOAD # XYZ123
   Dallas, TX load 24,000 lbs
   Deliver to Jackson, MS

9. In the "Message to Customer" section write your remit to address like this:
   REMIT TO:
   XYZ TRUCKING LLC
   200 GOTTA GET IT ST
   ATLANTIS, GA 31093

10. Press save.

11. You will get brought to a new page now with the "loaded" invoice waiting to be sent off. You will see at the bottom a paperclip icon that says "Add notes or Attachments". **Click this**. This is where you will attach

you **PDF** files. Attach your **RATE CON**, and your **BOL / POD**.

12. Once you attach the files you are ready to send this invoice off for your money!

13. On the top right of the "**loaded**" invoice screen you will see **3** little dots. **Click here**. This will give you the option of "**Email**". Click on email.

14. **Once** clicked, you will be taken to an email screen. Make sure the email is being sent to their accounting department's email (this is why we set up a good customer profile!), if their email looks good, tap into the "**To**:" email bar after their email. This will pull up your keyboard (as if you were going to add another email). Once in this "bar" and with the keyboard pulled up, press the "return" button on your keyboard. **This** will put a comma after their email and allow you to write another email. Go ahead and enter your own email. I always include myself on the invoice emails to make sure that the email went through. ✔

15. **THAT'S IT. YOUR DONE. COLLECT YOU CHECK!** 💰

It sounds like a lot of steps, but it's super easy. I just did the most by explaining it in very easy to understand steps. This **whole process** once you master it takes no time at all. It's not a bad habit to contact the accounts payable department of the brokerage about 2-5 days after you send everything. Tell them you are checking on the status of your invoice and you want to make sure that they got all the paperwork they need. They will ask you for a **PRO** or **LOAD** number, just make sure you have it ready when you call. ✔️

I don't even call to check if they got my stuff anymore. If they start running late on my payment I'll call. **But** a lot of the loads I haul are for the same customers that I've dealt with before. I know they will pay and are good for it. But still, it is not a bad habit to give a follow up call to make sure they got it. This will help you get paid on time for sure for sure. 💰

It's also a good gesture to **include** your broker in on the **invoice** / **POD** email. Once you send the email off to everyone, make sure to call or email you broker and tell him or her that the load is finished and everything went perfect! And that you included them in the **POD** email just in case they need it. They will be impressed by how **quick** you move and will probably thank you and tell you to give them a call whenever for another load.

This is great customer service! ✔️

That's all there is to it! Now you know. **Whether** you already have your own authority or are studying getting ready to make the leap yourself, this is the good information to know. This is **exactly** how I bill my customers. My bills look professional and my invoice tracking system is easy.

I wonder how I would bill my customers if it wasn't for the owner operator in VA that I met?? 🤔🧔

It's because of him, that you get to do this way now too! **So**, go ahead and thank him right quick! **I know I am thankful for his advice**!

But that's what this is all about. <u>Steady growth</u>. <u>Listening</u> and <u>paying</u> attention. Asking the <u>right</u> questions to the <u>right</u> people. ✔

I spotted the owner operator out in VA **because** I could tell by his truck, trailer and his company decals that he was an <u>independent</u>. **Use** your vision like this to spot people out and strike up a little conversation! Let them know you just started, or that you're researching to get your own authority. **Ask** them if they have any advice or tips. Sometimes you will get stupid answers like "Quit while you can" or "you better save up some money", **but** many times too <u>you will get good advice to think about</u>. 👍

It helps to have **good** <u>enthusiasm</u> and to be <u>respectful</u> **too**. It also helps if you have a **specific** question like "How do you bill your customers if you don't mind me asking?" **These** direct questions will probably <u>get better answers</u>.

Get your knowledge! <u>Learn from these successful guys</u>. **Continue** to put all the information together and figure out how **YOU** want to do it. **This is your show!** <u>You're the boss!</u> 👉

Experiment with different tactics and methods until you crack the code for what works for you. ✔

Once you <u>crack the code</u>, **continue** to develop it and make it better. This is how you become successful! That's what I'm here for, to help you "**<u>crack the code</u>**" 😁.

Let's talk some more specifics. **The next chapter is "Carrier Packs".** You might have heard of these before. There's not much to it. I'll show you what it's all about. 🚚

CHAPTER 22: CARRIER PACKS

Carrier packs are simply the **forms** we as carriers fill out for the brokerages. **Carrier packs** are short for carrier packets. I remember starting out and being a little nervous about carrier packs, mainly because I didn't know what they were. I remember booking my first load, projecting myself as if I knew what I was doing lol. They asked me what email should they send the carrier pack to. I was like oh man here we go! I hope I can figure it out fast enough and my research has set me up right! I had my iPad and Apple Pencil ready to go! And sure enough, that set up still works great to this day! Not only did I get the carrier pack sent back in a quick manner**, I realized**, oh this isn't hard at all! 😁

If you're going to have your own authority, I do advise eventually getting an iPad PRO (preferably with its own cell signal) and an APPLE PENCIL https://amzn.to/3aqur0E **. This setup is perfect for filling out non-digital carrier packs.** ✔️

Each brokerage has their own style and method when it comes to carrier packs.

Carrier packs can be anywhere from 1 page to a contract over 15 pages plus. ✔️

Carrier packs are simply the brokerages way to collect all the necessary paperwork, information, and certificates on a carrier. 📝

Inside this carrier packet will also be the **main** binding contract between you and the brokerage. Once you fill out a carrier pack for a brokerage, you will rarely have to fill out another one. If your insurance has been renewed since your last haul with them, you will more than likely be required to send them an updated copy of your insurance and that's it. This is normal. But a lot of brokerages are moving to digital onboarding platforms now like McLeod Trucking Software - Trucking & Transportation Management Software | McLeod Software , Home Page - MyCarrierPackets.com , and RMIS rmisdirectory.com . **This digital onboarding process can be very convenient and even automatically update your insurance for you.** 😁👍

This digital onboarding process can usually be completed on your phone, but something like an iPad is preferred. The cool thing about this onboarding software is that it usually saves almost **all** your carrier information in the system. This way, when you get a new carrier packet from a brokerage that uses the same software, many of the pages will be pre-filled; Making less work and time for you.

Some of these carrier packs are more than 10 pages long. A lot of the information they ask for can be your company name, address, and email over and over again on multiple pages lol. **So**, it's real nice when it's already filled out. ✔️

BUT: You have to be prepared to fill out long carrier packs that are not digital. These days it's about 50/50. **50**% of brokerages still use traditional carrier packs which you fill out by hand and the other **50**% have moved to a digital onboarding process. 📄

The bigger brokerages are more so the ones going digital. Some guys will go into the truck stop, pay to receive the fax (sometimes 20+ pages), then pay $**2** a page to fax everything back. **COME ON**! We have ways around this now! That is not sustainable over time. That means for my **100** customers, I would have spent north of **$4000** if I did carrier packs <u>over fax</u>. Buy an iPad pro and an Apple Pencil! It will make your life so much easier and efficient. You'll make that money back in about a years' time of not paying and waiting for faxes. 😄

The carrier packs will request from you a few pieces of important paperwork. It is a good idea to have these documents **saved** <u>in an easy to access place</u>. I store mine all in its own folder inside the "**files**" app on my iPhone / iPad. These important documents will be requested by almost every brokerage.

They are:

1. Authority Certificate
2. Active Insurance Certificate
3. A filled-out W-9 for the active year you're in. <u>Form W-9 (Rev. October 2018) (irs.gov)</u>
4. And for good measure I add my Carrier profile that I made in Microsoft Word, exported as a PDF file. It has my company logo, phone numbers, email, billing address and etc. (this is not a requested item, but I do it for good show)

Everything else that they want will be in the carrier pack itself. They will ask you for your address, billing address, your email, how many trucks and trailers you have, what lanes do you run, where are you looking for backhauls at and etc. Each brokerage will be a little different in what they ask for. **They are basically just building a profile of you to have on file.** ✔

Some brokerages will ask for references; Especially **if** your authority is <u>still new</u> (less than 1 year old). **This** may be frustrating in the beginning because maybe you haven't hauled for anyone yet. But It's ok to put the names of just about anyone in here. **Anybody** <u>that can vouch for your character</u>. It can be your parts guy, your close friend, girlfriend, someone from your old company, a family member or etc. Don't let this bum you out in the beginning. Once you get your first **3** loads hauled, you will have **3** companies that can now vouch for you. It's not that big of a deal! 👍

I have noticed that when filling out handwritten carrier packs with my iPad and Apple pencil; It's **better** for me to link my Gmail to the "<u>mail</u>" app that comes default on apple products. I still use the **GMAIL** app for my main email communication, but also keep it linked to my "mail" app for signing documents. I don't know what it is with the Gmail app, but the "**mail**" app works way better for me when it comes to signing documents with my apple pencil. Once if fill everything out, I will attach my authority certificate, insurance, and signed W-9 and just select the option to reply to all. 😊

THE CARRIER BROKER CONTRACT ✔

This carrier broker contract almost looks the same for every brokerage. It's like they all copy and paste and use the same one, each with a couple of minor differences lol. **You** will fill out the date, write in your carrier name, MC number, and sign it at the end. I usually <u>initial</u> every page on the bottom right just to speed up the process of getting approved. In some contracts it is mandatory that you initial the bottom right of every page. 👍

This is your chance to read through the contract and make whatever change you want to. I don't usually cross anything out, but some guys do. <u>Just know</u>, the more you cross out, the longer it will take to get you approved, and many brokerages will just **deny** to work with you if you <u>don't agree</u> to all their terms. It's pretty crazy, but kind of the way it goes. **Maybe** one day we can pool together to make Brokerage Carrier Contract reform. We just want **simpler**, more **balanced** <u>contracts</u>. But until then, you kind of got to do what you got to do

CERTICATE HOLDER ✔

If you have your own authority, you will eventually come across this term "<u>certificate holder</u>". Your broker might tell you something like "ok, once you get the carrier pack in to me, we need to be listed as a certificate holder as well". This is normal. **All this means is**, <u>their company will be listed on your insurance certificate</u>.

What this does for them is; It allows them to get <u>notified</u> if there is a **change** or **lapse** in your insurance coverage. The way I make them a certificate holder is, I call up **OOIDA** (my insurance company), I <u>ask</u> for truck billing, once in the truck billing department I tell them that I have a customer that needs to be **added** as a <u>certificate holder</u>. I tell them the name of the company, usually the company will already be on file, I make sure the address is right, and they will either fax or email it for me. **I always choose email**. I give them the email address of the broker that I'm working with, then I ask to be included in the email (just in case the other one doesn't go through). <u>That's it!</u> That's your **Certificate Holder** or "**CERT HOLDER**" as brokers call it in emails sometimes.

SUMMARY ✔️

That's all there really is to it when it comes to carrier packs! Just have your main documents in an easy to access place, have a way to fill out the handwritten carrier packs, read through your contracts if you want to and that's it. It's pretty easy!

Sometimes it is annoying writing your company name over and over again on different pages of the packet, but it's all good. The more carrier packs you do, the easier and quicker you will get at doing them. There are only **3** or so main digital onboarding services that brokerages use. **So**, there's a good chance that you will come across different brokerages that use the same software. **This** is good for you because most of your carrier packet's will be pre-filled for you! Pretty easy now that you now right?? 😁

Having your own authority isn't that complicated, I **think** it's the fear of the unknown that scares most people off. I had these same concerns in the beginning but I kept on doing research. Having your own authority consists of small things like "**carrier packs**" that sound complicated but really aren't. But if you don't know, you don't know! I'm so glad I got the idea to write this book! I get to show you the way! I get to show **how** a lot of this stuff isn't that complicated. You get to see it for yourself in advance. You get to hear it from a seasoned owner operator. And I get **$27** for my instruction and my initiative to write all of this into a book 😁! That's a pretty good deal if you ask me! **We both get to win**!

I know my book has been super long, but I'm really taking **10** years of **real advanced experience** and jamming into one book. Some of these topics I **have to** describe in the detail that I have. I want to make sure you understand. I want to make sure you **OVERSTAND**!

I want to make sure that you are <u>prepared</u>. ✔

I want to make sure that you are **way more** <u>equipped</u> now than before you came through my course.

I want to make sure that you have the knowledge to make great decisions.

I want to **increase** your confidence!

I want to make sure that you are shown the pros and cons of different decisions and methods.

I want you to have all the cards in your hand that I didn't have when I started.

I want you to win!

<u>I want your family to be proud of you!</u>

I want you and your family to be financially stable because of your success!

I want you to be the <u>owner</u> of land, the <u>owner</u> of your equipment, and the <u>owner of your life</u>!
✔ ✔ ✔ ✔

Let's continue, I will talk about <u>rate contracts</u> next. This will be another quick chapter. **You're blazing through it now**! Once you build this great foundation, everything you build on top of it has a greater chance of standing the test of time. That's what you're doing right now. <u>Building</u> a great foundation for your success in trucking and for your success in life! You are putting in the work. You are separating yourself from the pack. **You are outworking your**

competitors. You are taking <u>initiative</u>. You know what you want. **Or** at least by now you realize how important it is to know what you want! You are creating the habits in your mind that will take you off the old path, and onto your new path! **The path that will lead you to what you want.**

CHAPTER 23: RATE CONS

Rate cons are short for <u>rate contracts</u> or <u>rate conformations</u>; also called <u>rate sheets</u>. These are the contracts you will get after you book a load. These rate cons are the contract you and the brokerage make for a certain load. This contract may be one page, it may be multiple pages. It may be **digitally** accepted or it may be **handwritten** only. This is where having the **iPad PRO** and **apple pencil** come in again (or something similar).

This contract will have; The rate that was agreed on, the pick-up and delivery times, the address', the weight, the pick-up number, the load number, the information of where to send your invoice and POD, and any other information particular to this load. **Make** <u>sure to read</u>, <u>double check</u> and make sure **everything is right** on your rate cons. **Because** once you sign, the load is yours now, exactly how it's written in the contract.

Expect to get a rate con within **5** to **15** minutes after booking a load. Anything longer than **15** minutes, I would call to make sure they are still on top of it. If you're not too busy then maybe you can wait on it; But it's kind of **fishy** if they don't get back to you within **15** to **30** minutes without good reason.

Sometimes I will have a broker who is on lunch break, we book a load, and he tells me it will be another **30** minutes until he gets back to his office. <u>This I understand</u>, and is ok in book, **especially** if I'm pre-booking a load and have time. **But** if I'm empty now and I want to get moving, I might tell him; "That's to long for me to wait, but do call me when you get back in your office, if I'm still available I will do the load."

If you book a load towards the closing of a business day, say **5** or **6**pm, you **may not** get a rate con <u>until the next day</u>. This is ok and is normal. 😁

You'll have to learn to trust your gut instinct as you gain more experience. You have to trust your gut wether this broker is taking too long to get back to you with a rate con or not. **Sometimes** the broker really doesn't have the load yet and is working to lock it down from the shipper. **Sometimes** they are waiting to see if they can move the load for cheaper too. <u>Usually</u>, I draw the line right around **30** minutes of waiting **IF THERE'S** no good reason to wait.

I will call one more time, ask what's going on, and say I'll wait **5** more minutes; Then I will have to keep it movin…. This is one reason I prefer to book loads with posted rates. **When** a load has a <u>posted rate</u>, this tells me that the broker is content at moving the load for that price. **Therefore**, there is usually way less drama on loads with posted rates. **They are not trying to find carriers to do it for cheaper because they already moved it for the rate they wanted**. ✓

When you book loads with no posted rates and get a great rate, you want that rate con fast! The longer time goes by, you can **almost bet** <u>they are looking for a cheaper carrier</u>. **Especially** if that brokerage has a reputation for doing these types of things (which is usually the bigger brokerages). I almost never prebook loads with no posted rate.

If I book a load with no posted rate, I'm looking to put it on my trailer asap! ✓

Once I'm loaded, <u>I know that I'm good</u>, and that the load is mine. I usually won't deadhead very far on those loads posted without a rate either; **Especially** if I get the feeling they might be trying to get it moved for cheaper.

When you get your rate con, make sure to review all the important information. Make sure that the rate is right; Make sure that the pickup and delivery times are right as well. Make sure that the tarp size is right (if flatbed). Make sure there's **no weird stipulation** or **deal** they are making you agree to in the <u>notes</u> or <u>in the fine print</u>. And that's about it!

I will cross stuff out on rate cons if it's not right. Like if it says deliver at **7**am but we agreed to a first come first serve (**FCFS**) before **4**pm; I will cross out **7**am and write **FCFS** before **4**pm <u>as discussed</u>. **It** doesn't happen often with good brokerages like the ones in my customer list, but if that rate con says deliver at **7**am, and you deliver at **8**am, you <u>could</u> get a rate reduction or a back charge of some kind.

This especially happens in some of the bigger more sharky brokerages that I won't really name on here for the sake of "defamation", but ask around and look at <u>TruckersReport.com Trucking Forum | #1 CDL Truck Driver Message Board (thetruckersreport.com)</u> ; You'll find out who these companies are eventually. Once you find out who these **over-sharky** companies are, I would avoid them like the plague. I have quite a few brokerages that **I will not haul for**, <u>period</u>!

I don't care <u>how good the load is</u>. I'm not taking the **risk** of getting hit with bogus freight claims, charge backs, and refusing to pay me because of some made up freight claim and stuff like that. I will not name the brokerages because of "defamation" but I wish I could! A couple of them are pretty obvious though, if you ask around enough, <u>you'll find out quick</u>. **Ask** guys "which brokerages would you not haul for", and keep tabs of who people say and why. Then as you go, make your own list of brokerages that don't meet your standard, and don't haul for them! ✔️

So, look over and check your rate con very well, cross out and make changes if need be. **Usually**, you won't get much kick back for making casual changes to the rate con. <u>Of course</u>, you can't just mark the rate out and put an extra thousand dollars on it lol; But things like tarp size, delivery times, and etc, I will cross out if need be. I cross it out and write the correct thing next to it followed by "as discussed". 🔍✏️

Make sure the rate is right! You don't want to <u>accidently</u> sign the rate con for a wrong, lower than you discussed rate! It will be an **unnecessary** and **embarrassing** task to get them to change it back. You might even get kickback at this point. Because **technically** <u>you signed it</u>, and they don't have to fix it if they don't want to. If you find yourself in this situation, just approach your broker with **enthusiasm** and **confidence**, let them know that the rate in the rate sheet is not correct. Don't let them know you signed it already, just play it as if you haven't signed it. **Ask** for an <u>updated rate sheet</u>. Do what you can to avoid that altogether by just checking over the important details **BEFORE** you sign! 😁

Make sure you read and follow the little notes or instructions if there are any on the rate con. **Things like** "Carrier must provide a check call by 10am everyday while in transit", there may be a list of little nit-picky things like this followed by a

"OR THE CARRIER COULD RECEIVE A $100 REDUCTION IN RATE PER OCCURANCE".

Just be careful and check the little fine print. **Usually**, brokerages won't stoop to this low level as long as you're communicating and doing a great job on their load. **But do be aware**, and its good practice to go ahead and follow those little instructions so you eliminate any chance of rate reductions or etc. **Most** times I will just talk to my broker and ask him or her if they wants check calls while I'm in transit, usually the answer is no. **If you prove yourself early on** in the deal with good communication, usually the broker will cut you free to do what you want. Things like emailing when you get on site for pick-up, and emailing or calling when you are loaded and in-route can make a big difference. 🔑

Rate contracts protect you and they protect the brokerage. **Contracts** are good in my opinion for almost any type of business. A **contract** helps keep people straight on their end of the deal. A **contract** is proof in court that a deal was made. This protects you to the rate that you agreed to. I've never had to go to court or nothing over a load, but none-the-less, this contract would be proof if need be. 📃✔️💰

Signing rate cons and reviewing rate cons are super easy. Just search for the main things like **rate**, **delivery** and **pick-up times**, **weight** and etc. Make corrections if you need to. I do my signing of rate cons in the "mail" app inside my iPad, I click on the **PDF** file and sign with my Apple Pencil https://amzn.to/3agur0E . Once I sign the document, I just hit "reply to all". 📇

Many rate cons now are digital, and don't require a physical signature. You just type your name in the box (on your phone or tablet) and press submit. It will **automatically** generate a default signature and time stamp it. And **that's** it when it comes to rate cons. About as simple as it gets! Make sure the deal looks good on paper, sign it, and be on your way to making more profit!

Just be careful of what you sign and pay attention to the little deductions that can hit you with, and you should be fine! ✔

In the next chapter I will share with you the exact fuel card I use. Since fuel is pretty much the biggest cost we have in trucking, it is **VERY IMPORTANT** how you source your fuel, and who you decide to use as your fuel card provider. Let me show what I do. On to the next chapter! 🚛🚛

CHAPTER 24: FUEL CARD

This will be a short chapter, but a <u>very</u> <u>important</u> one.

Fuel is easily the biggest day to day expense that we spend on to run our business in trucking. <u>Saving big money</u> at the pump will really help to increase your profits and enforce your desire to be successful. ✔

I save upwards of $**3000** to $**6000** a year in fuel off a $**250** membership. And to think, some owners won't get involved in this fuel card operation because it costs $**250** or $**350** to get in! **Come on!** <u>This is business</u>. You got to spend money to make money. **Invest wisely**. With enough trial and error, I eventually found the **BIG DOG** in the trucking fuel card game. Their name is **NASTC** <u>Home | NASTC - The National Association of Small Trucking Companies</u>.

NASTC is an association, kind of similar to **OOIDA**, but their main focus is providing us independent owner operators and small fleets with the <u>most competitive fuel pricing available</u>. **David Owens**, the owner, has built his company from the ground up. We (**NASTC**) are now the largest customer of **TA Petro**. This is why we get the same discount if not better than the big fleets. I remember David Owens saying in his orientation there is over **10,000** of us over at **NASTC**. The discounts I get at **NASTC** are the <u>same</u> or **BETTER** than the fuel discounts I got a Landstar! **That's incredible**!!!! That was one reason I was hesitant to leave Landstar. I would convince myself that "well, I'm paying a big percentage to Landstar but we got some of the best freight and fuel discounts out here". **Now**, I get the same fuel discounts if not bigger discounts with **NASTC**. <u>Little did I know</u>! 😁

The only other fuel card I tried was **RTS** fleetone. They were not too bad. One thing I liked was that I had access to the **RTS** credit checking inside their app. That was very helpful in the beginning until I found out how to credit check on my own. The thing I didn't like the most about **RTS** was, their discounts are at Pilot and Flying J. As mentioned in my book already with many reasons, as an owner operator I really prefer the TA Petro. 😊

The **RTS** discounts weren't that great either in my opinion. I think I would get **.12** to maybe **.20** cents off the pump price. At **NASTC** I consistently see **.25** to **.50** cents off the pump price, in certain locations where the fuel prices are really hiked up like TA Jessup, MD (Baltimore South) I will see close to a **$1** off the pump price. 😄

In my opinion, **NASTC** is the way to go <u>hands down</u>. **They** offer other services if you need them too. Services like drug testing consortium, driver programs, office management, software and more. You will also get discounted tire pricing too. It's not as good in as a full-blown national tire discount from a big fleet, but it helps for sure.

NASTC has their own app and you can check the prices off fuel along your route or anywhere on the map in a very convenient fashion. The app performs very well and I use it often! 😁

To become a member, you can either pay full price, which I think is $**350**, or you can attend a new members orientation and your price will be $**250** a year for the <u>lifetime of your membership</u>. During this orientation you will probably meet **David Owens** and others of the **NASTC** team. You will be shown what other products and services they have available.

This orientation is about **6** hours give or take. They hold the orientation in the **Nashville**, TN area or at either or at the big truck shows (GATS in Dallas, TX & MATS in Louisville, KY). I attended orientation at the Great American Truck Show in Dallas. I was already planning to attend the show, so I did a 2 for 1 and went for orientation too. 😁

I do not regret my decision to team up with NASTC <u>at all</u>! ✓

They have been **GREAT**! I will recommend them to any owner operator who's serious about lowering their overhead and being successful! I do not get any commission from them (YET!); I truly **use** and **love** <u>this company</u>. They really get it right! They **understand** the <u>difficulties</u> of our business and have a ton of respect for us. They understand great customer service too. They treat us great and **David** is always batting for us against the big guys to make sure we get the best deals as an association.

David has many things in the <u>pipeline</u> that his is working on for us **like** preferred pricing and service at TA Petro. He has a vision of making every **TA** and **Petro** a **home trucking terminal** to us <u>single owner operators</u>. Preferred pricing, preferred service, great perks and more! **David Owens** runs a great operation! <u>That's why he is so successful</u>. He loves our trucking business and is a stand-up guy. I've met and conversated with him personally. ✓

In the next chapter we will discuss IFTA. Are you ready? Guess what? It's not that complicated either 😁! If you keep good records on the miles that you travel in each state, you won't even have to pay anyone to file your IFTA for you! Let's

456

take a jump into **IFTA**. You may be surprised how quick we will cover it. I'm telling you, **IT'S SUPER EASY!** 🚚

CHAPTER 25: HOW I FILE IFTA

International Fuel Tax Agreement aka IFTA. This is the system that was put in place to make sure that each state gets its fair share of fuel tax collected. Every time we buy fuel at the pump, some of the cost that's built into the pump price is the state's fuel tax. **Each state has its own fuel tax rate.** If you drive **200** miles through Tennessee, Tennessee will want to collect the fuel tax on each one of those **200** miles at the end of the quarter. This is true in every state except Oregon. Since I've had my own authority, I haven't been to Oregon. I don't go that far west while trucking anymore. **So**, I don't know exactly how Oregon works. I think they do not charge a fuel tax, but an annual permit fee instead. But none-the-less, every other state wants to collect on their fuel tax. $ ⛽

If you fill up with fuel in a state that has high fuel tax like **Pennsylvania**, and only travel **50** miles in the state, then drive your next **1000** miles in other states that have a lower fuel tax; You would be getting a refund of some of that money you paid at the pump in **PA**. 💵

The opposite is true too. If you fill up in **New Jersey**, and drive all the way across the PA turnpike without fueling, you will have to pay **PA** back at the end of the quarter for the miles you traveled in their state with paying a fuel tax. ✔️

All in all, it pretty much always averages out. Some times when I file, I'll get a $5 to $60 dollar refund. And sometimes I'll end up owing $5 to $60 dollars. Sometimes I'll either owe or get a refund less than $5 dollars lol.

TO FILE IFTA IS EASY <u>USING THE STATES WEBSITE</u>.

IT'S A LITTLE HARDER IF YOU DO IT BY MAIL; BECAUSE YOU HAVE TO ADD EVERYTHING UP YOURSELF MANUALLY. THE ONLINE VERSION IS JUST PLUG AND PLAY AND DOES THE MATH FOR YOU!

Filing online makes it super easy!

IFTA filings are due by the end of the next month following the end of fiscal quarter.

<u>For example</u>. **JANUARY – MARCH** is fiscal quarter number 1. Your **IFTA** report for this period is due by the end of April.

APRIL – JUNE is fiscal quarter number 2. Your **IFTA** report for this period will be due by the end of July.

JULY – SEPTEMBER is fiscal quarter number 3. This report will be due by the end of October.

OCTOBER – DECEMBER is quarter number 4. The **IFTA** report for this period is due by the end of January.

The main thing you will need to be responsible for each quarter is your fuel receipts, and the miles you drive in each state.

You keep <u>fuel receipts</u> to keep up with the GALLONS of fuel purchased in each state. And to calculate MPG

(miles per gallon). 🚚 **(THIS CAN be done digitally now through your fuel card provider and physical receipts are not needed.)**

And you keep track of the <u>miles traveled per state</u> so you can report the miles you traveled in each state and to calculate MPG as well. 🚚

Now with ELD's this is easier than ever! 😄

Keeping fuel receipts is easy. Just keep a big plastic bag and throw your fuel receipts in there and forgot about. Do keep them out of the **sunlight** though so they don't fade! I have **3** drawers for clothes in my truck, I use the whole bottom draw for <u>fuel receipts</u>, <u>receipts that I'm claiming for taxes, and for my finished BOL's</u>.

I dedicate this whole drawer for this activity. **So**, as soon as I get a new receipt, I toss it in this drawer. When I get home from over the road, I take all of these papers out and take them into my office. I separate my **tax receipts** and put in them in my tax bag. I take all the **fuel receipts** and put them into a file folder. And I take my **BOL's** and store them off to the side.

This covers keeping up with receipts. Some people like to use apps to scan them in, and that's cool too! Some people run reports off their fuel card, and this is fine too. Just make sure you have a system in place that works for you; A system that will accurately keep up with your fuel receipts. Whether you <u>pay</u> somebody or not to file **IFTA**, you have to have this information anyways. By keeping up with your receipts you're already **25%** done with filing **IFTA!** 😄

The way I keep track of my miles traveled in each state is by using my **KeepTruckin ELOG**. All I have to do is log onto my customer profile on a computer, select **IFTA**, choose the dates for the quarter that I'm reporting on, and run the report. It's that easy. ✔

It will generate a file that shows me how many miles I traveled per state. Regardless of the **ELD** you use, it should have a way for you to generate these types of reports; If not consider getting a different ELD provider! 😄

This is one of the best benefits of having an **ELD**. Or you can keep track of your miles the old school way, with pen and pad 📝. And that's fine too! Reset your odometer when you cross a state line and when you leave that state, look at your odometer, and write those miles down.

Next you add up the total gallons purchased in each state. ✔

What I do is have a notebook and pen, and write down the **state abbreviation** with a **hyphen** next to it. Then I put the gallon total next to the hyphen.

For example: If my first receipt is from **Georgia** and it's for **45.6** gallons, I will write on my paper **GA – 46**. You can only use whole numbers for gallons, no decimals. Anything .5 and above gets rounded up, anything .4 and below gets rounded down. If my next fuel receipt is from **Mississippi** for **72.4** gallons, below where I just wrote **GA – 46**, I will write **MS – 72**.

It will look like this on paper.

GA - 46

MS -72

I will <u>continue</u> to do this for each state until I finish the last fuel receipt. If I have multiple fuel receipts in the same state, I just continue the tally on the same line I started. If I had another **50.5** gallon receipt for **Georgia**, I would add it like this.

GA – 46, 56

Do this for each state you have fuel receipts in. Once you finish your last receipt, simply <u>add up</u> the total gallons for each state. Once you get the totals, <u>circle</u> them so you won't misplace the numbers on your paper. Then you add up all the gallons from each state to get a "**total gallons purchased**" number. These are the numbers that you will need to file your report. You are now **75%** done filing your own **IFTA**.

Now that you have **all the numbers you need** which are; <u>Total gallons purchased, gallons purchased per state, total miles traveled, and miles traveled per state</u>. **Log** into your <u>state's</u> particular department of revenue site that handles your **IFTA** account. I can't speak that every state will have online portals and calculators like this, but I know here in **Louisiana** we do. Make sure to check. <u>If you can file online it will be a breeze</u>! 😁

Find where on the website to begin filing your report. Select the time period (<u>which fiscal quarter</u>) that you will be reporting for. **Everything** from here is just fill in the blanks. Since you already did the "<u>hard</u>" part of gathering **all the numbers**, <u>the rest will be easy</u>. 😊👍

When it asks for total miles traveled, put that number in. 📱

When it asks for total gallons purchased, put that number. 🔢

It will ask you what type of fuel, select Diesel. ⛽

It might ask you if you are closing your IFTA account, select no. 🔢

From here on, you will be adding jurisdictions (states) one at a time. When you add each state, it will ask you for the total miles traveled and total gallons purchased. Fill this information out for each state according to what you wrote down on paper. 📝

After you've added the last state, press submit or finished and you're done! ✔️

It will automatically do the math for you and let you know if you owe or will get a refund. If you owe, it will let you make a payment right there through there portal (probably with an extra card fee added). I think Louisiana will let me hook up my bank account for **ACH**, I just never got around to doing yet. Maybe I will later. **That's it, you're done**! You just filed your own **IFTA**. Easy right! There's no real reason to pay someone to do this for you, especially with how easy it is with online filing. 😁

If for some reason you **can't** file online, you will have to file the old-fashioned way, on paper, by mail, and with you doing all the math. The math is not complicated but it's a little tedious and takes about **30** minutes to an hour sometimes to get it right; Compared to **15** minutes with online file. If you do find yourself filing by mail, your state will send the instruction form in the **IFTA** letter they send you each quarter. Just follow the instruction letter step by step and you will be fine. It is slightly complicated but I've done it many times. Make sure to get it "<u>postdated</u>" at the post office. This will ensure that if the mail runs late, you will not be fined for a late filing. **BUT**: I just recently started E-Filing and it's so much better! 😄👍

You see now, that the only real time-consuming part is adding up the gallons off your fuel receipts. ✔️

But this is something you have to do regardless. **So**, if you <u>already</u> have to get this information to give to an **IFTA** filing service, you might as well take the next little step and E-file it yourself! I don't know how much those services cost, probably $**20** to $**40** per filing is my guess. But still, that's like "<u>taking candy form a baby</u>". All they are doing is keying in the information you give them, and having the states website do the auto-calculation! This takes **15** minutes! Maybe less, maybe a bit longer if you're <u>new</u> to doing it.

Keep that money in your pocket and <u>buy you a nice dinner</u>! All you need is the total gallons purchased, total gallons purchased in each state, total miles driven, and total miles driven in each state. Plug them into your states **IFTA E-FILE**, and **BOOM**! You're done. <u>SIMPLE</u>! Now you can file your own **IFTA**. You're really getting the lay of the land now! Some of this is pretty easy right? 😄

In the **next chapter** I will briefly discuss **ELD's** and which one I use and why. If you've been reading along from start to finish, you already know what **ELOG** I'm using; But none-the-less, I built my book so you can skip around in it too! **So** maybe you haven't seen what **ELOG** I use yet. If you haven't skipped around then **GOOD FOR YOU**! If you have skipped around, <u>that's fine too</u>! Get what you need first. The rest will be here waiting on you. 🚚🚚

CHAPTER 26: WHICH ELD DO I USE

I use the **KeepTruckin ELD now called MOTIVE**. KeepTruckin | Fleet Management Software, ELD, Dash Cams, GPS. I really use their product and have been **very much** impressed by it. I also use their dash cam too. I think I pay right around $**600** a year for everything. **So**, it's not cheap, but it's not crazy expensive either. And surprisingly, I really like their product. 😁

I spent **YEARS** on Qualcom / Omnitracs with Landstar; I was never too impressed. The units would always look good, but the ones I had would freeze pretty often and do other weird stuff.

When I first got my authority, I chose to go with **VDO Roadlog**. I really enjoyed **VDO** too. It was a standalone unit, hardwired into my diagnostic port. It was a one-time fee of $**500** dollars or so, and it always worked great; It never failed on me once. The online software they add for **IFTA** and record keeping was great too. Too bad they decided to shut down their operation. I don't know if they got paid money to stand down; Or if the one-time purchase units weren't drawing enough income to sustain the rest of the operation or what. **VDO** partnered with **KeepTruckin**. The one company I told myself I would never go to lol 😁. They had a deal for all of us **VDO** guys, no up-front equipment costs and a couple of other perks. I called them up, even after talking on and off for a couple days, I was still skeptical. 😶

I eventually decide to make the deal and get on board with **KeepTruckin**; Even though technically I'm exempt from **ELOGS** because I have a **1999** motor. But I like the **ELOGS** for a couple reasons. One being, the ease of keeping up with traveled miles per state for **IFTA**. And the other is for **legal** reasons. If I ever have to **present** myself to a judge and jury in the case of a fatality accident; My logs have to be on point or they might say I killed the person **because** I wasn't supposed to be there. 👉

A good lawyer will **fight** the case that if I didn't cheat on my logs, I wouldn't of been at that **particular place** at that particular moment. **And** if I wasn't there, the other person would still be alive. **Even** if the other person was drunk driving or **whatever**, it doesn't really matter. If your logs are bad, you might be charged with vehicular manslaughter. I know this sounds extreme but just be careful. I know that on paper logs, the temptation for me to drive off my own common sense would be there; And I would probably cook my book a little bit. **So**, for me, the **ELD** helps keep me straight. 👉😎

I never thought I would like a phone ELD. But KeepTruckin is great!

Onto the features and the app itself. **The app is great**! It has a very easy to understand interface. Everything seems to be in the right place. To do daily vehicle inspection reports is **very** easy. It will even remind you if you forgot to log a vehicle inspection report. This is a nice feature. **And** they don't remind you in an annoying way either. ✔️

It is very easy to add your **BOL** number in; They have a section called "**forms**" that's easy to access where you can easily update this mandatory info. I like the fact while driving, I can see my **14** hour clock, **11** hour drive time, **8** hour break, and **70** hour clock all at once. This really helps when taking calls on my posted truck and checking my hours on the fly.

Especially if it's a longer load they are calling me on, and I'm unsure exactly how much time I have on my **70**. To view your recap hours is <u>very easy</u> and clear to understand. I also like the fact that if I pull over to grab a bite, and if I forget to log off duty, I can log myself off duty inside the restaurant on my phone! This is nice to have as an option to remotely change your duty status. 😄

The hardware its self is nice and of <u>high quality</u>. I have not had one issue with my KeepTruckin set up. ✔

The <u>dash</u> <u>camera</u> seems to work very well too; And has something like a 3 year warranty on it. **This is nice**, because most of the dash cams that I've had end up not working after about a year or 2 of use. The dash cam work seamlessly with the app. It's always a good thing to have a forward-facing camera. It's always good to have video evidence in the case of **having** to defend yourself legally. Don't hold me to it, but I think the between the **dashcam** and **ELD**, <u>it records speed as well</u>. **So**, if you get a bad ticket for speeding and you were not speeding, you have **video** and **GPS speed** <u>data to prove it</u>. ✔

Overall, I'm super satisfied with **KeepTruckin** and I definitely recommend it. It has not froze up on me, and has performed perfectly! Check them out if you haven't already. You may like it this much too! In the **next chapter** I will share with you how I manage the paying of my tolls. 🚚

CHAPTER 27: TOLLS

I'm not going to bore you on this chapter with how much tolls cost all around the country but I will provide you some of the resources I use and the device I use to pay tolls. ✓

I'm pretty sure we've all heard of **EZ-PASS** by now. But getting an **EZ-PASS** can be a **little tricky** for a solo owner-operator. **Well**, at least it was for me when I started. The solution I found was **Illinois I-PASS**. The **I-PASS** works everywhere that **EZ-PASS** is accepted.

The **I-PASS** can be obtained easily from the Home - Illinois Tollway and managed through the Welcome - Get I-PASS website. Unlike getting a regular **EZ-PASS**, the **I-PASS** is very easy to get and set up. 😊

You just create an account, upload your vehicle information, let them know you are a **commercial** vehicle, load your account with a debit / credit card and wait the **7** to **14** days or so it takes to get the transponder. ✓

In the Welcome - Get I-PASS website you will be able to set all your preferences. You can set your auto refill threshold; I think I have mine set to refill at **$25** with an auto refill amount of **$150**. Another cool thing about this website is that at the end of the year, you can easily run a report to see how much money you spent on tolls so you can claim them on taxes. 📝

Another thing about having a transponder set up is; You get discounted toll rates. **Especially** when traveling through places like the **PA** turnpike. I get a significant discount off the **PA** turnpike, **NJ** turnpike, the **GW** bridge in **NYC** and etc. The savings are another great way to add efficiency to your operation and lower your overhead. ✓

What looks to be another good alternative to I-PASS is **Best Pass** Bestpass® | Save Time and Money with One-Invoice Toll Management .

This will cover tolls and pre-pass at the scales. I might eventually sign up with them since their transponder works with the **TX tag** tolls. I do **Dallas** and **Houston** pretty often, and end up paying by tolls by mail. **Dallas** and **Houston** traffic can be pretty crazy at times, and I'm getting to the point where I'll just rather pay the $7 to $15 dollars to bypass it lol. I was just looking at a coverage map of **Best Pass**, and it looks like it works pretty much everywhere!

When it comes to tolls, I used to be one **of** those guys that would always look to avoid the tolls and "**save money**". But in my experience, bypassing tolls doesn't always save money. Usually, to avoid tolls, you have to go an extra **50** miles or, through a way more difficult terrain, through small towns and etc. This is especially true if you're in **PA** or **WV** avoiding tolls. I don't play around out there anymore! Those roads are too dangerous and hilly for me, I'll just stay on the big road and work the cost into my rate. 😁

This doesn't mean I will take toll roads for the fun off it though! If it's only **30** to **50** miles more for me to run I-**80** in **PA**; I will drive up to I-**80** instead of paying the $**200** or so dollars that it costs to ride all the way across the turnpike. 💵

If I'm going to **JFK** in **NYC**, or to southern **CT**, depending on where I am, I will skip all the Baltimore, Harve De Grace, DE, and NJ tolls by staying on 1-**81** to I-**78** to I-**287** and catch I-**80** into that area. This way I'm only paying for the **GW** bridge. 👍

If I'm going to **JFK**, I will also consider going I-**78** to I-**95** for a short section, and grab the I-**278** Goethals Bridge into Staten Island, take the **278** through Brooklyn, grab the I-**495**, then the **678** straight into **JFK**. ✔️

Tolls in **NYC** take some time to figure out; Especially when it comes to bridges like Verrazano Bridge (used to be free to get off Staten Island, but now costs going both ways since DEC 2020), the Robert Kennedy (Tri-borough), Throgs Neck, and Bronx-Whitestone each cost $**30** on **EZ-PASS** and $**50** if pay by plate. These bridges cost going both ways too. **So**, make sure you work this cost into your rates when going into the **NYC** area. The old rule is this "It costs to get into New York, but it's free to leave". Take the famous GW bridge, it costs to come into NY, but is free to cross into NJ.

If I'm going to **middle CT**, or **MA**, or anywhere north east of these points, I will travel up a little bit further to the Tappan Zee / Cuomo bridge, or even the Newburg Beacon bridge if possible. This is especially true if I'm in **PA** on I-**80** coming into the north east. I will probably split off at I-**81** in Wilkes-Barre and grab I-**84** all the way across the Newburgh bridge into **CT**. Not only is this a way cheaper bridge, but I get to skip all the **NYC** and sitting in the parking lot known as the Cross-Bronx Expressway! 😄

So, yes, I will do my share of smartly avoiding certain tolls, or lowering my costs by taking good routes with slightly more distance; But at the same time, I will not be petty when it comes to tolls. That's why you got to have a **I-PASS**, **EZ-PASS**, or a **Best Pass** so you get these toll discounts and handle your business! 👍💰

Some of these off-toll roads in PA and WV are straight <u>crazy in terms of terrain</u>! Especially if your loaded heavy.

Me personally, I will stay on the toll road! My days of ducking and dodging tolls are long gone! There's nothing wrong with dodging tolls, **just be careful**, <u>make sure that it's worth it</u>. That **$100** you save might very well cost you **$50** additional in fuel, lost time, and more wear and tear on your truck.

Play it smart. Work smarter not harder! Work the cost of tolls into your rate, or book freight that more than covers the cost of your tolls. ✔️

This is not a deal breaker of a topic, but this is how I do it. At the very least, **seriously consider** <u>partnering up</u> with a transponder provider of some kind so you can get your **discounts** and <u>increase</u> your **profits** even more! The **next chapter** will be the dreaded conversation of **TAXES**! It is a part of every business. Luckily for us, there's a ton of tax deductions that we can take. But it's up to you take keep up with all your receipts and do some good accounting at the end of the year. I will share with you how I do it! Let's continue! 🚚

CHAPTER 28: TAXES

The conversation we all love, taxes! (sarcasm 😄) We work **hard** for the money and want to keep <u>as much of it as possible</u>. We already pay a **2290** heavy high way tax, fuel taxes, we pay a heap for **IRP** plates, insurance and more. There's nothing wrong with not liking the reality of taxes, but there is something wrong **if you** <u>ignore</u> the reality of taxes. 📢

It really depends on **your** <u>record keeping skills</u> as to how smoothly your tax filings will go. The more **accurate** and **organized** you keep track of your expenses, the better it will be.

Don't be concerned of taxes, paying taxes just means that you're making money and showing a profit. ✔

Don't get into the hype of buying stuff to avoid taxes. If you spend $**10k**, it doesn't mean that you knocked $**10k** of your tax bill, it just means you will not pay taxes on that $**10k** dollars. Taxes on that $**10k** would be about $**1500** to $**3000** give or take.

So, would you rather spend $10k to avoid paying $3k, or pay $3k and keep the other $7k? 👻 ❓ (stuff to consider)

The money not spent (for a tax deduction) will be **much more** <u>money kept</u> then the taxes you have to pay on that same money. Now, if you've had a great year and you need some tires or new brakes on all the way around, and it's the end of the year, **that's fine**, make your investment, <u>but don't be buying stuff just to buy it</u>! 😄 because it doesn't knock your tax bill down by the SAME dollar amount you spent.

The **main** key to paying the least amount of taxes is good record keeping. Make sure that you keep track of **EVERY** receipt, <u>online</u> <u>invoice</u>, <u>bill</u>, and **etc**! What I do is keep a **big 5-gallon plastic bag** in my office and I <u>fill it up</u> with receipts (the Rawze method!). I have a bottom drawer in my truck that's dedicated to holding fuel receipts, BOL's, and expense receipts for taxes. If I'm on the road and I buy something for the business, I **toss** the receipt into this drawer until I get home. Once I get home, I separate the receipts and put the tax receipts into the big freezer bag I just mentioned.

I USUALLY TAKE OFF THE FIRST OR SECOND WEEK OF JANURARY TO COUNT UP ALL MY RECIPETS, GET MY TOTALS, AND FILE MY TAXES. ✔️

I don't play around when it comes to getting taxes done. On the **first** or **second week** of a new year, I take about a <u>week</u> or so off to count up all my receipts and do taxes. I may not take it to my tax CPA to file it yet, but I will have all my numbers counted up and ready for my CPA. 🌴

The first thing I do is take all my receipts out my bag one by one and place them into different categories onto my bed. The categories I will separate them into are:

1. FUEL
2. MAINTENANCE
3. PARTS
4. TOOLS AND SUPPLIES
5. MISCELLANEOUS
6. COMMUNICATIONS (PHONE BILL)
7. OIL AND ADDITIVES
8. INSURANCE
9. TOLLS
10. TIRES
11. HOTEL
12. PARKING
13. ACOUNTING / LEGAL FEES
14. HOTEL
15. TRUCK WASH
16. SCALES
17. OFFICE
18. LOAD BOARDS
19. ADVERTISING (CAN BE COMPANY T-SHIRTS AND ETC)
20. PER DIEM (I JUST WRITE HOW MANY DAYS I WAS OTR IN THIS FILE)

Once **everything** is in its separate categories; I will us a calculator with a printer on it to add up the totals of each category. Once I finish a pile of receipts, I will place the **printed** total and all receipts in a file folder **for** later storage in my file cabinet. I do this for each category until finished.

On the file folders, on the tab I write "the year, and the category". Then on the front of the file folder on the top right, I write the **total $ amount** for the added-up receipts. I will continue to add to this number as I find and get my hands on more expenses that are not yet printed out. ✔️

<u>Next</u>, is the "**big clean-up**".

<u>**I search high and low for everything that I bought off the internet and for expenses that I don't have physical receipts for**</u>.

I go to my **Amazon account** and make sure I print off my purchases. I will screen shot the purchase, and print it out so it can be added back into the category that it belongs.

I will pull up my **phone bill**, and print it out (you can claim a certain percentage of your phone bill, basically whatever percent that you think you use for business, I usually claim bout **50**% of my phone bill.)

I go online to my **I-PASS** account and print out a summary of what I paid in tolls. I go to my Gmail account.

I have a subfolder in my email I named "**INVOICES**". This is where I move my invoices for things I purchase online. I go through these and print them out.

I go onto my **load board accounts** and print out the billing summary.

I call up **NASTC** and get a yearly summary of what I spent on fuel.

I remember things like my **Drug Testing Consortium** and I call them for an emailed invoice.

My **NASTC** membership fee.

I call up **OOIDA** and get a summary of everything I spent with them on insurance.

I go to my permit book and see how much I paid for **IRP**, take a photo and print it!

I print all of this stuff out. I go back to my file folders, and place the new printed receipts into the folders they belong and add in the new receipts to the working totals I already wrote on the outside of the file folder.

THE PART ABOVE IS THE PART THAT TAKES ME THE MOST TIME.

Because it's **so** important that I don't leave **ANY** money on the table. I want to make sure that I remember and find **EVERY** thing that I spent on business. The more money you can prove you spent on business, the lower your tax burden will be. That's why I take a week off. **2** days might go by after I finish, and I'll still be   remembering things that I forgot. I've got better at keeping notes in my phone as I buy things throughout the year that I might forget come tax time as well. I make a note in my iPhone's "notes" app titles "(**THE YEAR**) **TAXES**". Whenever I buy something digital, or something that I may forget, I write it in this notes app. Then when its time for me to count up my expenses for taxes, this will be one of the last things I look at to make sure I didn't forget everything. ✔

This is why I **really** advise doing your taxes as soon as possible in January. That way you can get it mostly finished and you still will have time to remember if there are expenses you may have forgot. There's been times when a whole week will go by and I'm like "**oh yeah**! <u>I forgot about those tires I got online</u>" or something like that. **MAKE SURE MAKE SURE**, you find <u>every little thing</u> you purchased in that "fiscal" year so you can lower your tax bill. 🗝

PER DIEM is an <u>important</u> deduction we get in our trucking business. You will get a $**50** or so dollar credit for each night you spent away from home. I use my logs on my **ELOG** software to do this. I will print out a little calendar and just go day by day on the software, circling the days I was over the road on my printed-out calendar.

After I have all my days circled, I **add** up the totals for each month and write it on that same paper by the month that I added up. Once I add up each month, I add up all the months to get a **total amount** <u>of days OTR</u>. Actually, now as I write this, I think I will just go ahead and print the calendar out and leave it in my permit book. Then I will circle the days I'm over the road in real time; That way I don't have to go back into my **ELOG** software day by day to get an accurate count. ✔

One thing I used to do was get one of those **free calendars** from **TA** and stick it on my dash. I would circle each day I was over the road. Then at the end of the month, I would tear that page off and place it in my permit book for later. **Whatever way you choose to do it**, <u>just make sure that it gets done</u>! You really want this tax break! I end up getting about a $**5k** to $**15k** tax credit off per diem every year. <u>It's super helpful</u>! If you spend a lot of time on the road, it will definitely help out, maybe even more than the numbers I just said.

The **trick** during this whole process is to **stay organized** <u>so what you wont cluttered or overwhelmed</u>. It's not that hard as long as you keep track of all your receipts, store them in a reliable place, count them all out into separate categories, file them in file folders, find all your online purchases, add those back in, and store them in your file cabinet. 💾

This way, if you ever get an **IRS** audit; Your records will be clean as a whistle! The auditor should be very impressed with your organization, printed tallies, and your ability to quickly provide documents. If your auditor says "You claimed $**5250** in <u>parts</u> this year, will you show me those records?". You want to be able to go **straight** to that folder, and <u>produce</u> those records.

You **don't** want all your receipts <u>separated by the month</u>. If your receipts are separated by the month, your receipts for "parts" will be **scattered** all over the place. It will **look** <u>real bad</u> fumbling for all those receipts while the auditor sits there looking for more discrepancies. By having everything separated by **category** and filed in file folders, you are way more prepared for a potential **IRS** audit. ✔

It is recommended by the **IRS** that you send in a **1040 ES** (estimated) payment <u>every quarter</u>. Some years I do, some years I don't. It's up to you. There will be a slight fine if you don't send in estimated payments but it's usually not too much; I think my fine is usually about $**100** or so if I don't send ES payments.

If you are not confident in your **saving** and **budgeting** <u>skills</u> yet; I would advise sending in at least $**1k** every quarter to the **IRS** in the form of a **1040 ES** payment. For me personally, I know when I look at my bank account; All of that money **isn't** <u>technically mine</u>. I always know in the back of my head that about **10%** to **25%** or so of my money may be needed to pay in for taxes. 🔑

I'm very disciplined <u>when it comes to money</u>. ✓

A lot of owners get caught in that **mentality** where they think that 'just because money is in the bank, that it's there's to spend'. Like mentioned in "Home Life and Budgeting", I set financial floors. **Once I set this floor**, <u>I don't go below it</u>.

I especially don't go below that floor for buying personal things that I want. If you set your floor at **$10k** dollars and you have **$13k** in the bank, then you "only have $3k". And even out of that $3k I <u>wouldn't</u> spend more than a couple hundred on personal things I wanted.

This grind takes times, and this discipline stage is a must. ✓ but you will break through

There are exceptions to this rule, but many owners mess up their hustle because they can't stay financially disciplined for a few years. This being hyper disciplined is the most important in the beginning of your business. And once you make it to the other side, being disciplined will have become a habit, and will still be necessary but will be less intense. 😁

In my opinion, if you don't have at least **$30k** to **$40k** in the bank, you shouldn't be spending much money on anything yet <u>except business</u>. What if you need a new motor (**$8k** to **$25k**)? What if you need a new transmission (**$5k** to **$10k**)? A differential (**$3k** to **$5k**)? A new turbo (**$800** to **$5000**)? If you had **$25k** in the bank and you where out here spending money and living your best life, look how quick you could back on the ground floor. 👻

My attempt is not to scare or belittle you, it's just to **prepare** you with the reality of this business. If you had **$25k** and you needed a motor, you will be wishing you kept saving your money. If you were up in that **$30k** to **$40k** range you could of took the hit and kept it moving. If you wanted to, you could of even put half of the big bill on a **0**% interest credit card (**18** month **0**% introductory rate). Then you would have been super fine.

I've been in this position before. That's why I **stress** saving like I do. At the time I was running **2** trucks at once. I had about **$25k** in the bank, thought I was doing fine. I was getting my operation down pretty good, making back some money off some recent repairs and etc. When both trucks were on the road, I would make in that **$4**k to **$7**k range after paying my driver.

For me, at that age, that was pretty good. Well long story short, my **09** Pete that my driver was driving started pushing coolant out the expansion / fill tank. This is caused by exhaust combustion usually because of a failed head or head gasket.

I went to a great shop of mine, but still ended up paying a little north of **$20k** for everything. But I put new injectors in, fueling actuators, and etc. I bought quite a bit of things I didn't need; But that's pretty much how I also do, I make the **investments** when I'm down and already in there to reduce labor cost.

I had plans of putting that truck right back on the road as another million-mile motor. My driver ended up in a relationship with an owner operator at Landstar and she politely thanked me, said she was sorry, but she must follow her heart! Lol I get it! It's all good. 😄

Now I'm **$20k** into the rebuild, the trucks are paid for at least, and I was not looking to hire another driver! I could see how **3** to **5** trucks would do pretty well. But **2** trucks with me driving full time, doing payroll, making sure all the withholding taxes were right, learning her state laws of NY when it comes to income tax and unemployment tax, booking her loads, booking my loads, **YEAH, I'M GOOD**! I make more money now (profit) by myself with way less work than I did back then with 2 trucks on at Landstar.

The point is, see how quick my **$25k** turned into nothing? Luckily, I had a private lender for **$10k**, and I put the rest on **0**% interest credit cards and paid the cards off within the **18**-month **0**% time period; And I paid my lender off within **2** years as well. What if I didn't have my lender? What if I didn't have great credit?

CASH IS KING. THE MORE CASH YOU HAVE, THE MORE POWER YOU HAVE IN YOUR DESTINY. ✔

I'm not suggesting be money crazy and skip the good and simple things of life; But do find that balance, especially if you want longevity in this business. I didn't take a real vacation until about **7** years into trucking lol. My wife and I drove all the way down to **Key West**, FL. We stayed down in **Old Town** off Duval st, and enjoyed every minute of it! Since then, we've been to **Orange Beach**, AL, and **Grand Canyon**. With many trips to GA and Jacksonville, FL in between to see family and etc. 😁

Once you reach a certain point financially, **your** pretty much good. That still doesn't mean go blow your money; But you can start to ease up and enjoy life more with trips, food, hobbies, going out and etc.

You just got to be smart with your money. ✔️

I always say, it's a lot quicker to spend money than it is to make it! If you have **$75k** in the bank, **GREAT**! But you can't afford to buy that **$65k** brand new F-150 Lariat with cash. Technically you could "Afford" the truck, but that would leave you with next to nothing in cash. 🗝️

Cash is currency, currency is electricity, with electricity if you are not on, you have no power. 🤐 💯 💰 ✔️

Do you see what I'm saying? I don't really love or lust money, but I understand the **power** of money. I understand, that with enough money I can **leave** the rat race and **blaze** my own trail! I understand the value of money. I like freedom. The more financial freedom you have, the less you have to rely, depend, or play other people's games for money. You work hard for your profit. **Keep stacking it up before you get to spending**. Even when you do spend, be reasonable. I paid cash for my **2**nd truck. I paid cash for my **home** and **land**. Every time I made a big cash purchase, I made sure never to go below that **$30k** to **$40k** floor. ✔️

If you enjoy your freedom, you will make sure that a big purchase won't put your business in jeopardy! To do this, you will be more frugal and more disciplined than most. While they point fingers and maybe think you work too hard and are too tight with money; They are going to be wishing they were more like you once you blaze past them in life and never have to look back! 😄👍

People would ask me from the age **21** to about **25**, why don't you get a car? Why don't you get an apartment? I didn't care, because I had a plan. And at **25 / 26** years old, I dropped in and **paid cash** <u>for my first acre of land and home</u>. **2** years later I paid cash for the additional acre and home that touches my original property. No bank loans, no mortgages or nothing.

What do these people say now 😕? "God has blessed you so much, and you're doing so good" **Hmmm**.

Funny how God tends to bless those that help themselves! ✔️

<u>It takes patience when you have a vision</u>. **That's** why I talk so much in my book about knowing what you want. The more you **increase** <u>your desire</u> of what you want, it becomes an **obsession**. Once this **obsession** is created, your vision and the path **to get there** <u>gets more and more clear</u>.

I knew I wanted to <u>buy my home outright</u> and I was willing to stay on the road until I had enough cash to make it happen. That was what I wanted. **This was my desire**. I became obsessed (in a good way 😄). The more confident I became in what I wanted, the path to get there became **more** <u>and more clear</u>. And because I met my vision halfway every time, it happened. Would my desire of came true if I was always blowing my money and not taking saving serious? (no!)

I created generational wealth. Now I will always have a place to live. Do you see how much more **important** this is compared to buying new shoes every 2 weeks, going on vacations and etc? The way I am, I wouldn't even be able to truly enjoy myself on a vacation if I knew I couldn't really afford it and was not in a strong enough place financially. 🔑

BE DISIPLINED! FOR YOURSELF, AND FOR YOUR DREAMS! KNOW WHAT YOU WANT! CREATE YOUR FINANCIAL FLOORS! BE AWARE OF TAXES AND BUDGET YOUR MONEY ACCORDINGLY! ✔️

Let's **recap** taxes since I went off on a bit of a long but necessary rant.

Keep your receipts for <u>everything</u>. I don't care if it's for paper towels or candles. If it goes in your truck, chances are you can claim it for a business expense.

Don't lie on your taxes by claiming stuff that's not real. You may get ahead in the beginning, maybe you never get audited; But the **IRS** is not one to play with.

They will <u>backdate</u> the interest on the money you were supposed to pay, they will take your house, they do not care, they play for keeps. Avoid this madness **by** being <u>true</u> in your reports and by keeping **good records** stored in your file cabinet or digitally in folders if you choose to scan in your receipts. **Find a method that works for you and stick to it**! I shared with you my method, it may not be preferred to some, but it works perfect for me. Don't wait around until **April** to try and get all your stuff together! 😄

I like to have <u>all my receipts</u> counted up by the **second week** of **January;** And I like to have my taxes filed with my **CPA** by mid-February. This way I know what I owe and have until **April 15** to make my payment.

Take **initiative** in your taxes. **Keep every receipt!** Remember long and hard for everything that you spent that you don't yet have a paper receipt for. Everything from your tolls to your fuel.

If you're leased to a company, go through your settlements and count up every deduction and claim it. ✔

If you are leased to company, it may be a good idea to count up your settlement expenses once a month **so** it's not such a big job at the end of the year. Or maybe your company will print you an annual report of everything you spent on deductions. They have the software and should be able to run the report. They might say 'they can't even print it', though they probably could lol. Either way, ask them! If not just make sure to **include** <u>your deductions</u> in your expenses for taxes.

Make sure to find a good **CPA** that knows the trucking business and our specific deductions like **per diem** and **depreciation** (if your buying 'new to you' equipment, this deduction will help get your tax bill down). I used a **CPA** company that **Prime Inc** recommended called Abacus CPA's out of **Springfield**, MO. They were pretty good, I used them for years. It **wasn't** a very personal experience, <u>but it was good</u>. I would always have different people working my taxes each year. I would get a call from this person, then a call from another person saying that they're now taking over my return. But they knew **depreciation** and **per diem** good and was good on everything else; They specialized in trucking. I would pay about $**550** a year for them. Oh, and it would take weeks and weeks my filing finished. 😶

Eventually, I did what I always wanted to do and found me a **LOCAL CPA** that is great in trucking. I pay her the same price of about **$550.** I schedule an appointment with her, and we are done within about 30 minutes! She sends in my report to the Fed and State and we're done. She knows her stuff and is fast!

No more waiting weeks for me 😄. I come with all my **totals per category** printed out on one page. I have another couple pages of all the brokerages I worked with and the **totals** I collected from each. On this same report I add up the **grand total** of all money received. If you are leased to a company, this will be in the form of a **1099**. I take these **2** reports up to my **CPA** and she has all the info she needs to file for me. Which is basically, expenses and income. ✔

If you can find somebody that's **local** that knows trucking taxes, that would be great. The tax programs like **Turbo Tax** are getting easier and easier to use too. I might end up filing my own taxes one of these years but at this point I'm fine.

It's always been my theory too; That sending in your taxes by an accredited and respected CPA will make you less likely to be audited. I don't have any hard proof to back this up, **but** its been a theory of mine for a while! If you don't have a local **CPA** yet, or are still on the road and just living with family you can try **ATBS**; They seem to have a good reputation in our industry. I have never used them personally but I have a friend that does. Trucker Tax Services, Accounting for Truckers, Trucking Consulting | ATBS

A lot of people fall short when it comes to taxes, don't be one of them! ✔

Take taxes serious. **Always remember**, the money you have in the bank may not all be yours come tax time. Be aware of this and spend and budget accordingly. If you have **$40k** at the end of the year, pretend that you really have more like **$32k** to **$38k**. Some years I pay nothing in taxes, some years I've paid as much as **$7k** to **$15k**.

Just be careful, keep all your receipts, save your money, make quarterly 1040 ES payments direct to the IRS if you want / need to, don't forget your online purchases that you did towards business, your LLC renewal fees, IRP, and etc.

Anything that you spent on trucking, keep up with it. Do what you need to stay organized, **even** if you have to keep notes in your phone throughout the year and place emails into an "INVOICES" subfolder folder. You got this! If you are leased and have to wait on your **1099** to come in; You can still get all your expenses counted up early.

You do not want to be on the wrong side of the **IRS**. They will "haunt" you forever with wage garnishments and crazy interest rates that can really gobble up your profit money that you wish to save up.

Be organized ✔

Be proactive ✔

Take initiative ✔

Don't take taxes lightly ✔

As long as you are prepared, don't blow your money throughout the year, and keep good records, you should be fine! ✔

If you use it on, in, or for your trucking business, chances are you can claim it on taxes. 😁

CHAPTER 29: LLC OR NOT

As a single truck owner operator, this is not a very important subject because an LLC will not provide you with any real asset protection in the case of a lawsuit.

Why? Because if you're the owner and the driver, the **company** can get sued of course; But **you** can still be sued personally.

Whoever the driver is can get sued personally. 👆

If you plan on expansion and adding more trucks in the future, then yes get an **LLC**! If one of your drivers were to get in an accident, your company could get sued, but not you personally unless you were deemed complicit in the act.

A single truck owner operator with an **LLC** will get taxed as a "pass through entity"; Which just means that even with an **EIN#** it will be your **SSN#** at the end of the day that gets taxed. I have an **LLC** despite there not being a real advantage. It gives my company and brand a more professional appearance. I think brokerages take you **more serious** when have an **LLC** compared to a **DBA** (doing business as) or having nothing at all. And I guess if you wanted to go for business credit, having an **LLC** may will help.

There's **no** <u>real need</u> to pay someone to get your **LLC**. It can be done **easily** on your states "**SECRETARY OF STATE**" website. Just find the website, make an account, check for name availability, and fill in the blanks. It'll usually cost right around in that $**100** range. It's not that big of deal lol. It's especially not a big enough deal to be paying someone $**250** and $**300** to it for you. <u>Keep that money in your pocket!</u> Filing for an **LLC** is about as easy as it gets. ✔️

You can save **even more** money by designating yourself or a family member as your "**REGISTERED AGENT**". In the process of setting up your LLC, you will be asked who is your registered agent.

I didn't know for years that I can just make myself the registered agent! 😁

When you or a family member becomes the registered agent, it's only $**30** here in **Louisiana** to renew my **LLC** each year. This is compared to the almost $**200** or so a year I would pay Abacus to do this same service! That's ridiculous! They are making a killing! $**150+** in profit just to press a few buttons on the state website to renew my **LLC**. I'm in the wrong business <u>LOL</u>! **So**, keep this in mind. If you are setting up your own **LLC**, you might as well make yourself the registered agent; That way you can <u>renew</u> your **LLC** every year on your own for way cheaper than what it would cost some one to do this simple task for you. 👍

To touch back on the **liability** issues as a driver, I must say a few things. Since you can get **sued** <u>personally</u> as a driver with a **LLC** or not, you must be **VERY** careful. 🔫

We all work so hard out here, we put our lives on the line, we teach ourselves all this new stuff for a business most of us didn't know nothing about until we got into it, and we really put in the blood, sweat and tears to make this all happen.

Don't make it easy on <u>NOBODY</u> to take this away from you. ✔️

Drive slow, <u>stay away from everybody</u>. The further back you stay in your own bubble, the less likely you will be to ever get in an accident. When you back up a night, try **TA** and **Petros**, the parking lots are so much bigger and you won't have to make such a difficult back up maneuver just so you can rest. It never hurts to get out and look when backing up, I know I still do! 😁

Drive defensively. But in certain situations, drive offensively. For example, if you're approaching a **tight** <u>right-hand turn</u>, take up **as many lanes** as you need on your left to make the turn. Ease your way into blocking traffic until everybody **realizes** what you're doing, then take your turn. There's no need to put yourself in trouble for the convenience of others. Once they realize what you're doing, they can't do nothing but give you the room and respect what you're doing. 🚚🚚

Keep a dash cam on and recording in your truck at all times.

PROTECT YOUR ASSESTS SINCE YOUR LLC TECHNICALLY WON'T. ✔️

Do you see what I'm saying? Stay away from the crowd, be careful, take your time, keep video proof. Make it **IMPOSSIBLE** as possible for anyone to take what you worked so hard for. 🔒💪✊

Next, I'm going to take this long journey into a "sum everything up" chapter I got called "**Morale**". We all want to be happy. We all want success. But sometimes the desire for success can <u>blind</u> us from the happiness along the way. Congratulations on getting through my book!!!!

Hopefully it didn't take too long for you to read it. I know it's a long read; It's a ton of information that I had to explain in as much detail as I felt necessary. This is **10** years of <u>raw</u> experience jammed into one presentation. It's taken me 4 months to complete this task. It was over **4** months ago that I decided I was going to make my book a reality! It's been 4 months since started to write chapter 1 "A Week in my Shoes"! My eyes have been getting blurry from staring into the computer screen so much! I wanted to create a book that will stand the test of time. I wanted to make the **most complete** <u>source</u> of hard-to-get information in our trucking business. **I'm officially an author now**! Not to mention that, in the process of writing this book, I wrote 3 more books at the same time lol! The journey keeps going, I'm tryna tell ya! 😁 **INITIATIVE**

I hope that I have been able to clearly explain the many unclear and unknown topics in trucking.

I hope I've been able to provide you with extreme value.

I hope I've been able to give you great insight.

I hope I've given you many ideas for running your business.

I hope I have increased and expanded your mentality and the way you think.

I hope I have encouraged you to be more self-reliant.

I hope I have encouraged you to be more responsible.

I hope I have encouraged you to be a fighter.

I hope my confidence has become your own now.

I hope that with my story and testimony you now have a more clear vision.

I hope that you find the strength within you to be great.

I hope you that you take serious these lessons so that you can find success.

I hope you learn to take control of your sub-conscious mind and guide it to assist you in creating greatness.

I hope your mental health will be great.

I hope you that you choose the right truck now.

I hope you choose the right operation now.

I hope you book even better freight with better strategies now.

I hope you start clearing $3k to $5k a week now after fuel.

I want you to be the owner of land.

I want you to have the title to your truck and trailer.

I want you to experience the same freedom that I do.

I love life, and I wish for you the same. 😄

Let this book of mine be a turning point in your life.

A point where you dig deeper than ever before to bring out the best you! 🌴

The **you** that's <u>blasting with enthusiasm</u>! The **you** that <u>knows what you want</u>! The **you** that doesn't let negative emotion create your reality! The **you** that has the confidence to buy tools and fix stuff! The **you** that tells brokers EXACTLY what it is that you want. The **you** that other people look up to!

CHAPTER 30: MORALE

Let's just define morale real quick, "The **state** of the spirits of a person or group as shown by confidence, cheerfulness, discipline, and willingness to perform the task at hand" and also "The **moral** or **mental condition** as regards to <u>courage, spirit, zeal, hope, confidence, and the like</u>".

Morale in this business is very important. ✔

Why? Well, we already learned in the "Mentality" chapter that negative emotions attached to thoughts get broadcasted into the universe and the universe in turn creates the thoughts we broadcast.

By having **low** <u>morale</u> or a **negative** <u>outlook</u>, we in turn begin to **create** that same reality over and over again for ourselves. Just as enthusiasm is contagious, so is low morale.

If you handle yourself towards others with low morale, you will probably get a low level of results back. ✔

And there's something about this world where; If certain people see you with a low morale, they will use you as a punching bag and will attempt to get over on you over and over again. I don't know why, but I guess it's just the animal nature that's inside of some people. 👎

<u>Low morale can leak into every part of your life and really cause havoc</u>. ❌

Your business deals may begin to suffer.

You might seem to get truck breakdown after breakdown.

You may find yourself more irritable and spouting off at the people you love.

You might find yourself aging faster.

You might find yourself becoming depressed.

You may find yourself uninterested in life.

You may stop smiling as much.

You might resort to having a negative perspective on everything.

You may begin to lose hope in people.

You might forget why you started this business in the first place.

You might forget how excited you were when you first got your LLC and truck and the world was yours for the taking!

Those are **SOME** examples of how this thing called low morale can just come in and get to tearing down everything you love. <u>Trucking can be very hard</u>. The lifestyle we experience in trucking can make us feel distant at times. There can be a lot of quiet time where you are left alone and to think to yourself (I enjoy this actually! 😄). But in this **silence**, there is possibility that one begins to doubt themselves. **Doubt** can turn into fear. **Worry** can also turn into fear.

Once **fear** sets its roots in you, it can be hard to remove it. Fear is a negative emotion. Whatever emotion plus your thoughts is what will create your environment. If you're in a negative emotion such as fear, you create this type of reality. This can be extra stressful especially in the beginning when you're figuring out maintenance, your truck, maybe dealing with breakdowns, and maybe dealing with a lot of breakdowns (like me in the beginning! 😄). If you let that worry of a truck break down turn into a fear, that is not good! ✕✕

I speak from experience. My first couple years in the business was so rough because I didn't know what I was doing. I knew business to a certain degree, I knew basic math, I had common sense; But I was still a **22**-year-old kid who knew **nothing about** mechanics except that the truck uses oil and coolant!

 I would let the dealerships tell me what was wrong so that they could produce a big bill for me with very little fix. I started with an emissions motor that already had **600k** miles on it. So, you already know now what type of problems I was facing and didn't even know it. **EGR** cooler, bad sensors that made bad **DPF** and **DOC** filters, **EGR** valve, Turbo, Aftertreatment injector, turbo actuator, air compressor, my clutch went out early on me **LOL**. It was hard to get a break in that truck! <u>But my ambition wouldn't let me stop</u>. With every defeat, I found out why and became stronger. **But I still had fear**. Because I had broken down so many times, it just became a habit to check my dashboard for a check engine light. Eventually I out a piece of electrical tape over the check engine light so I would stop looking at it.

As I got stronger **financially** and with **experience**, <u>the fear got weaker</u>.

As I bought more **tools** and started **really working** on my own truck, <u>the fear got smaller.</u>

As I got **mentors** and **people who believed** in me, <u>the fear shrunk even more</u>.

It wasn't until I read "Think and Grow Rich" by Napoleon Hill (are you tired of me bringing him up yet lol?? 😄) https://amzn.to/2LTaBhZ that I truly understood the mechanics of what was going on in my mind; How it created my reality and how I could control it. I've always been a spiritual person, **so** the concepts in Think Grow Rich was like a <u>catalyst</u> to make everything else I studied and learned in life come into full action.

Wouldn't you rather create from Faith, Desire, Obsession, Enthusiasm and Hope <u>instead</u> of creating with Fear, Envy, Jealousy, Doubt and Worry ⁉

It's like cooking a great meal, right? A great meal is going to take great ingredients. Look at the ingredients of Fear, Envy, Jealousy, Doubt and Worry. What good can you really make with them?? You might be telling me; Andrew I don't create with these ingredients! If this is truly true, then perfect! You are ahead of the pack for sure! But let me show you where the problem is. <u>Many of us don't even realize</u>, these **ARE** the ingredients we are using. Let me explain. 🤐

The **conscious mind** <u>is but the gardener</u> 🕵️. And the **subconscious mind** <u>is the Earth where the gardener plants his or her seeds</u>. 🌍

You know how they say in science that we humans only use like **10**% of our brain? Well, check this out for size; There have been studies from neuroscientists that have shown that only **5**% of our cognitive activities (decisions, emotions, actions, behavior) is <u>conscious</u> whereas the remaining **95**% is generated in a <u>non-conscious</u> manner. 🤔

To me, this means that **95**% of the mind that most of us don't use, controls the **5**%. In order for the **5**% to control the **95**%, <u>it takes a lot of work and discipline</u>!!!! If you just be like "oh I got faith" once every couple of days; Don't really expect that to convince the other **95**% of mind (the subconscious) that it is true?? The **subconscious mind** <u>only pays attention to thoughts that have emotion attached to it</u>. And it MUST be convinced! Convincing takes time and **constant** faith, desire and positive emotion. 🖐️

If you want that faith to work, you have to be faith. ✔️

You have to be <u>actively</u> involved in controlling your thoughts with faith every day!

The subconscious mind is no fool, it's been around forever. 🖐️

If you tell your **subconscious mind** that you have faith or desire <u>for only a moment</u>; Then go right back to **low key** doubting and worry; Then guess what your subconscious mind will believe and broadcast to the universe? 🛰️ 🪨

Your **subconscious mind** will broadcast that you do not have faith; and that you must **want** worry and doubt because that's all you focus your energy on! 😵‍💫

SEE HOW THIS WORKS! Your **subconscious mind** is like the "middle-man" between you and God, and or you and the universe.

Whatever emotion you truly hold onto the most is what gets taken by the subconscious mind and broadcasted into the supreme intelligence language that the universe speaks. ✔️

Whether this **language** is light, magnetism, electricity, frequency, I don't know exactly. But I do know that this language is advanced and our **subconscious mind** knows how to translate our desires to the creation process of this universe. 🔒

The **subconscious** isn't going to lie to the universe. There must be a big punishment of some kind or **it's** just not possible in universal law; kind of similar to how **2** same sides of a magnet will not attach to each other. 🧲

This is why if you have a moment of faith or hope, but your dominant energy is doubt and worry, your **subconscious mind** is not going to broadcast the little faith you just had. Your subconscious mind doesn't believe you! **So**, instead of faith you are now broadcasting doubt, worry, fear, envy, jealousy and all that type of stuff. We are dealing with electricity, magnetism, electrons and neutrons lol!

What your **subconscious mind** broadcasts is literally becoming attracted to you and is entering your life. 👑

Your **conscious mind**, the one you think with throughout the day, might be like "I don't want these things in my life, I just want to be successful, loved and happy" **but** your emotions say otherwise and your **subconscious mind** doesn't believe you. You say you **don't** want these things to happen to you, but they continue to happen because it's what you attract.

KNOW ME right here, THIS ALL TIES INTO MORALE; Give me another moment! But the great thing is; IF you're willing take initiative and control of your own thoughts from now until forever, you can be on the right side of this attraction process. You can literally broadcast and receive the help and breaks you need to get what you want. You have figured out exactly what you want by now right?? I've only said it a hundred times in book lol! 😁

HERE'S THE TRICK: YOU LITERALLY HAVE TO CONVINCE YOUR SUBCONSCIOUS MIND. ✔️

Just because it's a trick I'm not saying that it's easy. But the good thing is; Once you **convince** your subconscious mind of who you are and what you want, it's hard to convince it otherwise. You have to convince your subconscious mind that you truly want what you want, that you are great, that you have an attractive personality and more! That's why some people win and some people lose in this life. The people that win, whether they realize it or not, have convinced their **subconscious mind** of who they are and what they want. Their **subconscious mind** then broadcasted that message into the fabrics of existence and it became so.

But just like a gardener; If we want a beautiful crop, we must actively pull the weeds, plant the seeds, water the seeds, and maintain the growth. 🧑‍🌾

The **weeds** are the negative emotions of <u>doubt</u>, <u>worry</u>, <u>fear</u> and <u>the others</u>. Even once you convince your subconscious mind, it will still take;

Daily maintenance of pulling the weeds out.

Daily maintenance of planting new seeds (dropping the seed of desire in the ground over and over again!).

Daily maintenance of watering the seeds, (learning new information pertaining to your desire)

Daily maintenance of maintaining growth (putting in the work to make your desire happen)

They say a <u>new habit</u> takes **21** days to create and, in my experience, this is pretty accurate. Napoleon Hill describes a **habit** <u>being like a path</u> in the woods or a trail of some kind. The habit we have is like the path that is already cleared, it's the easy path. 🥾

Most people won't walk off the trail in the woods because the bushes are too thick and it would take too much effort to walk through and or to clear. But what if the cleared path **doesn't** lead to where you want to go. What will you do? Take the easy way to a place you don't like, or put the work in to clear a new path to where you want to go?

And just like the path in the woods that needs to be cleared, **so** does the path in our minds need to be cleared to get to where we want to go! That's why it takes **21** days! It takes a while to clear the new path. And that's why **many people** fail in making new habits because they get tired of clearing a new path, they think it's not working or worth it, and return back to the easy comfortable path that they know.

THIS REALLY TAKES <u>DISIPLINE</u> AND <u>WORK</u>. DISIPLINE OF THE MIND. AND DISIPLINE OF YOUR THOUGHTS. THAT'S WHY YOU NEED YOUR SUBCONSCIOUS MIND ON BOARD TO HELP YOU MAKE YOUR NEW PATHS IN LIFE! 📔 🏝

A lot of our habits **come from** our <u>upbringing</u> and from the <u>early years of our life</u>. Then the **next set** of habits are formed as we attend public school. The next set of habits from in the late middle school to high school years. And for a bulk majority of people, their new habit making stops around this point. You will have some that go to college, you will have some that have children, and they will probably create some new habits based off these experiences but that's about it.

Then you have the **successful** people who <u>never stop</u> clearing new paths, and making new habits. The universe is **constantly expanding**, why shouldn't we be constantly expanding too? I know that I keep expanding and **building** <u>bigger</u> and <u>better</u> paths in my mind and I challenge you to do the same! 😁

Take this book for example! I didn't know I was going to write this book one year ago. But in the **constant expansion** of my <u>mind</u> and <u>desires</u>, I was shown the idea, and now I've helped clear a big path for you and everyone else who reads this book and takes it serious! Life is so **incredible** once you take yourself to the places you want to go. Life is so incredible when you work **with** God and not against God. **The most high created all of this**, and all of this is governed by universal law!

If we want to be co-writers in our destiny, we have to work with God and the universal laws that govern creation, not against them. ✔

Old habits are the **hardest** to leave. They are the **most** deepest and wide paths in our mind. The habits we pick up as a child and through trauma are the deepest. Habits like this are the ones we slip into and don't even realize it. Habits like **self-doubt**, **hate**, **jealousy** and **more** can be picked up as a child because of our environment. If you have kids, please be mindful of this, and create great habits into the minds of your young ones, because once you get grown it can almost impossible to leave the deepest paths that are built into who we are.

But I'm here to tell you, IT IS WORTH IT! Do a self-audit of yourself; Go back into the deepest parts of your mind and habits of who you are. If an old habit or tradition you picked up as a kid no longer serves you in the direction towards your desire, then let it go! **Be a trailblazer** and create a new path of tradition for yourself and for everyone that comes after you! **BE GREAT**! Don't hold onto to old traditions because you think you're supposed too. Yes, keep the traditions that are positive, and build from those; But the next generation won't even know about the traditions that don't work because you wrote them out! **Now the next generation gets to start off strong** and improve upon your habits, methods and

<u>traditions</u>. **AND SO, GREATNESS IS BORN! IN YOUR WILLINGNESS TO PUT THE WORK IN TO CONTROL YOUR OWN THOUGHTS!** 😄

I'm telling you all of this because once I really started to crack this code is when **my success** <u>catapulted into greatness</u> that I didn't think I could reach so fast! Everything in my life got better.

I started to make better deals than ever before.

I started getting more breaks from people and situations than ever before.

I stopped breaking down all the time lol.

I started to meet greater people and forge better relationships.

And most importantly, I finally knew what I wanted in life.

I finally took control of my thoughts and emotions. I finally **figured out** <u>the master key</u>. I searched near and far for the meaning of life since as far back as I can remember. And I still do. That's why I know, controlling your own thoughts is **KEY** to your success in both business and happiness. 🔒

YOU MUST MAKE YOURSELF BELIEVE YOURSELF!

YOU MUST CONVINCE YOUR SUBCONSCIOUS MIND THAT YOU ARE GREAT AND ARE ALLOWED TO HAVE WHAT YOU WANT!

DO THIS BY MIXING STRONG FAITH INTO YOUR THOUGHTS!

DO THIS BY KNOWING WHAT YOU WANT AND ATTACHING A BURNING DESIRE TO IT!

DESIRE WHAT YOU WANT SO MUCH UNTIL YOU CREATE THE EMOTION OF OBSESSION!

YES, THIS WILL TAKE 21 DAYS, MAYBE LONGER!

YES, YOU WILL FEEL WEIRD IN THE BEGININNG LIKE IT'S NOT WORKING!

YES, YOU WILL HAVE TO STILL PULL WEEDS AND WORK ON IT AFTER YOU CREATE YOUR NEW PATH!

BUT IS IT WORTH IT? YOU BETTER BELIEVE IT!

ENTHUSIASM IS CONTAGIOUS!

ENTHUSIASM IS A POSITIVE EMOTION!

YOU ATTRACT WHAT YOU PUT OUT.

MAKE SURE YOU KNOW WHAT YOU'RE PUTTING OUT SUBCONSCIOUSLY.

One thing I must say is this too; **The church has made it hard for many of us** to feel righteous in wanting things. The church kind of taught us that if it's God's will, then it will be. The church has kind of gave us the spirit of "if it's meant for me then I will get it" or "I shall not want" or "God will bless me with whatever he blesses me with".

For many years I **thought** it was not ok to say "I want". I really thought I was not allowed to want, I thought it was unrighteous and was being like a spoiled kid if I wanted stuff. I thought to be a man, you just had to keep pushing and hope for the best. **FORGET THAT LOL!** 😁

Let me tell you what I figured out; If you are a <u>righteous</u> person, <u>then what you want is righteous too</u>; Therefore, what you want <u>IS</u> GOD'S WILL! ✔️

You see how this works! **So**, as long as your heart is pure and your intentions are good, CLAIM OUT LOUD WHAT YOU WANT! Know what you want! Desire what you want! It is my opinion and inner-standing that you are not doing anything wrong or unholy by wanting what you want! **If anything, you're doing that exact opposite**! <u>You are walking in extreme faith</u>. Keep on walking, running, riding, flying and do whatever you do with this extreme faith! They say "God helps those who help themselves". Show God that you are worthy of this universal help by walking in **extreme faith** <u>towards what it is that you desire</u>. Meet God half way, and if it seems like God hasn't shown up yet, keeping pressing forward with even more faith and desire.

People tell me all the time how blessed I am, and I say thanks, yes God is good. But to myself I think sometimes "If is sat on the couch for **6** months straight and did nothing, watch how much God would bless me then lol!" It's funny how some folks will look at your success as if you were the lucky one. As if God blessed you and not them because you're the 'lucky' one. 🖕

Or is it, you're the one that met God halfway, and walked in **extreme faith** towards your desire (your blessing)? Or is it because you're the one that put the work in?? **I'M JUST SAYING LOL!** 😬

This is all **important** <u>when it comes back to trucking</u>. If your morale is low, people don't care about you. Brokers don't care about you; They give you low rates, and it feels like there's nothing you can do about it. I've been there and have done that! 😁

When you allow **negative emotions** to dwell in the deepest parts of your mind and body; You create and attract that world to you in real life, even if you pray from time to time and have some good thoughts. **A little prayer is not enough**. A little faith is not enough. You literally have to <u>hack</u> into your subconscious mind, be a bully, and make your subconscious mind believe your conscious mind. <u>Only then</u> will become a master of yourself and of your destiny. Only then will you be able to **truly implement** and use all my great methods and specific tactics I have given you through my entire book. 🤑💰💪🧠💯✔️🎩

The **better** you get at hacking into your subconscious mind, the more you will enjoy life and find success and happiness. **But it takes you**! <u>I can't do it for you, nobody can</u>. **All** someone like me can do is lead you to the palace and show you how to get in. It's up to you to do the work it takes to get inside! 😁

Keep your truck clean, **invest** into little things like candles and air fresheners that will make your truck more nice and smelling good. Invest into a fridge if you got room. It's so nice to have cold spring water on demand in the summer. Invest into some good perfume or cologne! <u>Make yourself smell like money</u>! ✔️

Buy some new socks from time to time. Slipping into new socks when coming out of that truck stop shower can sure boost my morale lol! **Organize** your tools and personal belongings. Like they say, "<u>cleanliness is godliness</u>". The more clean and organized you are, the less likely you are to get stressed and irritable about little things. ✔

Keep track of your receipts. Make notes in your phone for online purchases that you need to remember for taxes. All these different little things that I've been sharing with you in my book will help you in increasing your morale.

You have to keep your spirits up out here. But not in a fake and artificial way by going on spending sprees and over indulging on food. **But by knowing what you want and handling your business** LIKE A BOSS! When you know that you're doing right, that you smell good, that your trucks clean, that you got all your tools organized, and etc; It's going to much more of a natural thing to sustain **HIGH** morale! 😁

You know the saying right? "A **wise man** will tell you he knows nothing, and the **fool** will tell you he knows everything". In the grand scheme of things, we are but a pebble in the ocean, a grain of sand on the beach. We do not know how to travel the universe or how far it goes; we don't even know all the animals that live in the depths of the ocean. It's **silly** for man to act as if he knows everything. Most adults don't even know how to control their own thoughts and emotion. Most adults don't even know how to keep themselves healthy half the time.

I think we all just need to take a **step back** and be thankful for Earth, the air we breathe, and this amazing human body we have; And admire it for the incredible creation that is. I think we need to admire nature and it's beauty more as well. **As technology improves**, we tend to get further from nature, further from what sustains us and provides us nourishment. Many of the health and psychological problems we have today didn't much exist when we were closer the earth; I think it was because we were more grounded. 🌍

Technology can be a great tool, <u>but it is a double edge sword</u>. Just as much as it creates opportunity for some, it creates depression and anxiety for others. Just as much as social media allows us to connect with new people, it can disconnect us from real interaction with each other. 🎯

I really hope the youth of today can keep their innocence long enough to have a developed imagination. Kids are exposed to so much so quick now through the internet. It's good to grow up quick in certain regards; But once a kid see's certain things, they start to **lose** their imagination. <u>It's your imagination that allows you to dream.</u> 📓

The problem is, <u>too many people are dreaming other people's dreams because of this lack of imagination</u>. They are dreaming other people's dreams as if it's their own. They do this because they were influenced on social media to do so. **Social media is a tool**. It shouldn't be a **measuring stick** that we use to <u>measure</u> ourselves up against another person. A lot of the people that look like they are happy on social media are not that happy in real life. A lot of the people that look rich and successful on social media are not rich and successful in real life. 📱🤔 but either way doesn't matter.

People don't really like to post their bad days, and their not so good-looking pictures lol! It's ok to be mellow. **It's ok to not be** "<u>turnt up</u>" <u>every second of the day</u>. We are running a rat race and don't even realize it. We are trying so hard to keep up with everyone else's "happiness" that we burn ourselves out, become depressed, feel like we can never do it, and stop dreaming. 👍✔💯😶

The more we as people can find love and peace within ourselves, the more the world will know love and peace as well. I'm sure you know the saying "If you want others to love you, you must truly love yourself first"? It's true! And the same is true for respect as well. If you don't respect yourself, other people will feel like they don't have to respect you either. I wish this world wasn't so "dog eat dog" and we are getting better I think, but the reality of it is, you got be careful and learn how to play the game. 🔒

Who are the ones that win the game? Who wins the game are the ones who believe in themselves the most and that puts the most work in. **Success is when opportunity meets preparation**. Don't worry so much about how you measure up against other people in the social media world, just pay attention to your own happiness and what's in **your** bank account! That's the only opinion that really matters LOL! What does your bank account have to say about it 💰😄🔇💿? I do suggest having multiple bank accounts too, just in case one gets hacked or something crazy, you can still operate and handle business while you get it resolved.

You have prepared yourself a ton by going through my course. If I were to know all of this when I was just **21** getting started, I would have been a beast super quick! But remember, everything in my book is just words until you put my words into action. **Knowledge is not power, applied knowledge is power**. Simply knowing is not enough. Success is when opportunity meets preparation. I speak **so much** about mentality because that's almost the biggest part of preparation, is having the mentality to make, take and capitalize on opportunities.

Keep your head on straight my friend and you will be all right! Keep reaching for greatness. Only surround yourself with greatness. Find you some friends that are doing what you do and support each other with good morale! Follow me on social media. Check out my posts! I'm new to this social media. I have 17 followers at the time of me writing this book LOL. I'm one of those people whose somebody in real life and left social media a long time ago and have enjoyed the peace. I've been around the world and back so to speak and now I got something to give! 😄

"A wise man **will make more opportunities** than he finds." – *Francis Bacon*

"If opportunity doesn't knock, **build a door**." –*Milton Berle*

"Most people miss opportunity because it is dressed in overalls and **looks like work**." –*Thomas Edison*

"As I grow older, I pay less attention to what men say. I just watch what they do."
— Andrew Carnegie

"People who are unable to motivate themselves must be content with mediocrity, no matter how impressive their other talents."
— Andrew Carnegie

"No man becomes rich unless he enriches others."
— Andrew Carnegie

"All human beings can alter their lives by altering their attitudes."
— Andrew Carnegie

"You cannot push anyone up a ladder unless he is willing to climb a little.
"
— Andrew Carnegie

"Do your duty and a little more and the future will take care of itself."
— Andrew Carnegie

Peace n LUV> MUCH SUCCESS

Made in the USA
Monee, IL
29 October 2024

68879448R00301